9193
9.50
0090

Armies in
Low-Intensity Conflict

Armies in Low-Intensity Conflict

A COMPARATIVE ANALYSIS

Edited by

David A. Charters and Maurice Tugwell

BRASSEY'S DEFENCE PUBLISHERS

(A member of the Maxwell Pergamon Publishing Corporation plc)

LONDON · OXFORD · WASHINGTON · NEW YORK
BEIJING · FRANKFURT · SÃO PAULO · SYDNEY · TOKYO · TORONTO

UK (Editorial)	Brassey's Defence Publishers Ltd., 24 Gray's Inn Road, London WC1X 8HR, England
(Orders)	Brassey's Defence Publishers Ltd., Headington Hill Hall, Oxford OX3 0BW, England
USA (Editorial)	Pergamon-Brassey's International Defense Publishers, Inc., 8000 Westpark Drive, Fourth Floor, McLean, Virginia 22102, USA
(Orders)	Pergamon Press, Inc., Maxwell House, Fairview Park, Elmsford, New York 10523, USA
PEOPLE'S REPUBLIC OF CHINA	Pergamon Press, Room 4037, Qianmen Hotel, Beijing, People's Republic of China
FEDERAL REPUBLIC OF GERMANY	Pergamon Press GmbH, Hammerweg 6, D–6242 Kronberg, Federal Republic of Germany
BRAZIL	Pergamon Editora Ltda, Rua Eça de Queiros, 346, CEP 04011, Paraiso, São Paulo, Brazil
AUSTRALIA	Pergamon-Brassey's Defence Publishers Pty Ltd., P.O. Box 544, Potts Point, N.S.W. 2011, Australia
JAPAN	Pergamon Press, 5th Floor, Matsuoka Central Building 1-7-1 Nishishinjuku, Shinjuku-ku, Tokyo 160, Japan
CANADA	Pergamon Press Canada Ltd., Suite No. 271, 253 College Street, Toronto, Ontario, Canada M5T 1R5

First edition 1989

Library of Congress Cataloging in Publication Data

Armies in low-intensity conflict: a comparative analysis/edited by David Charters and Maurice Tugwell.—1st ed.
p. cm.
1. Low-intensity conflicts (Military science) 2. Military history, Modern—20th century. I. Charters, David. II. Tugwell, Maurice.
U240.A76 1988   355'.0215—dc 19   88–22219

British Library Cataloguing in Publication Data

Armies in low-intensity conflict: a comparative analysis.
1. Small scale military operations, 1945–1987
I. Charters, David   II. Tugwell, Maurice
355.4
ISBN 0–08–036253–2

Printed in Great Britain by A. Wheaton & Co. Ltd., Exeter

Preface

Since the end of World War II, Western armies have been configured to fight mechanised conventional (and nuclear) battles against similarly-structured opponents. Yet, in that time, these armies have fought relatively few conventional wars. Instead, they have been assigned to missions which encompass the entire spectrum of low-intensity conflict: peace-keeping, internal security, counter-terrorism, hostage rescue, unconventional warfare, special operations, and counter-insurgency. As will be shown, some armies adjusted better than others to these largely unexpected, unorthodox requirements.

The aim of this book is to demonstrate how Western armies have learned to adapt to unconventional roles and missions in the post-1945 politico-military environment of low-intensity conflict. The main body of the study consists of five case studies of armies involved in low-intensity operations: the United States, Israeli, French, Canadian and British forces respectively. Each case attempts to explore the nature of the army; its institutional processes and methods of incorporating experience and change, including training methods; development of tactical and strategic doctrine, and of specialised skills and units; operational experience; and assessment of the army's ability to adapt and the forms adaptation takes. The study opens with an historical survey of the problem of army adaptation to changing forms, methods and weapons of war. The conclusion offers some general propositions on how armies adapt, the criteria for effective adaptation, and the consequences of adaptation with respect to the ability of armies to conduct conventional operations.

The editors and authors wish to acknowledge gratefully the assistance rendered by their own and other institutions. Special thanks are due to the Public Records Office, Kew; the Ministry of Defence Library (Central and Army), London; the Army Historical Section, Ministry of Defence, London; Patricia Methven, Archivist, Liddell Hart Centre for Military Archives, King's College, London; the late Colonel Jonathan Alford, International Institute for Strategic Studies; and the Reference and Documents Staff of the Harriet Irving Library, University of New Brunswick. Andrew Rasiulis of the Directorate of Strategic Analysis, Department of National Defence, Ottawa, was very helpful in providing the administrative support and oversight essential to the success of the original research. His encouragement was instrumental in the decision to submit the report for publication. Stalwart secretarial support was provided by Deborah Stapleford and Thelma Clarke. Linda Hansen endeavoured to render the page proofs correct and consistent. Finally, we owe a debt of thanks to our Literary Agent, Mark Hamilton, for his perseverance and patience.

The editors and authors wish to advise readers that this is a revised version of a study that was performed under contract to the Canadian Department of National Defence. The opinions expressed in the publication are those of the editors and authors and do not necessarily represent those of the Canadian Department of National Defence, or the British Ministry of Defence.

Use has been made of the following (British) Crown Copyright source material and its reproduction is with the permission of the Controller of Her Britannic Majesty's Stationery Office:

Imperial Policing and Duties in Aid of the Civic Power (1949);
British Army Journal/Review (1953–73);
A Handbook on Anti-Mau Mau Operations (1954);
The Conduct of Anti-Terrorist Operations in Malaya (1954, 1958);
Notes and Information on Training Matters (1955–72);
Keeping the Peace (Duties in Aid of the Civic Power) (1957);
Keeping the Peace (1963);
Land Operations Volume III Counter-Revolutionary Operations (1969).

Crown copyright material in the Public Record Office is reproduced by permission of the Controller of Her Majesty's Stationery Office.

Contents

About the contributors   ix

Chapter 1

Adapt or perish: the forms of evolution in warfare   1

MAURICE TUGWELL

Chapter 2

The American response to low-intensity conflict: the
formative period   19

SAM C. SARKESIAN

Chapter 3

Israeli defence forces and low-intensity operations   49

GUNTHER E. ROTHENBERG

Chapter 4

From Algiers to N'Djamena: France's adaptation to low-
intensity wars, 1830–1987   77

MICHEL L. MARTIN

Chapter 5

Peace-keeping and internal security: the Canadian Army in
low-intensity operations   139

DAVID A. CHARTERS AND JAMES LEBLANC

Chapter 6

From Palestine to Northern Ireland: British adaptation to
low-intensity operations   169
DAVID A. CHARTERS

Conclusions   251

Index   257

About the Contributors

David A. Charters is Director of the Centre for Conflict Studies at the University of New Brunswick. He received his PhD in War Studies from the University of London, where his dissertation examined the British Army's counter-insurgency campaign in Palestine, 1945–47. He has since published numerous studies of military aspects of low-intensity conflict.

James LeBlanc is currently the Executive Assistant to the Ambassador for Disarmament in the Canadian Department of External Affairs. He received his MA in International Peace and Security Studies from Carleton University, and contributed to this project prior to taking up his present position.

Michel L. Martin is Professor of Law and Political Science at the Université des Antilles-Guyane and at the Institut d'Etudes Politiques of Toulouse (France). He is Visiting Guest Scholar at the University of Chicago. He has written extensively on African politics, military affairs and has recently published a book on American foreign policy. He is the representative of Europe at the board of directors of the Inter-University Seminar on Armed Forces and Society.

Gunther E. Rothenberg is Professor of Military History at Purdue University. He has published extensively in the field of military history, including a volume on the anatomy of the Israeli Army, in which he served in 1947–48.

Sam C. Sarkesian is Professor and Chairman of the Department of Political Science at Loyola University of Chicago. He served in the US Army in Korea and Vietnam, retiring in the rank of Lieutenant Colonel. His major publications have examined the place of the military in society and its role in low-intensity conflict. Dr. Sarkesian is currently Chairman of the Inter-University Seminar on the Armed Forces and Society.

Maurice Tugwell is Director of the Mackenzie Institute for the Study of Terrorism, Revolution and Propaganda, an independent research centre based in Toronto, Canada. From 1980–86 he served as

Director of the Centre for Conflict Studies at the University of New Brunswick. After a lengthy career in the British Army, retiring with the rank of Brigadier, he received his PhD in War Studies at the University of London. He has published a number of books, articles and other studies of armies in low-intensity operations.

1

Adapt or Perish: The Forms of Evolution in Warfare

MAURICE TUGWELL

Change, as Heraclitus observed some 2,500 years ago, is the only enduring certainty.[1] Dealing with change and evolution is a necessary part of everyday life. For national leaders, whether political or military, the ability to anticipate change and to adapt successfully when it occurs is an important and sometimes vital gift. For want of this talent battles have been lost and empires have crumbled.

There appear to be two main forms of military adaptation. The first is the product of military genius. An outstanding national or military leader sometimes originates a new method of conducting war, as Napoleon did. He saw how the *élan* of revolutionary troops could be translated into victory on the battlefield by shock effect. Fast-moving infantry, mobile artillery and audacious tactics achieved the desired results. The new mobile guns were a gift from the Gods but Napoleon knew instinctively how to capitalise on the gift. For the rest, the adaptations flowed from his inspired imagination. We may call this innovative adaptability.

The contrasting and commoner form is reactive adaptation. This is required whenever new or unforeseen events or conditions upset existing military doctrine. 'Adapt or perish' is the motto, as commanders at all levels seek answers to novel problems. Against Napoleon, the Russians used scorched-earth policy, geography and climate, while the British developed and subsidised coalition warfare.

Changes requiring new responses may arise almost accidentally, or they may be carefully planned by one of the combatants. Prior to World War I, all the European armies had access to the latest weapons. They knew the effects of machine-guns and modern artil-

1

lery. Yet most did not foresee the compound effect of these developments upon the nature of warfare. Even technical innovators were unprepared and both sides groped towards doctrinal adaptation to the new conditions. Other changes came about by design, such as the use of poison gas and tanks. Technical surprise imposed an urgent need for adaptation by the unwitting side, but often the army employing the new weapon was also surprised by its potential or limitations.

New weapons have changed warfare through history, even though military establishments have often resisted the opportunities presented. Innovation has often followed upon discovery or invention, such as the development of bronze weapons and armour in Mesopotamia in about 3500 BC, the making of the compound bow, the introduction of iron weapons in Asia Minor around 1400 BC and the invention of blast-furnaces in China nearly two-and-a-half millennia later. The discovery of gunpowder and its use in guns eventually changed the nature of warfare, as did all the devices which flowed from the scientific and industrial revolutions of the 18th and 19th centuries.[2]

The effectiveness of armies and their weapons depends in part on their mobility, in part on their protection and in part on the way they are commanded and controlled. Developments in mobility and protection have possibly changed the nature of warfare as much as new weapon design. In about 1800 BC the invention of the spoked wheel with friction-reducing hub and axle permitted the use of horse-drawn chariots in war.[3] Waves of barbarians equipped with these mobile fire platforms overran all the civilised lands of the Middle East between 1800 and 1500 BC. Their prowess depended on a combination of firepower, armour and mobility. An archer equipped with a compound bow stood beside the driver and both were protected by bronze. Nothing could stop them; they could shower arrows on opposing infantry or outflank them with ease.[4]

Chariots dominated warfare for a millennium. Then the Assyrians mounted two soldiers astride the same horse, one to control the animal, the other to shoot. As man and horse became as one, a single rider learnt to drop his reins while using both hands on his bow: cavalry became queen of the battlefield. Ironically, this innovative adaptation by the Assyrians contributed to their downfall. Their enemies adapted in the reactive sense so effectively that they overtook the innovators. In 612 BC cavalrymen played a key role in the sack of Nineveh and the destruction of the Assyrian empire.[5] Horseback warfare was well suited to the steppe nomads and, in William H.

McNeill's words, 'announced the onset in the Middle East of a new era in military matters which lasted, in essentials, until the 14th century AD'.[6]

Nomad cavalry retained the mobility and firepower of the charioteers but forsook the armour. Between 500 and 100 BC the Iranians bred powerful horses which could carry an armoured rider equipped with new-fangled stirrups.[7] This was a striking adaptation but one not much copied at the time. It was not until 732 AD, under Charles Martel in France, that armoured cavalry came into its own. Virtually invincible, these knights gave rise to feudalism and the entrenchment of local power.[8] Reactive adaptation took four centuries, coming eventually in the form of a sophisticated crossbow which could knock an armoured knight off his horse.[9] The era of invincible cavalry was drawing to a close, to be extinguished by muskets and cannon. Mobility in battle has always been conditional upon battlefield survival.

But other forms of mobility were less constricted. Fast movement between cities and the battle area meant rapid mobilisation, deployment and resupply. Inland waterways and railroads revolutionised this type of mobility. So long as she retained command of the sea, Britain was able to supply her land forces in the American War of Independence, an experience which proved valuable in the later wars against Napoleon.[10]

Mobility returned to the battlefield with the internal combustion engine, which made possible the truck, tank, armoured personnel carrier and aeroplane. Strategic mobility has been most recently influenced by air transport and rapid deployment over thousands of miles is now a reality. Reactive adaptation to these developments has tended to take two forms: the provision of special weapons to render such movement on the enemy's part costly or impossible; and a scramble to make one's own army equally mobile.

Command, control and communications, known today by the shortened form C^3, decide the usefulness of new weapons and improved protection or mobility. Command implies leadership, originality and inventiveness, the qualities that permit both innovative and reactive adaptation, as well as the ordering of campaigns and battles. Command also inspires doctrine, which governs the way one's troops go about the business of war, and loyalty, which plunders the current ethos—be it religious, patriotic, revolutionary, ideological or mercenary—to underwrite military *esprit de corps*. These are timeless assets: innovation in command can only take the form of military genius. Control and communications combine to translate command into action, and in these fields change constantly occurs.

There must always have been some means of control and communication in warfare, however rudimentary. Tribal organisation and discipline, manoeuvre by hand signal and voice, and cohesion born of a common urge to survive, sufficed so long as warfare was confined to relatively small groups. As armies grew larger, C^3 posed problems. William McNeill thinks the Assyrian kings were the most successful practitioners of the art of bureaucratic management of armed force in the early Iron Age.[11] Ranks, standard equipment, fixed organisation, supply, systematic innovation, discipline, and radical rationality characterised their approach to C^3.

All empires and armies have developed control and communications of one kind or another. Often, strictly military needs have been subordinated to the overriding requirements of domestic politics, economics and administration. The roles of monarchs and high priests have sometimes distorted control and communications within the military; or the needs of agriculture and city commerce have imposed restrictions on efficient mobilisation and organisation.

Before the scientific and industrial revolutions, simple social organisation sometimes produced the best military. In the 13th century Genghis Khan united almost all the steppe peoples into one single command structure. He arranged his army on a decimal system with units of 10, 100, and so on, led by battle-tested commanders. Defeated steppe enemies could readily be incorporated into the victorious horde. As the Mongols overran north China and central Asia, they adapted their organisation and tactics to make best use of new weapons encountered, be these Chinese explosives, Moslem siege engines or southern Sung warships.[12]

If the Mongols' C^3 depended for its success upon simplicity, the emerging professional armies of medieval Europe relied on the efficient management of sophisticated and often expensive resources. McNeill describes how a remarkably flexible and efficient system of warfare, relating means to ends according to financial as well as diplomatic calculations, came into being in Italy's Po valley by the end of the 15th century.[13] Relationships between civil and military elements in Italian society were stabilised, while armies learnt to co-ordinate the actions of bowmen, pikemen and cavalry. And whereas the Mongols were skilled at adapting for their own uses the inventions of others, the Europeans began to pull ahead of their Chinese and

Moslem rivals in inventiveness and in the development of social and economic infrastructures that would later spawn an industrial revolution.

In the 17th century the Dutch pioneered drill as an important control system. It was discovered that a well-drilled army with a clear chain of command from top to bottom made for peace at home and victory in foreign wars. Long hours of repeated drill made soldiers more obedient and efficient in battle. Because the requirements of a frightening and potentially demoralising battle had been practised hundreds of times in peace, and could therefore be performed with the mind, as it were, in neutral, unit cohesion was strengthened. As muskets replaced pikes and crossbows, drills enabled high rates of fire to be maintained and the fire to be applied most effectively—in volleys.[14] Prince Maurice of Nassau, captain-general of Holland and Zeeland, also divided his army into 550-strong battalions, further sub-divided into companies and platoons. Personal ties between leaders and followers were established, and the capacity of the commander to manoeuvre his men by passing orders down the chain of command was much improved. Drill also reinforced unit *esprit*. The precise, massed performance of complicated movements created strong social bonds and a sense of invincibility. The regiment became a very special social group, a warrior tribe with its own traditions and values.[15] The other European countries reacted to these developments by copying the Dutch. Reactive adaptation inside Europe widened the military proficiency gap between Europe and the outside world.

By the end of the 18th century weapon innovation and the increasing size of armies were beginning to overwhelm existing control and communication means. Management was lagging behind. The French recognised the importance of accurate maps as a prerequisite for regaining control. As maps became available, the need arose for military specialists in map reading, planning, and preparing written orders. In 1765 General Pierre Bourget established a school for training *aides-de-camp*. Before the end of the century, the divisional organisation had been introduced. Maps, a staff organisation and the divisional structure permitted France to field larger armies than had hitherto been practical, and paved the way for the 1793 *levée en masse*.[16] Napoleon inherited new tactical doctrine which authorised battlefield manoeuvre in column, line or by skirmishing. By selecting a combination of these tactics, he was able to outmarch and outmanoeuvre enemies. During his revolutionary wars,

Napoleon made use of newly-invented balloons and the semaphore telegraph, both useful C^3 assets.[17]

In Prussia, the Great General Staff was created between 1803 and 1809, raising the status of the military intellectual in a profession traditionally dominated by privilege and class. This staff was responsible for contingency planning—a radical departure at the time. Their role was to predict all possible future military campaigns and to plan for them in peacetime. This naturally led to a requirement for intelligence and for logistical planning; innovation in these fields has ever since proved of crucial importance. Scharnhorst, Gneisenau and Moltke were prominent in this managerial revolution. Prussia also introduced conscription in peacetime, enabling a relatively small nation to play in the major league.[18]

The Prussian innovations led to success against Austria and France in the second half of the 19th century. They were copied to greater or lesser extent by other Western armies. But by 1914 the scale of war had once again outstripped C^3. The modified Schlieffen plan, on which the Germans relied to achieve a rapid victory over the French and British, demonstrated both the brilliance of German staff planning and its narrow vision. No one had foreseen that ample firepower and a total lack of armour would together severely restrict mobility, nor was the effect of total war mobilisation understood in advance. Their combined effect was stalemate. In the long series of costly battles intended to break this stalemate, C^3 was generally inadequate. Although there was constant innovation in all fields, including command and control, 1914–18 was an age in which the engines of destruction were far ahead of armoured mobility and reliable communication. Thus, it proved difficult to adjust doctrines to new weapons because all too often schedules and control broke down under the strain of battle. There were all manner of reactive adaptations, such as messages dropped from aeroplanes, but technology was incapable at the time of providing full answers to the C^3 problem.[19]

By World War II, most European nations had these answers although some used them better than others. The *blitzkrieg* reunited firepower with mobility because reliable armoured vehicles were available. Field radios permitted control to be maintained over fluid, fast-moving battles.[20] More recently, C^3 has become so advanced that a president could, if he so wished, speak direct to the leader of a squad in battle on the far side of the globe. Needless to say, such technology has its disadvantages: all intermediate commanders can easily be reduced to the level of spectators. Political judgements may distort sound military planning and misdirect the mission. The art of high command in today's C^3 environment may require a determination not to misuse the means of control and communications—a reactive adaptation against an over-abundance of technology.

Change in one area, be it weaponry, mobility, armour, C^3 or intelligence, is liable to affect the *status quo* in others. In a technological age, man is to a large extent able to command the direction of research and invention. But this controlled evolution is forever being upset by random, unexpected, scientific breakthroughs, and by unforeseen secondary effects. Adaptation of research programmes in the light of such developments, so that finite resources are applied in the most profitable directions, has become an important part of national or alliance decision-making.

One novel form of adaptation is to develop an intelligence apparatus capable of monitoring all military developments by potential adversaries. This safeguards the nation so equipped against being caught off guard, and provides it with the fruit of the rival's scientific investment at a tiny fraction of its cost. According to journalistic reports, the USSR has adopted this course and made it work so efficiently that she is conceivably able to incorporate new American technology into Soviet weapons before it has reached the production stage in the USA.[21] Another novel form of adaptation is to persuade one's adversary, on such grounds as morality, efficacy or cost-effectiveness, to abandon certain forms of weapon development or doctrine. By such means—which must of course be deceptive and indirect—a technological or policy disadvantage may be reduced or erased.[22]

Weapons, mobility, protection, control and communication decide the way any particular war is fought. They do not decide the nature of the war, its purpose, or limitations on aims, means or geographical confines. The command element affects these matters; sometimes one commander is able to decide in advance on the form of conflict, forcing his opponent to conform. New types of war have, therefore, required adaptation by armies to meet new challenges and unfamiliar problems.

Armies have always had to look in two directions. As the principal instrument of force in the hands of the state, an armed body of men will, when necessary, be called upon to quell internal disturbances, to 'keep the peace' at home. Whether this call is made lightly, or only as a reluctant last resort, will depend on the history and traditions of the particular country, as well as on the efficiency and reliability of lesser instruments of force available, such as militias, police and *posse comitatus*. In 1812, Wellesley's expeditionary force to the Peninsula was fewer in number than the regular soldiers required to suppress violence in Britain.[23] The same might be true for the Soviets in Eastern Europe if a major war were to break out tomorrow.

Some internal military duties are so limited in scope that they may be seen as diversions rather than forms of conflict. But serious revolutionary challenges, sustained political violence at a low level of intensity and civil war are conflict forms requiring armies to adapt their tactics in response. Regular armies vary in their attitudes to such duties. Where an officer corps is politicised in the Western meaning of the term, that is to say they are into politics for what they can get out of it, the internal role comes naturally. Where the military ethic subordinates the army to political control, either through democratic or ideological conviction, there is often a reluctance to become involved in internal operations. Officers know how demoralising and divisive such duties can be and prefer that the state devote sufficient resources to police and militia that the need for military intervention does not arise. Such officers also tend to regard the external role of defending their country against foreign threats as the 'proper' function of the military. Indeed, there is perhaps a feeling that the greater the level of the threat, the more 'proper' the military role. Nuclear weapons may have dented this notion, but there is little doubt that most professional armies are more comfortable with the idea of fighting at least to the limit of all available conventional arms, than with coping with 'one hand tied behind the back'.[24]

One may speculate that one reason for such preferences is the relatively clear-cut distinction in such 'high-intensity' circumstances between politics and war. The first has presumably failed and, from a soldier's perspective, can be put aside in favour of the second, which is the realm of the military professional. Such is, of course, never quite the case but at least at the operational level the soldier is on his own, free to act in accordance with military priorities and procedures.

These priorities have also been subject to change. War may be total, requiring the complete submission or destruction of the adversary, or it may have limited purposes. Limited war has tended to move in and out of fashion throughout history.[25] It is attractive when the overall *status quo* is acceptable to the nations concerned, or when its overthrow is seen as too difficult or too dangerous to attempt. Richard Preston and Sydney Wise describe the moderating trend in warfare that affected Europe by the beginning of the 18th century and attribute this to moral revulsion arising from the atrocities of the Thirty Years' War and the accompanying realisation that such wars were no longer a worthwhile means of achieving political ends.[26] Limited war may shift the balance between adversaries or remedy a perceived injustice: it does not as a rule overthrow the *status quo* by demanding unconditional surrender. Of course, a war may be limited for one participant while at the same time being a matter of life and death for another; both the Korean and Vietnamese wars displayed this asymmetry.

Adaptation to limited war can sometimes be demanding on soldiers. The army with more advanced weapons and an abundance of supply is apt to resent the controls that may be applied to the level of force permitted. For some, the very idea of limited objectives is unsoldierly and improper. General Douglas MacArthur lost his command in Korea because he resisted President Truman's instructions limiting his options north of the Yalu River.[27] Yet the limits of the post-World War II period were really the same as those of the early 18th century: total war had become politically nonsensical. If the experiences of 1914–18 and 1939–45 were not enough, the advent of the nuclear weapon in 1945 removed reasonable doubt. Nevertheless, within professional military ranks, war without limit retains its hold over the mind not so much as a desirable or logical resort but as the norm, the standard against which other forms of war are measured. With all-out war at the centre of professional attention other (lesser) conflict forms inevitably become peripheral. The process of adaptation to such lesser forms must seemingly be continuous, or be repeated anew each time a crisis arises. Alternatively, an army may divide its resources and energies between high-intensity and low-intensity challenges by forming special commands to deal with each.

Pulls upon the military, then, come as it were in two dimensions: up and down the scale of force between limited and all-out warfare; and inwards and outwards between the domestic arena and the overseas war. And there is a third, lateral dimension yet to be considered, in which the profession of arms is pushed or pulled sideways between wars dominated by the clash of arms and wars dominated by the clash of ideas.

Of course, ideas are always instrumental in war-making. One monarch makes up his mind to conquer, another decides to resist, and there is war. The soldiers follow out of loyalty, fear, greed, habit or because they have no other option. If loyalty is instrumental in making men fight, clearly some body of ideas has brought this about—patriotism, personal obligation to a lord or monarch, and tradition being typical sources of this sentiment. To this extent, all wars are wars of ideas. But because, in what may be termed 'normal' conditions, both opposed armies have such loyalties, these balance out: neither commander believes that he holds a monopoly of virtue. The loyalties that hold such armies together are not easily transferred and little effort is made to subvert. The outcome of battle therefore hangs upon the clash of arms.

Ideas become weapons in their own right when they have the potential to inspire the rank-and-file to revolutionary ardour, and thus to energise an army, making it capable of feats a less inspired army might never accomplish. Such ideas are often millenarian, mystical, dogmatic. Adherents become true believers, immune to rival appeals, even fanatics. If there are waverers, the discipline of the belief system keeps them in line. The tendency towards totalitarianism is obvious. This weapon is sharper still if it has the ability to subvert adversary rank-and-file.

Because millenarians believe that they possess a monopoly of truth and virtue, they cannot easily accept any *status quo* that deprives others of the revolutionary beliefs. For tactical reasons they may sometimes adopt limited forms of warfare but their reasons for so doing are subversive of the rationale described earlier. Their aims are not limited, only their means. This holds true so long as the body of ideas retains its power in undiminished form over adherents' minds: once the spark dies, the army reverts to a more 'normal' status, schisms occur and leaders may in time come to accept limited objectives as well as limited means. Clearly, an army inspired by ideas poses a challenge that calls for adaptation by potential adversaries. Whether the ideas come packaged as religion or political idealism, they represent a novel politico-military threat.

Imperialism in its prime created a body of ideas of considerable power.[28] It transforms nationalism into a crusading, reforming force and clothes aggression in the self-righteous mantle of liberation. The superior condition of man at the imperial centre justifies the subjugation of lesser breeds, that they may learn better ways.[29] By modern standards, the body of ideas inherent in imperialism is intellectually weak and morally unacceptable. But this has not detracted from its operational power, described by Colin Vale when he wrote that 'for some reason the world stands paralysed before the onward thrust of the successful empire. This has been true of all ages and of all empires'.[30] Of course the body of ideas bound up in the imperial concept relies for its effectiveness on organisation, manpower and the matériel means of warfare. But the forces which carried Alexander to India, the Romans to Britain and the British to the ends of the earth had a moral as well as a physical dimension, and in its loose, incoherent way the imperial dream may be listed among the ideas that help to win wars.

Religion, when militant, provides a far more coherent body of ideas and sharpens the edge of struggle. Fired by the new Islamic teaching, the Arabs of the 7th century poured out of Arabia and spread East and West. They invaded Visigothic Spain in 710 AD and, during the same year, moved beyond Persia to enter the Hindu-Buddhist kingdom of Sind. Religious belief inspired unity and faith, at least during the early years.[31] The passionate loyalties of Europe's inter-Christian wars showed how, even after a faith had split into rival sects, the emotive power of its several parts endured.[32] Today, the revival of militant fundamental Islam in Iran has illustrated the special quality of menace that a religious threat poses to the outside world. The hostage-taking at the US Embassy, the blatant attempt to subvert Iraq through her Shia population and the terrorist martyrs of the Lebanon testify to a total indifference to norms, laws, agreements and conventions that exist beyond the bounds of Islam. The outside world has no moral standing and its opinions are without importance. Moreover it is damned by God: only by conversion can its people save themselves. Thus, to greater or lesser extent, religious wars are revolutionary.[33]

Revolts, coups, insurrections and revolutions are as old as history. The relatively new ingredient is political idealism, a desire to advance history towards absolute betterment. Jacques Ellul writes:

> Until 1789, revolutions were attempted and occasionally achieved, but never romanticised. Then the era of the revolutionary epic began. Revolution, in the person of the revolutionaries, started to look at and admire itself, to grimace and disport in the mirror. The myth of revolution was about to descend on the modern world.[34]

Ideology provides revolution with a body of ideas capable of transforming the shape of war. The early defection of non-commissioned officers and men from the French Guard demonstrated how ideas robbed the French monarchy of security without a clash of arms: an instrument of force fell apart in its owner's hand. When the revolution succeeded, the problem of controlling the forces it had unleashed remained. The *levée en masse* was part of the answer: it removed the mob from the street and directed its anger outwards.[35]

Marx provided new ideological justification for revolution and Lenin incorporated his theories within a body of ideas—Bolshevism—which inspired, justified, engineered and consolidated revolution.[36] This ideology combined the moral force of a religion with an operating code of power. To a Bolshevik, the outside world has no moral standing. Moreover, it is damned by history: only by conversion can its people save themselves. This body of ideas, created in the first quarter of this century, is now the dominant belief system imposed upon more than one third of the world's population.

Nationalism, generally speaking, is a conservative force, providing the strength to resist attacks from without rather than inspiring foreign adventures. But nationalism denied can create a body of ideas of great force. Germany under Hitler succumbed to an ideology, National Socialism, which borrowed Bolshevik operating codes and married them to the worst excesses of frustrated German nationalism. Brutal and anti-intellectual, the Nazi system nevertheless inspired a generation of Germans. Only the racial, fiercely Germanic component of the ideology deprived it of greater subversive appeal outside the Reich.[37]

In the post-World War II period, reawakened or, in some cases, newly created nationalism was for 25 years the major revolutionary standard-bearer. The loyalties that the European imperial powers had so carefully fostered amongst their colonial subjects, and which for so long had persuaded such peoples to look to the imperial centre as the proper focus of their allegiance, disintegrated under the impact of revolutionary nationalism. The more this force was resisted or suppressed, the greater became its strength. In Algeria the rebels, like the Nazis before them, borrowed Bolshevik operating codes, but deliberately rejected the ideology. They also refused Islamic identity, preferring to remain simply nationalist.[38] But in Indochina, the nationalist revolutionary leaders were communists too, and so led their country, like China, into an ideological form of governance. The Zionists, in their revolutionary struggle against alien control of the Holy Land, summoned assistance from every sympathetic Jew in the world. Theirs was a body of ideas, in part religious, in part frustrated-nationalist and in part political-idealist.

The legitimising notions that drive nations, revolutions or world movements often begin as fresh, original, even innocent thoughts, only to be brutalised by struggle, institutionalised by successor leaderships uncertain of their positions, and bureaucratised by hangers-on. When legitimacy and internal stability rely overmuch on some crusading ideal, and especially when national security seems threatened by the continued health of rival external ideas and ideals, the religious or ideological origins may be transformed. The result, often, is a new imperialism, and the two belief systems merge.

The Moslem Arabs made 10 attempts over 70 years to conquer Sind, beginning between 634 and 644 AD, during the reign of the second caliph or successor to the Prophet. By the time of the final invasion, Islamic conversion had ceased to be the driving force. The aim was commercial-imperial; the invasion had to show a profit. Revenge was a secondary motive. But what was required from the people of Sind was not conversion to Islam, but tribute, taxes, treasure, slaves and women.[39] Napoleon redirected the French revolutionary explosion outwards, becoming imperial in title and deed.[40] In the 1970s and 1980s, Soviet Russia seemed to be following a similar course, gradually co-opting nationalism at home while using Marxist propaganda abroad to support an imperialism made more menacing by the Leninist operating code.[41] Thus can be seen the power of ideas strengthening the power of armies, and the success of those armies creating a myth of invincibility which is a force in its own right.

The challenges posed by the clash of ideas, particularly those that inspire revolution, have forced armies confronting them to adapt in several dimensions simultaneously. The scale of force employed may be that selected by the challenger to minimise his numerical or other disadvantages. He may regard the struggle as purely political but he may not abide by the rules of society which require that politics be non-violent. Thus, an army dealing with this threat is plunged into politics, not in the traditional sense of wishing to gain power but in the unwelcome, reactive sense of having to act apolitically in a political arena, and act without the advantages normally flowing from superior force.

The period 1945–70 saw the European imperial powers resisting and eventually accommodating revolutionary nationalism in one colony after another. The 19th century imperial myth had died, and there was no body of ideas to answer, let alone defeat, the nationalism that was burying it. Towards the end of this era, the United States, an ardent opponent of the imperial myth, was herself caught up in countering revolutionary nationalism in Indochina, and came to resemble an imperial power. The legitimising body of ideas for this involvement was the containment of communist expansionism. But this was outflanked by Vietnamese nationalism and by the revolutionary myth referred to by Ellul, which insists that revolutions are always irresistible and just.

In his New Year sermon for 1972, the Most Reverend Dr. Daly, Bishop of Ardegh and Clonmacnois in the Irish Republic, observed that one of the sad paradoxes of our time was that the de-mythologising of war had been accompanied by what amounted to a re-mythologising of revolutionary violence.[42] Even so-called pacifists in the West are these days apt to display ambivalence over revolutionary violence, whilst denying the legitimacy of force in the defence of sovereignty.

In many of these struggles, particularly France's war in Algeria and America's in Vietnam, armies had to adapt to, or at least to accept, the domestic dimension of revolutionary warfare. They, or their governments, had to face in two directions at once. The US troops defending the Pentagon against flower people were to the mid-20th century what Wellesley's home-bound regiments had been to the early-19th. The Israelis in the same period adapted from being the revolutionary opposition, to defending the fruits of victory, to dealing with internal subversive threats. Canada's armed forces were deployed briefly to counter a domestic terrorist threat, and the British army has had to adapt to a seemingly permanent secondary commitment in Northern Ireland, where it faces an internal threat inspired by frustrated nationalism, religious bigotry and radical socialism. The notion that 'suppressing violence' at home is a military task belonging only to history or to the Second and Third Worlds, is no longer tenable.

Thus in all three dimensions—scale of force, the domestic and political, and the significance of ideas rather than arms—Western armies are having to adapt to new and often unwelcome conditions. And it is not as though the forces propelling such changes are tangential. The revolutionary myth dominates all modern international affairs, particularly East-West relations, where the Leninist code changes everything. Limited forms of war can no longer be seen as evidence of limited aims: they have become tactical means towards strategic ends. This presents a challenge that stretches each dimension to its limit, combining politics with force, internal threats with external, and the power of armies with the power of ideas.

Notes

1. 'Nothing endures but change', attributed to Heraclitus, 540–480 B.C.
2. William H. McNeill, *The Pursuit of Power: Technology, Armed Force, and Society Since A.D. 1000* (Chicago: University of Chicago Press, 1982), pp. 9, 26, 39, 223–306.
3. McNeill, *op. cit.* pp. 9–10.
4. McNeill, *op. cit.* pp. 11–14; Montgomery of Alamein, *A History of Warfare* (London: Collins, 1968), pp. 34–6.
5. McNeill, *op. cit.* pp. 13–15; Montgomery, *op. cit.*
6. McNeill, *op. cit.* p. 15.
7. McNeill, *op. cit.* pp. 18–19.
8. Richard A. Preston and Sydney F. Wise, *Men in Arms: A History of Warfare and its Interrelationships with Western Society*, 4th ed. (New York: Holt, Rinehart and Winston, 1979), pp. 67–9.
9. McNeill, *op. cit.* p. 68.
10. McNeill, *op. cit.* p. 204; Jan Read, *War in the Peninsula* (London: Faber, 1977).
11. McNeill, *op. cit.* p. 13.
12. Montgomery, pp. 369–77; Peter L. Brent, *The Mongol Empire: Genghis Khan: His Triumph and His Legacy* (London: Weidenfeld and Nicolson, 1976).
13. McNeill, *op. cit.* p. 77.
14. Preston and Wise, *op. cit.* p. 107; McNeill, *op. cit.* pp. 117, 125–39.
15. See Morris Janowitz and Roger Little, *Sociology and the Military Establishment*, rev. ed. (New York: Russell Sage, 1969), pp. 77–99; Bryant Wedge, 'The Individual, the Group and War' in Winnick, Moses and Ostow, eds., *Psychological Bases of War* (New York: Quadrangle, 1973).
16. Theodore Ropp, *War in the Modern World*, new and rev. ed. (New York: Collier Books, 1962), pp. 101–2; McNeill, *op. cit.* p. 162; Preston and Wise, *op. cit.* pp. 183–5; Henry Barnard, *Military Schools and Courses of Instruction in the Science and Art of War* (1872; repr., New York: Greenwood Press, 1969).
17. McNeill, *op. cit.* p. 196; Montgomery, *op. cit.* pp. 345–51; Christopher Hibbert, *The French Revolution* (London: Allen Lane, 1980).
18. Preston and Wise, *op. cit.* pp. 206–8; Ropp, *op. cit.* 162–70; McNeill, *op. cit.* p. 217; Barnard, *op. cit.*
19. Ropp, *op. cit.* pp. 239–50; Preston and Wise, *op. cit.* pp. 265–72; McNeill, *op. cit.* pp. 317–19; Montgomery, *op. cit.* pp. 461–4.
20. Montgomery, *op. cit.* pp. 499–502; Preston and Wise, *op. cit.* pp. 295–7.
21. See Donald L. Farrar, 'Technology Transfer: Pros and Cons', *Military Science and Technology* vol. 4, no. 7 (July 1984), pp. 44–8; Ian Mihai Pacepa, 'Rumania Steals Western Technology', Institute on Strategic Trade, *Current Analysis*, September 1984; A. E. Cullison, 'Soviets take fast path to High-Tech advances', *Journal of Commerce*, 17 July 1984, p. 4; *Wall Street Journal*, 24 July 1984, p. 1; *Defense Watch*, March–April 1984, pp. 12–13; Henri Regnard, 'The Theft of Western Technology', *Journal of Defense and Diplomacy*, April 1984, pp. 44–8, 64; Victor Keegan, 'Open Secrets', *Manchester Guardian Weekly*, 10 June 1984, p. 9, 'In key areas the USSR is applying American technological advances faster than the US is able to do.'
22. From a growing literature in this field, see Subcommittee on Oversight of the Permanent Select Committee on Intelligence, *Soviet Covert Action (The Forgery Offensive)* (Washington, DC: USGPO, 1980); Joseph D. Douglass Jr., 'Soviet Disinformation', *Strategic Review*, Winter 1981, pp. 16–25; Richard H. Shultz and Roy Godson, *Dezinformatsia: Active Measures in Soviet Strategy* (New York: Pergamon Brassey's, 1984).

23. T. A. Critchley, *The Conquest of Violence: Order and Liberty in Britain* (New York: Schocken Books, 1980), p. 55.

24. Concerning civil-military relations, see *Civil/Military Relations* (London: RUSI Seminar Report, 1973); *The Armed Forces in Modern Society* (London: RUSI Seminar report, 1973); Janowitz and Little, *op. cit.*; Stanislav Andreski, *Military Organization and Society*, rev. ed. (Berkeley: University of California, 1968); Morris Janowitz, ed., *The New Military: Changing Patterns of Organization* (New York: Norton, 1964); S. E. Finer, *The Man on Horseback* (London: Pall Mall, 1962); Samuel Huntington, ed., *Changing Patterns in Military Politics* (New York: Free Press of Glencoe, 1962); M. R. Van Gils ed., *The Perceived Role of the Military* (Rotterdam: Rotterdam University Press, 1971); Kurt Lang, *Military Institutions and the Sociology of War* (Beverley Hills: Sage, 1972).

25. For discussions on limited war, see Morton H. Halperin, *Limited War in the Nuclear Age* (New York: John Wiley, 1963); Bernard Brodie, *War and Politics* (New York: Macmillan, 1973), pp. 63–112; Morris Janowitz, *The Professional Soldier: A Social and Professional Portrait* (New York: Free Press, 1960), pp. 303–21.

26. Preston and Wise, *op. cit.*, p. 133.

27. Brodie, *op. cit.* pp. 81–91.

28. See Charles Reynolds, *Modes of Imperialism* (Oxford: Robertson, 1981), pp. 124–71; Norman Etherington, *Theories of Imperialism* (London: Croom Helm, 1984); Raymond F. Betts, *The False Dawn: European Imperialism in the Nineteenth Century* (Minneapolis: University of Minneapolis, 1975).

29. Never better expressed than by Kipling:

> Take up the White man's burden,
> Send forth the best ye breed—
> Go, bind your sons to exile
> To serve your captives' need.
>
> *The White Man's Burden* (1899).

30. Colin Vale, 'Boer War III: The Soviet Imperial Factor in South Africa', *South African International Quarterly* vol. 13, no. 3 (January 1983), p. 187.

31. Montgomery, *op. cit.* pp. 135–41; Gustave E. von Grunebaum, *Medieval Islam* (Chicago: University of Chicago Press, 1946).

32. Ropp, *op. cit.* pp. 39–40; Preston and Wise, *op. cit.* pp. 109–13; Montgomery, *op. cit.* pp. 265–79.

33. See, for instance, G. H. Jansen, *Militant Islam* (London: Pan Books, 1979).

34. Jacques Ellul, *Autopsy of Revolution* (New York: Alfred Knopf, 1971), p. 86.

35. McNeill, *op. cit.* pp. 188–92.

36. See Nathan Leites, *A Study of Bolshevism* (Glencoe, Illinois: The Free Press, 1953).

37. Nathanael Greene, ed., *Fascism: An Anthology* (New York: Thomas Crowell, 1968), pp. 39–112; Gilbert Allardyce, ed., *The Place of Fascism in European History* (New Jersey: Prentice-Hall, 1971), particularly pp. 67–94.

38. Alf Andrew Heggoy, *Insurgency and Counterinsurgency in Algeria* (Bloomington: Indiana University Press, 1972); Alistair Horne, *A Savage War of Peace* (New York: Viking, 1977).

39. V. S. Naipaul, *Among the Believers: An Islamic Journey* (London: Deutsch, 1981), p. 125.

40. Harold C. Deutsch, *The Genesis of Napoleonic Imperialism* (Philadelphia: Porcupine Press, 1975).

41. See Edward N. Luttwak, *The Grand Strategy of the Soviet Union* (New York: St. Martin's, 1983), particularly pp. 72–107.
42. Quoted *Irish Times* (Dublin), 3 January 1972.

2

The American Response to Low-Intensity Conflict: The Formative Period

SAM C. SARKESIAN

The US Army has been involved in low-intensity operations at home and abroad since the American revolutionary war.[1] To deal with this form of warfare it created *ad hoc* special forces, which were quickly disbanded at the cessation of hostilities or termination of the mission. During the two decades following World War II the US military experimented with various special units and operational concepts searching for some type of permanent structure and acceptable doctrines. The Vietnam War signalled the end of the formative period and, ironically, witnessed both the high point and low point of special units and special operations. From then up to the present, the concept of special operations and units organised for such purposes have become institutionalised in the military system.

The purpose of this Chapter is to analyse the formative period in which the American military developed a capability to conduct special operations, identify the conceptual basis and organisational designs for this capability, explore the meaning of low-intensity conflict, and link these to the evolution of the current American military posture for low-intensity conflict. Most of the attention will be on the US Army, although other services went through similar, if less important, developments with respect to low-intensity conflicts.

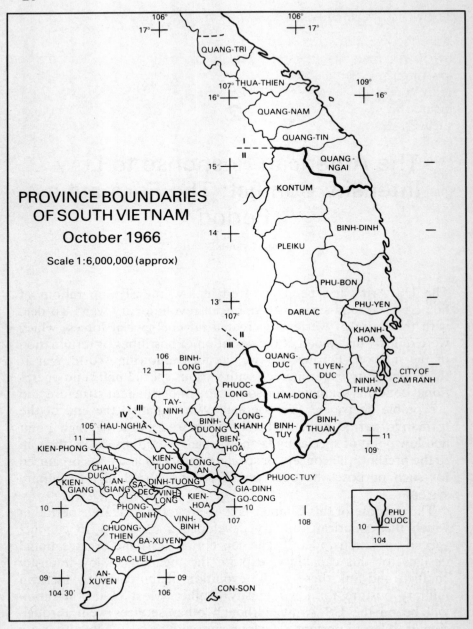

PROVINCE BOUNDARIES
OF SOUTH VIETNAM
October 1966

Scale 1:6,000,000 (approx)

Conceptual and Organisational Issues

An effective military capability for low-intensity conflict integrates two issues: first, an understanding of the nature and characteristics of low-intensity conflicts, and second, organisational strategies that reflect that understanding.[2] Low-intensity conflicts as conceived here include shows of force, but stop short of limited conventional wars such as Korea and the Falkland Islands. However, low-intensity conflicts should not be viewed as conflicts that are less deadly or violent than conventional wars. Rather, the term primarily identifies policy directions and characterises the nature of the conflict. The diagram below (Fig. 1) shows the broad outlines of the range of low-intensity conflicts in relation to other types of conflicts.

Figure 1[3A]

Low ← (Intensity interpreted in terms of policy) → High

Non Combat	Low-Intensity Conflict		Conventional War	Nuclear War
Shows of Force	Special Operations	Revolution/ Counter- revolution	Limited/ Major	Limited/ Major
Military Assistance	Counter- Terror Rescue Quick Strike			

**US Capability

← Good → ← Poor → ← Good →

'Special Operations' encompass counter-terror missions and are primarily highly special contingencies undertaken by skilled conventionally-trained units such as the Rangers and Delta Force. These include such actions as hostage rescue, quick strike and withdrawal operations, and vanguard operations (such as in Grenada). These missions are generally characterised as follows: target identifiable, short duration, narrowly focused, and highly specialised. Doctrines appropriate for these missions are, more or less, variations of existing doctrines for small unit operations, long-range patrols and strike forces. In brief, special operations are primarily rooted in conventional doctrines already well established within existing military institutions.

Revolution and counter-revolution, however, differ significantly from all other forms of conflict conceptually, organisationally, and in their strategic and tactical aspects.[4] The response to these requires different command structures, different training and operational planning, different targets and intelligence. Most important, such conflicts differ in missions, personnel, and resources. Effective response also requires a mix of civilian-military efforts and a high degree of co-ordination and control. This Chapter will demonstrate that, in the context of American foreign policy execution, the US Army's Special Forces have been the units best suited to undertake such missions. However, it will also show that the value of such forces was not always appreciated, and that the forces were misused. This can be attributed both to professional resistance to special forces from within the army, and to a failure by civilian and military leaders to understand the nature of revolutionary war.

The International Context: US Policy and Strategy 1945–60

A serious study of American capability in low-intensity conflict must be done in the context of political and strategic conditions. American politico-military policy and strategy are guided by expectations and demands emanating from the political environment and perceived external threats. Policy fixes the goals and strategy determines the means; both determine the course of military doctrine and influence the evolution of concepts and organisational development.

The elation of the allies over the defeat of Germany and Japan was short-lived. The Yalta conference in 1945 seemed to establish the basis for amicable relations between the Soviet Union and the West. The Declaration on Liberated Europe provided for self-government and free elections in Eastern Europe. Indeed, the United States seemed to have accepted the Yalta conference in spirit as well as in law. However, the policy and strategy of the Soviet Union resting on its Marxist-Leninist ideology proved totally incompatible with the West. The contentious environment was reflected in the United Nations and exacerbated by Soviet power projections around its immediate periphery and in Europe. As John Spanier notes, 'The American dream of post-war peace and Big Three co-operation was to be shattered as the Soviet Union expanded into Eastern and

Central Europe, imposing its control upon Poland, Hungary, Bulgaria, Romania and Albania'.[5] Soviet expansion and pressures also occurred outside Eastern Europe, in Iran, Turkey and Greece.

Two major events marked the growing American concern over and reaction to Soviet expansionism. After 18 months of witnessing the expansion of Soviet power, America tried to establish a countervailing policy and strategy. First, the Truman Doctrine was proclaimed in 1947, intended to contain and counteract the Communist revolution in Greece and relieve Soviet pressure on Turkey. The following year the Communist coup took place in Czechoslovakia. As Ray Cline recalls:

> It is hard to remember how menacing the Soviet encroachments appeared. In February 1948 the Communist coup in Czechoslovakia succeeded and then in March the popular and well-known Foreign Minister, Jan Masaryk, jumped—or was pushed—from a window to his death. The shock in the United States was tremendous.[5]

Second, the United States embarked on a programme to strengthen Western Europe: the Marshall Plan, the North Atlantic Treaty Organisation (NATO) and the commitment to establishing a framework for a US-Western containment of the Soviet Union in Europe became the mainstays of US policy and strategy. Thus, from the outset, threats against American security and the Western alliance were perceived by the West to focus on Europe and emanate from the USSR.

Within a short time ominous signs appeared in Asia. The 'loss' of China to the Communists, the proliferation of Chinese-type revolutions in many parts of Southeast Asia, and the Korean War, all seemed to indicate a coherent Soviet bloc strategy to 'defeat' the United States, the West and their allies. In reaction to the fall of China, the United States tried to establish a NATO-type containment in Asia. Despite the Communist victory in China, however, many officials in the United States felt that the Chinese brand of Communism would eventually clash with the Soviets. Nonetheless, the Truman Administration viewed Communism as a monolith. There followed a publicly proclaimed American defence perimeter in Southeast Asia designed to contain China, but this perimeter excluded Korea.

At the same time, a number of revolutions (insurgencies) broke out, the most notable in French Indochina. Indeed, shortly after the Communist take-over of mainland China, Viet-Minh forces led by Ho Chi Minh, began a series of successful engagements against French forces in North Vietnam, culminating in the French defeat at Dien Bien Phu in 1954. In the United States, the 'never again' school emerged, committed to the view that American ground forces should not be used to fight a land war on the mainland of Asia.[7] As if to reinforce the American concern with Europe, the French involvement in Indochina was linked directly to European politics, dispelling notions that such wars posed a different and more difficult challenge to the West. Perhaps most important, decolonisation began in earnest, eventually creating an international political environment of competing ideologies, regional power centres and many fragile political systems. Finally, the success of the Maoist revolution legitimised wars of national liberation. Castro's revolution in Cuba set the stage for revolutions in Latin and Central America.

The Korean War signalled a sharp demarcation from the post-World War II period and opened a new phase of international politics. The Soviets had developed atomic weapons by 1949 and, by the time the Korean War ended, they had a delivery capability and had tightened their grip on Eastern Europe. At the same time, Stalin's death in 1953 plunged the Soviet system into a leadership struggle that was not resolved until 1955 and institutionalised only in 1958 with the appointment of Nikita Khrushchev as Premier. Although the new leaders in the Kremlin proclaimed 'peaceful co-existence', many in the West were convinced that co-existence was just another name for Soviet aggression in a different guise. Confrontations over Berlin, the Soviet intervention in Hungary, conflicts in the Middle East (Suez crisis), heightened tensions in the Formosa Straits, and the increasing tensions in Europe between East and West, seemed to confirm Western fears, while reaffirming the Soviet view that the world was moving towards socialist predominance. Indeed, it did appear that in a short span of one decade the nature of world politics was tilting away from the Western notion of world order.

The 1950s saw the firm establishment of an American policy of containing Communism. (The now famous 'Mr. X' article written by George Kennan outlined the basis for such a policy).[8] One component was the creation of a series of alliances around the rimland of the Soviet Union. These included, for example, the Central Treaty Organisation (CENTO) comprising Turkey, Iraq, Pakistan, Iran, and Britain; and the Southeast Asia Treaty Organisation (SEATO), comprising the United States, Britain, France, New Zealand, Australia, the Philippines, Thailand, and Pakistan. Together NATO and CENTO provided an alliance of states extending from Norway to Iran and Pakistan. While none of the new alliances had the strength and commitment of NATO, they did provide an ideological posture, arrayed against Soviet expansion, which some called 'pactomania'.[9]

Another component of American policy put into place in the early 1950s coincided with the election of President Dwight Eisenhower. John Foster Dulles, Secretary of State, felt that the idea of containment was insufficient. He stated that 'the aim of American foreign policy . . . should not be to coexist indefinitely with the Communist menace; it should be to eliminate that menace. The purpose of American policy should be a rollback of Soviet power'.[10]

But the Eisenhower administration's policy was that the United States should not become involved in local ground wars, as had been the case in Korea. Rather, its strategy was based on its ability to strike the Soviet Union or mainland China with American air and sea power armed with massive atomic weaponry, should there be local aggression anywhere supported by either of these powers. The Eisenhower-Dulles policy of 'brinksmanship' was given credit by some for bringing an end to the Korean War.[11]

The final component of American policy was the Eisenhower Doctrine. As a result of the Suez crisis and the subsequent withdrawal of British, French and Israeli forces, President Nasser of Egypt gained a significant amount of prestige in the Middle East. At the same time, the Soviet Union appeared to gain the most from the apparent disarray between the American, British, French and Israeli governments. In an attempt to gain some leverage and establish a more consistent policy, the Eisenhower administration supported a 1957 Joint Resolution of Congress which declared that the independence and integrity of Middle Eastern nations was vital to American interests. The resolution further stated that the United States was '. . . prepared to use armed force to assist any nation or nations requesting assistance against armed aggression from any country controlled by international Communism'.[12] Although it was an ambiguous policy, the Eisenhower Doctrine, as it became known, did delineate between pro-West and pro-Soviet states. 'It helped Washington abandon Nasser and construct a pro-American, anti-Communist, anti-Nasser bloc forcing the states in the Middle East to choose between Cairo and Moscow on one hand, and Washington on the other.[13]

The primary American strategy of the 1950s, then, was based on nuclear retaliation in response to major and local wars. This 'new look' dominated the decade, particularly in the aftermath of the Korean War. Even during that war, however, the major focus of American strategic concern was Europe and the possibility of Soviet aggression there. This is not to suggest that the Korean War did not have some impact on American policy and strategy. As Robert Osgood points out, 'the great impact of the Korean War on Western strategic imagination springs from the fact that the war undermined the preoccupation of strategic thought and plans with general war and challenged the basic premises underlying the preoccupation'.[14] He goes on to say that 'the Korean War, therefore, compelled the proponents of containment to cope with a form of warfare—local conventional war by Soviet proxy—that could neither be deterred nor won by US central war capacity'.[15]

Yet, even after the Korean War, the eyes and thoughts of American civilian and military policy remained fixed on Europe and the Soviet heartland. The Soviet acquisition of atomic weapons and the maintenance of large land forces in Eastern Europe were sufficient cause for American concern. American policy and strategy did not long retain serious interest in local conventional wars. Indeed, for most, 'the Korean War was to be regarded as an aberration and American land forces would not be committed again to fight conventional battles with Communist hordes in Asia unless it became necessary in the national interest'.[16]

Should Communist threats occur in any part of the world challenging its interests, the United States would choose the time and place to retaliate. But the Soviet threat and American strategy made it necessary constantly to upgrade nuclear weapons in order to maintain American superiority. The capacity for massive retaliation required constant attention to developing more and better strategic weapons and demanded a strategy that raised the destructiveness of war to its highest level.

These components of American policy and strategy during the 1950s were based on perceptions that the Soviet threat was uppermost, translating into a primary American concern with the European battlefield. Nonetheless, increasing unrest in the Third World, the impact of decolonisation, the French struggle in Indochina, and the institutionalisation of the Communist regime on the mainland of China emerged as serious challenges to America's European-oriented politico-military posture.

American Defence Posture

The demobilisation of the American military which began immediately following World War II led to a considerably weakened military posture. In 1945, the United States Army had 89 divisions consisting of eight million servicemen. 'By 30 June 1947, the Army was a volunteer body of 684,000 ground troops, and 306,000 airmen (the Navy was meanwhile reduced to a strength of 484,000, the Marine Corps to 92,000).'[17] In 1950, the strength of the Army was further reduced to 591,000, organised into 10 divisions. The monopoly of atomic weapons evolved into a defence posture which relegated ground forces (non-strategic forces) to secondary status. A strategy was designed based on the air- and sea-delivery capability of atomic weapons against any aggressor. As General Ridgway has written: 'Two factors stimulated this thinking—the earnest desire of the nation to cut down on its military expenditures, and the erroneous belief that in the atomic missile, delivered by air, we had found the ultimate weapon.'[18]

Some improvements had been made in American defence organisation following World War II. The National Security Act of 1947 provided for a centralised defence machinery and a Central Intelligence Agency (CIA). The new national security establishment prepared the groundwork for a post-World War II defence posture with a National Security Council paper NSC 68 (1950). This document '. . . surveyed the strategic position of the United States in relation to Russia's acquisition of nuclear weapons . . . the study was designed to foster a common outlook within the government'.[19] It provided for increases in defence spending and the strengthening of America's nuclear forces.

During the period 1945–50, the Army struggled to define its role, as the primary focus for defence shifted to air and sea forces capable of delivering atomic missiles. It saw its primary role in a non-atomic battlefield. In an atomic war, the Army viewed its role as ancillary to atomic delivery forces; this resulted in a doctrine that focused primarily on a European-type battle environment. Thus, much of the doctrinal debate within the Army centred around the use of tanks, the organisation of battlefield defence positions, and 'mop-up' operations following an atomic exchange. For some, the US Army was seen primarily as a home guard. As one authority observes, 'between 1945 and 1950, a number of changes thus occurred in Army doctrine. Despite these alterations, much remained the same . . . Army doctrine was oriented toward a European-type battlefield—an orientation which varied only slightly during the next 30 years'.[20] In fact, until the Korean War, organisation, equipment, and tactics generally followed the experience in World War II.

But, the combat capability of the American Army had so deteriorated that, upon entering the Korean War, General Ridgway stated: 'We were . . . in a state of shameful unreadiness when the Korean War broke out . . .. The state of our Army in Japan at the outbreak of the Korean War was inexcusable'.[21] Occupation duty and reliance on the 'bigger bang for the buck' had taken their toll. The Korean War seemed to confirm the weak American military capability—at least during its initial year. The military remained basically in its World War II frame of mind. With the exception of atomic weapons, much of the equipment and weaponry was of World War II vintage. Moreover, the severe reduction of manpower initially limited America's ability to respond to the North Korean offensive. Nonetheless, improvements had been made in American defence organisation. Additionally, air and sea capabilities had been improved. As the Korean War progressed, the American military learned to adapt to North Korean and Chinese tactics, not however without casualties and local defeats. This adaptation was primarily in using conventional tactics more effectively and employing better trained and disciplined troops.[22]

Yet, at the end of the Korean War 'the official position was that no real changes in doctrine had occurred or had been necessary'.[23] But it seemed clear that certain changes had occurred in doctrine—changes that were to affect American operations in Vietnam. 'The Army had become accustomed to massive amounts of firepower which came at the expense of mobility . . . [it] focused upon attrition at the expense of manoeuvre and its offensive spirit.'[24]

By the late 1950s, the Soviets had launched an operational intercontinental ballistic missile (ICBM) and the Sputnik. The US response, bordering on near panic, was to mobilise massive resources for space vehicles and missile weaponry. The Soviet accomplishments had the effect of driving American financial resources, weapons designs and doctrine towards strategic considerations and threat perceptions focusing on the Soviet Union. Although there was some attention to the possibility of conflicts outside the European context, 'the domination of the 1950s by the nuclear threat tended to cast a shadow over developments in other areas'.[25]

The military adapted its posture accordingly. Because of the emphasis on air and sea forces, the notion of military capability rested primarily with the Air Force and the Navy. The Army was reorganised around the 'pentomic' division consisting of battle-groups; relatively self-contained and semi-independent units designed for the atomic battlefield. This attempt to adapt to the atomic age resulted in lack of coherency between doctrine, organisation, tactics and weaponry. Among other things, 'the technology lagged behind the doctrine, and strategic concepts raced ahead of tactical realities'.[26] By the end of the 1950s, the Army again reorganised in an attempt to overcome earlier difficulties. Organisational structures focused on heavy and medium divisions, partly as an answer to increasing concerns about non-nuclear wars. Thus emerged the concept of the dual-capability army, designed to fight both nuclear and non-nuclear wars.

But it was not until the early 1960s that a serious effort was made to expand American conventional military capability, even though in the aftermath of the Korean War the strength of conventional NATO forces had been increased. The Kennedy administration laid the groundwork for 'flexible response' on the premise that forces armed and trained for nuclear warfare were not suitable for non-nuclear wars. Massive retaliation was de-emphasised and emphasis placed on the military's ability to respond across a broad conflict spectrum. This strategy continued into the Vietnam War period, when it proved inadequate in producing a political-military condition acceptable to American civilian and military policy-makers.

Unconventional Warfare and the Development of Special Forces

The combat weakness of the American military during the immediate post-World War II period was more than matched by the inadequate and virtually non-existent capability in unconventional warfare. Despite the World War II exploits of various military organisations functioning as guerrilla units, engaging in behind-the-lines missions in Burma and the Philippines, and the activities of the Office of Strategic Services (OSS) in Europe, no serious effort was made to continue such capability after the war.

The Truman administration moved quickly to abolish the OSS. 'In

the rush to tidy up administrative matters, the Bureau of the Budget
. . . which had always been unhappy with Donovan's unconventional
style, strongly urged prompt abolition of the OSS.'[27] This was done
by Executive Order on 1 October, 1945.

Not only did such actions reflect historical American antagonism
towards special units, and an absence of perceived requirement for
them, but also the 'bigger bang for the buck' philosophy presumed
that modern weapons and an atomic monopoly could easily substitute
for human resources. These national decisions had their parellel in
the US Army. 'The Army was going through one of its cyclic phases
of anti-élitism almost invariably associated with peacetime.'[28] With
the reduction in Army strength and concern with defence
expenditures, 'there were simply no spaces for élite units, such as the
once-proud Ranger battalions'.[29]

Any remaining capability was scattered in various agencies. A
research and analysis section (R and A) was transferred to the
Department of State,

> and transferred to the Secretary of War [were] the S-1 Branch and X-2, plus
> whatever else was left over after demobilisation. Since the paramilitary services of
> OSS phased out rapidly, what the Army got was an independent organisation
> (called SSU—Strategic Services Unit) containing espionage and counter-espion-
> age elements.[30]

The SSU is rarely mentioned in Army history. Indeed, lack of
military interest in the SSU and its missions made it an anomaly in a
peace-time America. Little was done and the unit sank into oblivion.

The establishment of the National Security Council, the Department of Defense and the Central Intelligence Agency signalled a
more systematic approach to intelligence and covert operations. In
1947, NSC 4 authorised the Director of Central Intelligence to
undertake covert psychological operations. This was followed by
NSC 10/2 in 1948, which directed the CIA to create a formal covert
political capability. According to Ray Cline, however, these functions were not sought by the Agency. 'CIA entered into covert action
operations under pressure from leading US officials of the day to
support basic US foreign policy.'[31]

The attention to intelligence and covert operations at the national
level prompted the Army to re-examine its own posture. This
followed two tracks: the Army's capability in psychological warfare
and its capability in unconventional warfare. With regard to the first
track, immediately following World War II the US Army response to
unconventional warfare and covert operations found its place in

psychological warfare within the Plans and Operations Division of the War Department and later G-3 Operations in the Department of Defence. But even here little was done except to study its feasibility, to lay the groundwork for some elements to be incorporated into school curricula, and to create a small detachment for the conduct of psychological warfare.[32] 'On the eve of the Korean War, it [the Army] had made "only a start" toward development of a psychological warfare capability.'[33] The establishment of a formal unconventional war capability within the military was precluded for a variety of reasons, ranging from CIA missions to conventional military perspectives. The military perceived its role as supportive of other agencies whose responsibility included unconventional operations.

Regarding the second track, the Army undertook a number of studies examining unconventional warfare and ways in which it could establish such a capability. These ranged from the feasibility of establishing an airborne reconnaissance unit to the possibility of including courses on subversion and espionage in service school curricula. In the process, the Army sought to combine two different types of capabilities and missions. It was thought that the capability of the airborne reconnaissance unit should integrate OSS experience in World War II and Ranger/Commando missions. 'From an "OSS point of view", this organisational concept should have been unacceptable. It attempted to lump together missions and capabilities of Rangers and Commandos with those of Special Operations and Operational Group elements of the OSS. It combined the tactical with the strategic.'[34] Upon close examination, these studies revealed a misunderstanding of unconventional warfare and conceptual confusion over the distinction between Ranger and Commando type operations, which were tactical in nature—the quick strike variant, and long-term OSS-type activities which had been carried over to the post-war era, albeit in a different guise.

In reviewing these studies, the Joint Chiefs of Staff (JCS) objected to the development of a military capability in unconventional warfare or in creating special units for such warfare. The NSC had already given this mission to the CIA. While the JCS were agreed that the military should support CIA activities wherever and whenever feasible, they did not consider unconventional warfare a major military concern.

There was also a professional basis for the JCS position. Historically, military systems have frowned upon the permanent establishment of special units for unconventional operations; it was feared that élite units would attract the best people and thus deprive the standard units of quality leadership.[35] Equally important, military professionals were educated in the grand battles of major wars. Little attention was given to unconventional conflicts, considered peripheral to the major thrust of military professionalism. Moreover, career success was (and is) primarily through the standard command and staff ladder. Finally, and particularly important, covert operations and unconventional warfare were closely tied into intelligence and political activities—which were anathema to conventional military minds. As Colonel Francis Kelly has observed,

> An élite group has always appeared within the Army during every war in which the United States has been engaged . . .. As surely as such groups arose, there arose also the grievances of the normally conservative military men who rejected whatever was distinctive or different or special . . .. In the conduct of conservative military affairs, revisions of current military modes are frequently resisted with missionary zeal and emotional fervor simply because they mean change, they are different. . . .[36]

Thus conceptual confusion and misunderstanding established the basis for Army thinking on such matters, and this continues to the present day. The other services followed similar patterns. This is not to deny that there were some military men who saw the importance of developing an American capability in low-intensity conflict and who recognised the distinctions between OSS and Ranger/Commando type operations. It was this core of military men who were the prime movers for the establishment of the Special Forces, not without help, however, from the international security situation and from a few civilian policy-makers.

For much of the 1950s and until the early 1960s, the American military responded hesitantly to the increasing revolutionary conflicts occurring throughout the world. Nevertheless, the North Korean use of guerrilla forces in the Korean War forced some response. As a result, the American military pieced together several units and developed *ad hoc* tactics to create an unconventional war capability.

> Limited though it was, however, the Army's activity in this field—particularly the doctrinal confusion that marked its tentative thinking on unconventional warfare and its early interaction with CIA/OPC—is important for a full understanding of the subsequent developments that contributed to the creation of Special Forces. The first of these developments was the outbreak of war in Korea.[37]

Although conventional combat was the main characteristic of the

Korean War, a different challenge emerged:

> With thousands of North Korean guerrillas harassing the Eighth Army's rear, behind-the-line activity on the part of the United States became a tempting course of action in an effort to retaliate in kind. But the OSS was gone, the CIA did not have a similar capability, and Special Forces was not yet born. It was necessary to paste together in some haste an organisation to do the job of unconventional warfare.[38]

This 'pasting together' produced several types of special units ranging from Wolfpack, designed to conduct guerrilla operations within North Korea, UNPIK (United Nations Partisan Infantry Korea) to the 8240th Army Unit and a variety of other units designed to establish escape and evasion nets and agent entry capability. However, these units added little to American military effectiveness. The lack of training and inadequate co-ordination, but more importantly the lack of understanding of the nature of unconventional warfare, precluded an effective unconventional response.[39]

The Central Intelligence Agency developed its own unconventional activities in Korea under the Joint Advisory Commission Korea (JACK). Led by a military officer assigned to the CIA, JACK covered the entire spectrum of unconventional warfare. In an effort to achieve a greater degree of co-ordination between the military services and the CIA, CCRAK (Covert, Clandestine and Related Activities in Korea) was established, controlled by the Commander in Chief, Far East (CINCFE). However, this organisation had no real authority over CIA personnel nor did it succeed in eliminating duplication of efforts or in correcting 'amateurish' unconventional war operations.

Towards the end of the Korean War, several contingents of Special Forces officers were sent to Korea, a number being assigned to these 'paste together' units. Nonetheless, there was little if any appreciable increase in the effectiveness of unconventional warfare activity, not only for the reasons noted earlier but also because such doctrine and tactics as there were for special operations were obscure and conventionally oriented. Also, there were too few trained Special Forces officers to make a difference late in the war. Perhaps equally important, there was no central Special Forces headquarters in Korea to plan and co-ordinate unconventional operations.

Ranger units were employed in Korea, but these were organised and trained for hit-and-run raids, commando type operations and long range patrols reminiscent of World War II. These units operated in close conjunction with front line infantry units.

The experience in Korea did little to create enthusiasm for unconventional warfare within the conventional military. The relative ineffectiveness of such operations in Korea and the focus of military professionals on conventional command and staff structures, combined with the persistent concern with the Soviet threat in Europe, encouraged the continued neglect of unconventional warfare during the latter part of the 1950s. The view that unconventional warfare was an adjunct of conventional operations exerted an important and lasting influence.

Thus, the confusion over special operations and unconventional warfare continued, but with an added dimension. Previously Special Forces missions and those assigned to Ranger/Commando type units were amalgamated. Now Army doctrine dictated that such missions were an inherent part of conventional operations. For a better understanding of how these misconceptions developed and their implications, it is necessary to look at the activation and evolution of Special Forces.

Special Forces and Unconventional Warfare Doctrine

The creation of Special Forces and the development of unconventional warfare doctrine evolved during the Korean War. Ironically, these were not aimed at the challenges of the war but at the Soviet Union.

> NATO was scarcely a military reality, and the Berlin blockade highlighted the difference in firepower between the US 1st Infantry Division and three light armoured cavalry regiments and some 100 Russian divisions across the iron curtain. Top-level intelligence was convinced that Stalin would attack no later than 1954. In some desperation, the Army at long last turned to guerrilla warfare concepts as a possible 'equaliser'. The captive peoples of Eastern Europe were the target of American hopes to neutralise at least some of Stalin's divisions.[40]

Much would take place before the Special Forces were activated, beginning with the creation of an Office of the Chief of Psychological Warfare (OCPW) in 1951. This comprised 'three major divisions: Psychological Operations, Requirements, and Special Operations'.[41] The Special Operations Division and the mission assigned to the Psychological Warfare Office set the stage for the creation of Special Forces at Fort Bragg in 1952. Although strong opposition persisted within the Army hierarchy against a special warfare focus, the Army

Chief of Staff, General J. Lawton Collins was supportive, as was General Robert McClure who had informal links to the White House. These factors helped in overcoming the obstacles to the formation of Special Forces. 'In an obscure corner of the sprawling post at Fort Bragg, a Psychological Warfare Centre had been established, very much outside the mainstream of airborne infantry life.'[42] Within this Centre the 10th Special Forces Group was born. There was some resentment because of the link between Special Forces and psychological warfare units but it was McClure's belief that, owing to the resistance of other services, as well as from within the Army itself, Special Forces would not be created unless the two were linked.[43] Psychological warfare had legitimacy; Special Forces did not.

The 10th Special Forces Group was initially organised around the operational team concepts of the OSS. When it was activated, an 'A' Team of Special Forces consisted of 15 men (including two officers). This FA Team, as it was known, reported to a higher level FB Team, designed to control two or more FA teams in a particular area. The next highest level was the FC Team which controlled teams in a single country (later the FC Team became Special Forces company head-quarters). The FD team was organised to control the activities of teams in two or more countries.

Each member of the FA teams was trained as a specialist with skills ranging from operations, intelligence and demolitions to field medical care. Additionally, the men were trained to operate with foreign equipment. The training was designed to qualify men to operate in small, isolated teams within a foreign environment for long periods of time. The official mission of the 10th Special Forces Group was:

> To infiltrate its component operational detachments to designated areas within the enemy's sphere of influence and organise the indigenous guerrilla potential on a quasi-military or a military basis for tactical and strategic exploitation in conjunction with our land, sea and air forces.[44]

By late September 1952, some thought was being given to adding special operations missions (Ranger/Commando) to Special Forces as a result of the Korean experience. The heavy casualties suffered by the Army's Rangers in Korea resulted in their deactivation. In an effort to retain some special operations capability, consideration was given to the formation of Special Forces Ranger Companies. However, under the organisational arrangements for the Special Forces, this was not deemed feasible and was abandoned. At the end of 1952, it seemed that the Army had finally delineated Special Forces from special operations. But, in fact, confusion still underpinned the concept of Special Forces. As one of the Army's earlier experts on unconventional warfare recently observed, 'It was indicative of the US Army's basic misunderstanding of what Special Forces really are, that official lineage of Special Forces is traced back to the First Special Service Force. The OSS was a more legitimate ancestor of today's Green Berets'.[45] The most glaring example of such misunderstanding at the operational level occurred when the 10th Special Forces Group was assigned to Germany. Planners in US European Headquarters assessed the effectiveness of the Group by the number of men the unit could put 'on the line' at the onset of war.[46]

By the late 1950s, the idea of using Special Forces against the Soviet and Eastern bloc countries appeared less likely. The lack of serious Western response to the Hungarian revolt in 1956 seemed to imply the acceptance of spheres of influence between the East and West. But there were other reasons. The continuing emphasis on strategic and conventional capability with respect to the Soviet Union gave little credence to special operations. Further, it was difficult for a democratic system to accept the idea of American soldiers fomenting revolution and conducting guerrilla operations against another state. Also, the conventional American military remained hostile to Special Forces. This was well illustrated in the attempt to get official approval for the 'green beret' as an official item of the uniform for the Special Forces.[47] Not only was there a great deal of official resistance but a number of high-ranking military officers reacted vehemently to such a proposal. The combination of these factors reinforced the resistance to the development of a serious low-intensity conflict capability and perpetuated the misunderstanding of such conflicts, particularly revolution and counter-revolution—the heart of low-intensity conflicts. Thus, Special Forces lost some of their original purpose and earlier thrust.

Shortly after the Korean War, the Special Forces reached their nadir. Even with the commitment of the 10th Special Forces to Germany, the activation of the 77th Special Forces at Fort Bragg and the 1st Special Forces in Okinawa, the total strength of the Special Forces stood only at about 2,000. These small numbers hardly mattered to conventional military posture and capability. Indeed, Special Forces were considered to be on the periphery of the military system. The careers of professional military officers were hardly helped, and often hindered, by association with Special Forces.

Moreover, Ranger/Commando units were increasingly seen as appropriate for all forms of low-intensity conflicts. The missions of such units were presumed to be so closely related to Special Forces that it was difficult for most military men to draw a clear distinction between the two. The conduct of 'little wars' was equated to the special missions of Ranger/Commando units. In doctrinal terms, it was expected that all military operations, regardless of their nature, would operate in conjunction with tactical forces on the ground. Special operations became the catch-all for all aspects of low-intensity conflicts and, in turn, were seen as adjuncts to conventional operations, in which both Special Forces and Ranger/Commando units could be employed.

With the presidency of John F. Kennedy in 1960, Special Forces began a period of growth that extended into the Vietnam War. Supported by the President, whose view of Communism included concern for Third World revolutions, Special Forces took on a new mission, which completely subordinated its original purpose and put aside others. Counter-insurgency became the catchword of the early 1960s. Rather than the conduct of unconventional warfare behind the enemy's lines, the Special Forces changed their orientation to countering guerrilla forces which operated in support of enemy forces in friendly countries. At the same time, there occurred a conceptual shift and doctrinal realignment focusing on counter-insurgency.[48]

Mao's revolution in China became the model for counter-revolution as well as for revolution itself. The Indochina War fought by the French against Ho Chi Minh and the Viet-Minh was seen as an extension of the Chinese revolution. Yet, as one authority concluded:

> The most difficult obstacle facing the Army as it attempted to prepare for counter-insurgency operations was the mental redirection and re-education required of its officers and soldiers, most of whom had only been exposed to nuclear or conventional tactical doctrine . . . . The elusive ideal of identifying goals of military action within counter-insurgency was thus overwhelmed by the more immediate task of developing tactical organisations, equipment and doctrine . . . most tactics for counter-insurgency remained extensions of, or resembled, small-unit tactics for a conventional battlefield.[49]

But the fact that President Kennedy took the lead in stressing the development of a counter-insurgency capability opened the floodgates.

> The services rushed new field manuals into print, and the commercial publishing market brought out new books on resistance, insurgency, and guerrillas. The

writings of Mao, Che and Giap neared best-seller status, although it remains doubtful that many of those who acquired the books actually read them or that, of those who did, many grasped their lessons. The nation's 'think tanks', from Santa Monica to Washington, joined in the chorus with a great rash of new studies. If there was a surfeit of information about the subject, there was also a genuine enthusiasm, one reason for which was that, on paper, counter-insurgency seems both logical and practical. Practice, of course, was and is something else.[50]

Andrew Krepinevich, however, makes the telling point that much of this literature was ill-conceived, and hence, next to useless for the purpose of educating the army about counter-insurgency.[51]

President Kennedy's emphasis on unconventional warfare and his efforts at revitalising Special Forces seemed to signal the beginning of what many felt was a turn-around in the fortunes of special units and special warfare capability, and some shift in the European emphasis. However, the emphasis in counter-insurgency doctrine and training was almost exclusively on military aspects of unconventional warfare. Guerrilla war, hit-and-run raids and intelligence activities became primary missions.[52] But the centre of gravity of revolution and counter-revolution—the most difficult of low-intensity conflicts— was (and is) the political-social milieu of the indigenous system. There was little that prepared the American military for an effective role in such conflicts. Not only were conflicts such as the Indochina War and Mao's revolution in China misread and misinterpreted, but conceptual confusion that had begun in the 1950s became more pronounced. Guerrilla war, insurgency, special warfare—all of these terms became entrenched in the lexicon of American military terminology.

The fact of the matter is that none of these terms aim specifically at the roots of wars such as Indochina and Vietnam. Revolution and counter-revolution are more appropriate concepts. These include a broad spectrum of politico-psychological components. Revolution includes guerrilla war but only as an adjunct. Its primary purpose is the overthrow of the existing system by the use of unconventional war combined with political mobilisation and political action. Terrorism and propaganda are major vehicles of the revolutionary process, but the purpose of the armed units is to protect the revolutionary leadership and cadre and to create an environment in which the revolutionary political system can operate.

Revolution and counter-revolution appeared to bring a totally new dimension to American views on unconventional war or special operations. Equally important, most American civilian leaders had little understanding of the Third World environment, much less of revolution and counter-revolution. Looking through conventional lenses from within liberal democracy, the concept of revolution and counter-revolution became distorted and misunderstood. Few military and civilian leaders appreciated the fundamental distinction between guerrilla war, insurgency, and revolution/counter-revolution. Those who did, found it almost impossible to translate their understanding through the military and civilian bureaucracy into doctrine and appropriate training. The experience of General Edward Lansdale in the Philippines and later in Vietnam in the 1950s is telling in this regard. Of his experience, Lansdale writes:

> People's wars are not for fighters with short attention spans . . . I concluded that Americans who go out to help others in people's wars must understand that these struggles are composed of the means that shape the ideological end. Essentially, they are conflicts between viewpoints on the worth of individual man.[53]

Unfortunately, Lansdale found that most military and civilian leaders had little understanding of these issues and persisted in viewing such conflicts from a conventional perspective.[54]

The Vietnam War

Vietnam represents a key reference point in the development of US unconventional war strategy, doctrine and organisational structures. While much has been published about the US experience in Vietnam, there remains a pressing need for a systematic and analytical assessment of the Vietnam War. Nonetheless, there is sufficient material from which to build tentative assessments and to establish a basis for historical study.

Special Forces operations in Vietnam did make some attempt to aim at the social-political centre of gravity of revolution and counter-revolution. This is particularly clear in the 1961–62 period, when the Special Forces operated under the CIA in the Civilian Irregular Defense Group (CIDG) programme, which was demonstrably effective in Darlac province.[55] Most Special Forces personnel were aware of political and psychological components of low-intensity conflicts. They also recognised that a long period of time was required to develop effective counter-revolutionary systems. Moreover, many Special Forces professionals were sensitive to the thin line between moral and ethical conduct in such conflicts. Mistakes were, of course, made in Special Forces operations. There were also some whose sole commitment to Special Forces in Vietnam was to obtain a record of their assignment—the ticket-punching drive. Underneath it all, conventional troop commanders remained highly sceptical of the utility of Special Forces. Nowhere is this more evident than in the reorientation of Special Forces away from the CIDG pacification programme and toward unconventional special operations in support of conventional offensive action. The change in emphasis was congruent with the Army's approach to counter-insurgency, but it had a devastating impact on the CIDG programme.[56] In any case, the Vietnam experience undermined any attempts to develop an effective long-range US capability in unconventional conflicts.

The Post-Vietnam Era

There is a considerable body of opinion in both military and civilian quarters that places little value on the United States experience in Vietnam with respect to future low-intensity conflicts. Though it is true that policy-makers should not necessarily be bound by the past, it is also true that forgetting the 'lessons' of Vietnam is to invite similar results. If one reviews the history of the United States military operations, for example, against the Seminole Indians (1836–43), in the Philippines (1898–1901) and in Vietnam (1964–72), one is struck by a number of similarities regarding politico-military strategy, military operations and insurgency forces. Unfortunately, there has been little historical analysis for the purpose of developing doctrine. Indeed, the military in particular has a singularly short institutional memory. To reduce the gap between past experience and current and future operational contingencies, there must be an analysis of doctrinal relevance *and* irrelevance of the lessons of Vietnam, both political and military, as these may apply in future conflicts.

Without belabouring these matters, providing another perspective on the war or engaging in a review of the literature, it is useful to make several observations relevant to this study. Firstly, the Vietnam War developed into an asymmetrical relationship between the United States on the one hand and the Viet Cong and North Vietnamese on the other. While the United States was engaged in a limited war, for the revolutionaries and counter-revolutionaries it was a total war. Secondly, conventional military wisdom, training and traditional professional education were clearly inadequate to meet the challenges of the politico-military dimensions of unconventional conflicts. Thirdly, American domestic political attitudes were crucial in affecting the American military role in Vietnam. The crescendo of criticism from domestic political groups had a decided effect on the policy options available to the political leadership. All these factors compounded the asymmetry of the relationships in Vietnam. Fourthly, US military intervention in support of a governing élite or political system that does not have some minimum level of internal support is likely to erode indigenous public support for the existing system. Fifthly, the American experience in Vietnam remains an important influence in the world perspective of military and civilian leaders and, as such, has an important influence on politico-military strategy for unconventional conflicts. Lastly, the Vietnam experience stimulated a military preoccupation with the conventional environment of European wars. This is reflected in hardware and tactics as well as in professional military education and training.

Regardless of recent events, therefore, the US military intervention still weighs heavily on the minds of important political actors. As Osgood noted:

> . . . the popular disaffection with the Vietnamese war does not indicate a reversion to pre-Korean attitudes towards limited war. Rather it indicates serious questioning of the premises about the utility of limited war as an instrument of American policy, the premises that originally moved the proponents of limited war strategy and that underlay the original confidence of the Kennedy Administration in America's power to cope with local Communist incursions of all kinds.[57]

Most important, as demonstrated in Vietnam, the employment of force for any length of time requires popular support. Without it, military intervention of any type will quickly lose its legitimacy.

This is best reflected in the statement of General Fred C. Weyand. Writing in 1976, he noted:

> Vietnam was a reaffirmation of the peculiar relationship between the American Army and the American people. The American Army really is a people's Army in the sense that it belongs to the American people who take a jealous and proprietary interest in its involvement. When the Army is committed the American people are committed, when the American people lose their commitment it is futile to try to keep the Army committed. In the final analysis, the American Army is not so much an arm of the Executive Branch as it is an arm of the American people. The Army, therefore, cannot be committed lightly.[58]

In sum, the involvement in Vietnam indicated that US policy-makers (civilian and military) had difficulty in understanding and appreciating the nature of unconventional posturing of US forces, and the designing of strategy through conventional lenses precluded the effective designing of tactical operations and those aimed at the 'essence' of revolutionary conflict. Additionally, the democratic socialisation process and the linkages between the military and American society made it extremely difficult to provide the necessary training and conflict analysis appropriate for counter-revolutionary involvement.

In this context, the Clausewitzian notion of war with its centre of gravity on the destruction of the enemy armed forces is open to question in the conduct of counter-revolution. Yet, such a notion is at the core of US military doctrine and organisational strategy. As the Vietnam War showed, response to unconventional conflicts are the most difficult for the United States and its military establishments.

The advent of sub-state and state-supported terrorism in the 1970s and 1980s, however, again turned the attention of the American military to the organisation of special units capable of conducting hostage rescue and counter-terror operations. Moreover, serious conflicts in the Third World, particularly in Central America, forced the American military to give renewed attention to unconventional warfare capability. A second 'counter-insurgency craze' had come into being. But this latest concern is in danger of producing yet another cycle of confusing concepts and organisations whose missions amalgamate special operations and revolution/counter-revolution.

The creation of the First Special Operations Command and the establishment of a Unified Special Operations Command are major steps in the right direction.[59] This is also true of the establishment of an Assistant Secretary of Defence for Special Operations and Low-Intensity Conflict. Yet there appears to be little in the US posture that comes to grips with the central issues that are relevant to the broad concept of unconventional conflicts. The intermixing of special operations with low-intensity conflicts—Ranger/Commando type units with Special Forces—is indicative of this problem. Aside from counter-terror contingencies, there is little in the present posture that provides strategic options and doctrinal guidelines that synthesise political, military and psychological environments of unconventional conflicts. Further, there is little agreement on where and how Special Forces should be used, aside from military training and assistance.

Moreover, professional and organisational resistance to the idea of creating a contingent of special units remains: an élite force concept is anathema to most mainstream military professionals. Élite forces have been historically resisted by the military system. This is reflected today in the general attitudes and perspectives of the US political-military system. There are some noteworthy exceptions, including the fact that the Special Forces have been established as a separate branch.[60] It remains to be seen how far such developments will go. More important, there remain many questions regarding the shape of the politico-military structure that evolves for unconventional conflicts and the strategy and doctrines for the conduct of such conflicts. Thus, the decade of the 1980s may be the start of realistic assessments and effective US strategy for unconventional conflicts. Yet it may also be the continuation of conventional interpretations of unconventional operations and another counter-insurgency era rooted in the mistakes of the past. But all of this is another story and not part of the formative period, but rather a result of the formative period.

Conclusion

Throughout the formative period, the American response to low-intensity conflict was completely submerged beneath the perceived strategic threat from the Soviet Union and later from mainland China. The atomic and nuclear battlefields were based on a European scenario. This was broadened to include a strategy of massive retaliation against the Soviet heartland should the Soviets engage in aggression anywhere in the world. Flexible response followed, as the Soviets developed their own nuclear capability, neutralising the concept of massive American response. American capability in low-intensity conflict must be seen in the context of these strategic concerns and threat perceptions.

The response to low-intensity conflict has been fashioned by a conventional American politico-military strategy that was formed during the immediate post-World War II period. The introduction of nuclear weapons, Soviet military power and expansion, combined with decolonisation and the rise of Communist China, changed the international security situation following the Korean War. But even with the experience of the Korean War behind them, Americans tended to view the world through conventional lenses rooted in a mind-set more appropriate to the World War II era. This posture was reaffirmed by important characteristics of the American political system. Wars were seen as a struggle between good and evil. Thus, Americans tended to perceive wars as a challenge to democracy and the American way of life, to be met by mobilisation of manpower and resources and a drive for total victory. The idea that wars could be fought for limited objectives or for political posturing was far removed from the American mentality.

Moreover, the US military is governed by a well-established concept of civilian control. Reaching back to the Founding Fathers, the constitutional provision of civilian control of the military has not been seriously challenged. Indeed, it is well embodied in the military value system. It follows that American military men and women are (and were) expected to perform within the context of democratic rules and norms, with all of the moral and ethical implications these suggest. Thus, the 'good guy—bad guy' syndrome characteristic of World Wars I and II prevailed, with the United States expected to enter a conflict as the 'good guy'. In such circumstances, it is presumed that the identification of the enemy is unambiguous and that American intentions and purposes are clear. Unfortunately, guerrilla war, insurgency, revolution and counter-revolution hardly adhere to such simplistic, liberal-democratic notions. In brief, a conventional lens is used to assess low-intensity conflict, leading to policy, strategy and doctrines rooted in conventional organisational postures, conceptual misunderstanding and doctrinal confusion, all in the context of constraints imposed by the American political system.

In this respect, conceptual and doctrinal confusion regarding low-intensity conflict evolved from a number of factors. First, there exists a doctrinal view based on the notion that low-intensity conflict was (and is) an amalgam of special operations (Ranger/Commando missions) and Special Forces-type missions. It was assumed, therefore, that units trained and organised for hit-and-run raids and long-range patrols, for example, could readily undertake all kinds of low-intensity conflict missions. Similarly, many viewed Special Forces as a 'super' Ranger/Commando organisation when, in fact, Special Forces missions were more similar to OSS operations during World War II.

Another component of this doctrinal confusion was the presumption that low-intensity conflict, as originally conceived, is an adjunct to conventional operations. Even when some attempted to draw a distinction between special operations and Special Forces missions, it was presumed that guerrilla warfare (the initial primary mission assigned to Special Forces) was an adjunct to conventional operations. Although there has been some improvement in the organisational direction for low-intensity conflict, even as recently as 1986 the American military still placed special operations units and Special Forces units under the same command.

Perhaps the most fundamental issue is still conceptual: disagreements and confusion over the nature of, and response to, low-intensity conflict. Special operations, guerrilla war, insurgency, revolution and counter-revolution are generally conceived in similar terms. Yet, as has been shown, they differ considerably in their strategic and tactical dimensions as well as in their civilian and military components. These conceptual problems, in turn, are reflected in the composition, planning and training of forces designed for low-intensity conflict.

Many of the conflicts in the Third World and those in which the United States has (and may have) a vital interest are revolutionary in nature. Consequently, counter-revolution should be a major mission for Special Forces-type operations, but this need not exclude a 'revolutionary' mission. In this respect, revolution is more than guerrilla war and insurgency; it is a total war against the existing political system with its main 'battlefront' within the political-social milieu. Political mobilisation, psychological war, propaganda and terrorism, are major means of revolutionary conflicts. Armed conflict is important, of course, but it is primarily an adjunct to the major struggle. Political mobilisers and cadres are more important, in the long run, than battlefield soldiers. This is a view that has been, and remains, difficult for American civilian and military leaders and officials to grasp.

The formative period institutionalised most of the doctrinal confusion and conceptual misunderstandings that exist today. Moreover, the hesitancy with which planners approach the establishment of low-intensity conflict capability reflected the political and military constraints placed on such operations. Conventional military wisdom, superpower threat perceptions and lessons of the grand battles of the past dominated military professionalism. Civilian policy-makers hardly did any better, viewing guerrilla war and low-intensity conflict as something 'undemocratic' while expecting to counter such warfare according to democratic rules and conventional military posture. Those few within military and civilian circles who understood the nature of low-intensity conflict found it difficult to translate this into realistic policy, strategy and organisational capability.

Organisational resistance, conceptual misunderstanding and doctrinal confusion of the formative period have yet to be overcome. Not only is this seen in current policy debates regarding American involvement in Third World areas but it is reflected in the persistent downgrading of those within the military who are committed to a career in low-intensity conflict. While some of this is changing, there remains the danger that a serious response to low-intensity conflict will emerge as a conventional version, with all of the mistakes and misunderstandings of the formative period replayed in a modern guise.

The lessons of the formative period also show that, at best, incremental changes are the most that can be achieved within American military organisations. Such changes are likely to be closely linked to the underlying traditions and philosophical substance of American democracy. A system committed to the principles of liberal democracy, giving birth to a military resting on absolute civilian control, and whose military traditions and heritage are based primarily on 'regulars' fighting 'regulars', cannot adapt readily—if at all—to low-intensity conflict, particularly to its most challenging form, revolution and counter-revolution. Only when civilian leaders in the United States understand the character of low-intensity conflict, particularly revolution and counter-revolution, and this in turn is transmitted to the American people at large, can there be an effective conceptual, organisational and doctrinal adaptation to such conflicts. It is not that this cannot be done; it is that it is difficult and demanding, testing the moral and ethical fibre of the democratic system.

Notes

1. See Sam C. Sarkesian, *America's Forgotten Wars: the Counter-revolutionary Past and Lessons for the Future* (Westport, Conn.: Greenwood Press, 1984).
2. For a detailed discussion of these issues see Sam C. Sarkesian, *The New Battlefield: The United States and Unconventional Conflicts* (Westport, Conn: Greenwood Press, 1986).
3. Adapted from Sam C. Sarkesian, 'American Policy and Low-Intensity Conflict: An Overview', in Sam C. Sarkesian and William L. Scully, eds., *US Policy and Low-Intensity Conflict; Potentials for Military Struggles in the 1980s* (New Brunswick, N.J.: Transaction Books, 1981), p. 6.
4. See John Shy and Thomas W. Collier, 'Revolutionary War', in Peter Paret, ed., *Makers of Modern Strategy* (Princeton, N.J.: Princeton University Press, 1986), pp. 815–62.

5. John Spanier, *American Foreign Policy Since World War II*, 9th ed. (New York: Holt, Rinehart and Winston, 1980), pp. 17–18.
6. Ray S. Cline, *Secrets, Spies and Scholars; the Essential CIA* (Washington, D.C.: Acropolis Books, 1976), p. 98.
7. Spanier, *op. cit.* p. 77.
8. 'The Sources of Soviet Conduct', *Foreign Affairs*, vol. 25 (July 1947), pp. 566–82.
9. Paul Y. Hammond, *Cold War and Détente: the American Foreign Policy Process since 1945* (New York: Harcourt, Brace, Jovanovich, 1975), pp. 87–90.
10. Spanier, *op. cit.* p. 72
11. *ibid.*, p. 75.
12. Hammond, *op. cit.* p. 124.
13. *ibid.*, p. 125.
14. Robert E. Osgood, *Limited War Revisited* (Boulder, Colo.: Westview Press Inc., 1979), p. 6.
15. *ibid.*
16. Maurice Matloff, *American Military History* (Washington, D.C.: U.S. Government Printing Office, 1969), p. 573.
17. *ibid.*, p. 531.
18. Matthew B. Ridgway, *Soldier: The Memoirs of Matthew B. Ridgway* (New York: Harper and Brothers, 1956), p. 190. See also Robert A. Doughty, *The Evolution of US Army Tactical Doctrine, 1946–76; Leavenworth Papers* (Fort Leavenworth, Kansas: US Army Command and General Staff College, August, 1979), p. 2.
19. Hammond, *op. cit.* p. 62.
20. Doughty, *op. cit.* pp. 6–7.
21. Ridgway, *op. cit.* p. 191.
22. An excellent work on the Korean War is Robert Leckie, *Conflict: the History of the Korean War, 1950–1953* (New York: Avon Book Division, 1962).
23. Doughty, *op. cit.* p. 12.
24. *ibid.*
25. Matloff, *op. cit.* p. 578.
26. Doughty, *op. cit.* p. 19.
27. Cline, *op. cit.* p. 85.
28. Charles M. Simpson III, *Inside the Green Berets: The First Thirty Years* (Novato, Calif.: Presidio Press, 1983), p. 14.
29. *ibid.*
30. Cline, *op. cit.* p. 87.
31. *ibid.*, p. 97.
32. Alfred H. Paddock, Jr., *US Army Special Warfare: Its Origins* (Washington, D.C.: National Defense University Press, 1982), pp. 44–68.
33. *ibid.*, p. 60.
34. *ibid.*, p. 71.
35. Eliot A. Cohen, *Commandos and Politicians: Elite Military Units in Modern Democracies* (Cambridge, Mass: Harvard Center for International Affairs, 1978), pp. 53–65, 70–74.
36. Colonel Francis J. Kelly, *Vietnam Studies: US Army Special Forces, 1961–1971* (Washington, D.C.: Department of Defense, 1977), p. 160.
37. Paddock, *op. cit.* p. 81.
38. Simpson, *op. cit.* p. 15.
39. *ibid.*, pp. 15–16. For an overview of such operations, see Paddock, pp. 100–109. The author served in one of these units during the Korean War. Some of the commentary here is based on this experience.

40. Simpson, *op. cit.* p. 15. The author served in the 10th Special Forces Group during this early period. Part of the commentary here is based on this experience.
41. Paddock, *op. cit.* p. 90.
42. Simpson, *op. cit.* pp. 19–20.
43. Paddock, *op. cit.* pp. 151–52.
44. *ibid.*, p. 149.
45. William P. Yarborough, Foreword, in Simpson, *op. cit.* p. xvi.
46. Simpson, *op. cit.* p. 48.
47. *ibid.*, pp. 29–33.
48. Douglas S. Blaufarb, *The Counterinsurgency Era: US Doctrine and Performance, 1950 to the Present* (New York: Free Press, 1977), pp. 52–56, 76.
49. Doughty, *op. cit.* p. 26; see also Andrew F. Krepinevich, *The Army and Vietnam* (Baltimore, M.: Johns Hopkins University Press, 1986), pp. 30–33, 36–37, 42–46, 108–12.
50. Simpson, *op. cit.* p. 67; Blaufarb, *op. cit.* pp. 70–71, 78.
51. Krepinevich, *op. cit.* pp. 38–42, 45.
52. Blaufarb, *op. cit.* pp. 76, 78–82; Krepinevich, *op. cit.* pp. 42–55, 108–12, 117–27.
53. Edward Geary Lansdale, *In the Midst of Wars: An American's Mission to Southeast Asia* (New York: Harper and Row, 1972), pp. 374–75.
54. Krepinevich, *op. cit.* p. 36 notes that in spite of his relevant expertise, Lansdale was out of favour with General Maxwell Taylor, then Chairman of the Joint Chiefs of Staff, and was excluded from any influential policy-making position.
55. *ibid.*, pp. 69–71.
56. *ibid.*, pp. 71–73, 229–33; for a more complete account of Special Forces operations in Vietnam, see Shelby L. Stanton, *Green Berets at War: U.S. Army Special Forces in Southeast Asia 1956–1975* (Novato, Calif.: Presidio Press, 1985).
57. Robert E. Osgood, 'The Reappraisal of Limited War,' in Eugene Rosi, ed., *American Defense and Detente: Readings in National Security Policy* (New York: Dodd, Mead and Co., 1973), p. 466.
58. As quoted in Harry G. Summers, Jr., *On Strategy: The Vietnam War in Context* (Carlisle Barracks, Penn.: US Army War College, 1981), p. 7.
58. Michael Ganley, 'Congress Creates New Unified Command for SOF and New Civilian SOF Chief', *Armed Forces Journal International*, November 1986, pp. 20 and 22.
60. Since Vietnam, however, standard command and staff career patterns have tended to discourage service in Special Forces. See Blaufarb, *op. cit.* p. 288; Richard A. Gabriel, 'No Light in the Tunnel: Can US Unconventional Forces Meet the Future?' *Conflict Quarterly* vol. 2, no. 2 (Fall 1981), pp. 5–6.

3

Israeli Defence Forces and Low-Intensity Operations

GUNTHER E. ROTHENBERG

Since 1945 the spectrum of armed conflict has ranged from large scale 'conventional' hostilities waged with ever more sophisticated weapons to protracted 'revolutionary wars' combining traditional guerrilla patterns with terrorism and Leninist techniques of revolutionary organisation. Indeed, such wars, one expert concluded, have 'now become the primary form of conflict'.[1]

Many contemporary armies have been compelled to prepare both for fighting conventional 'high-intensity' conflict and for 'low-intensity' anti-guerrilla operations. It is, however, wrong to assume that an army successful in one type of war is likely to be equally successful in another. Many armies have persisted in applying high-intensity methods to low-intensity operations. In 1962 the US Army Chief of Staff, General George H. Decker, insisted that 'any good soldier can handle guerrillas' and more recently a noted American military author insisted that 'military forces are designed, equipped and trained for a specific task: to fight and win on the battlefield'.[2] But victory on the battlefield calls for firepower and mass, command and control, and logistic support on a scale which may be wholly unsuitable for low-intensity operations against the guerrilla-terrorist in the opening stages of a revolutionary war. Armies trained for modern high-intensity operations, regardless of the individual quality of their manpower and matériel, have often found it difficult to improvise effective doctrines and methods for low-intensity operations, and as a result it has become common practice to assign these to special units.[3]

The Israeli Army, more properly the Israel Defence Forces (IDF),

49

CENTRAL MIDDLE EAST

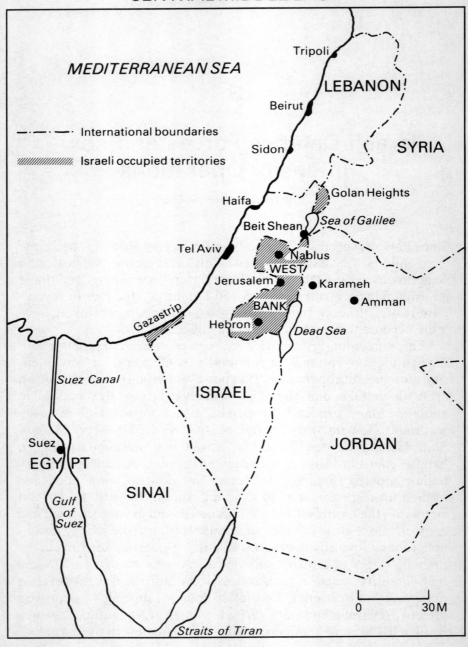

has arrived independently at the same solution. When formally established in 1948, the IDF inherited considerable experience in low-intensity operations from its clandestine predecessors. Internal circumstances and external aggression have, however, compelled it to shift to a high-intensity mode. Six wars have resulted in a combat doctrine that seeks to achieve rapid victory in the land battle by using armour and airpower to take the fight as soon as possible to the enemy's rear. This is reflected in the IDF's order of battle: 11 armoured divisions, 5 airborne, 1 regular, 15 territorial infantry brigades, and 650 first line aircraft.[4] While doctrine and force structure have proved sound in war, they clearly are not suited for low-intensity operations, specifically the constant terrorist-guerrilla threat facing Israel. With limited resources and manpower, IDF planners did not opt for a large, separate special forces establishment. Except for a few small *Sayeret* detachments and naval commandos, special operations have been carried out by personnel from the airborne (paratroop) and the regular infantry formations, backed by military and civilian intelligence agencies.[5] Overall, these dual-purpose units have proved most effective. The IDF, one German expert wrote, has provided an example of 'how to combat guerrillas and terrorists', and an American analyst commented that the 'total absence of a documentary record should not cause us to overlook the outstanding success of the Israeli Army in virtually extinguishing both guerrilla and terrorist activities in the Gaza Strip and the West Bank'.[6]

It should be noted, however, that these comments apply primarily to IDF operations within the territory of the state and the areas occupied since the June 1967 War. By contrast, rear area security following the invasion of Lebanon in 1982 has been much less impressive. One explanation is that local protection here has often been handled by logistic and administrative personnel, largely reservists, who are not fitted for anti-terrorist operations. But there is a larger dimension to this pattern of success and failure. In a democracy, success in fighting a low-intensity war against terrorist-guerrillas, almost always a lengthy and often costly process, depends on popular support. If the guerrilla-terrorist needs the people, the water in which the guerrilla fish swims, the government needs popular support to sustain prolonged operations. And this may well depend on the perception of the threat posed by the adversary. If the British gave up Ireland, the French Algeria and Indochina, and the Americans withdrew from Vietnam, it was not because their armies were clearly defeated, but because these powers felt that the political and economic costs of continuing were totally out of proportion to any benefit derived. By contrast, in Israel there is a strong consensus that the terrorist-guerrillas intend to liquidate the state and its people and therefore public opinion has, with some minor exceptions, supported a firm line regardless of costs.[7] No such consensus, however, exists regarding a continued IDF presence in southern Lebanon.

Development of Combat Doctrine Prior to 1949

Formally established in May 1948, the IDF has been described as the 'organic continuation of the *Haganah*'.[8] After World War I, a British administration had replaced Turkish rule in Palestine, but Arab riots in 1920 convinced the Jewish population, the *Yishuv*, that it could not rely on a foreign army for protection. That year, the United Labour Party founded the *Haganah* (Defence), and although in time the organisation broadened to include most elements of the *Yishuv*, it always retained a special affinity with Labour Zionism. The Arab riots of 1929, in which the Jews suffered heavy casualties where there were no self-defence units, changed the *Haganah* from a loose collection of local groups to a national organisation. Although forced underground by the British, the *Haganah* established a national command and by 1938, with a total Jewish population of about 500,000, it boasted a membership of some 35,000 men and women. Even so, the organisation was poorly armed and trained, the national command weak, and the *Haganah's* fighting doctrine was limited to static self-defence.[9]

   The Arab Revolt of 1936–39 compelled modifications in combat doctrine. The concept of 'self-defence only' was already under challenge from the *Irgun Zevai Leumi* (National Military Organisation), a radical splinter group which advocated retaliation to Arab attacks. Moreover, some younger *Haganah* commanders had begun to chafe under the operational restraints. Their opportunity came when the British administration decided to utilise the *Haganah* and established the Jewish Settlement Police (JSP) which enrolled several thousand *Haganah* members as 'supernumerary' constables and thus created a quasi-legal framework. In late 1936, utilising the *Haganah*-JSP framework, Yitzhak Sadeh organised a mobile JSP patrol, *ha-Nodedet* in the Jerusalem hills, and the following year the *Haganah* national command sanctioned field companies, *Plugoth sadeh* or

FOSH, to attack identified terrorist bases. Because of ideological misgivings within the national command, however, this experiment was discontinued in February 1939.[10]

By this time, however, Captain Charles Orde Wingate, a regular British officer seconded for special duties, had formed a joint British-Jewish force, the Special Night Squads (SNS). His mission was to secure the Iraq-Haifa oil pipeline against sabotage, but Wingate interpreted his orders broadly and with night raids and ambushes managed to clear most of northern Palestine of Arab bands in 1939. An ardent Zionist who had spoken of the SNS as the foundation for a future Jewish army, Wingate was banished from the country that year, but his operational doctrine—hitting the enemy when he least expected it—was transmitted to the *Haganah* by SNS troopers such as Yigal Allon and Moshe Dayan. Sadeh, of course, had already advocated similar ideas, but the *Haganah*, unsure of itself at this time, accepted them only after they were endorsed by a regular officer.[11]

Wingate's influence was most pronounced in the *Haganah's* shock companies, the *Plugoth mahatz* or *Palmach*, formed by the Jewish authorities in 1941 as a last ditch defence for the *Yishuv* in case of a British withdrawal from the region. For nearly two years, this force, not exceeding 2,000 young men and women, trained with British support or at least tacit acquiescence and, while never called upon to carry out their original purpose, *Palmach* personnel participated in British operations in Syria, Iraq and the Western Desert, and also mounted some missions into occupied Europe.[12]

Because British support had been limited, and in any case ended late in 1942, *Palmach* units had to combine military training with agricultural work on various *kibbutzim*. Here, with Sadeh as the first commander and guiding ideologue, the ideals of the collective agricultural communities and military requirements merged to create a new type of soldier, an egalitarian fighter, tough, highly motivated, and self-sacrificing, with leaders expected to be first in the attack and last to retreat, a concept that became an IDF tradition. Training and fighting doctrine, elaborated by Wingate and Sadeh, stressed personal initiative—the individual is the smallest combat unit—and emphasised surprise, rather than frontal assaults, mass and firepower. These tactics were well suited to a clandestine force with scanty means but they also were highly suitable for low-intensity operations.[13]

Widely considered an élite, and certainly regarded as such by its members, *Palmach* doctrine and ethos had an influence out of all proportion to actual numbers in the IDF. After 1943, rotation brought new personnel, largely recruited from *kibbutzim* and the Left-wing youth movements, into the organisations and, until its eventual dissolution five years later, the *Palmach* trained a substantial number of future senior Israeli officers who fought and directed the campaigns from 1947 to 1973.[14] By contrast, officers who had received their basic military education in various branches of the British Army—some 30,000 Palestinian Jews served in World War II—were less influential, even though David Ben Gurion, the Labour leader who became Israel's long-time prime minister in 1948, looked to these elements to provide the administrative skills and the discipline necessary in a conscript army.

From 1945, the *Palmach* was in the forefront of Jewish resistance against the British and at the same time it provided the mobile element countering renewed Arab attacks. This time, its operations were offensive, if clearly limited, though in contrast with the *Irgun,* the *Palmach* attempted to avoid unnecessary casualties. In 1948, when open warfare erupted between the new state and the five neighbouring Arab countries, the *Palmach* expanded to three small brigades and fought with distinction in the War of Independence.[15] In addition, *Palmach* officers trained and led many of the new IDF brigades. Even so, Prime Minister Ben Gurion was uneasy about the élite troops. The *Palmach* not only retained its own separate headquarters but on occasion questioned government orders and acted like an army within the army.[16] And this the Prime Minister was not prepared to tolerate. Moreover he feared that the élitism of the *Palmach* and its strong ties with the Left-wing of the Zionist Labour Movement might endanger cohesion of the new national Army. Determined never to tolerate 'any barrier or organisational distinction between one Jew and another in the IDF', he had used force to disband the *Irgun Zevai Leumi* in June 1948 and in September he broke up the *Palmach* headquarters; in the following year the *Palmach* brigades were the first to be demobilised.[17]

Ben Gurion's actions were resented and a number of promising young officers left the service, though some returned following passage of the 1949 Defence Service Law. With some modifications still in force today, the law created a unified military establishment, including ground, air and naval forces under a single Chief of Staff responsible to the Minister of Defence. All able-bodied men and women were to serve from two to three years and thereafter would be called up for varying terms of annual reserve duty. A small career cadre was to handle the technical aspects and, together with the active duty conscripts, formed the standing force, but the strength of the IDF was in its large reserve, organised not according to age but according to formation.

There were no special educational or social qualifications for officers selected from the ranks. Training was along British lines, though from the outset the IDF stressed initiative and improvisation over formal discipline. The Army was to have a dual function. More than a purely military institution, it was to be the school of the nation, integrating the mass immigration that followed the establishment of the state into Israeli society. This required a substantial educational programme. Moreover, the service law also required that following an initial year of training, all conscripts were to receive another year of agricultural training. This concession to Zionist labour ideology remained a dead letter. More successful was the establishment of the *No'ar Halutzi Lohemet*, (NAHAL—Fighting Pioneer Youth), legislation encouraging members of Zionist youth movements to join the Army as collective settlement groups. Placed in strategic locations, NAHAL outposts, together with the reservists of other frontier towns and settlements, were to provide the framework for a territorial area defence scheme.

During the first years of Israel's existence, these various objectives were hard to attain. Population doubled in three-and-a-half years, with many immigrants in poor physical and mental condition. Their absorption strained resources and the IDF was left short of funds. Conscription meant that new immigrants came to form the bulk of the Army, with the least educated often sent to the infantry. Short of funds, with obsolete weapons, and low morale, the combat capabilities of the IDF deteriorated in the early 1950s.[18]

The Paratroopers and the IDF Revival

Given the state of the IDF, it was fortunate that during this period the hostile Arab states were distracted by internal problems and were unable to mount a major attack. But such an attack remained a possibility. Therefore, considering Israel's limited resources, lack of defensive borders and strategic depth, IDF planners concentrated on preparing to deliver 'anticipatory counter-attacks' with the largest possible forces, something that until 1955 was practically impossible. Meanwhile, the General Staff gave only limited attention to security along the 593-mile Armistice Demarcation Line (ADL). Initially this was left to the Border Police, *Mishmar ha-gvul*, formed in 1950 within the jurisdiction of the IDF but transferred to the Ministry of Police the following year. Administratively, the Border Police was organised in three companies, enlarged to three battalions in 1954, and armed with light infantry weapons. Containing substantial numbers of Arabic-speaking Druze, conscripted at their own request into the IDF, the Border Police was useful but proved too weak to provide protection. And the area defence scheme also could not seal the border. New immigrant villages, populated by uneducated and unskilled oriental city dwellers, unused to discipline and the use of arms, could not contribute much against the increasing Arab incursions across the ADL.[19]

At first directed against property, these forays soon escalated to deliberate sabotage and murder. In 1950 there were 50 civilian casualties, 97 the following year, and 182 in 1952. After 1953, moreover, these actions were encouraged by Egypt and Jordan and financed by the Saudi government.[20] At first, Israel tried to stop the depredations by diplomatic means, using force only to repel attacks within its own territory. But when this proved useless, the government, in 1953, authorised reprisal raids, a course permissible in international law.[21] The primary purpose of these actions was to influence Arab governments. 'We cannot', General Dayan, the Chief of Staff, declared in 1955, 'guard every water pipeline from explosion and every tree from uprooting. We cannot prevent the murder of a worker in an orchard or a family in their beds. But it is in our power to set a high price on our blood, a price too high for the Arab community, the Arab army or the Arab government to think worth paying'.[22] At the same time, Dayan hoped that hitting back would raise army morale and improve combat effectiveness.[23]

The first reprisal actions, however, were disappointing. They were designed to inflict proportionate property damage rather than casualties and the conscript units involved frequently aborted action when encountering minor resistance. Overall, out of 85 retaliatory actions up to the end of 1953, only 38 were considered successful. The Chief of Staff, General Mordechai Makleff, decided that drastic change was needed, and, overriding the misgivings of several senior officers, established a special raiding force in the summer of that year.[24]

Ariel Sharon, a 23-year-old student at the Hebrew University and a former intelligence officer, was chosen to form a special raiding unit, designated as Unit 101. Comprising no more than 40 hand-picked men and in existence only for six months, the unit soon gained a reputation for toughness and success. Still, such operations could backfire. Following a specially brutal series of Arab killings, the government in October 1953 ordered a major reprisal, reinforcing Unit 101 with elements of the 890th Parachute Battalion, an untested unit. The action against Kibya, a village housing a concentration of infiltrators, resulted in the death of over 60 civilians, most of them women and children.[25] Although the government disavowed the raid as an 'unauthorised action by outraged citizens', foreign and domestic criticism compelled a change in policy.[26] Future reprisals, Ben Gurion ordered, were to be directed exclusively against military installations. This required larger strike forces and when Dayan succeeded Makleff as Chief of Staff, in December 1953, he combined the near-irregular Unit 101 with the paratroop battalion.

Originally Dayan, concerned that they might resurrect all the problems of the *Palmach*, had opposed the creation of special units. If he changed his mind it was because he hoped that a properly-handled raiding force would provide a role model for the rest of the Army.[27] By combining the combative spirit of Unit 101 with the formal discipline of the paratroopers he hoped to preserve the best qualities of both. Appointing Sharon, rather than the more senior paratroop commander, to lead the combined force suggested that, if he had to choose, Dayan would favour an aggressive combat spirit over formal discipline. Sharon and an extraordinary group of young officers, including several future chiefs of staff, moulded Unit 202 into a first class fighting body, consciously emulating the mystique of the tough French paras and the collective spirit of the *Palmach*. All men were jump trained, though this was primarily a rite of passage. Sharon's combat style emphasised the rapid and silent approach, followed by combat with submachine-guns, knives and grenades.[28] These tactics were well suited to night actions, producing maximum psychological shock, and obviated the need for artillery support which in any case was restricted to reduce civilian casualties. A French observer described Israeli paratroop tactics in one word: 'audacity'.[29] Following the *Palmach* tradition, officers of all grades were expected to lead in combat and they suffered severe casualties. 'I do not think', Dayan recorded in 1956, 'that there is a single veteran officer in the paratroopers who has not been wounded'.[30] The paratroopers replaced the *Palmach* in popular esteem and, with service in an élite unit regarded as moral duty conferring considerable prestige, the unit had no problem in attracting highly-qualified volunteers. Within the year it was expanded into a three battalion brigade.[31]

Until late in 1955 retaliatory reactions were mounted by small forces, rarely exceeding several platoons.[32] Even so, as Dayan had hoped, they raised general troop morale. In addition, Dayan saw to it that combat units, especially infantry, received better qualified conscripts. He emphasised the achievement of combat objectives and largely replaced the more rigid British-style tactical doctrine with mission tactics, giving great tactical latitude to all units. Casualties were less important than accomplishing the mission. All this, together with the example set by the paratroop élite, raised IDF combat effectiveness and during the large-scale actions of 1955–56 regular infantry as well as NAHAL fought very well.[33]

The paratroops achieved their assigned missions with soldierly efficiency, though whether reprisals actually were a deterrent remains a debated issue. On the whole they were more effective against Jordan, where they inflicted direct damage, and they had less effect on Egypt which cared little about the Gaza Strip.[34] Moreover, after Gamal Abdul Nasser came to power in Egypt, the Egyptian army commenced training the infiltrators, *fedayeen*, or self-sacrificers, as they styled themselves, and between September 1955 and October 1956 there were almost daily incidents with a casualty toll of 600 Israelis in 1956 alone. To counter expected reprisals, both Jordan and Egypt stationed regular forces near terrorist bases, and this compelled the IDF to employ larger forces.[35] Inevitably low-intensity operations escalated into battalion-size engagements and regimental battles. There was major fighting in the northern Sinai in November 1955, followed a month later by an operation to silence Syrian gun positions on the Golan Heights. There was also fighting on the West Bank. When new *fedayeen* camps were placed there during the summer of 1956, the IDF mounted four major strikes between 12 September and 10 October. The last, an attack against a police fort, resulted in substantial Israeli casualties. Dayan concluded that the IDF had 'reached the end of the chapter of night reprisal operations'.[36] He recommended massive daylight operations to 'capture commanding positions and make our evacuation conditional upon stopping of terror'.[37]

This reasoning contributed to Israel's decision to launch Operation Kadesh, the Sinai Campaign, two weeks later. To be sure, the elimination of *fedayeen* bases was only a secondary objective. The immediate causes for the war were apprehensions over Egypt's intentions, underlined by the acquisition of heavy Soviet arms, a build-up in the Sinai, and the closing of the Straits of Tiran.[38] In the event, victory in the Sinai temporarily eliminated the conventional threat and with a United Nations Emergency Force patrolling the frontier, *fedayeen* activities were curtailed.

The IDF Adapts a High-Intensity Mode

In the decade after 1956 the Arab states received vast quantities of modern arms from the Soviet bloc and, in the case of Jordan, from the United States and Britain. Israel, on the other hand, was able to acquire modern armour from France, Britain and the United States, and to equip her air force with French jets. IDF planners concluded that the Sinai Campaign had demonstrated not only the validity of the 'anticipatory counter-attack' doctrine, but also that if there was to be any kind of decisive victory it had to be achieved quickly before great power intervention nullified battlefield achievement. A further review of the campaign concluded that air superiority and armour had been decisive and that armoured formations should be employed in large numbers.

These conclusions modified the IDF force structure. Between 1956 and 1967 the Armoured Corps was substantially enlarged. New divisional formations were created, with mechanised infantry an integral component. Much stress was placed on absorbing new hardware, especially medium tanks, and on improving tank gunnery and maintenance. By comparison, infantry became somewhat less important. The paratroops and the one remaining regular infantry brigade, the Golani, were amalgamated and placed under a Chief of Infantry and Paratroops, forming a light infantry branch.[39] The shift to more sophisticated weapons and high-intensity warfare mirrored changes in Israel, which was rapidly becoming an industrial-urban society. There was a clear decline in the traditional Zionist ideology, though morale remained high. Career soldiers, conscripts and reservists believed that in a future war they would be defending their homes and families, and this motivated them to do their best in the service. Training continued to be conducted with great intensity and while the IDF was clearly moving towards a greater high-intensity operations mode, it still retained unique characteristics. Above all these included the citizen army character, together with the wide tactical latitude given to low level commanders, the stress on the principles of objective, surprise, and mobility, combined with the effective integration of intelligence into operational planning and the adaptation of weapons and formations for specific missions.

These characteristics were especially pronounced among the paratroops, now six brigades strong; trained to participate as assault infantry in the land battle, they could also adapt to low-intensity operations.[40] The paratroops remained an élite formation, composed of recruits with high mental and physical standards, and superior motivation. From 1965 on, they were again called for action against terrorist-guerrilla groups.[41]

The previous year the Palestine Liberation Organisation (PLO) had been founded as a loose combination of *fedayeen* and political groups. Though torn by frequent dissension, the PLO's main fighting branch, *El Fatah*, (Conquest) became the strongest and began operating in late 1965. From then until June 1967 it claimed credit for 108 out of 112 terrorist acts. Most of these involved small teams of infiltrators who avoided combat and concentrated on placing demolition charges and mining roads. Loss of life was not great, though 12 killed and 31 wounded was significant for a small country.[42] Israeli response followed the pattern of previous years. Initially it was defensive. Barbed wire fences were erected, mines laid and patrols stepped up. But 600 miles of frontier, winding across difficult country, could not be sealed off, especially with the terrorist bases in the West Bank sector of Jordan, close to major Israeli-Arab population centres. In addition, while the Egyptians bided their time for a major military confrontation, the Syrian army began to shell Israeli settlements from the Golan Heights.[43]

Israel resumed retaliatory actions early in 1966. Besides counter-battery fire and air strikes to silence Syrian gun positions, the paratroopers, on occasion assisted by light armour and sometimes artillery and air support, conducted six major retaliatory operations, four into the West Bank, one against Lebanon and one against Jordan. Syria, perhaps the main instigator, was considered too 'hard' a target for ground operations. Most of the actions were designed to inflict damage commensurate with that inflicted by the terrorists. In April 1966, however, following an incident in which the terrorists (*mehablim* as they invariably are called in Hebrew) caused multiple casualties, paratroopers demolished two villages in Jordanian-held territory and about 10 people were killed.[44]

But this did not stop the raids and General Ezer Weizman, then head of the Operations Branch of the General Staff, questioned the effectiveness of counter-strikes. 'In 1966', he argued, 'we can't carry out a 1955-style reprisal raid . . . going in at night, laying a few pounds of explosives, blowing up a house or a police station, and then clearing off'. This, he contended, would not deter Arab states from supporting the terrorists. 'When a sovereign state decides to strike at its foes, it ought to act differently. We have armour and we have an air force. Let's go in by day, operating openly and in force.'[45]

Weizman's views prevailed and in July 1966, following the killing of two civilians, the Air Force attacked heavy engineering equipment used by Syria to divert the Jordan waters, the first time that airpower was employed to answer a terrorist action. On 13 November 1966, following a mining incident which killed three soldiers, the IDF staged a massive armour and infantry attack, supported by air power, against Samua, a *fedayeen* base near Hebron on the West Bank. The strong deployment was designed to overawe resistance but triggered intervention by a Jordanian regular battalion, which was repulsed with the loss of 18 men. Meanwhile, intermittent artillery exchanges and air battles continued over the Golan Heights, culminating on 7 April 1967 with the downing of seven Syrian fighters.[46]

Once again terrorism led to increasingly heavy counter-actions, but the real cause of the June 1967 War was Nasser's belief that he was ready to challenge the IDF. He moved a large force into the Sinai, expelled the United Nations contingent and closed the Straits of Tiran. He expected aid from Syria and Jordan, with whom Egypt had military pacts. But while Arab forces still were deploying, the mobilised IDF struck and in six days drove the Egyptians back across the Suez Canal, the Jordanians out of Jerusalem and the West Bank, and the Syrians off the Golan Heights. A new geostrategic situation had been created.

Insurgency Containment in the West Bank and Gaza Strip

The 1967 War provided Israel for the first time with defensible topographic boundaries and some strategic depth. At the same time the new situation boosted prospects for a 'revolutionary' guerrilla-terrorist war. Israel now controlled some 26,000 sq. miles of Arab territory, the Golan Heights, the West Bank, the Gaza Strip and the Sinai, containing, together with the Israeli Arabs, a potentially hostile population of almost one and a half million. This mass, especially the 600,000 or so living in compact areas on the West Bank, represented a serious security threat, against which one analyst warned, the 'military brilliance recently displayed by the Israeli nation and its leaders will not be very relevant'.[47]

In fact, the various Palestinian guerrilla and terrorist groups had all the advantages for launching and sustaining a revolutionary war: a sea of friendly Arabs, sanctuaries and the overt support of friendly governments, almost unlimited access to arms, recruits and money, aid from the Communist world and various Left-wing and anarchist elements everywhere. Realising that for the present no Arab government could confront the IDF, the *fedayeen* leadership intended to build an insurgency infrastructure in the occupied territories, carry out acts of terrorism against Israel, eventually escalating into a full-fledged war of national liberation on the Algerian or Vietnamese pattern.[48] But analogies with Algeria or Vietnam did not hold. The population in the territories did not become the sea for the guerrilla fish and the IDF succeeded in 'virtually extinguishing both guerrilla and terrorist activities in the Gaza Strip and the West Bank'.[49]

Several factors determined Israel's success in preventing the insurgent movement from graduating into a major security problem. The PLO was internally divided and the various groups, competing for popular support, exposed themselves prematurely. The most important factor, however was the IDF's adaptability to low-intensity operations. One German observer noted that the underground experience of senior commanders enabled a 'near seamless transition from conventional war and combat tactics to guerrilla conflict'.[50] Dayan, now Minister of Defence, was resolved 'not to repeat the mistakes made by the US in Vietnam'. Neither he nor his successors had any illusions about winning the hearts and minds of the population, but realising that counter-insurgency had political, social, economic as well as military dimensions, they adopted a stick and carrot policy. The military government in the various territories was to leave the population alone as much as possible, while encouraging economic growth and well-being. To this end civilian elements of the Jordanian administration on the West Bank were left in place and the free movement of persons and goods, both across the Jordan River and in and out of Israel proper, was permitted. On the other hand, acts of terrorism, sabotage and subversion were to be put down firmly and at once.[51]

In the event, the PLO did not manage to get much beyond a conspiratorial phase. Within weeks of the end of the 1967 War, it called on the population to emulate the Algerian and Vietenamese models and sponsored attacks on Israeli personnel, vehicles and installations and on local Arabs co-operating with the military government. On the whole it amounted to little, mainly petty violence such as throwing a grenade, laying a mine, or firing a few shots at a patrol, combined with attempts to incite civil disobedience. Israeli reaction was swift and effective. The General Security Service (GSS) had seized Jordanian intelligence files and in co-operation with military intelligence and the Border Police, was able quickly to trace terrorist cells. Aware that brutality produced more rather than less resistance, the IDF measures were restrained. It was already Israeli practice not to apply the death penalty to terrorists and instead to provide incentives for surrender. Moreover, most West Bank Arabs, far from becoming willing recruits to *El Fatah*, gave the guerrilla-terrorists only the minimum of aid necessary to avoid being killed, while judicious bribery caused the betrayal of infiltrators and of weapons caches. But if there were incidents of armed violence, buildings used by terrorists were demolished, suspects were expelled across the Jordan and, in cases of civil disobedience, fines were imposed, schools closed and movement restricted. Generally the IDF kept large units away from population centres, but if there was a major incident, troops staged large-scale cordon and search operations. Backed by good intelligence, such actions often were productive. For instance, a search of the Nablus casbah on 13 February 1968, Operation Ring, resulted in the detention of 74 terrorists.[52]

Although neither terrorism nor civil disobedience could be rooted out completely, the IDF contained the insurgency in its earliest stage and forced the *fedayeen* to mount their armed effort from the other side of the Jordan River.[53] Syria, which provided most practical military support, was too wary of reprisals to allow operations to be launched from within its borders, but to the west and south, Lebanon and Jordan became staging areas for the PLO's infiltration efforts. Jordan, of course, had the longest frontier with Israel, its government was weak, and its population retained numerous ties with the Arab West Bank, and here *El Fatah* concentrated its strength, at one time an estimated 30,000 men under arms.

Deprived of an insurgency infrastructure on the West Bank, *El Fatah* sent small hit-and-run groups across the river. The IDF, in turn, attempted to intercept and destroy these groups. From the summer of 1968 until September 1970, the Judean and Samarean mountains and deserts, wild rugged terrain where temperatures in the lower elevations ranged around the 100° mark in the summer, saw a series of bloody encounters, sometimes called the 'battle of the paratroopers'.[54]

In this conflict the IDF employed passive and active means. Electronic detection devices, observation posts, minefields, trip wires and other measures were deployed along the frontier, especially in the 50-mile strip from the Dead Sea to the Beit Shean Valley south of the Sea of Galilee. Roads were built and outpost-settlements were established in the Jordan Valley and on the ridges to the west.[55] This defence belt was backed up by mobile fighting patrols, primarily drawn from the paratroops and increasingly from special forces, the *Sayeret* units.

Such 'special reconnaissance units' proliferated after the June 1967 War in all branches of the fighting army, but the most suitable and effective elements for low-intensity operations were the *Sayeret Golani*, recruited from the one remaining regular infantry brigade, and the *Sayeret tsanhanim*, the paratroop special force. Not to be confused with the regular division and brigade reconnaissance elements, these were semi-secret units but their reputation was soon established and once again it became a matter of considerable prestige to belong to such an élite body. Commanders had no difficulty attracting highly qualified recruits and, on occasion, when a soldier was refused acceptance, political strings were pulled to have him admitted. Such incidents, however, were rare, largely because the high demands of *Sayeret* service.[56]

Sayeret units had been formed because the bulk of the army, even the paratroopers, had become more and more trained and equipped for the more pressing demands of high-intensity operations. Moreover, low-intensity warfare, especially in the environment of the Jordan Valley, required troops at the peak of their physical condition, ruling out most reservists. Normally conscripts selected for *Sayeret* service are sent directly to a unit where they are trained and subsequently serve. Unless a recruit falls short of expectations, he will stay with his unit throughout his service, a practice which, together with the retention of longer-service NCO's and officers, contributes to combat cohesion. Interception of infiltrators requires an ability to make long forced marches with heavy loads across difficult terrain, and mobility is sometimes enhanced by inserting teams by helicopter. Marching power, coupled with knowledge of the terrain and enemy tactics remain, however, most important.[57]

Ambush and pursuit are carried out with the smallest possible numbers. One commander, it is said, proposed to take 20 men on a mission and was urged to take 40 to provide a reserve for emergencies such as carrying out the wounded. He is reported to have replied 'and who carries out the extra 20 men?'

Many *Fatah* teams accomplished little and returned with exaggerated accounts, but others, especially when cornered, fought fiercely. *Fatah* lost 550 killed or captured in 1968, 293 in 1969 and 308 in the first nine months of 1970. IDF spokesmen claimed that only one in five ever returned home. On the other hand, the IDF lost 138 men, including two senior officers, in action. Casualties were high because the paratroop tactics favoured the headlong rush into close combat, officers leading and, as early as 1968, Dayan ordered that intercepted guerrillas should be pinned down and given a chance to surrender; if this failed they should be eliminated by firepower rather than assault even if this required calling in artillery or an air strike.[58] These instructions went against the grain. Chaim Bar-Lev, the Chief of Staff and a *Palmach* veteran, informed the minister bluntly that neither he nor any other senior officer would refrain from going into action if they considered it necessary.[59]

Losses and aborted missions gradually eroded *Fatah* morale and the attempted guerrilla campaign degenerated into sporadic firing across the border, occasionally supplemented by Jordanian artillery barrages.[60] The IDF responded with counter-battery fire and air strikes which normally had the desired effect. Moreover, the IDF engaged in counterforce operations against the *fedayeen* bases. The objectives were in part retaliatory, in part pre-emptive, including a desire to drive a wedge between the Jordanian government and radical PLO elements. Of course, after 1967 the IDF was in a position to mount a rapid major ground offensive across the Jordan, but was constrained from doing so by the United States. On the other hand, the United States was willing to tolerate air strikes, limited ground and commando operations.

From early 1968, the IDF commenced 'active self-defence' to dissuade Jordan from offering shelter and aid to the *fedayeen* and to force them into the hinterland. In these operations the IDF employed all branches: artillery, mechanised infantry, paratroop and *Sayeret* units, supported by air power. On 21 March 1968 it mounted a

brigade-sized operation against Karameh, inflicting substantial casualties on a *fedayeen* concentration but suffering significant losses
including some armoured vehicles. Two weeks later, helicopter-
borne troops crossed the frontier south of the Dead Sea in hot pursuit
and destroyed a guerrilla complex near Dahal. Finally, both to prove
its capability and its will, the IDF mounted a major air strike against
Salt, a *fedayeen* centre east of Karameh, on 4 August 1968.
Moreover, to raise the cost of supporting the *fedayeen*, helicopter-
borne paratroops attacked and damaged a number of Jordanian
economic targets. These actions led to the evacuation of Jordanian
citizens from the Jordan Valley and to the eventual relocation of the
terrorist camps in the hills around Amman.[61]

Although some observers considered that Karameh, where the
fedayeen had put up a stout resistance, as a victory for the PLO,
others concluded that driving them out of the immediate vicinity of
the ADL represented a clear success for the Israelis. Moreover, with
Israel proving a 'hard' target, there was a split within the PLO with
groups favouring 'softer' targets gaining ground. Attacks on international air traffic began to multiply in 1969, culminating in the
hijacking of three airliners to Jordan in September 1970. In the event,
this incident provided King Hussein, who had come to fear the
fedayeen as a threat to his throne, with an opportunity to turn the
Jordanian Army against them. There now began a civil war in which
the PLO suffered heavy casualties when the King's troops eliminated
its main bases and, after fighting lasting into December, drove the
fedayeen out of the country. With casualties in the thousands, some
armed Palestinians crossed the Jordan to surrender to the IDF; most
who escaped went to Syria and Lebanon.[62] Terrorism from Jordanian
soil practically ended as of September 1970.

Following the pacification of the West Bank, the IDF turned its
attention to the Gaza Strip, crowded with some 400,000 discontented
and economically-deprived residents. In the first months after June
1967 the Gaza Strip had been largely left alone and the PLO had used
the time to move into the camps and neighbourhoods to recruit and
obtain control. Even so, action was limited to petty terrorism and an
attempted civil disobedience campaign fizzled out. In 1968 fighting
broke out among rival PLO factions, with the radical Popular Front
for the Liberation of Palestine (PFLP) gaining the upper hand. There
followed an increase in terrorism. In 1970 over 40 Arabs were killed
and 650 injured, while Israeli casualties numbered 20 killed and 50
wounded.[63]

The campaign to end this urban terrorism began in January 1971, as a police action rather than military low-intensity operations. Border Police units, including a strong Druze component, were moved into the Strip, while Army units prevented movement in and out of the area and naval craft patrolled sea approaches. Major cordon and search operations produced substantial finds of weapons and many arrests. Troops and police encountered little resistance in the Gaza Strip. There were, however, complaints that the Druze of the Border Police had used excessive violence and several were brought before disciplinary courts. Even so, the combined application of force and economic incentives, including the relocation of refugee camps and opportunities to work in Israel itself, produced results rather rapidly. Within six months incidents dropped off sharply and by the end of 1971 violence was contained, though not totally eradicated.[64]

Special Operations and the IDF, 1968–84

The special IDF units did not see much action in the Gaza Strip, but they were engaged during the War of Attrition (1967–70) along the Suez Canal. Besides patrolling the thin Israeli lines to intercept Egyptian commando raids, they made a number of spectacular deep penetrations. On 31 October 1968 an airborne raiding party destroyed two Nile bridges and an electric power transmission station 150 miles north of the Aswan Dam; in July 1969 paratroops and naval commandos captured Green Island, the southern hinge of the Egyptian air defence system, and destroyed its radar installations; and on 10 September paratroops and Armoured Corps personnel executed a mechanised raid along a 30-mile stretch of coastal road south of Suez. Finally, on 26 December 1969, seaborne paratroopers stormed a radar station at Ras Garib, some 250 miles south of Suez, to dismantle and bring back a new type of radar. While spectacular, these actions were subsidiary to a major conflict.[65]

By contrast, the presence of well-armed PLO groups in Lebanon, partly organised in semi-regular units with medium weapons, involved IDF special forces in a number of commando and covert operations. For the most part, though not exclusively, these were directed at the PLO camps ('neighbourhoods' is perhaps the better term) because the Lebanese government, though an unwilling host, was not in a position to oust or restrain its unwelcome guests. At first, the PLO used Lebanon primarily as a fund-raising and propaganda centre, but the PFLP had operational bases there and from the summer of 1968 began to mount operations against international and Israeli air traffic.[66]

Following two such attacks, on 28 December 1968 a small heliborne force led by Colonel Rafael Eitan, later to become Chief of Staff, descended on Beirut airport and destroyed 13 parked airliners. Although the attack was carried out without bloodshed, international opinion was outraged. More importantly, the raid did not deter the *fedayeen* who, virtually unhampered by an increasingly powerless Lebanese government, established fortified enclaves in several cities and converted the southern part of the country into the so-called *Fatahland* from where they fired into Israeli-populated areas and tried to infiltrate terrorist teams. The IDF responded with counter-fire and after particularly heavy attacks would mount air strikes against identified *fedayeen* bases. Patrols along the northern frontier were increased and an anti-infiltration fence was erected. From February 1972, IDF units crossed the border, patrolled a stretch 10 miles deep and attacked *fedayeen* groups.

Air strikes rapidly became the main tool for retaliatory and pre-emptive actions though, because the PLO had placed their bases in civilian neighbourhoods, they frequently inflicted substantial civilian casualties. At the same time, however, the IDF carried out some deep penetration operations. In February 1973 missile boats, helicopter-borne paratroopers and naval commandos attacked bases near Tripoli, and during the night of 9–10 April, PLO headquarters in the centre of Beirut were attacked. A small force of agents in place provided by the *Mossad* (Israel's equivalent of the Central Intelligence Agency), *Sayeret* teams, paratroops and naval commandos, a total of no more than 100 men, hit targets in Beirut while a diversionary operation was underway against Sidon. A number of PLO leaders were killed, documents seized and installations demolished. It was a well-planned and executed operation in the traditional IDF low-intensity mode, striking the enemy at unexpected times and in unexpected places.[67]

Even so, between 1967 and 1973 the IDF clearly continued its shift to high technology, high-intensity operations. High technology required greater conformity and the introduction of more formal discipline especially in the Armoured Corps, the backbone of the ground forces, causing one senior paratroop officer to grumble that 'if the tank crews proved themselves during this war, [June 1967] it was not due to their being correctly dressed in peacetime'.[68] Such grumbling, however, did not halt the changes and the October 1973 War, in which a surprised IDF managed to recover rapidly, drive back vastly superior forces and then counter-attack, seemed to validate the principal roles for armour, artillery and air elements.

The various armed Palestinian terrorist and guerrilla groups did not participate in the fighting. Moreover, much to the relief of the hard-pressed IDF, the occupied territories remained quiet even during the darkest days of the war, demonstrating the effectiveness of the IDF's counter-insurgency campaign. After the war, however, the various terrorist-guerrilla groups resumed activities aimed at producing maximum impact on Arab and world opinion. They mounted a series of daring, if suicidal, missions into Israel, while continuing the less dangerous course of international terrorism.[69] Operating primarily out of Lebanon where the PLO now had established a state within a state, terrorist groups carried out several brutal and bloody actions inside Israel. In April 1974 three terrorists killed 16 civilians in Kiryat Shemona; the following month they took schoolchildren hostage in Ma'alot, resulting in 24 pupils killed and 62 wounded during the rescue operations. In November, another small team seized an apartment building in Beit Shean, an action which saw four civilians killed and 18 wounded, while in December a bomb in Jerusalem wounded 24 people. In March 1975, finally, a seaborne attack into Tel Aviv itself caused serious casualties and cost the life of the paratroop colonel leading the final assault on terrorists who had gone to ground in a hotel.[70]

These penetrations were embarrassing, but the IDF did not consider them a major threat. Instead, impressed by the near disaster of October 1973, it concentrated on maximising its potential for a high-intensity land-air battle relying on armour, mobile artillery and airpower. While the IDF would continue to watch the frontiers, routine security was to be shifted to the Border Police, now 6,000 strong, and fully mechanised with armoured cars and armoured personnel carriers, and to the police, reinforced by a voluntary Civic Guard equipped with hand-me-down weapons. In case of a particularly serious terrorist penetration, of course, the army's special units would be called in.[71]

The IDF continued pre-emptive and retaliatory air strikes against PLO bases in Lebanon. Though often condemned as counter-productive, the government held, and holds, that it lacked other means to prevent or reply to terrorist attacks.[72] However, when other options were available, the IDF used them and demonstrated that it still could do the unexpected. This was the case on 3 July 1976 when, striking over 2,000 miles, a mixed force of *Sayeret, Golani*, and paratroop units, rescued 105 hostages held by the PFLP at the airport in Entebbe in Uganda.[73]

But this was an exception. After 1975 the PLO acquired heavy arms and turned its bases in Lebanon into strongholds that no longer could be attacked by special forces alone. For that matter, air strikes also had less effect and IDF planners increasingly believed that only massive ground operations could eliminate the PLO which, if equipped with medium artillery and multiple rocket launchers, for the first time was regarded as a military as well as a terrorist threat. In 1978 and again in 1982 the IDF undertook major operations into Lebanon. The first, in March 1978, was a three brigade offensive which chewed up some semi-regular PLO units and damaged its infrastructure, but when international pressure forced the Israelis to withdraw, the PLO returned to the region. The second operation, launched on 6 June 1982, was even more ambitious. The plan appears to have been not only to remove the PLO challenge to Israel in southern Lebanon, but to help the Lebanese Christian forces to establish a strong central government, and to expel both the PLO and the Syrians from the entire country.[74] The initial IDF advance was rapid. Sweeping aside PLO and Syrian resistance, it reached Beirut in a few days, but then was forced to halt under pressure from the United States. From then on the plan began to fall apart and two years later, while the IDF was still in occupation of a good part of southern Lebanon, it also faced domestic dissidence, lowered morale, and above all, attacks from various local and PLO factions.

This time, acting as an occupation force on alien ground, the IDF found it difficult to contain insurgency. Intelligence was harder to come by and the troops, for the most part regulars and reservists from armoured and support units, appeared to lack the skills required for low-intensity operations. Especially in and around Sidon, the major city in the Israeli-controlled zone, these rear-area troops seemed unable to deal with mounting guerrilla attacks. In late December 1983, therefore, a paratroop *Sayeret* unit was deployed in Sidon. Within six weeks it managed to reduce the number of attacks and inflict substantial casualties on the guerrillas. As its commander explained, while the guerrillas enjoyed the advantages of superior intelligence, knowledge of terrain and initiative, these could be offset by aggressive patrolling, high mobility and rapid response. The enemy, he concluded, had become more cautious, realising that he was 'facing professionals—not the amateurs before us'.[75]

Conclusion

This commander's assertions illustrate the case for assigning special units to low-intensity operations. Though ideally all troops should be able at least to hold their own against guerrilla-terrorists, in practice special operational skills are required. And this has been the experience of all modern armies, though some have adapted better to low-intensity operations than others. In the case of the IDF, adaptation to low-intensity warfare has been facilitated by historical experience and the continued unremitting guerrilla-terrorist threat. It has been compelled simultaneously to develop effective forces for high-intensity war while maintaining the capability for low-intensity operations. It has managed to do so by maintaining a 'light infantry' establishment that can participate in battle, but also can provide personnel for special units. This has been made easier because the IDF has been able to retain wide popular support. In a recent study of 17-year-olds about to begin their military service, 90 percent indicated that they believed that this was a necessary obligation, while a follow-up study indicated that an equal percentage preferred service in an élite combat unit.[76] Such attitudes enable the IDF to procure adequate high quality manpower for the special units which have become the necessary backbone of low-intensity operations.

Even so, a recent analysis by a competent American observer of Israeli operations in Lebanon suggests that conscript forces have potential problems in conducting a protracted low-intensity conflict, especially when the perception of an immediate threat to national security has been diminished. Evidence, he writes 'suggests that no one has found a satisfactory answer'. Neither the French in Indochina or North Africa, nor the Americans in Vietnam could use conscript forces freely. 'Conscript armies', he concludes, 'are simply not very good for conducting sustained low-intensity operations', arguing that for these purposes a special force, employing special tactics and techniques, very likely unacceptable to the larger political body, may have to be created. Such units would be permitted to operate along semi-independent lines, perhaps following the example of Unit 101. But whether the Israeli public is likely to condone such activities is, he concedes, an open question.[77]

Reuven Gal, a former Chief Psychologist of the IDF, concurs with these observations, though not with the recommendation. He notes that throughout its relatively short history, the IDF and its self-image has undergone a number of fluctuations and trends. Since 1967, he observes:

[there is hardly] a soldier who has not had to take his turn serving in the occupied territories . . . .. This service resembles a police action more than a military mission. On occasion, when the occupied Palestinian population's demonstrations become vehement and violent this duty turns into one of the worst.

Gal continues to point out that soldiers, regulars and reservists alike, 'have a strong distaste for these duties' and though they carry out orders, 'their motivation and morale is affected'. The prolonged occupation in Lebanon added to these problems, though the withdrawal began in 1985, leaving the army with a more clearly defined mission, the actual defence of close-by Israeli territory has alleviated these particular problems. Gal concludes that the IDF is acutely aware of these problems and is trying to repair damage done. The main challenge, he perceives, is to ensure that the IDF will remain representative of the best in Israeli society.[78]

Finally, an Israeli sociologist observed recently that thus far, despite severe internal strains, Israel has not become a garrison state, but has managed to maintain the routine life-style of an open society, accepting routine conflict and a continuing low-intensity struggle, (which he designates as routine conflict) as an acceptable norm. And the reason that the 1982 Lebanon War aroused such intense controversy within the social system and the framework of the IDF as a whole, was that the 'boundaries between active warfare and routine conflict were blurred'.[79] It would appear then that for a society and its army to engage in long-term low-intensity conflict requires this conflict to be accepted by the mass of the population as just and necessary.

Notes

1. R. Clutterbuck, *Guerrillas and Terrorists* (London: Faber & Faber, 1977), p. 16. *Cf.* the formulation by R. Thompson, *Revolutionary War in World Strategy* (New York: Taplinger Publishing Co., 1970), pp. 16–17.
2. H. G. Summers Jr., *On Strategy. A Critical Analysis of the Vietnam War* (Novato: Presidio Press, 1983), pp. 73, 184.
3. E. N. Luttwak, 'Notes on Low-Intensity Warfare', *Parameters* vol. 13 (December 1983), pp. 11–18; E. A. Cohen, *Commandos and Politicians: Elite Military Units in Modern Democracies,* Harvard Studies in International Affairs No. 40

(Cambridge: Center for International Affairs Harvard University, 1978), pp. 46–47.

4. M. Heller, D. Tamari, Z. Eytan, *The Middle East Military Balance 1983*, Jaffee Center for Strategic Studies, Tel Aviv University (Jerusalem: Jerusalem Post Press, 1984), pp. 121–23. *Cf.* I. Tal, 'Israel's Doctrine of National Security', *Jerusalem Quarterly*, no. 4 (Summer 1977), 45–47.

5. Communication by Professor J. L. Wallach, Tel Aviv University, 4 April 1984; R. Tophoven, 'Palästinensische Kommandos-israelische Abwehr', in R. Tophoven, ed., *Politik durch Gewalt, Beiträge zur Wehrforschung* No. 25 (Bonn: Wehr & Wissen, 1976), pp. 85–86.

6. *ibid.*, pp. 101–2; Luttwak, 'Notes', *op. cit.* p. 14.

7. H. Alon, *Countering Palestinian Terrorism in Israel: Towards a Policy Analysis of Countermeasures*, Rand Corporation Series in International Security and Arms Control N-1567-FF (Santa Monica: Rand Corporation, 1980), pp. 89–92. *Cf.* A. M. Burton, *Urban Terrorism* (London: Leo Cooper, 1975), p. 212.

8. M. Pe'il, *Min ha-Haganah le-tsva haganah* [From Haganah to IDF] (Tel Aviv: Zmora, Bitan, Moden, 1979), p. 263. *Cf.* E. Luttwak and D. Horowitz, *The Israeli Army* (London: Allen Lane, 1975), pp. 1–33; G. E. Rothenberg, *The Anatomy of the Israeli Army* (London: Batsford, 1978), pp. 13–38.

9. Luttwak and Horowitz, *op. cit.*, pp. 11–14.

10. Y. Sadeh, 'Ha-Nodedet', in B. Habas ed., *Sefer me'oraot tarzav* [Book of the 36 Riots] (Tel Aviv: Davar, 1938), pp. 518–19. Translated in Y. Allon, *The Making of Israel's Army* (New York: Bantam Books, 1971), pp. 136–38. Also Allon, 'Moreshet ha-FOSH,' in Z. Gil'ad, ed., *Sefer ha-Palmach* [Book of the Palmach] (Tel Aviv: Kibbutz ha-me'uhad, 1955), I. 49–53. For the dissolution of the FOSH see Y. Bauer, *From Diplomacy to Resistance* (New York: Atheneum, 1973).

11. M. Dayan, *Story of My Life* (New York: William Morrow, 1976), pp. 63–71. *Cf.* C. Sykes, *Orde Wingate* (London: Collins, 1959). The account of the then national Haganah commander is relevant. See Y. Rattner, *Hayai ve-ani* [My Life and Myself] (Tel Aviv: Schocken, 1980), pp. 29–42.

12. On Palmach operations during World War II see Gil'ad, Vol. I, *passim*. For the covert operations in the Western Desert there is P. Rabe, *Tobruk: ha-machlaka ha-germanit ba midbar ha-ma'aravi* [Tobruk: The German Platoon in the Western Desert] (Tel Aviv: Amihai, 1967). For missions into Europe see (Gil'ad) Zerubavel, *Magen ba-seter, mi-Pe'ulot ha mahteret ha-Erets-Israelit ba-milhemet ha-'olam ha-shniyah* [The Clandestine Shield, Actions of the Palestinian Underground in World War II] (Jerusalem: Jewish Agency, 1948).

13. In general see the accounts by Gil'ad, *Sefer ha-Palmach*, and Bauer, *Diplomacy to Resistance*. Training schedules and other documents in Allon, *Israel's Army*, pp. 139–48. For Sadeh's views see his pamphlet *Ma hidesh ha'Palmach?* [What did the Palmach Innovate] (Tel Aviv: Sifriyat ha-poalim, 1950).

14. Allon, *Israel's Army*, p. 24; Cohen, *Commandos*, pp. 32–34; A. Perlmutter, *Military and Politics in Israel: Nation-Building and Role Expansion* (London: Frank Cass, 1969), p. 36.

15. The standard account of the war is N. Lorch, *The Edge of the Sword: Israel's War of Independence, 1947–49* (Jerusalem: Massada, 1968). Documents in Allon, *Israel's Army*, pp. 153–93, 218–43.

16. M. Bar Zohar, *The Armed Prophet: A Biography of David Gurion* (London: Arthur Barker, 1966), pp. 148–49; Y. Peri, *Between Battles and Ballots: Israeli Military in Politics* (London: Cambridge University Press, 1983), pp. 54–57.

17. Rothenberg, *Anatomy of the Israeli Army, op. cit.* pp. 62, 71–76.

18. *ibid.*, pp. 85–88; Z. Schiff, *A History of the Israeli Army 1870–1974* (San

Francisco: Straight Arrow Books, 1974), p. 53.

19. S. Teveth, *Moshe Dayan: The Soldier, the Man, and the Legend* (Boston-New York: Houghton Mifflin, 1973), p. 248.
20. Alon, *Palestinian Terrorism, op. cit.* pp. 14–16.
21. M. Walzer, *Just and Unjust Wars* (New York: Basic Books, 1977), p. 216, concludes that reprisals are 'appropriate to periods of insurgency, border strife, cease-fire, and armistice'.
22. M. Dayan, 'Why Israel Strikes Back', in D. Robinson, ed., *Under Fire: Israel's 20 Year Struggle for Survival* (New York: Norton, 1968), pp. 122–23.
23. Dayan, *My Life, op. cit.* p. 173.
24. Rothenberg, *Anatomy of the Israeli Army, op. cit.* pp. 88–89; Schiff, *Israeli Army*, pp. 223–24. *Cf.* D. Margalit, *Yehidat kommando me'ah ve-ahat* [Commando Unit 101] (Tel Aviv: Moked, 1968).
25. Wealzer, *Just and Unjust Wars, op. cit.* p. 217. For a participant's view see M. Yenuka, *Mi-Kibya ad ha Mitlah* [From Kibiya to the Mitlah] (Tel Aviv: Bitan, 1969), pp. 5–11.
26. A. Avi-Hai, *Ben Gurion State Builder: Principles and Pragmatism 1948–1963* (New York: John Wiley, 1974), pp. 128–30.
27. Luttwak and Horowitz, *Israeli Army, op. cit.* pp. 100–2.
28. Training and indoctrination described by a future Chief of Staff, M. Gur, *Plugah Dalet* [D Company] (Tel Aviv: Ma'arakhot, 1977), pp. 3–18. Included among the original officers was the near legendary Meir Har-Zion, a man who did not hesitate to pursue his private vengeance when some Jordanian bedouin killed his sister. Dayan, *My Life, op. cit.* p. 425, described him as 'One of the chosen few'. A fine account of paratroop training and motivation can be found in M. Hastings, *Yoni: Hero of Entebbe* (New York: Dial Press, 1979), pp. 31–62.
29. J, Lartéguy, *The Walls of Israel* (New York: M. Evans, 1969), p. 23.
30. M. Dayan, *Diary of the Sinai Campaign* (London: Weidenfeld & Nicolson, 1966), p. 27.
31. Rothenberg, *Anatomy of the Israeli Army*, p. 93; E. B. Glick, *Between Israel and Death* (Harrisburg: Stackpole, 1974), pp. 22–27.
32. Teveth, *Moshe Dayan, op. cit.* pp. 241–42.
33. Dayan, *My Life, op. cit.* pp. 172, 178; Luttwak and Horowitz, *Israeli Army, op. cit.* pp. 116–17.
34. N. Safran, *From War to War: The Arab-Israeli Confrontation 1948–1967* (New York: Pegasus Books, 1969), p. 45.
35. Alon, *Palestinian Terrorism, op. cit.* pp. 18–19; Dayan, *Diary, op. cit.* pp. 4–10.
36. Dayan, *Diary, op. cit.* p. 57.
37. Dayan, *My Life, op. cit.* p. 210.
38. C. Herzog, *The Arab-Israeli Wars* (New York: Random House, 1982), pp. 111–14.
39. Rothenberg, *Israeli Army, op. cit.* pp. 114–30.
40. *ibid.*, and J. Lartéguy, *The Face of War. Reflections on Men and Combat* (Indianapolis-New York: Bobbs Merrill, 1979), pp. 324–25.
41. Cohen, *Commandos, op. cit.* p. 74.
42. Alon, *Palestinian Terrorism, op. cit.* pp. 21–30, 30–36.
43. R. Burrowes and D. Muzzio, 'The Road to War. Aspects of an Enumerative History of four Arab States and Israel, 1965–1967', *Journal of Conflict Resolution* XVI (June 1972), pp. 211–26.
44. Alon, *Palestinian Terrorism, op. cit.* pp. 38–39.
45. E. Weizman, *On Eagle's Wings* (New York: Sabra Books, 1970), pp. 102–3.
46. Rothenberg, *Israeli Army, op. cit.* pp. 131–33.
47. M. Howard and R. Hunter, Israel and the Arab World: The Crisis of 1967',

Adelphi Papers 41 (London: Institute for Strategic Studies, 1967), p. 43.
48. Tophoven, 'Palästinensische Kommandos', *op. cit.* pp. 76–80.
49. Luttwak, 'Notes', *op. cit.* p. 14. *Cf.* S. L. A. Marshall's introduction to B. E. O'Neill, *Revolutionary Warfare in the Middle East* (Boulder: Westview, 1974), p. iii.
50. Tophoven, 'Palästinensische Kommandos', *op. cit.* p. 84.
51. S. Teveth, *The Cursed Blessing. The Story of Israel's Occupation of the West Bank* (New York: Random House, 1970), pp. 32, 110, and *passim. Cf.* Peri, *Battles and Ballots, op. cit.* pp. 91–92.
52. Teveth, *Blessing, op. cit.* pp. 196–98, 209, 243, 253–55.
53. R. Tophoven, *Fedayin-Guerrilla ohne Grenzen* (Munich: Bernard & Graefe, 1975), pp. 70–72; O'Neill, *Revolutionary Warfare, op. cit.* pp. 73–74.
54. M. Harel, *Ha-Mirdaf shel ha-tsanhanim* [The Battle of the Paratroopers] (Tel Aviv: Modim, 1969), *passim. Cf.* J. Larteguy, *Walls of Israel, op. cit.* pp. 14–16; Teveth, *Blessing, op. cit.* pp. 347–48.
55. Tophoven, *Fedayin, op. cit.* pp. 72, 81–82, O'Neill, *Revolutionary Warfare, op. cit.* pp. 74–75; Alon, *Palestinian Terrorism, op. cit.* pp. 76–77.
56. Tophoven, 'Palästinensiche Kommandos', *op. cit.* pp. 85–86; Hastings, *Yoni, op. cit.* pp. 100–1, 112–15.
57. Described in Z. Schiff and R. Rothstein, *Fedayeen* (New York: McKay, 1972), pp. 93–99; Tophoven, *Fedayin, op. cit.* pp. 73–75.
58. Teveth, *Blessing, op. cit.* pp. 347–88; Dayan, *My Life, op. cit.* pp. 424–25; Schiff and Rothstein, *Fedayeen, op. cit.* pp. 79–80.
59. Larteguy, *Walls of Israel, op. cit.* p. 67.
60. Alon, *Palestinian Terrorism, op. cit.* p. 47; Dayan, *My Life, op. cit.* pp. 413–15.
61. O'Neill, *Revolutionary Warfare, op. cit.* pp. 76–77, 80; T. N. Dupuy, *Elusive Victory: The Arab-Israeli Wars, 1947–1974* (New York: Harper & Row, 1978), pp. 350–56.
62. On the response to terrorist attacks against international air traffic see J. Bowyer Bell, *A Time of Terror. How Democratic Societies Respond to Revolutionary Violence* (New York: Basic Books, 1978), pp. 58–70. On the Jordanian Civil War see E. O'Ballance, *Arab-Guerrilla Power, 1967–1972* (Hamden: Archon Books, 1973), pp. 137–60.
63. *ibid.*, pp. 171–75; Tophoven, *Fedayin, op. cit.* pp. 77–80.
64. O'Ballance, *Guerrilla Power, op. cit.* pp. 196–201.
65. Rothenberg, *Israeli Army, op. cit.* pp. 170–71. *Cf.* O'Ballance, *The Electronic War in the Middle East 1968–1970* (London: Faber & Faber, 1974), *passim.*
66. Schiff and Rothstein, *Fedayeen, op. cit.* p. 204. On the establishment of an autonomous territorial PLO base in Lebanon see I. Rabinovich, *The War for Lebanon 1970–1983* (Ithaca: Cornell University Press, 1984), pp. 34, 37, 40–42, 45, 50, and *passim.*
67. Tophoven, *Fedayin, op. cit.* pp. 83–85. Mossad co-operation in these and other strikes is discussed in G. Jonas, *Vengeance. The True Story of an Israeli Counter-Terrorist Team* (New York: Simon & Schuster, 1984), pp. 194–97. Like other such accounts of Israeli 'hit teams' and intelligence operations this source must be taken with considerable reservation.
68. Cohen, *Commandos, op. cit.* p. 74.
69. Alon, *Palestinian Terrorism, op. cit.* pp. 41–45, 65–66.
70. *ibid.*, pp. 65–67.
71. *ibid.*, p. 86. *Cf.* Y. Rabin, *Pinkas Sherut* [Service Folder] (Tel Aviv: Ma'ariv, 1979), pp. 519–21.
72. Thus Clutterbuck, *Guerrillas and Terrorists, op. cit.* p. 83.
73. The best account by three Israeli journalists is Y. Ben-Porat, E. Haber, and Z.

Schiff, *Tisah 139* [Flight 139] *op. cit.* (Tel Aviv: Zmora, Biton, Modan, 1976). *Cf.* Hastings, *Yoni, op. cit.* pp. 219–37.

74. Rabinovich, *War for Lebanon, op. cit.* pp. 121–23.
75. *Jerusalem Post International Edition,* 12–18 February 1984, p. 12.
76. M. Levin and D. Halevy, 'Israel', in R. A. Gabriel (ed.), *Fighting Armies. Antagonists in the Middle East. A Combat Assessment* (Westport: Greenwood Press, 1983), pp. 3–4, 17.
77. R. A. Gabriel, *Operation Peace for Galilee. The Israeli-PLO War in Lebanon* (New York: Hill & Wang, 1984), pp. 224–25.
78. R. Gal, *A Portrait of the Israeli Soldier* (New York: Greenwood Press, 1986), pp. 246–54.
79. B. Kimmerling, *The Interrupted System. Israeli Civilians in War and Routine Times* (New Brunswick, New Jersey: Transaction Books, 1985), pp. 200–2.

4

From Algiers to N'Djamena: France's Adaptation to Low-Intensity Wars, 1830–1987

MICHEL L. MARTIN

After having slipped to a minor status nation following World War II, France in the last twenty five years has re-emerged on the contemporary international scene as an influential if not leading power—and is widely acknowledged as such[1]—not least because of her increasingly visible military strength. The credibility of her nuclear deterrent in continuous expansion, the size of her military establishment, a fifth of which is deployed abroad, the range of her arms trade, and the magnitude of the military network she dominates, constitute some of most tangible signs of France's power. With the reduction of the US nuclear arsenal in Europe, France, now the only continental Western nuclear power, is bound to play the decisive role in the defence of Europe. In terms of technology, deployment, sophistication, the programmes to be implemented with the 1987–1991 military plan, adopted in April 1987, testify to this trend. Another aspect, sometimes passed over more unnoticed, of France's world importance, is the active military role, implying the use of force, that she consistently plays and seems determined to play, for the upholding of her interests outside Europe in various areas of the world.

In fact, no other state, except perhaps those of superpower stature, has been recently more engaged in what is considered as limited (or 'peripheral' as opposed to 'central') low-intensity conflicts than France.[2] In the last decade alone, French soldiers have intervened and fought in the Western Sahara, the Horn, the Central African

78

CHAD

LIBYA

● Aouzou

Aouzou strip

Tibesti
Mountains

Disputed
territory

NIGER

● Ouadi-Doum

16°

● Ziguey

Lake
Chad

CHAD

SUDAN

NIGERIA

● N'Djamena

0   150 M

CAMEROUN

CENTRAL AFRICAN REPUBLIC

Republic, Zaire and, recently, in Lebanon and Chad. In many ways, it is tempting to argue that France's readiness for external interventions, the range of her deployment capability and the instruments and techniques devised for low-intensity warfare, demonstrates an efficiency and a sophistication which could be matched by virtually no other state.

Such a posture is not a phenomenon of recent times. When considered in a historical perspective, it appears as the continuation of a pattern of military involvement which developed a century and a half ago; a pattern which itself was also characteristic with respect to the historical trends of the time. Indeed, from the day after the *naufrage* of the Napoleonic saga on the field at Waterloo, the intensity of belligerence on the European continent diminished significantly for the first time. By contrast with the preceding centuries in which warfare was dominant and pervasive, the 19th century, from 1815 to 1914, was a time of relative peace, what Karl Polanyi called the 'one hundred years peace'. France's participation in conventional wars followed this trend. During this period, it did not amount to more than five years or so of 'central' warfare, while from 1600 to 1815, the number of years of war was more than double the years of peace.[3] Yet, at least since 1830, France remained, in a more or less continuous manner, deeply engaged in limited low-intensity conflicts.

Interventions and wars in India and America and the campaign in Egypt in the 18th century were the first 'peripheral' conflicts in which France took part. They were the prodromes of an increasing number of successive operations which began with the conquest of Algeria in 1830, the expeditions in China from 1861–64 and in Mexico from 1862–66. This involvement accelerated by the end of the 19th century, with all of the interventions which accompanied the creation of France's colonial empire in tropical Africa, in Indochina and in North Africa. It continued afterward throughout the first half of the 20th century in Morocco, the Near East, and later with the wars of decolonisation in Indochina, Cameroon and Algeria.

This long history of 'peripheral' warfare which stretched from 1830 to the present day, reveals many different forms of interventions and conflicts. Low-manpower amphibious operations on the Senegal River in the 1850s, airborne rescue missions in Shaba in 1978, effective-intensive operations in Algeria in the 1840s and Indochina in the 1950s, air-strike missions such as those in Mauritania in 1977, and even police actions to maintain order, such as those in the former

Congo-Brazzaville, Senegal and Gabon in the early 1960s, are cases in point. They undoubtedly exhaust the composite spectrum of low-intensity conflict.

Yet, behind such diversity, it is possible from a more macro-analytical standpoint to isolate typological forms. On close inspection, the way contemporary unconventional wars are conducted, and the institutional posture they imply, appears as rather different from the earlier strategic and institutional modes. Most engagements which took place before 1960 present a fairly stable and uniform pattern, the principles of which had been devised as early as 1840 during the conquest of Algeria; for this reason it will be referred to hereafter as the *guerre algérienne* model. As for the post-1960 engagements, they affect a more polymorphous pattern but contrary to the preceding ones, have been restricted essentially to sub-Saharan Africa—hence the reference to the *guerres africaines*. In a way, it is not so much political and historical circumstances, though these cannot be ignored, which underlie the difference between these two types of warfare; the differences are also in kind and manifestations. The question, then, of France's present-day involvement in low-intensity warfare might stand to gain through discussion of a comparative historical perspective.

The *Guerre Algérienne*—1830–1960: the Dominant Mode of Low-Intensity Warfare

As we have seen, except for the wars in Italy and the Crimea, the Franco-Prussian conflict, and World War I, a total of less than 10 years of conventional or 'central' warfare, France participated mainly in 'peripheral' conflicts, and this in a continuous manner. Furthermore, except for the campaigns in China and the ill-fated expedition to Mexico, France's non-conventional military commitments were of a colonial nature. They were aimed at building and maintaining a large overseas empire which was to stretch from Indochina to Malagasy, from Equatorial Africa to North Africa, and was to be added to the remnants of her earlier colonial possessions in the Pacific, Atlantic, and Indian oceans.[4]

Although they have taken place in a wide variety of terrains, climates and over a relatively long span of time, in a context therefore of significant technological change, these military commitments clearly followed a fairly uniform and distinctive pattern. This can be ideally typified under the generic term of *guerre algérienne*, in reference to the way such a type of warfare evolved and was conducted at the time of the conquest of Algeria.[5] Indeed, it was amended to an important degree later on; yet the fundamental structure of this mode of war as conducted afterwards remained similar to that fashioned during the conquest of Algeria in the 1840s under the leadership of Marshal Bugeaud. In other words, it would be hypothesised that the *guerre algérienne* has served as the blueprint for later colonial wars in Indochina, 1875–1900, in Morocco from 1900–34, as well as for the wars of decolonisation in the 1950s and early 1960s in Africa and the Far East.

To be sure, the historian might question such a view by arguing that warfare as conducted in Bugeaud's Algeria could not, for instance, resemble warfare as fought in Lyautey's Morocco, for the former appeared rather as a 'savage' war, based on annihilation tactics. This is largely true.[6] Nevertheless if they had not been applied consistently, it was certainly during the conquest of Algeria that the new principles of warfare (military actions based on movement and psycho-political actions undertaken by a racially-mixed special corps of professional soldiers) were developed and began to be put into practice. The originality of the doctrine of the *guerre algérienne* can be approached from three levels, strategic as well as institutional.

The strategic and tactical aspects of the guerre algérienne

The main strategic tenets which dominated French military thinking in the middle of the 19th century were Napoleonic in essence. Indeed, a large portion of the officer corps at this time had been, in one way or another, formed, either by training or by field experience (especially in the case of the older generations in the higher ranks of the hierarchy) by the Napoleonic style of war.[7] Suited to the European continent and structured on the principles of revolutionary mass-organisation, this prevalent tradition was based on, among other things, static defence and relied upon mass manoeuvres of large columns and upon heavy artillery fire; it was conceived in the perspective of what Clausewitz called *die Niederwerfungs strategie*.

This was the strategy which the French adopted after the taking of Algiers on 5 July 1830, France's first military engagement since 1815. At this time the French expeditionary force and its leaders found themselves confronted with numerous issues. They had to maintain order in the conquered city and its vicinity. More important, they had to deal with the irredentism of the population in the hinterlands, exacerbated by France's policy of territorial appropriation. The results were bloody disasters. Sent into operation against rebellious groups, the heavy columns, slowed down by their own supply wagons, were the objects, unexpectedly, of 'hit-and-run' rear or flank attacks by highly mobile mounted forces. Material and human attrition rates, increased by the erratic nature of the terrain and climate, were always high. By the late 1830s, the gravity of the situation was made all the more dramatic for the French by the fact that the various fighting tribes which had hitherto lived in a state of reciprocal enmity, had federated, if not united, under the leadership of Emir Abd el Kader. Strategic and tactical adaptation was clearly overdue.

A new strategy had to be elaborated lest France lose her hold in Algeria. It was by a *soldat de l'empire*, Robert Bugeaud, appointed as the third governor and chief commander of Algeria, that an entirely new way of warfare was devised, through which France's position in Algeria could be consolidated. This new conception was more than a trial 'hit and miss' adaptation. In many ways it was thought out quite systematically and could be considered as a genuine, fully-fledged doctrine of low-intensity warfare. Bugeaud's vision derived both from the observation of the combat techniques of local native forces, his experience in the Peninsular War, as well as from his historical knowledge of the empire-building methods of the Romans, especially in North Africa.[8]

Casting aside all principles of continental warfare, Bugeaud advocated a *guerre de mouvement* based on offensive tactics. He was convinced that such a strategy was the only way to deal with an elusive and more numerous enemy. In his own words, 'The only system capable of subduing Algeria is that of mobility . . ..'[9] To enhance the mobility of the French troops so as to match that of the adversary, the equipment—both personal and collective—of the troops was lightened and simplified. Foodstuffs for men and animals were to be collected on the spot; necessary supplies, previously carried on wagons, were now hauled on horses and mules. The heavy column, the foremost instrument of Napoleonic warfare, lost its pre-eminence in the emerging strategy. Its role was restricted to forward penetration of the hinterlands or to smashing the heart of resistance strongholds. All other operations were undertaken by smaller mobile groups whose objectives were constantly to harass the enemy. The size of the columns, moreover, was reduced to 5,000 men with 1,200 horses and consisted of light infantry units covered by fast cavalry and light artillery; it thus acquired a new mobility. The advancing columns could also regroup swiftly in case of attack into square formation with mounted protection, thus eliminating the risks of rear and flank forays which had earlier beset the effectiveness of French forces.

A network of blockhouses, positioned at strategic points and connected by newly-built roads, was constructed to serve as warehouses and starting points for the launching of offensives and rescue missions. Static retrenchment was considered to be useless, and even dangerous given the climate, as well as detrimental to morale, so this notion was abandoned.

To ensure the efficiency of this new form of warfare and optimise the strength of these intensive yet limited offensives, careful strategic and tactical planning, as well as fluidity of communication and logistics, were emphasised. These developments allowed the French to co-ordinate simultaneous, convergent operations, which seemed the only way to extend control over the mountainous regions of the country. In this respect, Bugeaud's views, as spelled out in his report on mountain warfare, were quite innovative.[10]

Discipline and leadership were also critical for the success of this strategy, the more so since the enemy forces were always superior in number. Steadfastness, self-control and firing discipline became the hallmark of colonial military skill.

Although they developed on radically different territories, later imperial enterprises bore distinctly the tactical traits of Bugeaud's *guerre algérienne*. Governor Faidherbe's campaigns in Senegal in the mid-1850s, mounted to subdue the Mauritanians on the left bank of the Senegal River, to defeat Islamic uprisings or to control the Cayor coastal area, as well as his attempts to penetrate the upper-Senegal Niger regions, were the first successful applications of the *guerre algérienne* paradigm outside its natural environment. Faidherbe, who had served twice in Algeria where he participated in the Kabylie campaign, utilised light and mobile columns in a 'hit-and-run' fashion. In the fluvial region, moreover, against the Mauritanians or in the Haut-Senegal area, small fighting parties were launched from gunships steaming up the navigable parts of the river systems, to operate inland at a short distance from the shores.[11]

Then time and again, between 1883 and 1900, all over West and Equatorial Africa, Malagasy, Indochina, from sun-scorched Chad to rain-drenched Dahomey, from mountainous Tonkin at the Chinese border, to the delta area in Annam, small mobile units were launched from fortified positions, from mother columns or from river gunboats. Their tactics consisted of advanced reconnoitering, surprise and swift moves, disruption of the enemy troops forced out into the open or assaulted in their retrenchments; usually a bayonet and rifle affair conducted with a good deal of composure and firing discipline. The technique seemed so 'magical' to the enemy that they often sent spies into the French ranks to learn it. General Mangin's favourite *spahi* was one of Samory's spies.[12] Large-scale armed resistance, such as in West Africa under the leadership of imperial religious rulers, Mahmadu-Lamine, Samory, Behanzin or Rabah, to name some of the most conspicuous, was in this way dismantled and routed in the course of a few campaigns.

Generals Duchemin and Dodds, future generals Gallieni, Mangin, their men, the majors Archinard, Marchand and Gouraud, down to the last lieutenant, all followed Bugeaud's tactical path. So, later, did their heirs, in Morocco during the decades following the signing of the Protectorate and then in the Near East after the 1914–18 War; among them, one of the most outstanding, Marshal Lyautey.[13]

Mobility, Bugeaud's catchword, which extricated French troops from the hindering spell of static warfare and exorcised defeat, had become paramount. 'In Africa one protects oneself by moving', claimed Lyautey. In the Riff War, before reinforcements were sent in July 1925, small *groupes mobiles* and *bataillons de marche* succeeded, in relentless rescue operations, in preventing the collapse of local strategic posts on the line protecting Fez. The case of one of those battalions, from the 14th Algerian *tirailleur*, which in 60 hours covered more than 130kms and was engaged in three battles, is often recounted. To speed up action and its subsequent surprise effects, he and his associates made full use of the available modern technology and careful planning. Bugeaud relied on semaphor communications, *estafettes*, light carts and hauling by horse; his followers in Morocco used railroads, the motor car, even aircraft. Prepared with great attention, over a period of months, the operations—even the largest ones—were completed in a matter of a few weeks.

The columns were used only for approaches, penetration and mountain assaults. All other operations were conducted by thin advancing front lines—Lyautey coined the idea of oil patch progression—preventing any rear or flank counter-attacks. Thus, with limited manpower—and it was to grow smaller when reinforcements had to be sent to the front in France in 1914—Lyautey was able to gain control over large portions of the coastal and plain regions of Morocco.

The other aspect of Lyautey's contribution to the efficiency of the *guerre algérienne* deals with mountain warfare. Originally, the *guerre algérienne* was a flat land strategy; indeed, as already observed, Bugeaud had sought to adapt it to mountainous terrain when he undertook the Kabylie campaign. Yet the fact that the French had to mount several successful campaigns to control Kabylie demonstrated at the time the limitations of the strategy in reducing resistance. But Lyautey only elaborated on Bugeaud's views. He approached mountain warfare in terms of siege warfare. The starting point was the isolation of a sector of the range to be taken, and its encirclement at lowlands level by a continuous front. The front was to progress upward 'like a tide' occupying every gap in the mountain. This done, columns were then sent from opposite sides to cut the enemy from its lines before it was assaulted.[14] This strategy served also in the mid-1920s to deal with Abd el Krim irredentist forces in the Riff range, and again by Lyautey's able successor, General Huré, in mid-1934, in the pacification of the southwestern range of the Atlas and Anti-Atlas mountains. Although they relied on advanced weaponry—in the aforementioned campaign, Generals Catroux and Giraud, Huré's field commanders, resorted to air-bombing—the basic paradigm remained that of the *guerre algérienne*. In an article published in 1939, General Huré made it clear that Bugeaud's 1840 instructions had served as the framework of his own strategy in Morocco.[15]

Although the configuration of colonial warfare could be interpreted as having changed after World War I, as already presaged by the last stage of the Moroccan pacification, it can be validly argued that the basic military paradigm of the *guerre algérienne* remained at work. Before it lost its colonial character, becoming a large scale quasi-conventional and international war in 1950, the Indochina War was fought, and not without success, along these traditional lines. Light motorised columns of platoon size operating from a network of blockhouses or by amphibious approaches, after the initial mainland and riverine breakthroughs, characterised the campaigns for the reoccupation of South Vietnam, and the operations in Tonkin and Cochin-China after World War II. The same can be said for the Algerian War. After the ill-fated attempts to meet the rebellion by static-style defence with large-scale manoeuvres, and from the Battle of Algiers up to 1960, under the capable leadership of General Challe, most aspects of the strategy developed bore the imprint of the earlier colonial ways of warfare. Careful planning, speed in movement and surprise were decisive. Small highly-mobile units—the *commandos de chasse*, 60 to 80 men strong, modelled on the rebels' own units, the *katibas*—were sent on 'search and harass' missions against enemy forces with success. Larger enemy concentrations were met by *coup de massue* operations, undertaken simultaneously by several small units with helicopters and light armoured support, which, after first contracts, could then be dispersed to pursue the enemy. Although French military deployment in Algeria was significant in terms of manpower, the whole business of harrying was actually conducted by 35,000 men or so, that is less than 10 percent of the whole contingent stationed there.

The double-pronged assault, coded *Operation Jumelles*, in the Kabylie in July 1960 against the powerful *Wilaya 3,* demonstrated the efficiency of a tactic based on mobility and surprise. The operation was preceded by a surprise attack on the Hodna range (it was literally decided overnight on the basis of fresh intelligence information) where nearly 50 percent of the enemy forces were destroyed. Such an action, as well as those mounted earlier in the Western and Eastern Ouarsenis range in April, where between 40 to 50 percent of the enemy potential was also lost, undeniably forced the National Liberation Front on to the defensive, even to contemplating the possibility of military defeat. Had the planned *Operation Trident* in the Nementchas-Aurés region not been cancelled, with the recalling of Challe, the defeat of the rebellion might well have become a reality.[16] In many ways, these operations were also *du meilleur Bugeaud*, to use the formula which credited General Gallieni's earlier achievements in Malagasy and Indochina.

In sum, mobility, lightness, and co-ordination used in a strategy of manoeuvre and disruption permitted France to dominate a formidable empire with extremely limited manpower and a relatively low casualty rate.[17] Yet, tactics, firepower, heroism and initiative were only one side of the coin. The other side, with which it formed an indissociable whole—discussed separately here for the sake of convenience of the exposition—and which gave the *guerre algérienne* its unmistakable originality, was its politico-psychological dimension.

The psycho-political dimension of the guerre algérienne

No war, whatever its form, is entirely free of psycho-political elements and this is especially true for low-intensity conflicts. To be efficient, this type of warfare requires careful intelligence work, advance knowledge of the terrain and local cultures, contacts with the populations, and so on. In the case of France's *guerre algérienne*, however, this dimension had a particular salience. Even countries involved in similar conflicts and faced with similar situations, such as Britain, the Netherlands, or even Russia in Turkestan and the Caucasus, had never paid much attention to this aspect. In the end, for that matter, France's preoccupation with these psycho-political aspects of the war, or rather their ideological underpinnings, grew to such an inordinate extent as to contradict and defeat the very purpose they initially served.

Psycho-political action, as conceived by the French military, was not only a technique of administration but a direct, inseparable component of the military enterprise itself. Gallieni's 1898 instructions, for example, not only advocated the necessity of combining force with political efforts but further argued that 'political action was by far more important'.[18] This view—and in this regard there is no lack of testimony—was, from Lyautey to the revolutionary warfare propagandist of the 1950s, consistently upheld as the *ne plus ultra* of efficient warfare outside the European arena.

As seen in the preceding section, the *guerre algérienne* did not operate on a strategy of annihilation, but rather was based on a kind of *Ermattungsstrategie*, to borrow Hans Delbrück's formula. It was aimed essentially at harassing and disorganising enemy forces. And it could not have been otherwise. In terms of manpower ratio, the enemy forces always outnumbered those of the French. When he wrote in his memoirs: 'We are 98, waiting for 1,300 Mahdists; there is no disproportion',[19] Captain (later General) Baratier was not boasting but merely describing a common state of things at the time. Therefore, the battle had to be fought on the non-military as well as the military sides of the conflict, while the soldier's mission had also to be expanded beyond the conventional professional boundaries of combat and military roles.

The military operations of the conquest of Algeria cast a merciless shadow while its actors projected an image of *razzia* and instant glory-minded *soldatesque*, both alien to the sophistication of psycho-political thinking. Yet, it cannot be denied that, at the very same time, the political and psychological foundations of warfare were laid down. And the colonial soldier of later imperial enterprises only elaborated on these principles. With the establishment of various institutions for Arabic affairs, the early days of the conquest witnessed the first attempts to deal with the basic political necessities of the war; to wit, defining who was the enemy. Again, it was Marshal Bugeaud who sought to give this issue a comprehensive solution. His correspondence, notably with the War Minister, Marshal Soult, and with Duc d'Aumale, reflected this concern quite explicitly,[20] as did his instructions to subordinates.

The *Bureaux Arabes* that were created in 1841 represented the first fully-fledged institutionalisation of the psycho-political dimension of war. The Bureaux served primarily as intelligence-gathering agencies which allowed the military to engage in a successful diplomacy of exploiting local political dissensions, for instance with Mustapha Ismael, the Agha of Douair and Smala, or with Ben Gana, the *cheick el Arab* of Briskra during the campaign against Abd el Kader, (also of the treaty of La Tafna). But above all, the Bureaux were to operate as the *trait d'union*, in Captain Hubonnet's words, between the French and the local population.[21] Their role was to help in settling disputes, to build roads, to organise commercial centres and provide health care, and thus to win the support of the local population. Further to insure the French establishment in the countryside, Bugeaud also organised model farms and military villages. Of course, the reality often deviated from the irenic ideal that such reforms had implied. There had been abuses and scandals; heads of the Bureaux often behaved as feudal despots and the Doineau affairs or the Oued Mahouine massacre stained indelibly the image of the Bureaux and the whole psycho-political effort of the French.[22] Yet, it must be said that these failures flowed less from institutional deficiencies than from a lack of genuine sense of mission among a particular generation of soldiers.

It was nonetheless on the basis of these still rough, yet clear-cut premises that the political dimension of the *guerre algérienne* later developed. There were first the ever increasing needs for intelligence information and diplomatic actions on which the success of military operations depended. Interestingly, the French military was not content with playing off inherent local divisions. They also sought to win the co-operation of enemy troops and to integrate them into the French ranks. Successful examples of this policy were numerous, in Algeria and, more particularly, in Africa where nationalistic tendencies were non-existent. Colonial lore treasures the story of the enlistment in the Senegalese *tirailleurs* of several of Samory's off-spring. In recent times, during the Algerian War, the French took advantage of ideological dissension within the National Liberation Front and did not hesitate to arm dissenter groups such as BelHadj and Bella si Chelif. Rebels having surrendered and wishing to join the French were organised into auxiliary paramilitary units, the *harkas*, and armed for local and self-defence purposes.

But direct action on the terrain, at the level of local populations, became the pivotal objective of the psycho-political side of warfare. The French military developed the idea that it was not so much enemy propaganda which triggered the resistance of the population; rather, the population constituted the ground favouring the development of the rebellion. Rebellion fed on the disorganisation created by the first military actions; it is 'a plant which grows only on certain grounds', to use the image of General Duchemin, chief commander in Indochina in the 1890s.[23] There was no point then in trying only to eradicate the rebellion. Military actions had to be paralleled by social, economic and administrative actions which would prevent any disorganisation, and in consequence make the ground unsuitable for the rebellion to grow.

General Gallieni was among the first to systematise the views advocated by men like Duchemin and to give precedence to the psycho-political aspects of the military operation. His writings, as already pointed out, as well as his records in Tonkin and especially in Malagasy as Governor General, evinced such emphasis. Most of the southern part of the Malagasy Island was effectively conquered by non-military means. Gallieni was also responsible for carrying out on the institutional level the fusion of military and psycho-political actions which, in the first stages of the *guerre algérienne*, were separated both in time and space. He instigated a system of unified command whose basic unit was the *cercle militaire*. Whereas the heads of the *Bureaux Arabes* had no field responsibilities, the *commandant de cercle* was a soldier who had the role of administrator simultaneously engaged in judiciary, economic and educational activities. For the soldiers who had completed their service and wished to remain, the Bugeaud tradition of the 'military villages' was modified into a policy of dispersion into the local population.[24]

Lyautey, Gallieni's most able associate, expounded further the view of his mentor. In his celebrated piece on the colonial role of the army, he argued that military occupation consists of an 'organisation on the move' (*en marche*). Military posts were to be centres of various activities aimed to attract, educate and protect the local population and were designed to benefit the native people. They were not to be centres of occupation, but rather, centres of influence.[25]

For the next 50 years these conceptions would articulate the shape and conduct of France's 'peripheral' wars. Indeed, the colonial conflicts, which erupted after World War II in Indochina, Algeria, and Cameroon, were not the least illustrative instances of this persistent concern for the psycho-political dimension of warfare. In Indochina, in the early 1950s, many an officer found himself managing rice fields, trading the crops, running schools and hospitals, organising self-defence groups and instilling new life into local political institutions. His objective, once again, was to enlist the people's complicity, and, as one of them put it, 'to win it [the people] over and make my war its own war'.[26] The Algerian War witnessed an even greater emphasis on the psycho-political front. Not only did the French military seek to erode the legitimacy of the rebellion, it also sought to design a system of reforms aimed at reorganising and correcting the inadequacies of the country's social structure and its functioning. The military literally took over the ruling of Algeria. Through its own administrative network, the UAS (Urban Administrative Sections), and especially the SAS (Specialised Administrative Sections), the army supervised economic development, medical and social assistance, education and so on, and sought to modernise the civic, moral and professional outlook of the whole population. Women's clubs, trade schools, youth organisations were thus set up and directed by military officers all over the country, in an unprecedented effort to unify the people against the rebellion and legitimate the French presence.[27]

In sum, the *guerre algérienne* was as much, if not more, a psycho-political undertaking as it was a strictly military affair, in that 'victory' was always sought, buttressed and consolidated by non-military or paramilitary means. A great deal has been written on the 'dark' side of these methods. Some could, indeed, be judged as controversial if not repugnant. The *guerre algérienne* certainly resorted to the use of manipulation, intimidation, deportation and even terrorism. Here again certain of Bugeaud's more dubious methods of psychological warfare were adopted in Senegal, West Africa and Indochina.[28] This being said, the *enfumades*, economic retaliation and torture, cannot subsume the complexity of the psycho-political dimension of the war as practised by the French; nor do they do justice to the range of realisations achieved. An authority in French military history underlined the Kemalist nature of military reforms in Algeria; this term could just as well be applied to characterise many psycho-political undertakings by the army throughout the period considered here.[29]

In any case, the point in this section was not to assess the value of these accomplishments but to highlight the importance of the psychological and political components of the *guerre algérienne*. Its ultimate failure rested at another level. Enshrouded, as it came to be, in the ideological veil of revolutionary warfare, from a means it became an end. As such it led to confusion between local nationalisms and socialism and communism, between decolonisation and a threat to the free world, and as such rendered any compromise—the very objective for which it was originally devised—impossible. Furthermore, by implying a fusion of military and political roles, the psycho-political dimension of the *guerre algérienne* distorted the whole structure of civil-military relations on which rested the political control of the military, and brought a threat to the very institutional arrangement of the French political regime itself.[30]

The actors and institutions of the guerre algérienne

The third original aspect of the *guerre algérienne* was its particular institutional setting. The war was fought mainly by special corps and units, composed of racially-mixed troops of French volunteers and locally-recruited soldiers. They were commanded by French officers who had chosen to serve overseas and who exhibited a professional outlook somewhat different from that of their peers serving in France. These two aspects will be examined in turn, beginning with the utilisation of native recruits.

The military recruitment of native troops was certainly not an innovation, nor was it unique to France. Antillese, Senegalese or Indians, slaves and freed slaves, had been enrolled to serve and fight under the French colours during the *Ancien Régime*, the Revolution and the Napoleonic Wars, in Europe as well as overseas. The Royal

Africain, the *Corps des Laptots de Gorée*, the *Cipayes*, and the black Brigade formed (with slaves bought from the Sultan of Darfour) by General Kleber in Egypt, are some of the best known illustrations that can be mentioned in passing.

These early forms of recruitment and utilisation, however, differed significantly from those put into practice with the *guerre algérienne*. Previously these men, whose status was often disenfranchised, served as auxiliaries, performing general ancillary tasks or fatigue duties. There was, moreover, no continuity in their utilisation.[31] With the *guerre algérienne*, on the other hand, the military utilisation of natives became institutionalised and was to endure for more than a century until the early 1960s. They were recruited as conscripted or enlisted soldiers, integrated in the French armed forces rank structure, within which they could be promoted (though with some limitations). They fought in colonial wars but also in the wars in Europe.[32] These features, as well as the proven effectiveness of manpower under arms, single out the French experiment from those undertaken by other colonial powers, particularly Britain.

The reasons which motivated this doctrine of recruitment were diverse. The serious manpower shortage in the post-Napoleonic era which prevented any increase of the French contingent for non-European purpose, the necessity, moreover, to compensate for the demographic differential with Germany and to match German forces, the concern for minimising manpower costs, were the most commonly advanced reasons. But such a recruitment was also linked to the very nature and the functioning of the psycho-political aspects of the *guerre algérienne*. The use of natives, who were often former members of the enemy forces, was seen as instrumental in undermining the legitimacy of nationalist resistance among opposing forces and within the populations. Finally, it must be added that France's views of non-Western societies and cultures, views which placed less emphasis on colour and race than, say, those of Britain, Belgium or the United States, were elements facilitating the recruitment of native soldiers in the French ranks.[33]

Again, though in an unsystematised fashion, it was during the conquest of Algeria that the idea of a local military recruitment developed. Algerians were called up in order to compensate for the increasing manpower needs resulting from the extension of the operations and the difficulties in strengthening the French contingent (though this grew continuously until 1846). The existence of a mercenary network operated by the Turks, which recruited from particular social and cultural groups, such as the Azouaoua tribe, as well as the remnants, notably the Turco-Arab metis, the Koughoulis, of disbanded Turkish troops, availed the French of a local manpower pool and permitted the creation of the Zouave regiments and infantry *tirailleurs*. Soon afterwards, other tribal groups were recruited when infantry and cavalry forces were expanded. The multiplication of the number of *spahis*, originally the mounted units of Zouaves, resulted from the French policy of matching in mobility the Arab cavalry of Abd el Kader, but also was aimed at attracting the scions of the *grandes tentes* and retainers of tribal chieftains.[34]

These units were mixed in composition. French soldiers served in the ranks and French officers commanded them. They were juxtaposed with newly-established special French regiments, such as the *Chasseurs d'Afrique* (light cavalry units), the *Bataillons d'Afrique* (disciplinary battalions), and foreign regiments, like the celebrated Foreign Legion created in 1831.[35] Together, they formed what came to be known as the *Armée d'Afrique*, though, organisationally, they belonged to the French armed forces; after 1873, they made up the 19th Corps of the French Army.

Until the mid-19th century, the effectiveness of the native troops remained limited. In 1848, for instance, there were 6,600 Algerians in an army of 87,000 men.[36] The conquest of Algeria was, therefore, certainly a French war. Nevertheless, the idea of tapping the local populations for military purposes was instituted at that time and set the trend for the next 120 years. As early as 1885, the number of Algerians enrolled increased progressively; 40,000 served during the Franco-Prussian War, and in the early 1900s they formed a third of the total military strength in Algeria. With the establishment of the Protectorate of Tunisia and later in Morocco, both Tunisians and Moroccans served (although in smaller numbers than the Algerians) in the newly created Tunisian and Moroccan *tirailleurs* regiments. Between 1920 and 1924, 150,387 North Africans served in the French ranks.[37]

This policy of local military recruitment was also expanded to Black Africa and Indochina. In Africa, it was institutionalised at Faidherbe's initiative. It began in Senegal, where Senegalese had been serving episodically under the French colours since 1859, with the creation in the mid-1850s of the Senegalese *tirailleurs*. It was followed later by the establishment of new *tirailleurs* and *spahis* regiments all over the African continent; the Malagasy in 1885, the Haoussa in 1891, Soudanese in 1892. In Asia, the *tirailleurs* Anamites and Tonkinois were established in 1879 and 1884. All these units were attached to the French marine infantry and marine artillery units to form the *Armée coloniale*. It should be noted that many of these units had been fused together. This was the case in Black Africa with the celebrated *tirailleurs sénégalais* which were genuine interafrican units; a typical regiment, according to one source for 1926, was made up of 44 percent Voltaic, 38 percent Senegalese, 12 percent Malian and 6 percent Guinean.[38] Small in number at first, 17,000 in 1891 (14,500 Asians and 2,500 Africans), the size of these contingents increased later. In 1928, there was a total of 74,330 Blacks and Asians, that is, two-thirds of the colonial army. This figure has constituted a standard average throughout the period under consideration.

Geographical multi-purposefulness (*polyvalence*) was the crux of the policy governing the utilisation of these units. They were used all over the colonial empire to fight in the various conflicts as a result of its expansion. Algerians served in West Africa, Morocco and the Near East, black Africans in North Africa, North Africans and black Africans in the Far East. In 1919, of the 133,000 black Africans under arms, 27,000 were stationed in Africa, 15,000 in Algeria, 11,000 in Morocco, 10,000 in the Middle East and the remaining 60,000 in France.[39] This pattern of *polyvalent* service was maintained up to the 1960s. The Moroccan campaign of pacification called upon West Africans as well as Algerians. During the Indochina War in the early 1950s, one-third of the French expeditionary corps was composed of native troops, of which 30,000 were North Africans and 18,000 black Africans.[40]

A typical regiment of the *guerre algérienne* comprised 2,500 men, 20 percent of whom were French, with two percent officers. The French serving in the so-called *Armée d'Afrique* were enlisted men. In the colonial army, conscription had existed but since 1893 conscripts could not be sent overseas. The French policy was to avoid using French conscripts for overseas service. Conscripts had been called up during the Algerian War, but they were not sent into action. They were only committed for routine administration duties or police duties of the *quadrillage*; the actual fighting was carried out by professionals, a comparatively small group as we have seen, made up of colonial units and French professional troops.

Native troops were recruited through voluntary enlistments and conscription. Conscription of local troops was the object of numerous and heated debates. It was introduced slowly and operated on a selective basis. Proponents of conscription argued that it would help to constitute a reserve force, that it would prevent manpower transfers overseas and allow the reduction of the length of military service for French conscripts. The adversaries of conscription, who comprised a part of the military establishment as well as settlers, argued that conscription would be dangerous since it would result in developing the military skills of a sizeable part of the local population which could become a danger in case of uprisings. They pointed to the mutinous bent of native troops evinced by numerous incidents and cases of disobedience, such as in 1871 in Algiers, in 1912 with a rebellion of Moroccan soldiers, after World War I with Senegalese troops refusing to embark for the Near East, and in 1930 with the Yen Bay revolt in Indochina. Yet given manpower necessities, conscription had to be introduced. Tunisians were the first to be conscripted in 1881; the policy was then extended to Indochina, in Annam (1906) and Cochin-China (1908), then in Africa and in Algeria in 1912. Conscription, however, operated on a selective basis (generally on a lottery system) with a rather long-term period of service, of 3–4 years.[41] Many conscripts did re-enlist when their term ended. So, in the end, the bulk of the forces serving in the *guerre algérienne* were enlisted men.

The French were not as devoted to the idea of martial races for their recruitment policy, as were the British, yet evolutionary preconceptions on the warlike character of non-industrial societies were strong and indeed the military feats of the Abd el Kader, the Al adj Omar and other Samory confirmed such views. So it happened that the French often attributed better fighting capabilities to some racial groups than others. The Indochinese (though a distinction was made between Annamites—the bravest—and other groups) and the Hovas of Malagasy, for example, were considered to be intelligent and skilled in the more sophisticated paramilitary aspects of the war. Algerians were generally viewed as brave, yet less so than the Moroccans (called Lions), but a distinction was also made between the Arabs and the Kabyles who were judged as more intelligent. Among black Africans, considered slower-witted, the Soudanese groups were favoured for their fighting skills and endurance over those from the Gulf of Guinea. Within the Soudanese, the Malinkes and, above all, the Bambaras, seen as the 'cornerstone of our colonial edifice in Africa',[42] were the favourite choice; among the Peuls, the Toucouleurs were regarded as good soldiers though less disciplined than other groups.

Partly because of these beliefs in natural martial skills, partly because of the idea that training could be as well acquired on the spot, the military formation of native troops was brief (much more than in the British case) though intensive. It focused on basic training aimed at the proper handling of the bayonet and rifle. The manning of more sophisticated weaponry, principally the machine gun, was left to French soldiers, although many a native NCO had acquainted himself with more advanced technology. Training was also meant to assimilate the *parler tirailleur*—a kind of military pidgin—which facilitated not only the communication of orders but also the building of a sense of cohesion among culturally heterogeneous groups. The French also counted simply on the sheer psychological effects of the use of natives (in Europe it did shock the Germans both in 1870 and in World War I), especially playing on the North African and black African racial antagonisms. On the whole, such a policy of recruitment was successful. Native soldiers fought bravely, not least in the European wars—shouldering, to a large extent, the burden of suffering and death—and showed great loyalty to France. Many of them, at the time of independence, especially in Africa, found themselves torn between their allegiance to the French Army and the loyalty demanded by the new leaders who represented groups and ideas against which they had been fighting.[43] On the other hand, this experience has not been without effect on their political awareness and the roles that few of them were to play in the political as well as administrative and economic sectors of the newly decolonised territories.

Turning to the leadership of the *guerre algérienne*, French officers assumed in general the function of command. However, it must be stressed that, probably more than in other armies, native soldiers had opportunities to rise in the hierarchy. As early as the 1830s, provision was made to give Algerians commanding their troops a position in the French rank structure. Although the status of native officer was distinct from that of regular officer, the differences, which did not extend to pay, privileges or uniforms, diminished over time, and in any case did not apply to Africans or Algerians having become French citizens. After World War I, this effort was continued (see the Bill of November 29, 1926, and the decrees of January 1928 and April 1930), and culminated in the establishment of a special officer school at Frejus in the south of France.[44] Nevertheless, native officers were a minority, especially in the senior ranks of the hierarchy. Hence the leadership of the *guerre algérienne* was left to French officers.

Two stereotypes have traditionally served to depict the leader of colonial wars. On the one hand, the absinth-addicted and untidy adjutant of *la colo* as well as the racially-prejudiced hothead and over-ambitious officer; on the other hand, the romantic, cultivated leader, seeking refuge from industrial republicanism, or even the priest-like civiliser, concerned with the welfare of the colonies. The corrupted brutes of the conquest of Algeria, the altruistic educators of the Moroccan pacification; Bugeaud's men on one side, Lyautey's on the other. In sum, the *baroudeur* and the apostle; both were distinctive, and equally different from their peers serving in France. As always, the truth lies in between, though the model of the *guerre algérienne* leader, if one could be isolated, evolved from the first type to the second.

At first, indeed, the dedicated *Affaires indigénes* officer fashioned after Lyautey's model hardly seemed the heir of the men who had led the conquest of Algeria. Yet he was; but at that time his presence was still inconspicuous, given the comparatively poor quality of the recruitment of officers. In that period the military profession had very little prestige. The bulk of the officer corps had been promoted from the ranks. They came from lower-middle or middle-class backgrounds, with generally little education. In fact, the social profile of those coming from the military academy Saint-Cyr was not very different; their training had little value. Interestingly, these men came from those social groups whose expectations, though heightened, had not yet been fulfilled by the post-revolutionary changes, and who, given their poor education, were prevented from entering the most rewarding sectors of the civilian market.[45]

Hence, the traditional ideals of self-abnegation, honour and duty gave way to opportunism and ambition in the professional aspirations and outlook of these men. Offering many opportunities for quick promotion, glory, self-gratification, as well as special bonuses—a result of a policy aimed at attracting manpower for overseas service—the colonial campaigns were seen by the most ambitious and ruthless as a social and professional stepping stone. To some extent then, these attitudes affected the dynamic of the conflicts. Battles were needlessly engaged to satisfy a commander; diplomatic solutions were shunned. Vestigial military traditions, such as the *part de prise*, by which the combatants shared the spoils, incited an all-out warfare.[46] In such a context, the war escalated and fed on its own violence, the more so when the enemy saw it had nothing much to gain by evading all-out fighting.

Yet, the conquest of Algeria also saw the emergence of a new breed of officer. Nourished on Saint-Simonism and liberalism, they sought to approach warfare in a different way and tried to apply further some of the principles evolved in Bugeaud's instructions. Here the names of men like Marey-Monge, Duvivier, Bedeau, to mention some of the more remarkable, with their sense of duty and interest in the welfare of local populations, redeemed the image of their peers and prefigured what was to be the archetypal style of colonial leadership for the next hundred years.[47]

It was during the second half of the 19th century that this emerging profile developed. After 1860, the prestige of the military career rose again. Recruitment became less socially restricted. Educated and wealthy classes, as well as the more traditional and religion-oriented groups, ceased to shun the military career. Candidacies to military academies multiplied, Saint-Cyr's curriculum improved and the proportion of graduate officers increased. The military vocation became less mercenary and the new officers exhibited a greater sense of professional mission.[48] It was at this time that the concept of the social role of the officer evolved. This predicated that warfare could not be the sole professional end of the military and that its role must be pursued in times of peace and in other domains, social, moral, educational; these became the new principles on the basis of which the military legitimised its professional existence.[49] To escape the lingering rigidity and the increasing bureaucratisation of the institution, the most enlightened of these men chose to serve overseas, where their vision easily translated into the ideal of France's civilising mission. This ideal was also shared by men who went overseas because of their distaste for the emerging liberal industrial system of values, or simply by men animated with a patriotic fervour, which had no outlet in the duller metropolitan garrison life; for them an overseas mission was regarded as a means to contribute to the greatness, for some to the regeneration, of the homeland. Hence, whatever their motivation, sometimes politically ambiguous, all these men shared a new sense of professional duty and responsibility which extended beyond the sheer military realm.

Such a concept, and the pattern of behaviour it induced, were very much at odds with the more traditional and bureaucratic views and styles of most officers based in France. Correspondence and writings capture the feelings of these men and their sense of separateness from mainstream professional conventions. This is shown by the way they 'went native', by the special kind of relations—a mixture of paternalism, but also concern and respect devoid of any racist overtones, (of course there were as always exceptions and instances of brutality or mistreatment)—on which they asserted their leadership and commanded the loyalty of their men.[50]

Interestingly, despite the tremendous changes brought about in the country by World War I, it did not affect this professional conception. (The social recruitment of the military actually did not change much either, perhaps an adverse element for this continuity.) The Janusesque professional outlook persisted for another 40 years and continued to legitimate and feed the self-image of the colonial soldier, who in Indochina and then in Algeria, up to the early 1960s, remained that of an heroic leader as well as a civilising missionary.[51]

The particular aspect of the *guerre algérienne*, then, was as much the result of the outlook and origins of the men who led it as the product of a sort of functional adaptation to the circumstances of the moment.

Space is lacking here to discuss more deeply the character of this French mode of low-intensity warfare. Yet its originality was quite patent. In operation almost continuously from the end of the first half of the 19th century, the *guerre algérienne* lost its significance in the 1960s, though not through the erosion of its efficiency. The quasi-military victory on the field in Algeria would not have prevented France from ultimately losing this war. The '*guerre algérienne*' was an imperial type of undertaking which no longer had any meaning in the post-war era of national enfranchisement, world polarisation and internationalisation of conflicts. The now bi-polar international arena, under the umbrella of nuclear deterrence, had entered a period of ambiguous peace with peripheral confrontations from which most former colonial powers are abstaining, with the exception, paradoxically, of once more, France.

The *Guerres Africaines* in France's Contemporary Low-Intensity Wars

As observed earlier when considered strictly in terms of military activity, it is obvious that France's participation in low-intensity wars in contemporary times has not abated and is in direct succession to the past. The numerous interventions which took place, notably on the African continent, illustrate such a continuity. Within the last two decades and a half, France intervened more than twenty times in Africa and the Indian Ocean (Mayotta) and was also involved in actions in Lebanon (with the United Nations), in Tunisia and on the Suez Canal. As recently as September, 1987, some 1,500 French soldiers (they numbered more than 3,000 in the summer 1984 during the *Operation Manta*) were engaged in Chad on the side of Hissene Habré's troops in support of their campaign to drive Libyan forces out of the country;[52] it is clear that these activities differ both in nature and organisation from those which occurred in earlier times. To consider these interventions as mere neo-colonial variations on the perennial imperialistic theme is a useless cliché which obfuscates a number of significantly relevant differences.

Low-intensity conflicts: old and new

The *guerre algérienne* was a colonial mode of warfare. Engaged against local resistance and irredentism, its objective was the conquest and control of territories and populations without national identities. The post-1960s wars, juridically at least, are foreign wars, occurring on the soil of sovereign nation-states and involving sometimes external foreign powers.

Moreover, France's peripheral engagements formerly took place on a wide geographical spectrum, the Far East, the Middle East, Malagasy and black tropical and equatorial Africa. Today, however, they are essentially contained within the African continent; to be precise on a geographical space forming a reverse trapezoidal area within the sub-Saharan region, whose tips would be Dakar, Libreville, Kinshasa, and Djibouti.

The operational style also differs significantly in that earlier it presented a homogeneous pattern, while the present one consists of rather a protean ensemble of strictly military actions. These range from relatively large-scale interventions, combining mechanised infantry with air support, such as in Chad in 1983–84, to aerial pinpointed strikes such as those against the Polisario in Western Sahara, or from internal police action, as in Gabon in 1964, to airborne rescue operations, such as in Zaire in 1978. Given this variety in the actions undertaken and the circumscribed geographical nature of their location, the plural term *guerres africaines* will be used henceforth to subsume France's low-intensity military engagements in the contemporary period.

The *guerre algérienne*, furthermore, was a type of conflict which evolved on a comparatively low technological level (in contrast to that on which 'central' European wars were operated). Light infantry units equipped with small armament, were the basic instruments of warfare. Admittedly, as shown in the last stages of the Moroccan pacification, the Indochinese and Algerian wars, heavier and more sophisticated weaponry, such as armoured vehicles, helicopters, etc., were used. Yet—and despite the fact that the shape of these conflicts could be considered as anticipating the forthcoming pattern—the result of these engagements rested ultimately on the action of units whose combat effectiveness was precisely a function of their being small and lightly armed; technological abundance would have been unnecessary, if not counter-productive. In a way, there was not that much disparity in the *modus operandi* and the technological structure of General Challe's *commandos de chasse*, Faidherbe's small columns dispatched from river gunboats, and Lyautey's *bataillons de marche* in the Riff War. Today the situation is different. Apart from policing actions, most operations of the *guerres africaines* rely on stronger and more sophisticated fire-power. Sol-Air systems, precision-guided missiles of all sorts, jet-combat aircraft, speedy, light-armoured vehicles, etc., nowadays constitute common features of the technological landscape of the contemporary low-intensity conflicts; features, moreover, on which the success of the engagement increasingly rests. *Operation Manta* (1983–84) in Chad called upon an impressive array of the most modern armaments, including *Milan* precision-guided munition (PGM) and *Apilas* rocket launchers, AMX-10RC wheel-propelled tanks and AML armoured vehicles, *Jaguar* and *Mirage* F-1 aircraft, *Gazelle* attack helicopters with *Hot* missiles and *Breguet-Atlantic* observation planes.

There are several reasons for this new trend. Today, given the increasing organisational inter-relationships between the various sectors and services of the armed forces, technological change tends to spread more fluidly and affects the entire military institution. Also the necessity to maintain parity with allies and potential foes on the Central Front makes such changes a continuous imperative. Further, internal discrepancies in technological sophistication would not be manageable and could have negative counter-effects. Such was, for example, the situation in which the French military began to find itself during the Algerian War and to which, by resigning his commission as general chief of staff, General Guillaume tried to draw attention. The conduct of war in the archaic terms of the *guerre algérienne* impinged gravely on the central credibility of the French armed forces in general; several motorised and armoured divisions for example, had thus to be dismembered and their scheduled modernisation halted.[53] Another reason, actually at the crux of the difference, is that in contrast with earlier periods, adversary forces today are bound to be better armed and equipped, quantitatively as well as qualitatively. Local arms races and great power sponsorship (Soviet arms thus transited via Algeria, Libya, Angola) result in a greater availability of modern weaponry,[54] the manipulation of which, moreover, despite or even because of its sophistication, does not require specially developed skills.

Finally, there are two other key differences with the conflicts of the pre-1960 period. The first lies in the fact that in contrast to the colonial-style operations, the *guerres africaines* are conceived and engaged within the confines of an elaborate doctrine of security, itself derived from a particular geostrategical conception. The second difference is that while the *guerre algérienne* was carried out by a loose constellation of mixed units garrisoned and circulated throughout the whole imperial area, to which French-based forces could eventually be added, the *guerres africaines* are conducted and fought by a special deployment force composed of French professionals stationed, on the whole, on French territory itself.

Some of these features deserve to be given further consideration, to highlight the specific nature and dynamics of the *guerres africaines* as the French adaptation to contemporary low-intensity warfare.

Africa and French security

After 1945, it seemed clear that France, which had been considerably weakened by her experience of the second world conflict, would not be able to restore her imperial domination, nor re-emerge as a leading international power. The shape of events which developed in Indochina, and a few years later in North Africa, quickly confirmed those assumptions.

Yet it is quite remarkable that France was spared all of the consequences of this evolution that could not be escaped by most other European states. She was able to enhance her international status to the level of that of a major power and to uphold her pretence at worldwide vocation (summed up in the historical concept of 'civilisation') and related responsibilities. France's military presence around the world is a testimony to it. Besides the 50,000 men based in West Germany, another 30,000 or so are regularly stationed overseas; in 1983, including the troops sent to Lebanon and Chad, French forces abroad reached a total of 90,000, nearly a fifth of the entire military.

With regard to this rising status, her regained economic strength and her cultural weight as head of the Francophonic world are important factors, but not as much as her geopolitical assets. First, France managed to maintain and consolidate a vast network of possessions in the Pacific, Atlantic and Indian oceans: the *Départements et Territoires d'Outre-mer*, which include areas for nuclear experiments in Polynesia, and French, as well as European space programmes, in Guiana. Second, and above all, while posing as the advocate of the developing nations, France was successful in handling the decolonisation of her vast African territories in such a way as to secure a formidable sphere of exclusive influence, free of superpower interference.

Indeed the Gaullist scheme of an integrated political-military Euro-African fortress in the framework of the so-called *Communauté* quickly appeared incompatible with the expression of emerging nationalistic aspirations. But a formula keeping alive the spirit of the *Communauté* (meant here, incidentally, in almost the sense suggested by the German word *Gemeinschaft*) and the particularism of the relationship between France and her former African colonies, could be devised as a substitute. The name of this formula was *Coopération*, which instituted a sort of co-determinative management in the areas of diplomacy, economy and military affairs.[55] Extended successfully to African partners other than those formerly under French authority, it operates on the basis of relations going beyond the usual state-to-state relations, to take a personal, if not 'familial' tone.

It is indeed difficult, without expanding the argument, to convey the complexity of such an arrangement that the usual explanation—neo-colonialism—masked behind the flattering rhetoric of independence, only distorts.[56] In any case, the point to be underlined here is that this approach of Franco-African relations, established by General de Gaulle, was pursued without much significant change by his successors to power in France. Symptomatic of such a continuity was the renunciation by President Mitterrand, of socialist persuasion, of his earlier *tiers-mondiste* stance aimed at de-emphasising the African connection in favour of a wider and more egalitarian Third World policy. During his visit to Africa in May 1982, President Mitterrand made a point of reassuring France's traditional partners, proclaiming his willingness to preserve the consensus shared in matters of development. Later visits in 1983 confirmed this return to the earlier Gaullist orthodoxy.[57]

One of the key dimensions of *Coopération* is security. This is important, and probably explains also the special nature of the organisation of post-colonial Franco-African relations. It is striking, looking at recent French history, to observe how much the African continent came to be linked with France's own security. Other factors, such as economy and prestige, are more derivative.[58] Almost since the very beginning of colonisation, Africa had strategic significance. Besides offering control positions and bases, it rapidly appeared, as we have seen, as a reserve pool of manpower. After 1950, other important advantages emerged. Thus the African continent came to be considered as giving France, and Western Europe in general, the strategic depth that it lacks, as a theatre of operations to which it was possible to retreat, to regroup and to retaliate. World War II proved this role and it has been said that without Africa, France would not have been among the victors; Central Africa allowed the regrouping of the French Free Forces and the First Army which then began to push northward into North Africa and later southern Europe.[59] Moreover, Africa avails France with key raw materials, particularly strategic minerals now vital to the French defence system (uranium for example or special metallic components).

As a consequence of her perceived relevance to the security of France, Africa's defence then became tied up with that of France herself. Inevitably it became not only an integral element in the strategy and security of France, but one with a priority status in the agenda of France's defence programme. This is all the more true now that new threats have been arising. For example, the containment effects of NATO and the nuclear stalemate, revive the old Soviet threat of *contournement* summed up in the perennial Leninist formula: 'The road to Paris passes through Africa'. The new power-projection capabilities of the Soviet Union render this increasingly feasible. Moreover, the inter-African environment has evolved into a more volatile condition as a result of an unbalanced dynamic of power in the newly sovereign states.[60]

The political as well as the defence discourse, from General de Gaulle to President Mitterrand, testifies to such views. When he declared that the future of African interests is vital to the security of France, François Mitterrand echoed a feeling widely shared in the military and political establishments of both France and Africa, today.

The organisation of African security results from a series of bilateral and regional/multilateral defence agreements which integrate most Francophone states into the geostrategical structure of France, signed in the early 1960s.[61] Over the years, these arrangements have been renegotiated to provide more room for the expression of national sovereignty. Some states have changed their previous engagements, others have sought to diversify their dependency. As we shall see France also had modified the structure of her deployment. But, on the whole these modifications—sometimes regarded as the expression of a declining interest for Africa, perhaps wrongly so, had been foreseen, and somehow fit with the evolution of France's own capacities.[62] In the end, however, the basic significance of the system as a whole remained unchanged. Today, except for Guinea, all French-speaking states (Zaire, Burundi and Rwanda, former Belgian colonies, had joined in the 1970s) are linked to France through technical military assistance agreements, and six of them (Senegal, Ivory Coast, Gabon, Djibouti, Togo and Cameroon) also through defence pacts.[63]

These arrangements offered France a variety of special privileges, actually opportunities to play a key role in the diplomatic-military and internal dynamic of her former dependencies. Moreover, they allow a wide spectrum of actions. France is able to intervene militarily to protect or restore the *status quo* (or help in the birth of a new one) within a fairly flexible framework of legitimacy. But also they imply a whole set of preventive possibilities, operating 'upstream' of the security system. Thus, for example, the technical military assistance agreements provide the recipient countries with the training of local troops (both on the spot and in French military academies—in the early 1980s more than 2,000 African servicemen had been trained in France), their organisation and the furnishing and maintenance of equipment and armaments. Thus France is able to control the 'socialisation' of the local forces and the reproduction of a pattern of civil-military structure as well as political and diplomatic norms, congruent with the dominant system of values she has evolved.[64] France is also in a position to look over the flow of military technology in these countries and to some extent the inter-African balance of forces. Although a diversification of arms suppliers has been effected lately (and only in favour of NATO states who now supply 30 percent of the trade, compared to 10 percent in the 1960s), France remains nonetheless the main supplier state, providing more than half of the armaments to her former colonies, and nearly 70 percent of that to Zaire, Burundi and Rwanda, and 32 percent of the weapons of former British colonies.[65]

The defence pacts (together with the most secretive agreements regarding the maintenance of domestic order) to which are added various conventions regarding military bases and the garrisoning of French troops, constitute in principle the legal framework within which France's forces could intervene. However, it should be pointed out that the existence of such agreements is not necessarily a *sine qua non* for such an intervention. There was not a defence pact with Zaire for instance, when France mounted her airborne mission over Kolwezi. In the Central African Republic, the intervention violated the terms of the existing pact. In other instances, though all the conditions were met to justify an action, France abstained from taking any. In fact, in exactly similar situations, France adopted opposite attitudes. In 1964 she rescued Léon M'ba, then president of Gabon, from an attempted *putsch*, but the year before had refused to help in restoring civilian rule in Togo. More recently, in the Central African Republic, France deposed Emperor Bokassa to replace him with former premier David Dacko, yet she abstained from any action when Dacko fell victim to an army coup. On the whole, France acts with a great deal of freedom and pragmatism. The legitimacy of France's African role is not so much a function of its being specified or stipulated by these agreements as it is a function of an overall pre-contractual consensus (France would only intervene upon request of local regimes) within what is referred to as the *'pre carré' de la francophonie*.

If any pattern of intervention could be identified it would seem that in the early 1960s France essentially intervened (or chose not to, which was in that case a political act) in the area of domestic affairs under the form of police or maintenance of order actions. Later, this type of intervention became less salient, though it was not abandoned. Non-interference in internal political affairs seemed to have become the principle unless their evolution appeared to be jeopardising the expected stability. France, thus, in 1973 intervened in Niger to quell a mutiny, and in 1979 in the Central African Republic to evict Bokassa. The emerging pattern of intervention is rather related to crises involving possible external threats to the *status quo*. This shift might well reflect France's new unwillingness to intervene in purely internal affairs; President Mitterrand's policy is explicit in that regard. Yet again, in this domain abstention from action is itself an action; after all, most domestic changes that have occurred in the 1970s have not, on the whole, produced situations so hazardous to the geostrategic *status quo* as to justify intervention.

This change might well simply mirror France's increasing reliance on the less visible and cumbersome tools of influence existing 'upstream' of the intervention.

Though engaged on a case-by-case basis, and justified by an open range of reasons, all interventions are linked by France's ultimate concern for maintaining a modicum of stability in Africa, stability seen as one of the preliminaries to that of the wider geostrategic *status quo* in which French security is deemed to be rooted. The interventions constitute the ultimate and most cataclysmic recourses France disposes of, within a large array of measures by which influence can always be exercised.

The logistics of the guerres africaines

Given these considerations (and naturally those linked to the defence of external possessions), 'overseas defence' came to be compounded with the 'central' objective of the national defence in France's security doctrine. Since the Gaullist ordinance of January 1959, which reorganised French national defence, every official document, legislative, budgetary, political or strategic, has emphasised both these central and peripheral commitments. As a result, the organisation and the missions of the French military institution assumed dual structure. In addition to the forces responsible for the 'central' mission—the Nuclear Strategic Forces, the Forces of Manoeuvre, and the Forces of the Defence of the Territory, as they were called for some time—a force of intervention, whose name has changed from time to time (in 1981, for example, it was renamed Rapid Assistance Forces) but explicitly refers to this task, was assigned to overseas operations.

It should be emphasised that these systems of force were meant to be *polyvalent* (multipurpose, each one being able, in theory, to reinforce the other in the performance of its mission) by the end of the 1970s; at the same time, the old distinctions—forces of manoeuvre, forces of intervention—were de-emphasised. This was actually one of the objectives of the reform undertaken in 1975 and is certainly the purpose of the reform pursued after 1984.[66] Nevertheless the particular character of overseas intervention limits the extent of the *polyvalence*. The armoured divisions of the armoured mechanised corps could probably operate on the Southern Mediterranean flank, but hardly overseas; the same is true for some elements of the newly created Force of Rapid Action (the FAR). So although the airborne and marine infantry units which have been used for non-European interventions could be utilised on the north-central fronts, as their integration into the FAR seems to imply, the overseas fronts are their indisputable 'operational jurisdiction'.[67] Let us add again in passing that if the area of operation of these forces, as referred to in the legislative as well as strategic discourse, is *l'outre-mer* in general, they are actually specially tailored to act in Africa.

Moreover, the duality also appears in the doctrine of utilisation itself. There is today considerable speculation about France's attenuation, if not abandonment, of her 'sanctuarised' conception of security and her 'autonomous' use of her defence, in favour of a European extension, beginning with conventional forces and ending perhaps with her nuclear deterrent. However, since the middle of the seventies, France has been orienting her defence in a more European perspective, in which her full autonomy might be constrained. Yet whatever these trends, one observes that they do not affect the use of overseas deployment forces which still seem to be governed by a doctrine of full autonomy. This had been repeatedly reaffirmed by General De Gaulle and, indeed, by his successors, notably President Giscard d'Estaing.[68]

The success of effective crisis resolution depends on rapidity, today even more than in the past. In this regard, the 'fire-brigade' action as the key to effectiveness is an accurate analogy. In colonial times, the dispersion and the readiness of the units on the territory on which the crises were likely to develop, permitted effective handling most of the time. In times of independent sovereignty, such a strategy is, for obvious reasons, less feasible. Of course, technological changes, notably in the area of transport, facilitate a greater power projection from outside the territory, but with some restrictions.

To compensate for such limitations still being faced in the early 1960s, France relied on a *double détente* strategy, combining pre-positioning with projected intervention (*couverture à distance*). At a local level, a division of labour in the crisis control was instituted between local African forces—who, as we have seen, were organised, trained and armed by France in accordance with her own security conceptions—and French forces stationed in the African area. These forces, either in sequence or together, were to intervene in case of a crisis, thus giving time for the main intervention forces based in France to mobilise and arrive, should they be required. Critical, therefore, to the functioning and the effectiveness of this system was the pre-positioning of French forces in Africa and, of course, the provisions made in this regard.

The defence arrangements included such provisions. France was then able to have at its disposal seven military bases and naval installations (Fort-Lamy, now N'Djamena; Pointe-Noire, transferred to Libreville in 1963; Diego-Suarez; Port-Etienne; Douala; Bouar; Port-Bouet), transit and garrisoning privileges (in a hundred or so barracks), as well as air-space and stop-over rights. These facilities were to permit local deployment of French troops as well as reception and subsequent transit of the forces of intervention. The strength of pre-positioned troops was significant for a while. In 1962 there were some 70,000 French soldiers stationed in nearly 100 African garrisons; 1,800 in the Horn, 11,000 in 25 garrisons around Malagasy Island, 12,000 in 25 garrisons dispersed over Equatorial Africa, and 45,000 in 45 garrisons in West Africa. This network was articulated into two strategic zones, the headquarters of which were in Paris; the Central-West African and the Indian Ocean zones. These were in turn divided into four areas of defence with headquarters in Dakar, Abidjan, Brazzaville and Tananarive, with, in addition, the High Interservice Command of the Somali corps in Djibouti.[69]

Such a form of deployment was to be transitory. It was, indeed, financially and politically costly. In 1962, the cost of garrisoning French troops in Africa alone reached $172m., a relatively high sum for a state hard-pressed by the building of its nuclear forces at home. Moreover, it was somewhat too visibly 'neo-colonial' not to raise questions of its legitimacy, something France was well aware of. Many African states, though generally not opposed to France's policy, had been led, for internal political reasons, to demand the renegotiation of these arrangements. So, by the end of the 1960s, France adapted her overseas logistics, notably by de-emphasising the stationing of troops locally and by increasing her power-projection capabilities. The number of bases and military installations were reduced drastically. Four bases were retained: Dakar, Djibouti, Diego-Suarez and N'Djamena; after 1973, Diego-Suarez, now Antseranana, was replaced by a base in the Réunion and N'Djamena was evacuated. The role of these installations, as well as that of the smaller ones in the Ivory Coast, Gabon and the Central African Republic, changed. They were only to serve as *points d'appui* for intervening forces.

At the same time, the strength of French troops regularly stationed in Africa was reduced. It declined to 25,000 in 1965 over 40 locations and was then diminished further to 17,000 in the early seventies. In the mid-eighties, it reached 6,800 men, (3,500 in Djibouti, 1,200 in Senegal, 1,100 in Central African Republic, 500 in Ivory Coast and 500 in Gabon) to which 950 military advisers and the 1,300 men of the naval force of the Indian Ocean must be added. These figures still represent almost half of all French troops stationed on a permanent basis around the world.[70]

Such redeployment is not necessarily indicative, as is sometimes suggested, of a decline of France's interest and influence in Africa; nor was it forced upon her. French leaders seemed to have anticipated this evolution, and had relied temporarily on this 'neo-colonial' policy of only local presence as a bridge until the moment when the power-projection capabilities of the French armed forces would be sufficiently advanced. The Gaullist doctrine—see in this regard the declarations of Pierre Messmer, De Gaulle's defence minister—is explicit. Hence, only the means of exercising influence was changed, not the degree of influence itself.[71]

With progress, notably in the area of air-lifting, pre-positioning was less necessary and the 'couverture à distance' sufficient. A crisis could be handled almost as rapidly, by intervention forces flown in from France, locally-based forces serving only for the logistical purposes of receiving the intervention forces, and overseas military facilities as points d'appui. Moreover, it was also anticipated that part of the burden of crisis-control—notably for low-intensity crises, such as domestic disruptions—could be 'africanised'; handled, in other words, (now that their training and arming was well under way, if not completed) by the African forces themselves. This shift might then account for France's avoidance of intervening in purely internal affairs, at least as much as political and ideological considerations, though these should certainly not be minimised.

The instrument of the guerres africaines

The operations of the guerre algérienne were conducted by various special units which, without being institutionally separated from the armed forces at home, were autonomous and stationed overseas. Today, the instrument of France's peripheral wars is a more cohesive ensemble of units which are not dissociated from the French armed forces as a whole. Yet, though they could be enrolled in actions linked to European central wars, their main mission, like that of their colonial predecessors, is oriented toward overseas operations. It is likely that with the new 1984 reorganisation, these units will in future be more closely integrated into central engagements, but it remains true that they will continue to be the decisive instrument for overseas intervention.

The spearhead of the intervention forces comprises ground forces and marine infantry units. The Navy and the Air Force also play an important role. The Navy protects communications, provides transportation and, in certain cases, offers artillery and aero-naval support. Given the salience of rapidity of action, surprise and quick effectiveness, the Air Force fulfils a critical function in this type of engagement. With its sophisticated and powerfully-armed tactical fleet (the FATAC), with combat aircraft like the in-flight refuelable *Jaguar* and *Mirage* F1, the Air Force can be called in for long-range pin-pointed actions against concentrated forces, as against the Polisario forces in Western Sahara in 1977–78. With a vast array of sophisticated devices at its disposal (laser-guided bomb AS 30; anti-airstrip *Bap* 100 bomb; *Zuni* rocket and grenade-launcher bomb *Beluga*) it is capable of delivering extraordinary fire-power. The Air Force also offers the land forces close tactical support, reconnaissance and information missions and a wide range of air-lift capabilities including inter-continental transport, operational and assault aero-transport. To a large extent air power is an intimate component of intervention, not only at the logistical level but also the operational level.[72]

Intervention operations usually present an elusive system of opposing forces, a 'fluid' or diffuse battle-ground, so that the brunt of the action is shouldered by land forces which constitute the backbone of the force of intervention. Its first organisational element was established in 1962 out of the 10th and 25th Airborne Divisions and took the name of the Light Division of Intervention. It became the 11th Infantry Division in 1963. With a strength of 20,000, it was composed of three brigades, one airborne and one amphibious based in Brittany and another airborne based in the south-west, to which were added a light armoured, a light artillery and an engineering unit. This division was reorganised in 1971 and became the 11th Airborne Division, since when has been continually reinforced.[73]

On the eve of the 1984 reform, the French force of intervention was composed of several segments: the 16,600-strong 11th Airborne Division itself (with its headquarters in Pau), the 9,200 men of the 9th

Marine Infantry Division (with headquarters in Saint-Malo), the Foreign Legion Operational Group and the 31st Demi-Brigade based in Provence. The 11th Airborne Division is composed of two brigades (headquartered in Toulouse and Auch) with a total of six regiments of paratroop infantry, one light armoured regiment, one artillery regiment, one engineer regiment, one regiment of combat helicopters, a paratroop regiment of communications, command and Support units, and the 5th group of army light aviation (ALAT). As for the 9th Marine Infantry, it is composed of three marine infantry regiments, one army infantry regiment, one marine artillery regiment, one regiment of command and support, one light armoured regiment and one engineering company. In July 1981, the 31st Demi-Brigade (created in 1979) was converted into a full brigade (it became the 31st Brigade), specialised in amphibious and helicopter operations.[74]

The armament of these units has grown more sophisticated. They are now equipped with the latest weaponry; anti-tank *Milan, Apilas* and helicopter-borne *Hot* missiles, new reconnaissance and combat light armoured vehicles, S1G assault rifles, 20 mm guns, and third generation communication systems. *Operation Manta* mounted in Chad in August 1983, illustrates, as has been pointed out, the level of technology at which the French intervention forces are able to operate; the new swift and powerfully armed VLRA, with its 1,200 km autonomy, allows for long-range raids; *Gazelle* helicopters equipped with precision guided missiles serve to cover operations or deal with concentrated forces; *Bréguet-Atlantic* planes packed with the latest electronic and thermal sensing devices insure co-ordination of movement as well as localisation of enemy forces; it was in Chad also that the rocket launcher *Apilas* was experimented with for the first time.[75]

In 1982, the French government announced a large-scale military reform, which was to lead to a 'new model armed force'.[76] Its agenda was defined in the 1984–88 *loi de programmation militaire*, the fifth quinquennial military plan, passed by parliament in May 1983.[77] The reform, which mirrors new orientations in the French defence doctrine, notably at the level of a possible conventional participation alongside European and NATO allies, implies a profound reorganisation of the army to enhance mobility, multi-purposefulness and fire power; and affects the structures on which the intervention forces are based.[78] So, with the reorganisation of the battle corps of the First Army, of the Operational Defence of the Territory

(DOT), the creation of a tactical nuclear division, the key feature is the establishment of a rapid deployment force, FAR.[79] Endowed with a separate command structure, FAR will be 47,000 men strong and composed of five divisions: the existing 11th Airborne Division, the 9th Marine Infantry and the 27th Alpine divisions, and the newly-organised 6th Light Armoured, and 4th Aeromobile divisions. The 6th Light Armoured Division will be derived from the 31st Brigade and units from the First Army Corps. Seven thousand men strong, with seven regiments (two armoured, one mobile artillery, one engineering, two mechanised infantry, one command and support), it should be equipped with speedy modern armoured vehicles and mobile artillery. The 4th Aeromobile is to be a combat-helicopter division with 90 anti-tank helicopters, 30 support helicopters (*Gazelle* SA 341 anti-helicopters with 20 mm guns) and 80 helicopters for manoeuvres, in addition to an infantry regiment with anti-tank missiles.

Although FAR was created with the European theatre especially in mind—it was to give France forward power-projection to intervene quickly within the advanced lines of the NATO front—it was also designed to reinforce the capabilities for intervention in lower-intensity operations overseas. The newly-designed armoured division, with its important fire-power and versatility in manoeuvring, because of its fast vehicles could indeed conceivably be used in overseas warfare. In conjunction with units of the 11th Airborne and the 9th Infantry Division (the armament of which is also scheduled to be upgraded—in the last two years they have begun to receive the new ERC 90 *Sagaie* armoured vehicle equipped with a 90 mm cannon), it would undeniably add to the power and the effectiveness of French intervention capabilities overseas.

But until this reform is completed—and even when it is—the conduct of overseas warfare will remain to a large extent the exclusive commission of the 11th Airborne and the 9th Marine Infantry divisions.

The scope of actions these forces are capable of performing is wide. They can be engaged in so-called indirect actions, generally conducted by small teams of men, and involving training, operational advising, etc.; or direct actions, ranging up to brigade, or even bigger, military operations. The rapidity with which they are able to deploy and take control demonstrates the state of their preparedness and combat effectiveness. The operation in Zaire's Shaba province in May 1978, when the town of Kolwezi was occupied by Katangese rebels of the *Front National de Libération du Congo* (FNLC), is one of the best illustrations. Less than 48 hours elapsed between the ordering of the operation and the dropping of the first troops in the outskirts of the city, more than 7,600 km from France. In a few hours, they occupied key points; the dropping of a second wave the following day enabled the French to take full contol of the city. Until the end, the pace of the fighting never abated, day and night. The fire discipline permitted the routing of a relatively large enemy force— there were 4,000 rebels and some 700 French troops—without endangering civilian lives. More than 250 rebels were killed; on the French side there were five men killed and 20 wounded. Within three days nearly 2,000 Europeans were evacuated and the FNLC forces were dislodged from Kolwezi.[80]

The training of these forces is certainly the most exacting and relentless in the whole armed forces, both in time and thoroughness. They develop a highly flexible and dynamic form of combat and can adapt with the highest degree of effectiveness to a wide range of contingencies. An important part of the training is oriented towards speeding up the delivery and the operational readiness of the forces once they are airborne, and to encouraging a close co-ordination with other services, notably the air force. The men have made countless high altitude and night jumps and have developed astonishing capabilities for close-to-target assault jumps. Over Kolwezi, to save time, the men of the 2nd Foreign Paratroop Regiment, equipped with parachutes of a type they had never used before (they had been obliged to wear the American parachutes of the Zairean army), were dropped almost on the city itself instead of over the airfield six kilometres away as had been planned.[81] This demonstrates the high degree of inter-service collaboration of which these forces were capable.

Moreover, a great effort has been undertaken to give these troops preliminary experience of the actual conditions of the *guerres africaines*. Since 1965, full-scale manoeuvres have been regularly organised in various states of sub-Saharan Africa (with the *Gaur VI* operation in February in the southeast of Senegal) to test specific aspects of intervention, to enhance adaptation to the various hypothetical crisis situations, to uncover and remedy weaknesses in the system, and to allow co-operation with local African forces.

To prepare the troops for the great changes in climatic, cultural, and sanitary conditions, a programme of regular overseas tours of four to six months is regularly implemented for the various units.

Junior officers are often sent overseas for frequent short visits to become familiar with the people, the cultures and the terrain.[82]

Morale and fighting spirit are generally high in these units, both at home and abroad, even when the political atmosphere of intervention, as in Lebanon, is ambiguous. Interviews with men of the contingent deployed in Chad showed this clearly.[83] The military leadership, moreover, has proven highly competent. The higher echelon of the hierarchy had combat experience in Algeria and have an extensive knowledge of Africa. In general, the proportion of officers who are graduates of the military academy is higher than average; in the airborne units, an average of 65 percent of the officers come either from Saint-Cyr (30–35 percent) or the Inter-arms military school (also 30–35 percent), as compared with a general total average of 50 percent for the whole army officer corps. Surveys show that the majority of cadets with the best ranking in the entrance and finishing examinations at Saint-Cyr, who are also the younger officers, tend to chose a career in the most operational units of the armed forces, most of which are those comprising the forces of intervention.[84]

Less traditional in their institutional outlook, they show a high sense of initiative which is decisive in critical moments such as the first few hours of an intervention operation—generally spent in complete isolation. They also have a flexible and efficient weapon and deployment conception, useful in the unusual circumstances of operations where manpower is generally scarce and the field to be covered is large. In Chad, in 1983–84, the French somehow managed to deter the 5,000-man Libyan force, with 3,000 men holding a line 1,300 km long and 500 km deep.[85] Yet their restraint and discipline, their awareness of the right amount of force to be displayed and of the political realities of the operation testified to a considerable sensitivity, not without echoes of their colonial forefathers.

In many ways the sophistication of France's instrument of overseas intervention contrasts sharply with the techniques evolved in Africa by other intervening powers, such as the Soviet Union and more especially Cuba, which tend to operate on a more classical and static, therefore more visibly 'imperialistic', pattern. Together, the Cuban and East European (the Soviet Union included) forces constitute a total of nearly 50,000 troops and have been in Africa now for a decade.

The French style of intervention on the whole is flexible, low-key, and can be adapted to fit numerous different situations. Yet, for all its success, there are various constraints which could hinder its effectiveness and could jeopardise the policy that these interventions seek to carry out. And these constraints have been increasing since the mid-1970s.

The limit to overseas intervention

Clausewitz might well have been excessive in claiming that war is politics continued by other means,[86] yet, France's *guerres africaines* are certainly political actions pursued in the military realm. As such, they are not only bound by technical limitations, but also their legitimacy is limited by political constraints. This question has received a great deal of theoretical attention already, yet paradoxically, in the case of France, political constraints seem less binding than technical constraints.

In an era when the market value of military actions is at its lowest, a phenomenon particularly salient in the West, it is a fact that the level of political opposition, both international and domestic, to France's *guerres africaines* has remained somewhat inconspicuous.

In Africa, except for dissent regularly voiced by Marxist states, (to be exact, those in the southern part of the continent which nevertheless allowed interventions by 'non-colonialist' Cuba), public opinion on the whole has not been strongly negative. Nigeria, which denounced France's action in Zaire at the Khartoum Conference in July 1978,[87] avoided strong criticism when France flew her forces to Chad in August 1983 to deter Libya, whose actions were seen as a threat to the stability of the north western central countries of sub-Saharan Africa, among which is Nigeria. In fact, it seems that many African states, perhaps not always overtly, have welcomed French intervention. France's hesitation to intervene in Chad before August 1983 had even aroused nervous reactions and worries among Francophone states; some even thought, after France finally took up action, that it was either too late or too little. Until Africa puts together her own peace-keeping force—something which under the present circumstances is not likely to materialise—the chances are that external interventions will be accepted by African states.[88]

On the international scene, opposition was never adamant. Western attitudes in general have remained neutral, if not favourable. There has been very little open opposition; in fact, there was less opposition than interest, as demonstrated for example, by the British reactions.[89] The United States, which during the Carter administration shied away from any policy of intervention, supported and even assisted France. The French *legionnaires* at Kolwezi, for instance, were flown in American C-141 aircraft. Under the Reagan administration, such an attitude has been even more explicit. Indeed, it should be noted that President Reagan's insistence in July and early August 1983, that France should intervene in Chad against Libya, might perhaps have been a source of embarrassment for President Mitterrand and led him to delay France's military action. Given the fact that the American President considers Libya to be an agent of the USSR's policy, France had to avoid giving the impression of acting as America's agent or of operating in the East-West framework.

One touches here on one problematic aspect of the political constraints weighing on the French policy of intervention in Africa: namely, first, their being perceived as inseparable from Western interests and as such viewed in the perspective of East-West confrontation and, second, as a consequence contradicting the very principle of independence upon which the legitimacy of France's role in the area. Interestingly, this perception intermittently develops in the domestic political scene also. Interventions mounted under former President Giscard d'Estaing faced such criticisms from the Right as well as the Left. Gaullist, Communist and Socialist leaders together supported the accusation that France was becoming NATO's policeman, proxy power of the West or even the 'West's Cuba', to use François Mitterrand's formula at the time.[90] Yet, in general, the continuing concern of the French political leadership to demonstrate that such actions, as well as the situations from which they arise, are free of any Western entanglement, especially in acting on a case-by-case basis, have so far helped to dispel any serious doubts of Western collusion, and prevented these operations from becoming involved with East-West issues. The diplomacy employed over the intervention in Chad, illustrated by President Mitterrand's expressed impatience at American pressures, lengthy briefings by officials over the *sui generis* character of the issue, and the explicit remarks on the irrelevance of the situation to the East-West balance served this purpose, and not unsuccessfully.[91]

Moreover, French public opinion does not seem to have a particularly negative attitude. In 1978, a year in which France's policy of external intervention was active, polls showed that a little over one third of the respondents were opposed to French actions in Africa, and less than half were against sending troops in general. The engagements in Lebanon and Chad in 1982 and 1983 seemed to have been perceived positively.[92] Lately this consensus appears to have declined. A poll taken in February 1984 showed that 58 percent of the respondents disapproved of the presence of French soldiers in Lebanon and 47 percent favoured a withdrawal from Chad.[93] These figures, however, should not be taken at face value. Given the timing of the survey, they have to be seen as an expression of the widespread misgivings about the Socialist government and its policies in general, rather than as a specific and independent opinion of the single issue of external military intervention. Moreover, the survey was conducted in the wake of incidents which involved casualties both in Beirut, with the terrorist attack on the French headquarters, and in Chad, where in a counter-attack mounted against an enemy column which had penetrated the French lines, a *Jaguar* was shot down and its pilot killed.[94] Considering the ambiguity surrounding the mission of the French contingent in Beirut and the attitudes of the other powers involved, notably the United States, the French engagement there was bound to be viewed negatively. The death of 58 soldiers in the bombing of the French compound in the Hotel Drakkar on 23 October (before which time 18 men had been killed and 54 wounded) reinforced this feeling.[95] On the whole, French public opinion is far less dissentient than that of other European countries (*eg*, the little support Belgian Prime Minister Tindemans received during the intervention with the French in Shaba) or America in similar circumstances, especially in cases like the 'Manta' intervention in Chad which at the time of the poll had lasted an entire year. Finally, it should be noted that beside the positive and negative responses, a good third of the respondents voiced no particular opinion, which could be interpreted as being indicative of no specific opposition to the issue.

In sum, the political constraints which generally impede external military engagements are not manifest in the French case, and are certainly not severe by Western standards. In fact, they seem less constricting than the limitations which operate at the technical and military level, especially since the mid-1970s.

Without going into excessive detail which could lead the analysis too far afield and make it too discriminatory, this issue can be approached from five standpoints. First, when it is argued that political constraints are relatively less limiting, this does not by any means signify that the political legitimacy, national and international, of France's *guerres africaines* is immutable. It holds good in so far as they are circumscribed in duration as well as frequency.

The French format of intervention was drafted with this condition in mind. The ideal action is the pre-emptive pin-prick strike, seeking to nip the crisis in the bud, to avoid protracted warfare and the perennial risk of Vietnamisation. As we have seen, to reduce repeated actions, France sought to 'africanise' part of the crisis-resolution by relying on national armed forces which had been organised and trained in that perspective, reserving the French force of intervention for the least locally controllable problems.

In practice, however, this division of labour proved ineffective. For various reasons—perhaps the failure of French assistance, but also the politicisation of local officer corps, ethnic fragmentation, corruption, etc.—national armies have proved incapable of dealing with crisis. The deficiency and powerlessness of the Zaire military, though apparently one of the strongest armed forces of Africa, to deal with the Katangese separatists in Shaba in 1977–78 is a conspicuous, though not exceptional, example of this.[96] As a consequence of this weakness at the African level of the defence system, France could find herself having to rely more frequently than expected on her own devices.

Second, given the technological sophistication and effectiveness of modern weapons, which are more readily available, especially in the context of powerful surrogates, the technical level at which these crises are likely to ignite is bound to be high. Their treatment, therefore, especially if it has to be effective within a limited period, requires a massive and intensive mobilisation of technology. In the case of France's intervention forces, budgetary considerations set limits to such a mobilisation. What are these limitations?

Firstly, from a general point of view, given the economic constraints, both conjunctural and structural, and common to any contemporary industrial welfare state, the overall size of the defence budget, on the one hand, tends to be maintained at a relatively low level; on average under four percent of the GNP and under 17 percent of public expenditure. On the other hand, it increases only at a piecemeal rate. From 1974–87, the French military budget grew from 3.41 to 3.79 percent of the GNP; in 1987, it constituted 16.1 percent of all state expenditure. In such a context of inelasticity, any increase in the appropriation for one sector tends to affect, in a zero-sum fashion, the amount allocated to other sectors. Therefore, any policy of reallocation of funds can only be extremely measured.

Secondly, the pattern of appropriation between the various types of expenditures, as well as between the services, tends to penalise the ground forces. Since 1987, for the first time for twenty years, equipment expenditures have become higher than operational and personnel expenditures and should remain so for the 1987–1991 period. But it is by a small margin. Moreover, because of the centrality of nuclear deterrence in French defence doctrine, all the more salient that France will be the only nuclear power in Western continental Europe and that at some point in the near future will have to undertake an antimissile defence, an important part of the equipment appropriations will be absorbed by the nuclear programme itself. In 1984–87, this proportion amounted to 31.68 percent, a figure to reach nearly 35 percent in 1987–1991, which reduces concomitantly the appropriations available for conventional programmes.[97]

Thirdly, in any case, one should note that in the ground forces, though equipment expenditures have also increased, they remain at a lower level than operational and personnel allocations; this is linked to various parameters such as the comparatively sizeable volume of manpower, the needs for policies of manpower recruitment and retention, etc.[98]

Further, for some time, the increased funds made available to the Army after 1975 have served only to make up for delays in earlier development programmes resulting from the formidable costs (as well as unforeseen overhead expenses) of the building and expansion of the nuclear deterrent. Unpredicted inflation rates and costs subsequent to the emerging economic crisis have in addition penalised the development of the conventional programme of the Army.[99]

According to various sources regarding the development of major equipment and technologies, the situation of the Army will remain precarious in the future despite optimism about the new reform introduced in the 1984–87 quinquennial military plan and pursued in the following one. It is indeed probable that the estimated two percent annual increase in Army purchasing power will prove to be an unrealistic figure, since it has been calculated at a lower than real inflation rate and probably an overestimated economic growth rate. Hence the Army equipment programme, which, as pointed out by several *rapporteurs* of the defence commission, has been calculated '*au plus juste*', and therefore might be in jeopardy.[100]

Such financial constraints whose effects will necessarily be felt by the forces of intervention, could then expose France's preparedness for external intervention, particularly when several actions have to be undertaken simultaneously, as was the case in 1978 and 1983. In 1978, the Air Force, for example, found itself having mobilised more than

50 planes, comprising 10 percent of all the *Jaguar* aircraft and a fourth of the *Transall* transportation planes.[101]

Third, because of increasing technological needs for effective fire-power, the net load of the forces to be delivered to the overseas theatres of operation has been growing heavier, calling for greater air-lift capabilities. Yet the French air-lift system remains comparatively weak, both in capacity and speed. The necessity of calling upon the United States for air-lift assistance for the operation in Kolwezi in 1978 testified to this weakness. The French air transportation fleet is made up of 60 or so *Transall* C-160s and half-a-dozen DC-8s. Although their autonomy has been enhanced by the addition of extra tanks and in-flight refuelling devices, the *Transall* are far from matching either the *Galaxy* C-5A, *Starlifter* C-141, or the *Antonov* 22 that are used by the American or the Soviet air forces. The total air-lift yield then averages 1,300 tons for a 2,000 km range or 575 tons for over 5,000 km range. In addition, the C-160 system has been found to be inadequate in bridging the double needs for strategic and tactical aircraft.[102] The contracts signed with civilian companies offer only temporary and limited compensation. Civilian aircraft, moreover, are generally not equipped to haul military-type cargo and the cost of their rental always proves high.

Until new solutions are found (lately France has purchased four American C-130s), such a deficiency in the rapid projection of the forces could impinge upon the immediate treatment of crises before they extend in scope and in turn require a more massive, hence more politically problematic, deployment. On the other hand, reliance upon outside, essentially American, assistance would diminish the perception of France's action, notably by weakening its autonomy and dissociating it from the overall system of Western interests.

Fourth, operating at a high technological level and calling upon a fairly important manpower deployment, these actions are inevitably expensive and probably will be more and more so in the future. Although detailed data are scarce (in itself an indirect indication of the cost), available figures give a clear idea of the growing costs of such operations. For 1976–82, the annual average was 377.55m. francs (around $55m.). In 1978, it reached $65m. and in 1982, $69m. According to official statistics, the expenses incurred for *Operation Manta* and the deployment in Beirut in 1983 alone were estimated at $170m.[103] *Operation Manta* in Chad is an illustration of the spiralling cost of interventions overseas. The installation of French troops amounted to 500 million francs, roughly $60m. In the early days of the operation the cost of a litre of petrol was $14 and a DC8 round-trip flight between Chad and France cost $120,000. The modernisation of N'Djamena airfield and the adjoining base (Camp Dubut) was estimated at $200,000.[104] Such costs, especially in a context of financial austerity, as was the case in the early 1980s, are bound to limit French capabilities for overseas interventions both in frequency and duration.[105]

The last aspect of these constraints deals with manpower. We have seen that the strength of the intervention forces is around 30,000 men, but the effective number operationally available is far less. A little over half of the total personnel is conscripted—185,000 out of 340,000 in 1987—the Army in particular. Although the proportion of enlisted men over draftees has been increasing over time and its distribution within the military has been higher in operational branches, drafted personnel still make up a significant part of the composition of these forces. In 1983, there was still a total of 41.3 percent draftees in the 11th Airborne and the 9th Marine Infantry divisions. Since draftees are not to be sent overseas, the strength of manpower which can be utilised for external deployment and action is only 12,000–14,000 men.

As with the other constraints, this one limits the capacity for handling simultaneous, frequent or large-scale engagements. In 1978 and 1983, the French forces were somewhat over-extended. Tours of duty had to be stretched; many of the men in units involved overseas at these times had not spent more than two months serving in France. Since 1980, and particularly with the reorganisation currently in progress, an effort has been made further to 'professionalise' these units. In 1980, of the seven regiments of the 9th Marine Infantry Division, three were composed of volunteers and two others were to be partly volunteer; in 1983, the proportion of draftees fell to 32 percent, and draftees in these units were given the opportunity of signing up for overseas service. Moreover, a bill passed in July 1983 created a new category of personnel to enlarge the available operational pool. It was to be made up of draftees wishing to serve for 4–12 months beyond the mandatory one year in the branches of service of their choice, among which would include the units to be engaged overseas. It was predicted that by 1988, 10 percent of the army-drafted manpower would be made up of this category. Furthermore, the 1984 reform plans a general increase in volunteer personnel, 5,000 of those in the FAR itself.[106]

These measures, providing that they are developed as planned (which should not be taken for granted as the Army already seems unable to attract enough draftees for supplementary voluntary service)[107] will undoubtedly allow the forces of intervention to benefit from a larger manpower pool. But then the ultimate limits for expansion will have been reached. To go further would represent an institutional rupture, that is, a shift from the traditional conscript army model toward a quasi-all-volunteer force, a situation which the country does not seem ready to accept; many have already denounced the 1984 reorganisation measures as seeking to overhaul the old conscript army format.[108]

These remarks, which perhaps need to be developed further, nevertheless point to the nature and the variety of constraints which hinder the French capability for overseas low-intensity warfare. Although contingency measures could be devised to overcome some of the limitations, these cannot be eliminated entirely.[109]

Air-lift capability is a case in point. The *Loi de programmation* did schedule research and study for a new aircraft, but this would not be available before 1995–2000. On the other hand, purchase of foreign planes, notably American, does not seem feasible. This would create problems for the national aeronautical industry and, in any case, the available aircraft might not always serve adequately French needs: the C-130 *Hercules* is not that much bigger (though more powerful) the *Transall* (and the C-130 replacement, the C-17, is still in the 'pre-production' stage), the C-5A or the forthcoming C-5B goes beyond what is needed and the C-141 remains reserved for the American Military Airlift Command.[110]

Chad and After

By mid-November 1984 France, which had evacuated its forces from Chad, was confronted with Libya's deliberate violation of the Treaty of Tripoli, signed on 16 September by the two countries and which stipulated a 'total and concomitant withdrawal' of the two military contingents from the Chadian territory. Contradictory official declarations, dissimulations about the extent of Libya's violation (notably on the fact that there might even have been a reinforcement of her forces), President Mitterrand's trip to Crete to meet with Colonel Qaddafi, and other vacillations created a climate of malaise and confusion. This cast a serious doubt not only on France's political cautiousness, but also on her willingness fully to assume her military responsibilities. In the light of the often-quoted statement of former

Foreign Affairs Minister, Claude Cheysson, made after the signature of the treaty with Libya—'if they stay, we stay; if they come back, we come back'—France's indecisive attitude was indeed disquieting. The reactions of France's African partners, especially at the 11th Franco-African Summit held in Bujumbura—that was boycotted by leaders such as President Houphouet-Boigny of Ivory Coast or Seny Kountché of Niger (a country also under Libyan threat) who instead went to Washington—bore witness to the malaise of concerned African circles.

At the time, there had been speculation about a shift in France's willingness to assume her external overseas engagements.[111] Although, since 1982, President Mitterrand has followed the general policies of his predecessors over external engagements, it is clear that he prefers diplomacy to the use of force. In addition, if the so-called *tiers-mondiste* idealistic credo has made room for a greater pragmatism it has not for all that evaporated and continues to pervade influential official circles. In addition, so far as Chad is concerned, it cannot be denied that in the past France had supported Goukouni Oueddei against Hissène Habré, who is still remembered as responsible for the Claustre kidnapping and the shooting of a French military negotiator, and is perceived as having only a fragile legitimacy in his country. All these factors explain why in the summer of 1983 it took the French President so long to send French troops to Chad. By the time of their arrival, the Libyans had already occupied half the country. Moreover, the French were deployed in a strictly deterrent posture, whereas, it could realistically have been feasible— and this was the option proposed by the Air Force—to strike from the air, in a pre-emptive fashion, at the still undeployed Libyan columns in the north. The President's politically risky trip to Elounda to meet with Colonel Qaddafi, though undertaken with an awareness of the latter's duplicity, was motivated by the belief, if not the conviction, that he could, by lending the Libyan leader some legitimacy, lead him to complete the terms of the treaty on withdrawal.

These observations do not necessarily signal any significant change and subsequent developments demonstrated that it would have been premature to derive any definitive conclusion, from them. President Mitterrand exhibited firmness once troops were engaged in Chad, as after the GUNT-Libyan attack over Ziguey, within the French-controlled zone on January 24, 1984, when retaliatory measures were ordered together with the moving northwards to the sixteenth parallel of the French defence line. Technically, the *Operation Manta* itself was a success, since it prevented Libyan-supported forces of the GUNT to take over N'Djamena.[112] At the same time it created a climate which induced the near disintegration of the GUNT. The Treaty of Tripoli was diplomatically rational, preventing both risks of *ensablement*, given France's deterrent posture, and escalation, in other words of Vietnamisation. Moreover, if the French government seemed at the time uncertain about the Libyan position, it had declared that it would guarantee as before the defence of the 'Red Line' on the sixteenth parallel; *Manta* without *Manta* as it has been said.[113] Concomitantly, the whole French military formation was not repatriated, part of it was simply redeployed in Gabon, Cameroon and especially in the nearby Central African Republic; this allowed limited demonstration of force, the *'gesticulation'* in the French military jargon, as with the flying over N'Djamena of *Jaguar* aircraft in mid-November 1984.

Yet, as stated by François Mitterrand at the Bujumbura Conference, French troops, which had been kept out of the conflict for the next fifteen months, re-entered it in February 1986, after Libyan forces had carried out attacks in central Chad, south of the Red Line; the French aircraft then bombed the runway of Ouadi-Doum airport, one key facility used by Libya in the north of Chad.[114]

By November 1986, the situation in Chad had changed significantly. Hissène Habré's political legitimacy had been broadened and strengthened; in the Libyan-occupied north, many Chadians, including former guerrilla opponents of Habré, had rallied to his cause. This assessment of the situation led to a significant change in French policy. At the Lomé Conference, the French redefined the conflict as an international one, between Chad and Libya; it was seen no longer merely as a civil war between Chadian factions. Furthermore, the French government indicated that it would provide the increased military aid that would permit Hissène Habré to strike into the north. France actually went as far as to deliver airborne assistance of fuel, water, and ammunition to Chadian troops (Goukouni Oueddei's forces now allied to Hissène Habré, and waiting for reinforcements) under Libyan siege in the Tibesti, in the far northwest part of the country.[115] Between December 1986 and September 1987, Hissène Habré's national army recaptured virtually all of northern Chad, inflicting a series of spectacular defeats upon a clearly demoralised Libyan army.[116] On 24 September 1987 the OAU announced that Chad and Libya had agreed to a ceasefire, and that the claims to the disputed Aouzou strip—which Libya still occupied in part—would be settled by arbitration.[117] Apart from occasional yet extremely modulated operations in northern Chad, always responding to Libyan provocation, as in January 1987 with the delicate attack over the main radar of Ouadi-Doum airport, French forces, operating under the code name of *Epervier*, remained south of the 16th parallel, yet always close enough to provide assistance to Chadian troops.[118] The idea was to play on the battle fatigue of Libyan forces, and the dissensions with their Chadian allies, as well as rising discontent on the home front to force Libya on the defensive and help, with logistics, the Chadians to hold their newly conquered grounds.

The events of 1986–87 seemed to bear out the apparent wisdom of France's strategy. So long as the political situation in Chad remained unchanged, a re-intervention along the same lines as before September 1984 would have been meaningless as a way to force the Libyans out of northern Chad. Hence the only alternative to successful diplomatic pressures would have been a direct military confrontation with Libya. Though such defiance was viewed, notably among military circles who felt deceived, as therapeutic, it would certainly have had problematic consequences. Considering Libya's military strength, such a war would indeed have been something more than a low-intensity affair. As such, and given the likely costs—financial, technological and human not to mention politico-diplomatic costs (with regard to the Arab world especially and even African countries)—it would necessarily fall outside the realm of legitimacy traditionally governing low-intensity operations, on the international, as well as the domestic, scene.

This issue has certainly been already raised during the Chadian *face-à-face*. Experience has shown that Colonel Qaddafi's braggart diplomacy might not be taken at face value, but cannot be ignored either; he consistently advocated the expulsion of France from Africa and declared that he would make Chad the African 'Dien Bien Phu'. One could justifiably wonder what would have been the outcome of the Chadian confrontation had the Libyan regime not been besieged by all sorts of troubles; on the home front (unrest within the military establishment, economic difficulties induced by the costs of war, etc.) also on the war front (tensions with the Chadian protégés, also divided between themselves, and operational problems due to the over-extension of the logistical lines).[119] The attack on Ziguey in January 1984 and the French riposte also demonstrated the potential for escalation, the consequences of which could have been serious given the type and the sophistication of the weaponry and equipment to which the opposing forces resorted. As we have seen, France would have had to face, in such circumstances, increasing financial and technological complications which in turn could have hindered the overall readiness and effectiveness of her intervention system; hence the extreme carefulness of her responses, and the measure with which they were taken, when provoked by Libya, as in 1986 and 1987.

However, once Libyan forces blatantly violated the *de facto* partition of the country, it made strategic sense—both within Chad, and in respect of France's wider African strategic interests—to reintroduce French forces in a deterrent posture. Later, when politico-military 'correlation of forces' inside Chad shifted against the Libyans, the French contingent could play a more direct, albeit still 'supportive role', without a significant risk of escalation. Even so, it was a calculated risk; it is doubtful whether in December 1986, French military leaders and diplomats could have foreseen with certainty the remarkable outcome of the conflict that emerged nine months later.

As with other interventions overseas, the action in Chad highlighted the increasing complexity of the system of constraints within which France must and will have to operate to protect militarily her interests and influence overseas. The means to alleviate these limitations are tenuous. For the time being, attempts at drawing other nations into the solution of African crises within the Western or the European context have not been successful; the difficulties with Belgium in 1978 are a case in point.[120] Moreover, though it is admitted in France that African crises should be solved primarily by Africans themselves—this has been repeatedly reaffirmed since the Dakar and Paris summits in 1977 and 1978—the organisation of a permanent and effective inter-African system of peace-keeping failed, except for specific temporary cases such as the inter-African contingent established in Zaire in 1978. The institutional and operational obstacles are not insuperable, but ideological and political rivalries remain too sharp, as evinced by the failure to apply the protocol of mutual military assistance signed by members of the CEDEAO group (*Conféderation Economique Des États d'Afrique Occidental*) in West Africa or less recent projects sponsored by the OAU (Organisation of African Unity).

The earlier evocation of the technological issue of the Franco-Libyan confrontation leads us to a crucial yet elusive aspect of the theme discussed in this book, namely the future of low-intensity conflicts. In the case of France at least, the policy of overseas intervention would probably be modified if the dynamic of technological change was to accelerate and affect significantly the configuration of conflicts liable to develop overseas.[121] The appearance in these regions of nuclear weapons, whether produced locally or transferred from outside, would obviously be a case in point. France admittedly would have the resources to nuclearise her own forces of intervention. Back in 1977, Prime Minister Raymond Barre declared that there was no reason not to consider the idea of assigning tactical nuclear weapons to the French intervention forces. Today this would be even less problematic since the units of the newly created FAR could be easily equipped with 'neutronic' nuclear fire. But, because this evolution would mean a blurring of the distinction between low-intensity conflict, conventional war and nuclear war, it is obvious that the French policy of external military intervention would then operate on new parameters different from those governing any other classical 'central' type war. Then, even in the context of an emerging agreement over a limited use of nuclear fire for combat purposes, the legitimacy of any external intervention, potentially nuclear, would narrow. This, incidentally, is the objective that a school of African strategists advocating the nuclearisation of the continent seeks to reach.[122]

These considerations apart, such an evolution in the structure of 'peripheral' wars, without being an unrealistic hypothesis, still lies in the future. Until then, it is probable that France will continue, despite numerous and increasing constraints, to rely on military resources to deal with threats against the security and the balance of power in sub-Saharan Africa. The present ambiguities, if they exist, are not that significant; a bit of lassitude with an affair which lasted long enough. But at the Bujumbura conference, the French president reaffirmed that France would come to the assistance of countries to which she is bound by defence treaties to resist aggression. The conference of Lomé evinced the same spirit. And under the present circumstances, *Operation Epervier* is probably not the last of France's *guerres africaines*.

Notes

The author wishes to point out that a first version of this article was written in 1985. It has been extensively updated until the end of 1987. Yet the argument might reflect the previous pattern of analysis. The author expresses here his gratitude for the editor's material and editorial help.

1. Testifying of this new image, see the international opinion survey conducted in December 1983 and January 1984 by Gallup International; an analysis of the results was published in *L'Express*, 27 January–2 February 1984, pp. 12–23.
2. In this paper we shall consider under the heading of low-intensity engagements all conflicts in which France has been involved outside Europe in the 'Third Circle' to use General Poirier's terminology (*Essais de stratégie théorique*, Paris: Fondation pour les Etudes de Défense Nationale, 1982). They will be variously referred to as 'peripheral' wars (as opposed to European or 'central' wars) or external and overseas interventions.
3. The general question of fluctuations in length of belligerency has been discussed by various authors among which are Pitirin Sorokin, *Social and Cultural Dynamics*, vol. 4 (New York, 1939); Quincy Wright, *The Study of War,* 2 vols. (Chicago: The University of Chicago Press, 1943); see also for the case of France, Pierre Goubert, *L'Ancien regime,* vol. 2 (Paris: A. Colin, 1973), p. 112; and Michel L. Martin, 'Note de démographie militaire: Les variations d'effectifs en France depuis de quinzième siècle', *Revue des Sciences politiques* 8 (1983), pp. 21–35.
4. In this discussion we shall be led to refer to various episodes of France's colonial undertakings. Yet not to weigh down the argumentation, we shall not go into the details of the circumstances—political, international, etc.—surrounding these events. These will be considered known. The reader might refer to the existing literature which is plentiful.
5. The term *guerre algérienne* was used in a less extensive sense in Leland Conley Barrows, 'L'influence des conquêtes algériennes et coloniales sur l'armée français, 1830–1919', *Le mois en Afrique* 16 (December 1981—January 1982), pp. 97–127, and 17 (January–February 1982), pp. 125–48. The term is kept in France not only because it is meant to be the typological description of a way of warfare, but also not to be confused with the Algerian War itself (1957–1962), the last colonial war of France after which Algeria became an independent nation.
6. There is indeed no lack of historical evidence. It is stressed, moreover, that the deep nationalistic and Islamic militancy of the Arabs in Algeria helped to escalate the war. For a detailed analysis of these points see in particular Charles-André Julien, *Histoire de l'Algérie contemporaine: la conquête et les débuts de la colonisation, 1827–1871* (Paris: Presses Universitaires de France, 1964), pp. 270 *passim*. See also Stephane Gsell, George Marçais and G. Yver, *Histoire de l'Algérie* (Paris: Bolvin, 1927).
7. Pierre Chalmin, *L'officier français de 1915 à 1870* (Paris: Marcel Rivière, 1957).
8. *Cf.* his *Algérie: des Moyens de conserver et d'utiliser cette conquête* (Paris: Dentu, 1842) in which he discussed as an introduction the comparative methods of domination of the Carthagenese, the Romans, the Arabs, and the Turks; see also *Oeuvres militaires du maréchal Bugeaud, duc d'Isly* edited by Weil (Paris: Baudoin, 1894). Writings on Bugeaud in French are too numerous to be cited here; in English one can cite a recent work: Antony T. Sullivan, *Bugeaud, France and Algeria, 1784–1849: Politics, Power and the Good Society* (Hamden: Archon Books, 1983).
9. Cited by Julien, *Histoire de l'Algérie, op. cit.* p. 174.
10. *De la stratégie, de la tactique, des retraites et du passage des défilés dans les montagnes des Kabyles* was the title of the report. The pacification of the Kabylie however took several campaigns to complete. On Bugeaud's military views, see

Paul Azan, *Bugeaud et l'Algérie*, (Paris, 1930); Jean Gottmann, 'Bugeaud, Galliéni, Lyautey: The Development of Colonial Warfare', in *Makers of Modern Strategy: Military Thought from Machiavelli to Hitler,* edited by Edward Mead Earle (Princeton: Princeton University Press, 1941), pp. 234–59; see also Douglas Porch's article with the same title in the new edition of *Makers of Modern Strategy*, edited by Peter Paret (Princeton, 1986).

11. Leland C. Barrows, 'Louis Léon César Faidherbe (1818–1889)', in *African Proconsuls: European Governors in Africa*, eds. L. G. Gann and Peter Duignan (New York: The Free Press, 1978), pp. 51–79; 'L'influence des conquêtes algériennes et coloniales sur l'armée française', p. 117.

12. Reported by Charles John Balesi, *From Adversaries to Comrades-in-arms: West Africans and the French Military, 1885–1918* (Waltham: Crossroads Press, 1979), p. 24.

13. Campaign accounts by officers, in the numerous contemporary published memoirs make it clear.

14. Gottmann, 'Bugeaud, Galliéni, Lyautey', *op. cit.* p. 252 *passim.*

15. General Huré, 'Stratégie et tactique marocaines', *Revue des Questions de Défence nationale* 1 (July 1939), pp. 397–412; also cited in Gottmann, 'Bugeaud, Galliéni, Lyautey', *op. cit.* p. 235; also, General Catroux, 'L'Achèvement de la pacification marocaine', *Revue politique et parlementaire* 161, no. 479 (1934), pp. 24–46; for a more general view and analysis, see Douglas Porch, *The Conquest of Morocco* (New York, 1983).

16. There is a great deal written on the Algerian War though less on the way the fighting was conducted in the field. One of the best accounts of the war in English is probably Alistair Horne, *A Savage War of Peace. Algeria 1954–1962* (New York: The Viking Press, 1977); some of the data here have also been gathered from Philippe Tripier, *Autopsie de la guerre d'Algérie* (Paris: Ed. France-Empire).

17. The style of warfare developed in the colonies has influenced significantly the strategic thinking regarding the conduct of European wars; see Barrows, 'L'influence des conquêtes algériennes et coloniales sur l'armée française', *op. cit.* pp. 124–25.

18. From excerpt of Galliéni's instructions of 22 May 1898; quoted by (then Lt. Colonel) Hubert Lyautey, 'Du rôle colonial de l'armée', *Revue des Deux Mondes* 157 (15 January 1900), p. 316.

19. General Albert Baratier, *Au Congo: Souvenirs de la mission Marchand de Brazzaville à Fort Desaix* (Paris: A. Fayard, 1914), p. 101, quoted by Balesi, *From Adversaries to Comrades-in-Arms, op. cit.* p. 22.

20. See *Oeuvres Militaires du Maréchal Bugeaud* and *Lettres inédites du Maréchal Bugeaud*, edited by Capt. Tattet and H. Ferray-Bugeaud d'Isly (Paris: E. Paul, 1923).

21. *Souvenirs d'un chef de Bureaux Arabe,* 1858, cited in R. Peyronnet, *Livre d'or des Officiers des Affaires indigènes 1830–1930*, vol. 1 (Alger: Imprimerie algérienne, 1930), p. 84. For an introduction to the history of the Bureaux, see Pierre Chalmin, 'Les Bureaux arabes de leur création à la chute du Second Empire', *Actes du LXXIXe Congrés national des sociétés savantes: Histoire Algérienne* (1954), pp. 91–114; X. Yacono, *Les Bureaux arabes et l'évolution des genres de vie indigènes dans l'ouest du Tell Algérois* (Paris: Larose, 1953); Vincent Monteil, 'Les Bureaux arabes au Maghreb, 1833–1861', *Esprit* (November 1961), pp. 575–606.

22. Julien, *Histoire de l'Algérie contemporaine, op. cit.* pp. 337–41.

23. From an excerpt quoted by Lyautey 'Du rôle colonial de l'armée', *op. cit.* p. 313. See also Gottmann, 'Bugeaud, Galliéni, Lyautey', *op. cit.* p. 242; also J. Kim

Mulholland, '"Collaboration Strategy" and the French Pacification of Tonkin 1885–1897', *The Historical Journal* 24 (1981), pp. 629–50.

24. Joseph Galliéni, *Neuf ans à Madagascar* (Paris, 1908); Albert Ringel, *Les Bureaux arabes de Bugeaud et les cercles militaires de Galliéni* (Paris, 1923); Virgil L. Matthew, Jr., 'Joseph Simon Gallieni (1849–1916)', in *African Proconsuls*, eds. L. V. Gann and Peter Duignan, pp. 80–108; Gottmann, 'Bugeaud, Galliéni, Lyautey', *op. cit.*

25. Lyautey 'Du rôle colonial de l'armée', *op. cit.*; Gottmann, 'Bugeaud, Galliéni, Lyautey', *op. cit.* p. 247 *passim*; see also Porch's article in *The Makers of Modern Strategy* edited by Paret, and Kenneth Perkins, *Quaids, Captains, and Colons: French Military Administration in Colonial Maghreb, 1844–1934* (New York, 1981).

26. Quoted in Jean Feller, *Le dossier de l'armée française: La guerre de 'cinquante ans', 1914–1962* (Paris: Librairie Académique Perrin, 1966), p. 432.

27. In English, see Peter Paret, *French Revolutionary Warfare from Indochina to Algeria: The Analysis of a Political Military Doctrine* (New York: Praeger, 1964); Raoul Girardet, 'Civil and Military Power in the Fourth Republic', in *Changing Patterns of Military Politics* edited by Samuel P. Huntington (New York: The Free Press of Glencoe, Inc., 1962), pp. 129–41 in particular; and Horne, *A Savage War of Peace, op. cit.*

28. A. S. Kanya-Forstner, *The Conquest of the Western Sudan: A Study in French Military Imperialism* (Cambridge: University Press, 1969); Barrows, 'L'influence des conquêtes algériennes et coloniales sur l'armée française', *op. cit.* pp. 97, 117. See also the numerous pamphlets originated in the anti-colonialist milieux denouncing the excesses of the pacification, among which a scathing attack (perhaps not to be taken fully at face value) on Galliéni's policies in Madagascar by a member of the parliament, P. E. Vigné d'Octon, and recently re-edited as *La gloire et le sabre* (Paris: Ed. Quintette, 1984).

29. Girardet, 'Civil and Military Power in the Fourth Republic', *op. cit.* p. 138.

30. *ibid.*; also on the ideological implications see Paret, *French Revolutionary Warfare from Indochina to Algeria*, Chapter 7.

31. Among other writings, see Shelby Cullom Davis, *Reservoirs of Men: A History of the Black Troops of French West Africa*, Doctoral thesis at the University of Geneva (Chamber: Imprimeries réunies, 1934), Chapter 1; Louise Beaudza, *La formation de l'armée coloniale* (Paris: Librairie Fournier, 1939).

32. As a result of the application of the concept of the *Force noire* of which among others General Charles Mangin was the foremost proponent. On the participation of native troops in France's European wars, see Davis, *Reservoirs of Men, op. cit.*; and Balesi, *From Adversaries to Comrades-in-Arms, op. cit.* Chapters 4–6; for details on World War I see Marc Michel, 'Le recrutement des tirailleurs en AOF pendant la première guerre mondiale, Essai de bilan statistique', *Revue française d'Histoire d'Outre-mer* 60 (Winter 1973), pp. 644–60; and his thesis, *L'Appel à l'Afrique: contributions et réactions à l'effort de guerre en AOF, 1914–19* (Paris: Publications de la Sorbonne, 1982). Concerning World War II, see G. Bonnet, *Mémorial de l'Empire à la gloire des troupes coloniales* (Paris: Sequana, 1941); Jean Ingold, *L'Epopée Leclerc au Sahara, 1940–43* (Paris: Berger-Levrault, 1945); for a longer bibliography and comparison with the British experience, see Rita Haedrich, 'African Soldiers in World War II,' unpublished manuscript, 1976 (University of Chicago).

33. This point, noted by S. C. Davis, *The French War Machine* (London: Allen & Unwin, 1937), p. 129, should be emphasized against the conventional radical and other simplistic views which reduce often the reality of colonial relations in terms of racism only whereas the picture is far more complex in actuality; for such (yet well argued) view see William Cohen, *The French Encounter with Africans:*

White Response to Blacks (Bloomington: Indiana University Press, 1980).

34. For details on the establishment and the evolution of these units, see Paul Azan, *L'Armée d'Afrique de 1830 a 1852* (Paris: Plon, 1936); Julien, *Histoire de l'Algérie contemporaine, op. cit.* pp. 270–82; Barrows, 'L'influence des conquêtes algériennes et coloniales sur l'armée française', *op. cit.* p. 101.

35. The Foreign Legion was constituted with the remnants of the former Hohenlohe legion established at the time of the Restoration with the Napoleonic foreign regiments and the Swiss Guard.

36. Julien, *Histoire de l'Algérie contemporaine, op. cit.* p. 273.

37. Davis, *The French War Machine, op. cit.,* p. 121.

38. Myron J. Echenberg, 'Les migrations militaires en Afrique occidentale, 1900–1945', *Canadian Journal of African Studies* 14 (1980), p. 443. On the overall organisation, see Georges Pasquier, *L'organisation des troupes indigènes en Afrique occidentale française* (Paris: Larose, 1912); Davis, *Reservoirs of Men; The French War Machine, op. cit.*; Balesi, *From Adversaries to Comrades-in-Arms, op. cit.*

39. Davis, *The French War Machine, op. cit.* p. 141.

40. 5,400 French and 20,000 men from the Foreign Legion. To these were added as supplementary forces 100,000 Vietnamese. See Feller, *Le dossier de l'armée française, op. cit.* p. 441.

41. For a summary in English of these questions of recruitment, see Davis, *The French War Machine* and *Reservoirs of Men, op. cit.*; Myron J. Echenberg, 'Paying the Blood Tax: Military Conscription in French West Africa, 1914–1929', *Canadian Journal of African Studies* 9 (1975), pp. 171–92.

42. A. Marceau, *Le tirailleur soudanais* (Paris: Berger-Levrault, 1911), p. 3; cited in Balesi, *From Adversaries to Comrades-in-Arms, op. cit.* p. 44; for a general statement on the issue of racial recruitment in the military with a special emphasis on the English case, see A. H. M. Kirk-Greene, '"Damnosa Hereditas": Ethnic Ranking and the Martial Races Imperative in Africa', paper presented at the 1979 conference of the International Political Science Association, March 1979.

43. A great number of observations have been made on the native troops, their life, their behaviour, etc.; all officers having written on their campaigning in Africa had something to say on these questions. For a good summary and analysis, see Balesi, *From Adversaries to Comrades-in-Arms, op. cit.* Chapter 3 in particular.

44. For details see Balesi, *From Adversaries to Comrades-in-Arms, op. cit.* pp. 49–56; also Davis, *The French War Machine, op. cit.* Chapters 7–8. After 1946, new reforms were introduced: French military academies were opened to Africans, a special military academy, the EFORTOM was established to form African officers, and an effort was made to prepare young men at elementary and secondary school level. Though the number of African officers remained limited, in 1960, there were five colonels, six majors, 31 captains and 157 lieutenants of African origin.

45. See Chalmin, *L'officier français de 1815 à 1870, op. cit.* pp. 89 and *passim*; Raoul Girardet, *La société militaire dans la France contemporaine, 1815–1939* (Paris: Plon, 1953), Chapters 2–3; William Serman, *Les origines des officiers Français, 1848–1870* (Paris: Editions de la Sorbonne, 1979).

46. Julien, *Histoire de l'Algérie contemporaine, op. cit.* Chapter 6.

47. *ibid.*

48. Girardet, *La société militaire;* Louis Baron, 'Les idees coloniales et le recrutement des officiers sortant de Saint-Cyr dans l'Infanterie de Marine, 1872–1891' (Thesis, University of Paris), 1969. In English, see also Philip C. Bankwitz, *Maxime Weygand and Civil-Military Relations in Modern France* (Cambridge:

Harvard University Press, 1967) and David B. Ralston, *The Army of the Republic: The Place of the Military in the Political Evolution of France, 1871–1914* (Cambridge, Mass.: MIT Press, 1967).

49. *Cf.* Marshal Lyautey's celebrated piece, 'Du rôle social de l'officier français dans le service militaire universel', *Revue des Deux Mondes* (15 March 1891), pp. 443–58.

50. For a negative picture of French military behaviour toward African soldiers, see Geoffrey Gorer, *Africa Dances: A Book about West African Negroes* (New York: Knopf, 1935). This however should not be exaggerated, otherwise one would especially have difficulty then in explaining the loyalty and the patriotism of African soldiers, especially at times when they could have behaved otherwise. See also note 33.

51. The term here should be read in its religious meaning. For a long time, the officer's calling was literally conceived in religious terms and regarded as the fulfilment of a sacerdotal function; General Weygand compared the officer profession to priesthood. The missionary dimension of the colonial officer's role is also a consequence of the influence of the doctrine of 'social catholicism' in the French bourgeoisie. A comparative study (never undertaken yet) of the colonial officer and the catholic missionary would clearly evince numerous similarities, not only at the ideological level, but interestingly so at the organisational level as well; *cf.* for example, the structure of the mission post of Cardinal Lavigerie's *Pères blancs* and that of Galliéni's *cercle*.

52. France intervened in the 1960s in Mauritanie (1963), Gabon (1964), Cameroon (1964), Djibouti (1967), Chad (1968); in the 1970s in Djibouti (1974, 1976, 1977); Chad (1975, 1978); Mauritanie (1977, 1978), Mayotte (1977, 1978), Central African Republic (1979), Zaire (1977, 1978); in the 1980s in Chad (1980, 1983–84, 1986), and Mauritanie (1980). Space limitation prevents a discussion of the circumstances of these interventions. Details can be found in the various works cited hereafter. Moreover our argumentation bears upon overt military actions only and leaves aside a number of more covert operations at the diplomatic and political level involving intelligence agencies.

53. For details see Michel L. Martin, *Warriors to Managers: The French Military Establishment since 1945* (Chapel Hill: University of North Carolina Press, 1981), part 1.

54. Among most recent writings on this issue see Bruce E. Arlinghaus, ed., *Arms for Africa: Military Assistance and Foreign Policy in the Developing World* (Lexington, Mass.: D. C. Heath and Company, 1983).

55. Marcel Ligot, *Les accords de coopération entre la France et les Etats africaines et malgaches d'expression française* (Paris: La Documentation française, 1964); and Pierre Abelin, *Rapport sur politique française de coopération* (Paris: La Documentation française, 1975); Brigitte Nouaille-Degorce, *La politique française de coopération avec les Etats africains et malgache au sud du Sahara, 1958–1978* (Bordeaux: Centre d'Etude d'Afrique noire, 1982); Marcel Merle, 'La politique africaine dans la politique étrangère générale de la France', *La politique africaine du Général De Gaulle, 1958–1969*, edited by Dmitri-G. Lavroff (Paris: Pédone, 1980), pp. 145–67. See also Alfred Grosser, *La politique extérieure de la Ve République* (Paris: Seuil, 1965).

56. An illustration, in English, of such a view is Guy Martin, 'The Historical, Economic, and Political Bases of France's African Policy', *Journal of Modern African Studies* 23 (1985), pp. 189–208. Now for a more balanced view see Martin Staniland, 'Francophone Africa: The Enduring French Connection', *The Annals, AAPSS* 489 (January 1987), pp. 51–62.

57. On the African policy of France during the pre-Socialist presidency, see the

various essays in two collected works, Lavroff, ed., *La politique africaine du Général De Gaulle, 1958–1969*; and Samy Cohen and Marie-Claude Smouts, eds., *La politique extérieure de Valéry Giscard d'Estaing* (Paris: Presses de la Fondation nationale des Sciences politiques, 1985). Also J. L. Dagut, 'L'Afrique, la France et le monde dans le discours giscardien', *Politique africaine* 5 (February 1982), pp. 19–27.

On the first years of François Mitterrand's presidency, see Dominique Moisi, 'Mitterrand's Foreign Policy: The Limits of Continuity', *Foreign Affairs* 60 (Winter 1981–82), pp. 347–57; Daniel C. Bach, 'La politique française en Afrique après le 10 mai 1981', *Année africaine 1982* (Paris: Pédone, 1983), pp. 236–53. For a discussion of the return to continuity under the Socialists, Jean-François Bayart, *La politique africaine de François Mitterrand* (Paris: Karthala, 1984); see also *Le Monde* (16–17 January 1983). The shift in the African policy of Mitterrand's France after 1982 toward a return to the earlier military-diplomatic orthodoxy was symbolised by the resignation of Jean-Pierre Cot, head of the Ministry of Cooperation, and leading spokesman for the *tiers-mondiste* stand-point which implied a redistribution and 'demilitarisation' of France's relations in Africa. It remains that partisans of this view are not absent among the President's advisors. This, together with a certain distrust of Hissène Habré whose group has been responsible in the Claustre and Galopin affairs, explains in part the confusion of the French government in November 1984 when Libya, in violation of the treaty signed with France in September, maintained her troops in Chad.

58. Though the question of prestige and grandeur has always been linked to France's colonial experience, far more than economic issues; on this point see Raoul Girardet, *L'idée coloniale en France, 1871–1962* (Paris: Table ronde, 1972); Henri Brunschwig, *Mythes et Réalités de l'impérialisme colonial français* (Paris: A, Colin, 1960); L. H. Gann and Peter Duignan, *The Burden of Empire: An Appraisal of Western Colonialism in Africa South of the Sahara* (New York: F. A. Praeger, 1967).

59. Typical of this point of view, General Piollet, 'Le continent africain, atout maître de la stratégie française', *France Outre-mer* 266 (December 1951). By perusing the various professional journals of the time, the *Revue Militaire génerale*, the *Revue de Défense nationale* and particularly the documentation prepared at the Centre militaire d'Information et de Documentation sur l'Outre-mer, it is possible to see the extent of these conceptions in the military circles.

60. *Cf.* Dmitri-Georges Lavroff, 'Les enjeux Africains', *Défense nationale* 34 (December 1978), pp. 5–18; L. H. Gann and Peter Duignan, *African South of the Sahara: The Challenge to Western Security* (Stanford: Hoover Institution Press, 1981).

61. Maurice Ligot, 'La coopération militaire dans les accords passés entre la France et les Etats-africains et malgache d'expression française', *R.I.P.O.N.* (October–December 1963). See also the various other works cited about the *Coopération*.

62. Robin A. Luckham, 'Le militarisme française en Afrique', *Politique africaine* 5 (February 1982), pp. 96–97; for a slightly different view, see Pierre Lellouche and Dominique Moisi, 'French policy in Africa: A Lonely Battle Against Destabilisation', *International Security* 3 (Spring 1979), pp. 108–33; Edward A. Kolodziej and Birkanga Loukulutu, 'Security Interest and French Arms-Transfer Policy in Sub-Saharan Africa', in *Arms of Africa* edited by Arlinghaus, pp. 125–52.

63. For a systematic analysis of this issue, three works can be referred to here, a pioneering one, Jacques Guillemin, 'Coopération et intervention: la politique

militaire de la France en Afrique noire francophone et à Madagascar'. Doctoral dissertation, University of Nice, January 1979; Pascal Chaigneau, *La politique militaire de la France en Afrique* (Paris: Publications du CHEAM, Documentation française, 1984); and in English, John Chipman, 'French Military Policy and African Security', *Adelphi Papers* 201 (Summer 1985).

64. Moshé Ammi-Oz, 'La formation des cadres militaires africains lors de la mise sur pied des armées nationales', *Revue françaises d'Etudes politiques africaines* 133 (January 1977), pp. 84–99; also Guillemin, 'Coopération et Intervention', pp. 59–97; Pierre Dabezies, 'La politique militaire de la France en Afrique noire sous le Général De Gaulle', in *La politique africaine du Général de Gaulle*, pp. 229–61. Luckham, 'Le militarisme français en Afrique', *op. cit. passim*,

65. It should be noted that France provides between 80 to 100 percent of the armament of countries like Djibouti, Central African Republic, Senegal, Chad. See Chaigneau, *La politique militaire de la France en Afrique*, pp. 37–38.

66. The French military, today, is divided into three categories of forces: the nuclear strategic forces (the deterrent); the pre-strategic forces (tactical nuclear used as warning of a resort to the nuclear strategic forces); the conventional forces (to fight in Europe and outside Europe small or middle scale operations). Two key components make up the conventional forces: the armoured mechanised corps (with eight armoured divisions and two infantry divisions) and the Force of Rapid Action (with an aeromobile division, an armoured division, an alpine division, an airborne division and a marine infantry division, the latter two corresponding to the overseas deployment forces).

67. On the recent reorganisation see the subsequent section of the chapter.

68. There are numerous studies about the French defence doctrine; among the most recent and the most complete ones, in English, see David Yost, 'France's Deterrent Posture and Security in Europe' in two parts, in *Adelphi Papers* (Winter 1984–85) and (Spring 1985); see also note 78.

69. Guillemin, 'Coopération et intervention', pp. 58–118; see also Guillemin's articles derived from his dissertation in *Revue française d'Etudes politiques africaines* 186–187 (June-July 1981), pp. 43–58 and 188–89 (August–September 1981), pp. 31–44.

70. The exact figures on French troops deployed overseas and in Africa can be found in the various reports from the Defence Commission of the National Assembly and the Senate; see also Guillemin, 'Coopération et intervention', *Le Point* (19 September 1983', p. 62; Chaigneau, *La politique militaire de France en Afrique*, pp. 76–79; Chipman, *French Military Policy and African Security*.

71. See note 62.

72. For details see for instance the 'Dossier du Mois: L'appui aérien', *Armées d'Aujourd'hui* (July–August 1983), pp. 30–43.

73. 'Les capacités d'action extérieures', *Armées d'Aujourd'hui* (1980), p. 48; Guillemin, 'Coopération et intervention', *op. cit.* pp. 121–22.

74. *ibid.*

75. See *Le Monde* (18 February 1984), pp. 1 and 3; *Valeurs actuelles* (13 February 1982), pp. 24–26; *Strategic Survey 1983* (London: International Institute for Strategic Studies, 1984), p. 105.

76. The title of former Prime Minister Pierre Mauroy's speech at the Institut des Hautes Etudes de la Défense nationale, published under the title 'Vers un nouveau modèle d'armée', *Défense nationale* 38 (November 1982), pp. 9–28; see also 'La réorganisation de l'Armée de Terre: un entretien avec le Général d'Armée R. Imbot', in *Armées d'Aujourd'hui* 82 (July–August 1983), pp. 4–7; and *Défense nationale* 40 (April 1984), pp. 158–61.

77. For the general outlook see 'Projet de loi portant approbation de la loi de

programmation militaire pour les années 1984–1988', Assemblée Nationale, no. 1452, second ordinary session of 1982–1983. The reform and the *Loi de Programmation* have been discussed at great length in the press and specialised journals; summaries have appeared in *Défense nationale, Armées d'Aujourd'hui* and *Terre-Information* in 1983. See also *Le Monde* (16 December 1982) and (22 April 1983), and 'La France peut-elle encore se défendre', *Le Nouvel Economiste* (30 January 1984), pp. 36–42.

78. *Le Monde* (16 December 1982). On the new doctrinal aspects implied by the reform see (in English) Robert S. Rudney, 'Mitterrand's New Atlanticism: Evolving Attitudes Toward Nato', *Orbis* 28 (Spring 1984), pp. 83–101; Robin F. Laird, 'The French Strategic Dilemma', *Orbis* 28 (Summer 1984), pp. 307–28; Jolyon Howorth, 'Defence and the Mitterrand Government', in *Defence and Dissent in Contemporary France* edited by Jolyon Howorth and Patricia Chilton (New York: St. Martin's Press, 1984), pp. 94–134.

79. 'La force d'action rapide: Un entretien avec le Général de Corps d'Armée Gilbert Forray, commandant de la FAR', *Armées d'Aujourd'hui* (July–August 1983), pp. 20–22; 'The French Army: Shield and Sword for Europe?', *The Economist* (25 July 1984), pp. 37–40. For a doctrinal discussion on the European implications of the establishment of the FAR, see, among other writings, Lucien Porier, 'La greffe'. *Défense nationale* 39 (April 1983), pp. 5–32; Georges Fricaud-Chagnaud, 'L'Armée de Terre face à ses missions en Europe', *Défense nationale* 40 (May 1984), pp. 35–44; and François Valentin, 'L'arête étroite', *ibid.*, pp. 45–56; Dominique David, 'La FAR en Europe: le dire des armes', *Défense nationale* 40 (June 1983), pp. 27–49.

80. Michel Brissac, 'Kolwezi: un exemple d'Action entérieure', *Armées d'Aujourd'hui* (1980), pp. 46–47; Jacques L. Pons, 'Lessons of Modern History: The French Experience' in *U.S. Policy and Low-Intensity Conflict* eds. Sam C. Sarkesian and William L. Scully (New Brunswick: Transaction Books, 1981), pp. 145–46. For a general analysis of the issue, see Peter Mangold, 'Shaba I and Shaba II', *Survival* 21 (May–June 1979), pp. 107–15.

81. *ibid.*

82. Guillemin 'Coopération et Intervention', p. 125; Luckham 'Le militarisme français en Afrique; Les capacités d'actions extérieures', *Armées d'Aujourd'hui* (1980); see also *Afrique défense*.

83. *Le Monde* (18 January 1984), pp. 1 and 3; and despite also difficult sanitary conditions, *Valeurs actuelles* (10 October 1983), p. 44.

84. François Cailleteau, 'Elite Selection in the French Army Officer Corps', in *Defense and Military Institutions in Contemporary France* edited by Michel L. Martin, special issue, *Armed Forces and Society* 8 (Winter 1982), pp. 257–74.

85. *Valeurs actuelles* (13 February 1984), p. 25.

86. Alexander Atkinson, *Social Order and the General Theory of Strategy* (London: Routledge and Kegan Paul, 1981).

87. Mangold, 'Shaba I and Shaba II', *op. cit.* p. 111; Lellouche and Moisi, 'French Policy in Africa', *op. cit.* pp. 108, 125.

88. This is clear from the African press; see also *Valeurs actuelles* (15 August 1983), pp. 13–15; see also *L'Express*, 26 August 1983, p. 31. Again, in November 1984, the contradictions in the French official declarations and attitudes regarding Libya's violation of the treaty signed with France in September on a mutual military disengagement from Chad, created a great deal of uneasiness among Francophone African states about France's determination to protect the security of the area from destabilising encroachments.

89. Lellouche and Moisi, 'French Policy in Africa', *op. cit.* p. 124.

90. *ibid.*, pp. 108, 125.

91. See President Mitterrand's interview in *Le Monde* (26 August 1983); also *ibid.* 17 August 1983).

92. These are conservative figures; other surveys would show that only a fourth were against sending troops to Africa. See *Le Point* (12 June 1978); *Jeune Afrique* (6 December 1978) cited by Lellouche and Moisi 'French Policy in Africa', *op. cit.* pp. 124 n. 36 and 139 n. 66. See also *The Economist* (15 October 1983), p. 58.

93. From a Harris Poll conducted on 17 and 18 February 1984, in *Le Nouvel Observateur* (24 February 1984).

94. For details on the incident see *Strategic Survey*, p. 106. Afterwards the French changed the conditions of their fire and moved their lines up to the 16th parallel.

95. The French were to assist the Lebanese army and serve as 'interposition' force in Beirut which prevented them from playing an efficient role and from returning fire if attacked.

96. Mangold, 'Shaba I and Shaba II', *op. cit.* p. 109; and Lellouche and Moisi, 'French Policy in Africa', *op. cit.* p. 128.

97. See note 77,; also SIRPA, 'La programmation militaire 1984–1988', *Dossier d'Information* 72 (Octobre 1983) and *Le Monde* (20 April 1983).

98. The French ground force is still an *armée d'effectifs*. Only the Soviet Union has a population/military ratio smaller than that of France which is 163 (the Soviet Union's is 120). The ratio 'men to machine' is the highest in the industrial world. In the Soviet Union there are 47 men for one tank, 77 in the United States, 396 in France. For an analysis of this issue, see Martin, *Warriors to Managers, op. cit.* Part I.

99. Martin, *Warriors to Managers, op. cit.* Chapter 3.

100. *Cf.* the numerous analyses published in the press at the time, notably in *Le Monde* (5 May 1983); *Le Figaro* (19 May 1983); see also *Le Monde* (14 November 1986); 'Que vaut notre armée', *L'Express* (10–16 July 1987), pp. 37–44.

101. Lellouche and Moisi 'French Policy in Africa', *op. cit.* pp. 127–28, no. 56. 37–44.
     Defence Commission in Parliament; for technical details, see Claude Lemieux 'L'appui aérien transport', *Armées d'Aujourd'hui* (July–August 1983), pp. 39–41.

103. This evolution of supplementary expenses for external interventions between 1976 and 1982 in millions of francs: 43.7 in 1976; 187.3 in 1977; 590.63 in 1978; 473.61 in 1979; 345.55 in 1980; 385.73 in 1981; and 615.35 in 1984; from a report of the Defence Commission of the National Assembly on the 1984 Defence Budget. On the cost of the intervention in Lebanon and Chad, see *Avis présenté au nom de la Commission des Affaires étrangères, de la Défense et des forces armées sur le projet de loi de finance for 1984*, 'Section forces terrestres', Senat, 1er session ordinaire 1983–84, p. 65.

104. Data given in an interview with a member of a mission of investigation in Chad; *Valeurs actuelles* (10 October 1983), pp. 44–45.

105. It should be noted that to these costs are added those also incurred by the regular participation of French armed forces in non-military missions (rescue, assistance to foreign countries in time of natural disasters). Between 1977 and 1983, the annual average cost of such missions was $1m.; for 1979 and 1980 alone it reached a total of $4.4m.

106. See law no. 83–605 of 8 July 1983. According to the Army Chief of Staff, General Imbot, by 1986 a fourth of the army regiments should be either all-volunteer or partially all-volunteer units. See *Le Monde* (17 February 1984), pp. 1 and 10; for details *Défense nationale* 41 (April 1984), pp. 153–55.

107. *Défense nationale* 41 (April 1984), p. 154.
108. This is the case of the Communist Party; see *Le Monde* (1 February 1984), p. 10; *La Vie française* (10–26 February 1984), pp. 19–20; see also the criticisms developed against the increasing inegalitarian character of the conscription; *Le Monde* (26 November 1987), p. 29.
109. For a controversial analysis of France's problems in intervening, using Chad as an example, see Spartacus, *Operation Manta: Tchad 1983–1984* (Paris: Plon, 1986).
110. France, actually, had turned down the buying of C-141s in the late sixties under Pierre Messmer's ministry.
111. Though somewhat speculative at the time, the hypothesis of a complete change of the French foreign policy, characterised by a return to a pure-leftist orthodoxy had been advanced among opposition circles.
112. By success, is meant objective of the operation, *i.e.* preventing the Libyan and GUNT forces taking over the capital. The basic problem which created the situation, internal civil dissent remains unsolved. A great deal has been written on the internal difficulties in Chad, for a summary see for example, *Dossiers et Documents du Monde* (November 1983); Bernard Lanne, *Tchad-Libye: la querelle de frontières* (Paris: Karthala, 1982).
113. The situation could have led however to a *de facto* partition with the Libyanisation of the B.E.T. area and perhaps the opportunity for Libya to renew the same scenario in other countries, like Niger.
114. *Le Monde* (8–9 February and 5–6 April 1987).
115. See 'Tchad: le coup de main français,' *Le Point* (22 December 1986), pp. 33–35; *ibid.* (29 December 1986), p. 59.
116. See reports in *Le Monde* (9 January, 8–9 February, 29–30 March, 5–6 April 1987); *The Economist* (28 March, 5, 12 September 1987).
117. *Globe and Mail* (Toronto), 25 September 1987.
118. 'Tchad: ripostes sur mesure', *Le Point* (12 January 1987); pp. 48–49 *L'Express* (23 January 1987) and *Le Monde* (8–9 February and 5–6 April 1987).
119. The GUNT has always been riddled by factionalism which has lately—and this was a positive effect of the pressures created by *Operation Manta*—resulted in numerous fighting between at least five groups, not to mention fighting with Libyan troops whose morale and readiness was thus considerably affected. For summaries of this trend, see *Défense nationale* 40 (November 1984), pp. 183–85; *Le Monde* (16–17 November 1986); *The Economist* (25 October, 22 November 1986).
120. Lellouche and Moisi, 'French Policy in Africa', *op. cit.* pp. 192–232.
121. It should be observed that the military environment of sub-Saharan Africa is becoming more heavily armed. On this important issue see William J. Foltz and Henry Bienen, eds., *Arms and the African: Military Influences on Africa's International Relations* (New Haven: Yale University Press, 1985); Michel L. Martin, 'L'Afrique noire s'arme: note sur le développement militaire de l'Afrique au sud du Sahara' (forthcoming); for a statistical review, Pierre Viaud and Jacques de Lestapis, 'Afrique: les souverainetés en armes', *Dossier* n°16, Fondation pour les Etudes de Défense nationale, July 1987.
122. For a good analysis of this critical issue of the nuclearisation of Africa and the various related objectives and doctrines, see Pierre Viaud, *L'Afrique et la guerre nucléaire* (Paris: Edigeon, 1984); Oye Ogunbadejo, 'Africa's Nuclear Capability', *Journal of Modern African Studies* 22 (March 1984), pp. 19–43.

5

Peace-keeping and Internal Security: The Canadian Army in Low-Intensity Operations

DAVID A. CHARTERS AND JAMES LEBLANC

The Canadian Armed Forces are an almost 'invisible' institution in Canada. Small—about 84,000 regulars—and carrying little political weight, the armed forces are rarely and rather indifferently discussed in the nation's information media. Prior to 1970, when Canadians thought of their armed forces at all, which was not often, it was in terms of their exploits in the two World Wars. That is hardly surprising, given that the raising of large expeditionary forces was the only occasion when the Army drew heavily on the strength of the nation. The regular Army has always been small. Yet, it also has a long history of involvement in low-intensity operations, especially in the internal security role. Since 1970, it has been that role that has attracted the most critical public attention. Peace-keeping is another aspect of low-intensity operations in which Canadian soldiers have been involved since 1949. Simultaneously, Canada has maintained since 1945 conventional Army formations for service in general war. This study will endeavour to show how the Canadian Army learned to adapt to unconventional, low-intensity roles and missions in new politico-military environments while at the same time maintaining forces-in-being for conventional operations.

The study will consist of three parts. First, it will describe the Army as an institution since 1945. Most of the emphasis will be on the post-unification era, as this is the period in which the Army has been most active in the low-intensity role. The second part will discuss the low-intensity operations in which the Army has been involved and the

140

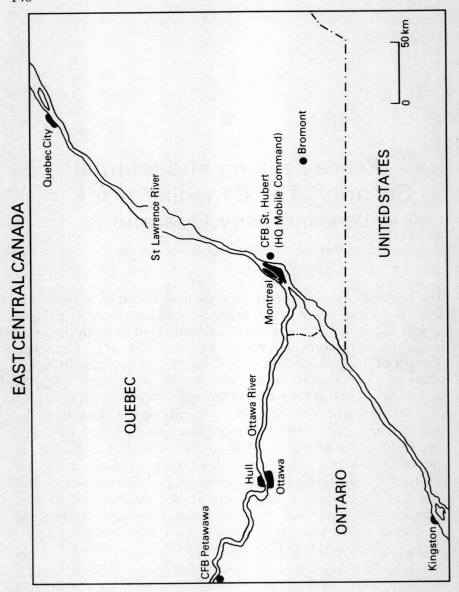

EAST CENTRAL CANADA

QUEBEC

ONTARIO

UNITED STATES

Quebec City

St Lawrence River

CFB St. Hubert
(HQ Mobile Command)

Bromont

Montreal

Ottawa River

Hull

Ottawa

CFB Petawawa

Kingston

50 km

0

demands made upon it in terms of adaptation and innovation. Finally, the study will attempt to assess the Army's ability to adapt to these roles and missions.

The Canadian Army Since 1945

The Canadian Army after 1945 was shaped by changing perceptions of Canada's security requirements and by defence policies which reflected—sometimes none too clearly—those changing perceptions. Objective and subjective conditions exerted their influence. The former included geography—the size of the country, its proximity to the United States and its distance from the world's trouble spots. Canada also had a small population and a relatively small industrial base. These two factors limited Canada's ability to maintain modern, expensive military forces.[1] The subjective factors were two: first, the decision taken after the war to pursue Canadian national security interests solely within the framework of collective security arrangements, and only with volunteer armed forces; and second, Canada's role in the Cold War, represented by Canada's membership in NATO and by close co-operation with the United States in continental air defence.[2] The Cold War exerted a unique impact on Canadian defence planning. Canada was to be defended on two fronts: in Canada and in Europe. This was later extended—temporarily—to Asia, during Canada's participation in the Korean War. Peace-keeping, which grew more out of Canada's option for collective security than out of the Cold War, developed from the 1950s into the 1960s as a major element of defence policy. It complicated defence planning and, in concert with other roles, stretched the Canadian Army's resources almost to breaking point.

All three services were reduced substantially following the end of the Second World War. In 1946 the government decided that Canada would return to its now traditional reliance on a small, all-volunteer professional force, supported by a large mobilisation base. The government envisaged an Army Active Force of 25,000, and a voluntary reserve of 180,000 which would provide two corps upon mobilisation. The operational element of the Army's Active Force was to be an airborne and air-transported brigade group known as the Mobile Striking Force. It was intended solely for the defence of Canada, especially in the North, where the perceived threat was from Soviet airborne landings, either as a diversionary attack, or as a prelude to further attacks on the continental United States.[3]

˙ That all changed in 1950, when two brigades were raised for service overseas–one for Korea under UN auspices, and the other for Europe, as part of Canada's contribution to NATO. The impact of Korea and NATO had two aspects: considerable expansion in size, and a substantial change in role. Regular Army strength reached nearly 50,000 in the early 1950s.[4] Both Korea and NATO demanded conventional all-arms formations—infantry, armour and artillery. Once the Korean War ended, the Army was earmarked almost entirely for NATO. In 1956, the UN Emergency Force commitment drew off nearly 1,000 men, and in 1964, Canada deployed a battalion group to Cyprus to participate in the UN peace-keeping mission there.

This piecemeal approach to defence policy and mission planning dictated that Canada's military commitments were acquired bit by bit, in an untidy manner that did not provide an overall focus.[5] Form followed function, and the diverse commitments produced unbalanced, divided armed forces whose roles were not mutually supportive.[6] These problems allowed for a number of possible solutions. The 1963 defence review and the integration-unification process which ensued, were supposed to provide that solution. Paul Hellyer, the new Minister of National Defence, decided that the remedy was reorganisation into a single, unified service. And although lip-service was paid to the need for flexibility and efficiency, the bottom line was cost. By Fiscal Year 1961–62 defence consumed 25 percent of the federal budget.[7] In his 1966 address to Parliament, Mr. Hellyer presented the problem—and the solution—in stark terms; if Canada was to continue to maintain its commitments it would either have to greatly increase defence spending or reorganise. The government, he said, had opted for reorganisation. Moreover, the forces were to be reduced in strength in anticipation that manpower savings could be traded off against increased equipment purchases.[8] Jon McLin suggested that this reorganisation represented an attempt to gain in 'distinctiveness' what was lost in relative strength.[9] If so, it was a significant price to pay for a dubious distinction. For the reorganisation-unification process opened the door to a decade of reductions in the defence budget and the real strength of the armed forces, and to a longer period of tinkering with defence policy, commitments, force structures and equipment. Yet the fundamental anomalies that had provoked the original defence review remained unresolved.[10]

The subsequent defence review, undertaken between 1969 and

1971, could be regarded as an attempt *ex post facto* to impose an independent Canadian strategic policy framework on decisions already taken and implemented for reasons of cost. It foundered between the conflicting positions of political realism and military function. Although it was possible to make a military case, however thin, for terminating Canada's participation in NATO and concentrating all Canadian forces at home, such a complete withdrawal was not possible politically. So the government resorted to half-measures, which neither rationalised Canada's commitments and resources, nor satisfied either critics or supporters of Canadian participation in NATO.[11] Moreover, in Canada it proved difficult to translate the priorities of 'sovereignty protection' and 'national development' into meaningful military roles and missions. Indeed, within the context and milieu of the 1971 Defence White Paper there appeared to be little justification for maintaining armed forces at all[12] but for the political reality which suggested that none of the existing military tasks could be forsworn in their entirety. It is hardly surprising, then, that the government felt it could safely freeze defence spending for three years.

In 1973, as a result of the severe problems resulting from the review and the spending freeze, the Department of National Defence (DND) instituted a modernisation and renewal programme. The total defence budget was to be increased by seven percent per annum for the next five years, the bulk of which was to be set aside for new equipment. However, the energy crisis and double digit inflation quickly rendered it a historical curiosity, producing a financial crisis at the DND.[13] The Department struggled to stay within the budget, slashing manpower, operations and training activities and deferring scheduled equipment purchases. This led to serious questions of military viability by 1974.

In November 1974 Defence Minister James Richardson undertook yet another review (the Defence Structure Review) to assess the tasks of the Canadian Armed Forces, the levels of effort at which those tasks should be performed and the organisation and resources required. The major findings were not disclosed in a new White Paper, but rather in a brief statement to the House of Commons on 27 November 1975. He reaffirmed not only the four basic 1969 defence priorities, but the existing manpower levels and the existing tasks and commitments of the Armed Forces.[14]

The net result of this for the Army was a degree of organisational and doctrinal confusion. In 1965 the Army became Mobile Command, a force which combined all Army field units in Canada (but not those in Europe) with some integral tactical air elements. The Command's mission was 'to maintain combat-ready land and tactical air forces capable of rapid deployment in circumstances ranging from service in the European theatre to United Nations and other peace-keeping operations'.[15] Mobile Command was to have three brigades: one for rotation to Europe, and two to be 'airportable'. An airborne regiment was also being formed.[16]

But Mobile Command became neither fish nor fowl. It did not rationalise Canadian defence commitments, which had been extended in 1964 to include peace-keeping in Cyprus and participation in the NATO Mobile Force, a multinational formation designated to deploy and fight on the European flanks.[17] Colin Gray later commented critically on the contradictory nature of the mobility requirements for Canada's diverse commitments:

> . . . the mobility and the flexibility that were the keynotes of Paul Hellyer's rhetoric in 1964 were belied by a series of procurement actions that seemed directed to the end of maintaining . . . a heavy brigade group . . . the acquisition of 1,000 M113A1 armoured personnel carriers provided cross-country (and amphibious) mobility, but no immediate possibility of air-portability.[18]

Nor could Canada's strategic mobility resources support the nation's commitments. Strategic airlift—23 C-130 Hercules and a handful of Yukon airliners—was insufficient, and government delay foreclosed the opportunity to purchase the C-141, a jet transport which combined strategic range (important for Canada), vehicle-carrying and paradrop capabilities. The two operational support ships built for the navy in the 1960s were designed to carry and disembark troops and equipment, but their primary mission was fleet replenishment. Moreover, a substantial sealift capacity was lost when the aircraft carrier *Bonaventure* was scrapped at the end of the 1960s.[19] Finally, the Canadian Airborne Regiment was formed without a clear mission requirement. It founded a role—'showing the flag' in the north—virtually by default.[20]

Simultaneously, the process of reducing the size of the armed forces was set in train. In 1968 Mobile Command's three brigades were converted into four smaller combat groups.[21] This was supposed to make them more readily air-transportable; in fact, all it did was make them weaker, less viable formations. The following year the axe fell again. In September 1969 the government announced that it would reduce the strength of the armed forces by 16,000 over the next three years to reach a strength of 82,000 by 1972. These reductions were to hit Mobile Command very hard. One combat group would be disbanded and five regiments were to be dropped from or replaced in the regular force order of battle. The brigade in Europe was also to be cut by half.[22] But the cuts did not end there. As noted earlier, by 1973 it was apparent that the defence budget could not keep pace with inflation and further reductions were required. By mid-1976, the strength of the armed forces had dipped to 77,900.[23] Later that year further reorganisation was announced. The airborne regiment, up to that time an independent formation, was to be moved from Edmonton, Alberta to Petawawa, Ontario, where, integrated with the existing 2nd Combat Group, it would form the core of the 'Special Service Force'.[24] The move took place in 1977.

In the second half of the 1970s the realisation dawned on the government that the armed forces had reached the point where reductions endangered effectiveness. In 1977 the government approved an increase in the authorised peacetime force level to 83,661, and in 1978–79 DND was permitted to increase personnel by 400 annually. At that rate, the authorised strength would be reached by 1989–90.[25] Yet, it quickly became clear that even this was insufficient. The 1980 Task Force on Unification of the Canadian Forces expressed the view that the Army's field formations would require 5–6,000 personnel for operations, but were manned at only a 3,500 level.[26] The Senate Subcommittee on National Defence revised that estimate downward in its 1982 report but only slightly: it identified an immediate requirement for 2,500 troops for Mobile Command, and a longer-term need for 6,400.[27]

In its report the following year the same subcommittee criticised DND for producing an 'undifferentiated list' of tasks for the armed forces, which set no order of priority and for which, in any case, there might be no resources to assign.[28] This lack of clarity was due to the confusion noted earlier about the application of military means to non-military tasks, and about Canada's participation in the military aspects of its alliance arrangements—NATO, in particular. For while Canadian defence ministers continued to insist that the 1969 priorities formed the basis of defence policies, international realities were forcing them to reassess the relative importance of those priorities. Most important for the Army was the fact that in the mid-1970s the government began to rethink its NATO commitment.[29] Once again, the Army was permitted to orient its thinking, organisation, training and equipment towards high-intensity warfare in the European theatre. Starting in 1974, a Combat Development Committee within DND began work on development of a 'Corps Concept' for the Army based on the requirement to be able to fight in a high-intensity combat environment.[30] The creation of a 'total force'—integrated regular and militia forces in divisional and higher formations, supported by mobilisation capability—was discussed informally at first, but as the corps concept took shape the government committed itself formally to a 'Total Force' programme.[31] In 1979 DND established a Mobilisation Planning Task Force; their work proceeded more slowly than anticipated and a draft plan was supposed to be ready by 1985.[32]

All this notwithstanding, the Army remained through the 1970s oriented to light or low-intensity missions, while being partly organised and equipped for the opposite end of the spectrum. The airborne regiment was a genuine light unit, while the brigade (or combat group) in Europe was a heavy or high-intensity formation once it was equipped with Leopard tanks. The other combat groups in Canada fell between these two stools. Operational experience, moreover, tended to blur the lines between low- and high-intensity mission profiles. The largest operational commitments—internal security operations in 1970 and in connection with the 1976 Olympics were clearly in the low-intensity spectrum. This, normally, would have been the case for peace-keeping operations as well, but in Vietnam and in Cyprus in 1974 Canadian peace-keepers found themselves in the midst of conventional or near-conventional wars. In Cyprus specifically, the peace-keeping forces were compelled by circumstances to 'stretch' the interpretation of their mandate to 'peace restoring', which involved the peace-keepers in combat themselves.[33] The Canadian commitment to the Allied Command Europe (ACE) Mobile Force on NATO's northern flank postulated, moreover, the deployment of an airportable battalion group followed by an air- and sea-transported combat group.[34] Of necessity, this would place relatively 'light' units (pre-positioned equipment notwithstanding) in a high-intensity combat environment. Combat arms training, furthermore, tended to concentrate on operations at battalion group or 'combat team' (company group) level. Although officers studied operations of higher formations at staff college, Exercise RV81 was the first exercise in 16 years to test troops in the field in operations above brigade level. Formation training thus institutionalised the anomalies of the Army's operational outlook.

D. G. Loomis has suggested that the reorganisation of the Canadian Forces in the 1960s was a masterful stroke, Machiavellian in its foresight and conception with respect to preparing the Army to respond to low-intensity conflict, particularly terrorism in Quebec.[35] He may be correct but from this vantage point the picture appears much less tidy. Defence policy, roles and missions, organisation, equipment procurement and operational experience were almost always out of phase with each other from 1964 onwards, certainly in so far as the Army was concerned. Even if the reorganisation had advanced from a sound conceptual base—a matter of considerable debate—subsequent force reductions, policy adjustments and commitments robbed reorganisation of any viability. However perfectly executed were the internal security operations noted above, the fact is they stripped the country bare of troops.[36] For the duration, the Canadian Army was deprived of the flexibility that was supposed to be the hallmark of Mobile Command.

In 1984, the Progressive Conservative Party came to power with a promise to 'rebuild' the Armed Forces. For a variety of reasons, it was slow to act on that promise. Two Ministers of National Defence came and went before the third delivered the long-awaited White Paper in June 1987. One of the central features of that policy document was its stated intention to resolve the 'commitment-capability gap' by rationalising Canada's NATO commitment, by making significant equipment procurements and by increasing military manpower; the establishments for the regular force and the reserves were set at 90,000 each. For the Army this will mean a continuation of the post-1950 practice of maintaining two 'armies': a European army, in the form of a divisional-size commitment to the NATO Central Front in West Germany (half of it based in Canada in a 'fly-over' posture) and a Canadian army, consisting of an integrated mix of regular and militia forces, to be used for sovereignty protection and 'defence of Canada' operations.[37] Although these proposals have generated a favourable response from many informed observers, and a start has been made on some of these programmes, there is also some scepticism as to whether the White Paper's promises will ever be carried to fruition. At this stage, it simply is too early to assess the impact of this change of policy.

Operational Experience and Adaptation

Peace-keeping duties and internal security tasks have comprised the sum total of the army's military operational experience since the end of the Korean War. In short, the Army has been engaged in low-intensity operations for the past 30 years. Several of these operations will be described and analysed.

To deal first with peace-keeping: the Army first became involved through the United Nations as a member of the Observer Group in India and Pakistan in 1949.[38] Many such operations involved only tiny detachments of personnel; this study will focus on the three largest operations exclusive of Korea: the United Nations Emergency Force (UNEF) in the Middle East; the Congo; and Cyprus. In November 1956 Canada took the lead in proposing and organising the deployment of an international peace-keeping force to the Middle East to supervise and enforce a ceasefire arising out of the Arab-Israeli war and Anglo-French intervention. A number of countries offered troops for the peace-keeping force, Canada among them. Most of the proposed contributions were of infantry, and it quickly became apparent that there was a vital requirement for a contribution of a technical support infrastructure. Because of the Canadian army's administrative capabilities and the fact that the proposed Canadian infantry contribution—the Queen's Own Rifles—was unacceptable in the face of Egyptian sensitivities, Canada provided the technical support for UNEF. The initial commitment of 300 service troops was increased in December 1956 to include: a signals squadron; an infantry workshop (RCEME); two transport platoons; and an RCAF communications squadron. In March 1957 this was supplemented further by an armoured reconnaissance squadron. From 1956–59, Canada also contributed a field hospital unit. The Army's contribution totalled 858 all ranks. In addition, a Canadian, Major General E. L. M. Burns, was the first commander of the UNEF. The tasks and duties of the Canadian contingent were essential to UNEF, if somewhat mundane. Only the reconnaissance squadron saw 'front-line' duty as a unit, patrolling the armistice line and the Egyptian-Israeli border. The rest were virtually all 'rear area' troops.[39] In mid-May 1967, the Egyptian government demanded the withdrawal of the UNEF. The Canadian contingent (at that time 795-strong) was withdrawn by air between 22 and 31 May 1967.[40]

From 1960–64, Canada contributed a bilingual signals squadron of 250 men to the UN peace-keeping force in the Congo, as well as an air detachment and a military police contingent of about a dozen men. The signallers provided communications staff at the UN forces headquarters in Leopoldville, and at up to seven outstations throughout the Congo. This maintained the communications link between force headquarters, military sector headquarters and the larger contingents.[41]

In March 1964 Canada deployed an infantry battalion group (including a reconnaissance squadron) to Cyprus to take part in what has since become Canada's longest-running peace-keeping operation. From April 1964 to September 1965 Canada also provided a brigade headquarters for the UN force. The mandate of the UN force was to prevent a recurrence of the Greek-Turkish Cypriot communal fighting that had precipitated the crisis and 'to contribute to the maintenance and restoration of law and order and a return to normal conditions'.[42] The Canadian contingent, with a strength of 1,087 (later increased to 1,149), initially comprised about one-sixth of the entire force, and was assigned to the Nicosia sector. The Canadian troops rotated to and from Canada on a six-month tour. From mid-1965, the size of the Canadian contingent was reduced slightly and the battalion group was redeployed to the Kyrenia district, where it remained until the end of 1969. Lessening tension on the island in 1968 allowed the UN force to reduce its strength by about 25 percent. The reconnaissance squadron returned to Canada at this time, leaving a total Canadian contingent of less than 600. Further reductions were made in 1973, at which time the Canadian contribution shrank to a battalion of 450, plus a small contribution to the UN force headquarters. During 1965–74, Canadian peace-keeping troops, at various times, patrolled the 'Green Line' separating the Greek and Turkish sectors of Nicosia and ran a convoy system on the Nicosia-Kyrenia highway.[43]

The situation in Cyprus changed radically in the summer of 1974. In July President Makarios was overthrown in a coup by Greek Cypriots, supported by the *Junta* in Athens. This was followed five days later by an invasion by Turkish regular forces. The Canadian contingent consisted at that time of about half of the Canadian Airborne Regiment. After some initial hesitation, this force was reinforced by deployment of the balance of the regiment bringing the contingent to a total of 859. The mandate of the UN force was altered by the facts of the situation, although in legal terms it had not changed. The Canadian contingent found itself involved in 'peace-restoring operations'; the most controversial of these was the seizure of Nicosia airport by UN forces in an effort to deny the contentious objective to belligerents. Canadian troops took part in this operation in conjunction with British elements of the UN force. As the crisis faded, the Canadian contingent was reduced in 1975 to its pre-crisis level, where it remained to the end of the decade. In 1975 Canada took over joint responsibility for the UNFICYP medical centre, and the following year was assigned to the Nicosia airport sector.[44]

In the field of internal security, the Canadian Army's history is much longer than that of peace-keeping. In the first 50 years after Confederation, troops were called out frequently to aid the civil power in the absence of standing police forces. They were also called upon to break strikes and intimidate strikers during that period and during the Depression. From 1940–80 the armed forces were involved in 15 operations on 20 occasions.[45] Three of these comprised responses to acts or threats of terrorism; the two that involved deployments of substantial forces will be discussed below.

The October Crisis

On October 5, 1970 in Montreal, the *Front de Libération du Québec* (FLQ), an underground radical movement committed to the creation of an independent Quebec 'state', kidnapped British trade commissioner James Cross. In exchange for Cross's life they demanded the release of jailed FLQ members, a large ransom, publication of their manifesto, and a flight to safe haven out of Canada. When the Canadian government stalled on most of their demands (except publication of the manifesto) a second FLQ cell abducted Pierre Laporte, Minister of Labour in the Quebec provincial government. Troops were deployed in Ottawa and Quebec and on October 16th, the federal government proclaimed the War Measures Act. Under the Act's sweeping powers police arrested more than 500 people, most of whom were later released since they were not involved with the FLQ. On October 17th, the FLQ murdered Laporte. Thereafter, the crisis gradually dissipated. Cross was located and freed in December, and his captors sent into exile. Laporte's murderers were apprehended later that month.[46]

Observers from as diverse perspectives as Pierre Vallières, (the Quebec separatist and ideological godfather of the *Front de Libération du Québec*—FLQ) and Major General D. G. Loomis have suggested that the reorganisation of the Armed Forces was specifically designed to deal with the contingency of putting down insurrections in Quebec.[47] The weight of evidence suggests however that reorganisation was undertaken without a clear idea of the ultimate objective of the process. That the military operation in October 1970 proceeded smoothly might be attributed more accurately to professionalism and training than to perceptive foresight. Moreover, the visible confusion amongst the Canadian political leadership over the management of the crisis[48] suggests that there was considerably less premeditation than Vallières and Loomis would have us believe.

Officially, the Army was called to assist the police forces, who were apparently stretched to the limit by the intensive investigative duties arising from the kidnappings.[49] The activities of October 1970 actually involved two distinct operations. On 12 October, two days after the second kidnapping, Operation GINGER commenced. This involved troops providing 'armed assistance' to the Royal Canadian Mounted Police (RCMP), another federal institution; it was not aid to the civil power. Between 500 and 1,000 troops from the 2nd Combat Group, normally based at Petawawa (about 100 miles west of Ottawa) relieved RCMP guards on VIPs, government buildings and other vital points in the Ottawa area. They also assisted the police in sweeps and searches. The operation lasted until 21 November.[50]

The operation in Quebec, code named ESSAY, was larger and more complex. An aid to the civil power operation, it commenced on 15 October and lasted until 4 January 1971. It involved some 5,000–6,000 troops of the 5th Combat Group, the Canadian Airborne Regiment, elements of the 2nd Combat Group and supporting arms and services. The forces had been placed on alert from the outset of the crisis and when the request for aid came (at 1245 15 October), the response was rapid: the first troops landed at Montreal by helicopter at 1405. The entire 5th Combat Group and the paratroops (flown in from Edmonton, Alberta) were deployed across the province by 2250. The build-up of the remainder of the forces in the province took several days.[51]

As the troops were being summoned, the Quebec provincial cabinet passed an Order-in-Council placing all police and military forces under the command of the director of the Quebec Provincial Police. Therefore, all armed forces operations were undertaken at the request and under the direction of the civil authorities. The chain of command went from the Police Director, to the Commander, Mobile Command (the Army), to the Commander, 5th Combat Group, which was the conducting formation. Units and troops thus received their orders through the normal military chain of command. To facilitate co-operation, the Army established a joint operational headquarters at the offices of the Quebec Provincial Police. On 16 October the federal government proclaimed the War Measures Act, giving soldiers and police sweeping powers of arrest, search and seizure without warrants and detention without trial.[52]

In fact, the armed forces carried out no arrests on their own; that task was left to the police. Most of the troops were deployed on static guard duties in Montreal, Quebec City and at other locations across the province. When required to assist the police in sweeps and raids, the Airborne Regiment provided helicopter- or vehicle-borne tactical teams which mounted the cordons around the search sites. They did not participate, however, in house-to-house searches. Deployment and subsequent operations entailed, as well, extensive air-lift and other air activities, including reconnaissance flights by CF-5 jet fighters. During the entire period of active duty, the forces fired only 10 shots, all warnings; there were no casualties from any of the incidents.[53]

The October Crisis was a watershed in Canadian history, although more for its political rather than its military consequences. Indeed, its military aspects have not been studied, at least outside the Canadian military establishment. Nonetheless, it seems fair to suggest that it probably attuned the Canadian military to their Internal Security (IS) responsibilities in a way that no previous operation had done. If so, then it was valuable preparation for the next major IS operation, the 1976 Olympics. It should be borne in mind, however, that at no time during the October Crisis did the armed forces come under attack by terrorists or rioters. The situation could not be considered comparable to that in, for example, Northern Ireland.

The Montreal Olympics

The Canadian Forces were involved in security planning for the Olympics from the earliest stages. In February 1972 National Defence Headquarters established an Olympics project office under the direction of a lieutenant colonel. Later that year he and his assistants attended the Munich Olympics,[54] where they received an object lesson in the consequences of inadequate security planning. The office of the Solicitor-General of Canada was the 'lead ministry' responsible for developing the National Security Plan for the Olympics and DND worked in close co-operation with it in preparing the plan. DND was to provide 'armed assistance' to the Office of the Solicitor-General.[55]

In May 1973 the Principal Committee of Public Safety for the Olympic Games (known by its French abbreviation CPSPJO) was formed, consisting of a police chairman, two representatives from the Canadian armed forces, and representatives from the four police forces immediately and directly involved in security operations for the Olympics—the RCMP, the Quebec and Ontario provincial police forces and the Montreal Urban Community Police. Its executive committee was responsible for developing, co-ordinating and executing the security operation plan, and reported to two higher committees, one comprising senior officers, and the other political ministers—municipal, provincial and federal.[56] Again, as in all Canadian internal security operations, the civil authorities retained ultimate authority.

The Olympic Games involved 24 competition, 59 training and three accommodation sites in two provinces, although concentrated in and around Montreal, Bromont (about 50 miles southeast of Montreal) and Kingston, Ontario (175 miles west). Some 12,000 athletes would have to be protected and surveillance and security provided for the hundreds of thousands of spectators, including large numbers of VIPs. The security task was formidable, involving site security at the above locations, escort of athletes in transit, VIP protection, security at points of entry and along the Canada-US border, and security of vulnerable points in and around Montreal and at other points in Quebec and Ontario. Original plans had envisaged the use of only 2,000 troops, but as the scope of the task emerged, it became clear that a much larger force would be needed.[57]

In September 1974 Major General Roland Reid was appointed chief of DND Olympic Coordination for Operation GAMESCAN, as the military operation came to be known. Mobile Command was designated to provide the major formed units for the security role at all Olympic locations. There they would work in close co-operation with the police forces and would have the powers of peace officers in order to enforce the law. Security afloat at Montreal and Kingston was assigned to Maritime Command while Air Command provided aerial security and air-lift. DND also provided personnel and matériel support for non-security operations. In all, DND provided 15,763 personnel, 9,085 of whom were deployed on security or security-related tasks.[58]

These functions were shared mainly between four Task Forces. Task Force 1, based on the 5th Combat Group and augmented by an infantry battalion and an airborne Commando (company), was responsible for: perimeter security at the Montreal Olympic Village and the Olympic Park; security of athletes in transit (which included searching the vehicles beforehand, route security and armed escort of the vehicles); security at various decentralised competition and training sites; protection of vulnerable points across the province of Quebec; and security patrols along the Quebec-US border. Some 4,000 troops were required to carry out these operations. Task Force 2, drawn from elements of the 2nd Combat Group and totalling about 1,900 troops, provided security at Montreal's two international airports, protection of VIPs and their baggage at hotels and in transit, and security at several training and competition sites in the Montreal area. Task Force 3 was made up of the airborne regiment (minus the Commando in TF1). They were to provide a commander's reserve for rapid response to incidents anywhere within the security forces' areas of responsibility. Task Force 4, consisting of 800 troops from 2 Combat Group, protected the Olympic Village itself, vulnerable points and VIPs at the Kingston, Ontario site. They also provided border security forces, vulnerable point protection in Toronto, and a standby force in Ottawa. Separate from the other task forces, one infantry battalion was assigned to protect Canadian Forces' installations in Montreal, to augment security along the New Brunswick-Maine border, and to provide additional security forces during the Royal Visit. Helicopter and jet fighter aircraft from Air Command provided airspace security over Olympic sites, route surveillance within the security corridor, and road convoy escort. At Montreal and Kingston, ships and helicopters of Maritime Command provided security and rescue forces for nautical events. To handle any terrorist incidents the various police forces provided between them about a dozen tactical assault teams, as well as trained negotiators and explosive ordnance disposal personnel. Nonetheless, the Armed Forces maintained a company-size assault force at the Olympic Park, in case a substantial assault capability should be required.[59]

Mobile Command exercised operational control of all land and air elements of the armed forces, but any action by the troops requiring the use of lethal force would have to be requested by the civil authorities, *i.e.* the police forces. Security intelligence was the responsibility of the RCMP Security Service. They conducted threat assessments over a long period prior to the Olympics, ran a Joint Intelligence Centre prior to and during the Olympiad, and conducted technical surveillance operations during the games. The intelligence cell at Mobile Command headquarters liaised with RCMP on operational intelligence.[60] Communications, on the other hand, were almost totally in military hands. The Armed Forces set up and operated the Olympic radio system and message centre and provided telecommunications support at a number of competition sites. In addition, Canadian Forces Communications Command, with the assistance of the Signals Regiment, communications squadrons, and signals personnel at headquarters, formation and unit level provided secure communications for the security forces.[61]

Contingency-planning was a joint government-police-military affair. The Olympic Games Public Safety Committee developed the basic security plan with input from all levels. Specific plans were developed for handling terrorist incidents (especially hostage-type actions) by means of negotiation, deception and assault. The basic plan and its sub-components were tested in a major command post exercise in April 1976—devised and directed by the Police and Security Branch of the federal Solicitor-General's Department. Modifications were made after the exercise and the plan was adjusted as necessary throughout the operation.[62]

There were no terrorist incidents associated with the Olympics, leading to the obvious lesson that an effective deterrent is better than a response after the fact. But to ensure that the deterrent was effective, it had to be massive: a total of 16,000 security force personnel were involved. The operation strained the resources of the Canadian forces to the limit and regular force units had to be augmented with 1,300 reserve personnel. Furthermore, the total security operation was expensive—approximately $100 million.[63]

Adaptation

There are two aspects of peace-keeping operations that render them distinct from most other military operations. The first is their non-combat 'constabulary' nature. The operational tasks consist largely of patrolling—on foot or in vehicles, the manning of observation posts (OPs), intelligence collection, and most important, mediation in localised disputes to prevent them from escalating into major incidents or crises. Although UN peace-keeping forces were usually equipped with personal arms and light crew-served weapons, it was UN practice that these be used only for self-defence, not for offensive action or retaliation. The concept of 'minimum force' was the operative principle.[64] This entailed a requirement not only for highly-disciplined troops who would not succumb to provocation or take the law into their own hands, but also for relatively junior commanders with an appreciation of the delicacy of the situation, the quick-wittedness to take the initiative in developing innovative ways of applying the slim peace-keeping resources to best advantage in any situation, and a flair for diplomacy and, if possible, foreign languages.

The second aspect of peace-keeping concerns its multinational character. UN peace-keeping forces have all been multinational enterprises; although individual national components normally functioned as distinct, autonomous units, they might share an operational area with one or more other national units. Moreover, the headquarters and service/support structure was invariably mixed. This has created problems of integrating administrative and staff procedures.[65] Clearly, this points to a requirement for officers and soldiers with experience in other multinational headquarters (such as NATO), with abilities to 'give and take' where compromise is required, and to improvise and adapt where standard procedures do not exist.

The character of peace-keeping operations might be summed up in one phase: *ad hocracy*; and it is clear that the Canadians do not feel comfortable with this approach.[66] The problem, as Canadians see it, is that, the *ad hoc* approach has pervaded every aspect of these operations, rendering an already difficult job even harder. The problems have included: faulty direction; absence of contingency planning; lack of training and experience amongst contributing contingents; hasty organisation, and difficult co-ordination. UN headquarters does not have an efficient peace-keeping staff to plan and co-ordinate operations. This has been particularly apparent in the administrative and logistic aspects of these operations. As late as 1978, when the 'Interim Force' (UNIFIL) was deployed into Lebanon, the UN still did not have a logistics contingency plan. In 1964, it was only the presence of well-stocked British depots in the Sovereign Base Areas that prevented the collapse of UNFICYP. Apparently, nothing was learned in the intervening 14 years. The joint Canadian-Polish logistics component of UNEF2 found that, despite assurances from New York, on arrival there were critical shortages of key supplies. Canadians had to air-lift several hundred tons of matériel to Egypt just to make the logistics contingent self-sufficient, in addition to being able to fulfil its logistic task for the peace-keeping force. On occasion, lack of matériel jeopardised or led to suspension of operations. On others, large quantities of matériel were destroyed in transit, or the UN purchased substandard goods from unscrupulous entrepreneurs. UNEF1 took two years to get its logistics up to standard; this was never achieved during the six years of UNEF2, nor in the Congo. The same could be said for the Lebanon operation. Generally, the UN peace-keeping force infrastructures suffered from a lack of standardisation or inter-operability in equipment, communications, administrative and tactical procedures.[67]

How, then, have Canadian troops adapted to this unorthodox operational environment? By most accounts, they have managed rather well. In 1958, Canada designated a specific infantry battalion (on a three-year rotational basis) to be the 'stand-by' force for UN peace-keeping operations. It was felt that the availability of several such units from a variety of countries would help to prevent crises from escalating to limited wars or further. These forces were to be organised for transportation by air and designed to satisfy the special needs of peace-keeping. The Canadian 'stand-by' battalion received two to six months specialised training for peace-keeping, and was exercised annually in co-operation with the Royal Canadian Air Force (RCAF) to check its state of readiness and its operational procedures for dispatch by air to overseas destinations. In the event, only in the case of Cyprus did Canada provide an infantry battalion to a peace-keeping operation; the specific battalion designated for such activity was called upon. In fact, the requirements for peace-keeping forces varied so widely that, beyond maintaining well-balanced, versatile forces, little advanced planning could be done effectively. This, and the limited resources of the Canadian Army, meant that the intention to designate, train and equip units specifically for peace-keeping was never a realistic option for Canada. More often, Canada was asked to provide technicians and specialists in the fields of signals, logistics and engineering—trades in which many other contributing nations might be weak. Consequently, the idea of a Canadian 'stand-by' force had to be broadened to consist of a contingency force brigade, from which required units or specialists could be drawn. The 1964 White Paper explicitly rejected exclusive designation of units for UN peace-keeping.[68]

By the 1970s, the Canadian government had worked out standard operating procedures for organising, mounting and deploying peace-keeping forces. According to General Beattie, within DND, the Director-General Military Plans and Operations would work closely with the Associate Deputy Minister (Policy) Group and the Defence Relations Office of External Affairs. This would ensure the drafting of plans and operations consistent with defence and foreign policy. Close contact would also be maintained with the military adviser to the Canadian Mission at UN Headquarters. As a situation developed that might require Canadian participation, DND and External Affairs would form a joint task force to monitor the situation and to provide agreed assessments and recommendations to the government. Given a clear idea of the type and scope of a proposed operation, DND could then develop a 'Canadian Contingent Model', and preliminary instructions for troop deployment—detailed check lists for staff action designed to ensure a smooth approach to mounting the operation. At command level, co-ordination cells or planning groups would be established.[69] At the earliest possible stage, National Defence Headquarters (NDHQ) would place elements of the stand-by force on notice to move, with preparations to commence at a specific date and time. The contingent commander, advance party and overseas airfield staffs are supposed to be able to move 48 hours after the date and time given in the warning order; the stand-by force and sub-unit advance parties are given 96 hours notice; and the main body, seven days. These times represent a mean or ideal, and have been shortened or lengthened according to the needs of the given situation. The issuing of the warning order also sets in train deployment procedures for air-lift and if necessary, sea-lift. Once the Canadian government has made the final decision to 'commit', the contingent commander and a recce party proceed to the theatre of operations to review the situation. Based on his assessment, the contingent commander will advise NDHQ as to the suitability of the force to the task. Thereafter, the appropriate operations order is issued and the force is deployed in a manner to arrive 'in theatre' by air in a 'tactical' configuration, that is, loaded and prepared to meet a 'worst case' situation.[70]

Peace-keeping operations did not require a significant change in tactics, so standardised training, briefing and screening procedures have been developed to fit into the broader army training programme. General Beattie has commented:

> In general, we have found that by training personnel for the 'worst case situation' of operations in defence of Canada or NATO environments, we can easily modify that training to adapt personnel to the peacekeeping environment . . . such special training emphasizes the constabulary approach, the exercise of restraint, use of minimum force as necessary, and the importance of self-discipline, tact, impartiality and negotiating skills in the resolution of conflict situations. In the case of formed units or formations, field exercises are conducted to practise personnel in procedures for preparation, mounting, movement, and tactical deployment of field elements in the theatre of operations.[71]

Canadian practice has been to expose all Army headquarters, formations and units to at least a degree of training in peace-keeping or security operations. This allows any unit to be made ready at short notice for peace-keeping duty. Normally, this training would amount to two weeks each year, except in the designated stand-by force which, as noted earlier, would receive two to six months specialised training. In addition, the unit would be exposed to refresher courses on subjects of particular value. Selected unit members are designated for refresher training in air movements. The units and soldiers themselves are trained in the following skills:[72]

1. crowd control and dispersal;
2. use of batons and shields;
3. protection of VIPs, convoys, buildings;
4. establishing military control of an area under UN authority;
5. road blocks;
6. cordon and search, and area search;
7. urban patrols;
8. mounting of guards and pickets.

In addition, refresher training for stand-by units might include sub-unit (platoon and section) tactics, unarmed combat, communications, military engineering, map-reading, first aid, hygiene and sanitation, security of stores and equipment, and environmental indoctrination. These troops would also take part in unit, sub-unit exercises, as well as a full-scale deployment and operations exercise, at least annually.[73]

It scarcely needs to be said that the kind of training for peace-keeping described above was also completely appropriate for internal security operations, or even for counter-insurgency as it was envisaged at that time. For example, the training exercises undertaken by the Canadian Guards in the mid-1960s blurred the distinction between training for peace-keeping, for internal security, or for counter-insurgency and anti-terrorist operations.[74] The government, to its credit, showed unusual candour when questioned in parliament as to whether such exercises were a possible prelude to sending Canadian troops to intervene as counter-insurgency forces abroad like, for instance, the US in the Dominican Republic. Defence Minister Leo Cadieux emphasised that Canadian troops had to be trained to deal with all types of civil unrest in Canada and that this type of training was also necessary for Canadian soldiers serving on peace-keeping missions, such as Cyprus or the Congo.[75] It was just as well that the Army had this training and the peace-keeping experience behind it in 1970, because under normal circumstances it would not have been prepared for the types of operations it carried out during the October Crisis. As Brian Cuthbertson points out, aid to the civil power in Canada had 'always been predicated on using troops to deal with riots and disturbances',[76] but in the October Crisis, there were no riots. Instead the soldiers were used to guard buildings and VIPs, to patrol, to carry out searches for arms, explosives and suspected FLQ supporters, and to provide formed bodies to threaten or use force if needed. The threat was entirely different from that anticipated in legislation covering aid to the civil power.[77]

1RCR was the unit perhaps best prepared for operations in October 1970, as it was deployed on rotation from Cyprus straight into the crisis. Sub-units were deployed to the Ottawa-Hull-Western Quebec region within days of arrival in Canada. One company protected VIPs in Ottawa; another, the hydro-electric grid serving the capital; the remainder carried out 'show the flag' patrols throughout the battalion area, which covered 3,200 sq. miles. A joint headquarters was established in Hull.[78] When not on operations troops were kept busy on training.

One field of importance, but not widely discussed, is intelligence. Because the nature of peace-keeping demands accurate information so that UN forces may anticipate and forestall incidents, the collection of intelligence by observation posts and patrols was of vital importance. The Army's Intelligence Corps was very small after 1945. It had gained limited operational experience in Korea. A decade later in Cyprus, the Canadian intelligence staff was headed by a succession of officers who were not career intelligence officers and few of whom had received any intelligence training. They relied heavily, and wisely, on the professional intelligence officers and NCOs under them.[79] The sharing of intelligence between elements of the security forces was a problem during the October Crisis;[80] a much better co-operative arrangement was established for the Olympics, if only because the relevant authorities had had time to prepare.

For the Canadian Army, then, the process of adaptation to low-intensity operations has not been radically different from the process of learning its principal roles. Once a requirement is identified and a commitment to it approved, it is largely a question of studying the task, developing procedures for it, preparing manuals, and training the units and personnel concerned. Exercises, training courses and staff college study integrate the subject into the Army's routine. This process also allows experience to be incorporated into training and preparations.

This is not to suggest that there have not been problems but these arose out of the larger Army experience in the 1970s and cannot be attributed solely to involvement in low-intensity operations. Chief among them was manpower, as noted earlier in this study. Defence policy decisions severely constrained the manpower available to the armed forces; peace-keeping commitments aggravated that situation by drawing off highly-trained officers and trades specialists from units that were already hard-pressed to maintain viable unit manning levels and skill standards.[81] In spite of Canada's declared commitment to make its UN-dedicated forces air-transportable, the Army has remained 'heavy' to a considerable extent, and there has never been sufficient Canadian air transport to deploy a peace-keeping force rapidly. The de-commissioning of the aircraft carrier *Bonaventure* also reduced considerably the strategic mobility of Canadian army units. During the Cyprus crisis in 1974 the Canadian government was slow to respond to the situation, leaving the Canadian force there in considerable jeopardy and ill-equipped to carry out its modified mission. The first Canadian reinforcements did not reach the island until 10 days after the Turkish invasion.[82]

By the latter part of the 1970s the Army had become something of a victim of its own success with respect to preparing for internal security duties. Both the October Crisis and the Olympics security operation had passed without the Army being required to use force against insurgents; either the threat did not develop to the point where military force would have been appropriate, or the deterrent effect of large troop deployments was sufficient. Moreover, given the relatively low terrorist threat to Canada and the development of police tactical units in all of the major cities, it could be argued that a significant military commitment to counter-terrorist operations was unnecessary. The specialised equipment required for IS duties is expensive and the Canadian forces had other priorities demanding considerable capital expenditure. Furthermore, training for IS took up time that ought to have been devoted to the Army's primary role: conventional war. Consequently, by the end of the 1970s, DND had reduced the time and money to be spent by the Army on IS, leaving the mission as much as possible to the police. IS training continued, but on a restricted basis; Army units were to retain capabilities for riot control, protection of vulnerable points, and carrying out certain tasks beyond police capabilities—for example, providing an armoured vehicle to assist police in flushing out a sniper.

In the first half of the 1980s Canada experienced a brief surge in international terrorist incidents. Most were bombings or shootings but there was one serious attack on an embassy which involved the taking of hostages—at the Turkish embassy in Ottawa in March 1985.[83] If the need was not already obvious, the apparent inter-service confusion which marred the handling of the siege[84] undoubtedly persuaded the government that Canada required some kind of specialised force for siege-breaking and hostage rescue. Since the special skills required already existed in the army, there was a strong case for it taking on the role. Indeed, it was argued that the Airborne Regiment, itself a unit designated and trained for special operations, was the logical choice for the mission.[85] Already overcommitted and understrength, however, DND apparently was reluctant to assign its scarce resources to yet another task. This may not have been the only consideration; legal and jurisdictional issues might also have been influential. In any case, the government assigned the role to the Royal Canadian Mounted Police in 1986. They have since created and trained a Special Emergency Response Team to carry it out.[86] It remains to be seen whether this was the correct decision. Nevertheless, for the time being it tends to reaffirm the pattern established in the late 1970s, in which the army would play 'second fiddle' to the police in the counter-terrorism role.

Conclusion

The first point to bear in mind in considering the Canadian experience is that, with the exception of the Cyprus crisis and a few isolated incidents in the Congo, Canadian troops have not really been 'tested' in the low-intensity role. They performed their peace-keeping duties largely without challenge—except in the administrative sense—and did not have to engage in combat against urban or international terrorists. It is thus very difficult to draw meaningful conclusions about the Army's ability to adapt. In general terms, the Army incorporated preparations for these roles into its normal training routine; only those units specifically designated for peace-keeping received intensive training. It managed to make its peace-keeping training 'dual-purpose' to cover the IS role as well. During major operations, when a significant proportion of the Army was committed to a particular task, training for that task continued 'on-the-job'. Difficulties encountered in maintaining skill levels and unit readiness for conventional operations had more to do with manpower shortages than with the difficulty or specialised nature of preparation for low-intensity operations. But this serves to highlight an important feature of such operations; they are manpower-intensive. The Canadian experience would tend to support the proposition that a professional army, properly trained, equipped and led, can adapt effectively from high- to low-intensity operations. However, to this should be added the proviso that commitments be matched to capabilities; a small army, such as Canada's can do only so much. An appropriate operational doctrine, no matter how fully absorbed by the army concerned, will be effective only if it can be matched by 'feet on the ground' when the army confronts a truly severe challenge from a thoroughly committed opponent.

Notes

1. Colin S. Gray, *Canada's Defence Priorities: a Question of Relevance* (Toronto: Clarke-Irwin, 1972), pp. 7, 14–16.
2. Canada, Department of National Defence, *Canada's Defence—Information on Canada's Defence Achievements and Organization* (Ottawa: King's Printer, 1947), p. 7; James Eayrs, *In Defence of Canada Volume III Peacemaking and Deterrence* (Toronto: University of Toronto Press, 1972; repr. 1977), pp. 22–24, 75–77, 84–101 *passim*, 138, 140, 149–51, 319–56 *passim*; C. P. Stacey, *Canada and the Age of Conflict: A History of Canadian External Policies Volume 2: 1921–1948 The Mackenzie King Era* (Toronto: University of Toronto Press, 1981), pp. 397, 406–408; John Hasek, *Strategic Assessment Team Occasional Paper 2/78 The Crisis in Canadian Defence* (Ottawa: Department of National Defence, 1978), pp. 1, 6–7.
3. Canada, DND, *Report* (Ottawa: King's Printer, 1946), p. 28; see also David Charters, 'Five Lost Years: the Mobile Striking Force, 1946–1951', *Canadian Defence Quarterly* vol. 7, no. 4 (Spring 1978), pp. 44–45; The wider policy context of these force structure programmes is discussed in Douglas Bland, *The Administration of Defence Policy in Canada 1947–1985* (Kingston, Ontario: Ronald P. Frye, 1987), pp. 13–17.
4. 49,278 by March 1952, an increase of 29,000 since June 1950. See Lieutenant Colonel D. J. Goodspeed, *The Armed Forces of Canada 1867–1967: a Century of Achievement* (Ottawa: Queen's Printer, 1967), p. 215.
5. Denis Stairs, 'The Military as an Instrument of Canadian Foreign Policy', in Hector J. Massey, ed., *The Canadian Military: a Profile* (Toronto: Copp Clark, 1972), pp. 86–118 *passim*; W. A. B. Douglas, 'Why Does Canada have Armed Forces?' *International Journal* vol. 30, no. 2 (Spring 1975), pp. 275–79.
6. Canada, Royal Commission on Government Organization, *Report Volume 4* (Ottawa: Queen's Printer, 1963), pp. 62–62, 66–69, 70, 88, 90.
7. *ibid.*, pp. 61–62.
8. Canada, Minister of National Defence, *White Paper on Defence* (Ottawa: DND, 1964), p. 19; The Honourable Paul Hellyer, Minister of National Defence, *Address on the Canadian Forces Reorganisation Act* (Ottawa: Queen's Printer, 1966), p. 13.
9. Jon McLin, *Canada's Changing Defence Policy 1957–1963* (Toronto: Copp

Clark, 1967), p. 7.

10. Canada, DND, *The Canadian Armed Forces Integration/Unification: A 1979 Perspective* (Ottawa: DND, 1979), pp. 15, 22; Task Force on Review of Unification of the Canadian Armed Forces, *Final Report* (Ottawa: DND, 1980), pp. 15–18, 19–24, 30–32, 57–59; see also Bland, pp. 35–85 on the command/management problems arising from the period of 'reform'; and R. B. Byers, 'Canadian Security and Defence: the Legacy and the Challenges', *Adelphi Papers* no. 214 (London: International Institute for Strategic Studies, 1986), pp. 32–33, 87 on the budgetary impact.

11. Nils Orvik, 'Choices and Directions in Canadian Defence Policy, Part I: the Present Defence Posture', *Canadian Defence Quarterly* vol. 9, no. 4 (Spring 1980), p. 9.

12. Colin Gray, pp. 43, 60, 124, 136, 158–68, 207–10, went so far as to suggest that Canada could drop virtually all of its conventional military roles without endangering its security. Rod Byers, in 'The Canadian Military and the Use of Force: End of an Era?' *International Journal* vol. 30, no. 3 (Spring 1975), pp. 284–96, did not go as far as Gray, but questioned the viability and necessity of maintaining conventional military forces for Canadian defence; Byers' 1986 study, however, suggests that he has changed his views on this issue; see pp. 9–12, 47–49, 72, 74–77.

13. Canada, DND, *Defence 1973* (Ottawa: DND, 1974), p. 16; *Defence 1974* (Ottawa: DND, 1975), p. 9.

14. Cited in full in Larry R. Stewart, ed., *Canadian Defence Policy: Selected Documents, 1964–1981* (Kingston, Ont: Queen's University Centre for International Relations, 1982), pp. 48–50.

15. Hellyer, *Address* (1966), *op. cit.* p. 19.

16. *ibid.*

17. Canada, *White Paper on Defence* (1964), p. 22.

18. Gray, *op. cit.* p. 27. The M113 was in fact airportable, but in the context of concurrent purchases (*e.g.* the M109 self-propelled howitzer) this does not detract from the thrust of Gray's argument.

19. David A. Charters, 'With the Wings of the Eagle: Canadian Air Mobile Forces, 1945–1970' (unpublished MA thesis, University of New Brunswick, 1973), pp. 197–203, 209–11; see also Gerald Porter, *In Retreat: The Canadian Forces in the Trudeau Years* (Ottawa: Deneau & Greenberg, 1979), pp. 43–46.

20. David A. Charters, *Armed Forces and Political Purpose: Airborne Forces and the Canadian Army in the 1980s* (Fredericton: Centre for Conflict Studies, University of New Brunswick, 1984), pp. 70–72.

21. Canada, House of Commons, Standing Committee on External Affairs and National Defence (hereafter SCEAND), 'Minutes of Proceedings and Evidence of the Revised Main Estimates 1968–1969 of the Department of National Defence', (Ottawa, 1968), pp. 574–75.

22. The Honourable Leo Cadieux, Minister of National Defence, 'Statement', (Ottawa, 19 September 1969), pp. 1–8.

23. International Institute for Strategic Studies, *The Military Balance 1976–1977* (London: IISS, 1976), p. 20. The IISS figures were based on strength as it was known as of July 1976.

24. SCEAND, No. 3 (1 December 1976), pp. 29–31.

25. R. B. Byers and Michael Slack, 'National Defence', in *Canadian Strategic Review 1983* (Toronto: Canadian Institute of Strategic Studies, 1984), p. 93.

26. Task Force, *Final Report* (Ottawa, 1980), p. 82.

27. Canada, Senate, Subcommittee on National Defence, *First Report: Manpower in Canada's Armed Forces* (Ottawa: Supply and Services, 1983), p. 30 and

Appendix A, pp. 101–107.
28. Senate, Subcommittee on National Defence, *Canada's Maritime Forces* (Ottawa: Supply and Services, 1983), p. 30 and Appendix A, pp. 101–107.
29. SCEAND, no. 31 (1 December 1975), p. 31 (Statement by Minister of National Defence), in Stewart, *Canadian Defence Policy*, pp. 50–51.
30. Major D. A. Gronbeck-Jones, 'The Combat Development Process in the Canadian Army', *Canadian Defence Quarterly* vol. 12, no. 2 (Autumn 1982), pp. 25, 27, 29.
31. Brigadier General D. G. Loomis, 'Reorganisation on the Basis of a Total Force Concept', *Canadian Defence Quarterly* vol. 5, no. 3 (Winter 1975–76) pp. 6–14; SCEAND, no. 4 (12 June 1980), p. 12, and *Minister's Statement: Defence Estimates 1983–84* (Ottawa, 15 March 1982), p. 20.
32. Task Force, *Final Report* (Ottawa, 1980), p. 71; Review Group on the Report of the Task Force on unification of the Canadian Forces, *Report of Findings and Recommendations* (Ottawa: DND, 31 August 1980), p. 23; SCEAND, *Minister's Statement*, p. 20; Chief of Defence Staff, 'Address to Annual General Meeting of Conference of Defence Associations' (Ottawa, 13 January 1983).
33. Henry Wiseman, 'Has New Life Been Breathed into U.N. Peace-keeping?' *Canadian Defence Quarterly* vol. 5, no. 1 (Summer 1975), p. 26. Major General Indar Rikhye insisted in a 1976 lecture that everything the UN forces did on Cyprus during the 1974 fighting was, in fact, within their original mandate. See 'Problems of International Peacekeeping', *Royal United Services Institute (RUSI) Journal for Defence Studies* vol. 122, no. 1 (March 1977), p. 8. See also Frank Gaffen, *In the Eye of the Storm: a History of Canadian Peacekeeping* (Toronto: Deneau and Wayne, 1987), pp. 98–104 for an account of Canadian actions in Cyprus during the crisis.
34. Brian Cuthbertson, *Canadian Military Independence in the Age of the Superpowers* (Toronto: Fitzhenry and Whiteside, 1977), pp. 210–17, 221–22.
35. Dan G. Loomis, *Not Much Glory: Quelling the FLQ* (Toronto: Deneau, 1984), pp. 70–79.
36. *ibid.*, pp. 142–43.
37. Canada, Department of National Defence, *Challenge and Commitment: a Defence Policy for Canada* (Ottawa: Supply and Service Canada, 1987), pp. 43–47, 49, 60–67.
38. McLin, pp. 206–207; see also Gaffen, pp. 165–67.
39. Goodspeed, pp. 248–49, 251–52; see also, Rosalyn Higgins, *United Nations Peace-keeping 1945–1967 Documents and Commentary. Volume I The Middle East* (London: Oxford University Press/Royal Institute of International Affairs, 1969), pp. 258, 304, 306, 314–15.
40. Higgins, *op. cit.* pp. 271–72, 294–95, 323–24; Commander W. A. B. Douglas, 'Canada and the Withdrawal of the United Nations Emergency Force', *Canadian Defence Quarterly* vol. 2, no. 3 (Winter 1972–73), pp. 46–50.
41. Higgins, *op. cit. Volume 3 Africa* (1980), pp. 89, 91; David W. Wainhouse, *International Peace-keeping at the Crossroads: National Support-Experience and Prospects* (Baltimore, Maryland: Johns Hopkins University Press, 1973), p. 208.
42. Higgins, *op. cit. Volume 4 Europe* (1981), p. 129.
43. *ibid.*, pp. 160–95 *passim*; Goodspeed, *op. cit.* p. 262; Wainhouse, *op. cit.* p. 369.
44. *ibid.*, pp. 139–40, 196–97; see also Major K. C. Eyre, 'The Future of UN Interpository Peace-keeping under the 1956 Pearson-Hammarskjold Formula: Conclusions Drawn from Personal Experiences in Cyprus, in the Tragic Summer of 1974', *Canadian Defence Quarterly* vol. 12, no. 1 (Summer 1982), pp. 31–36; Brigadier (ret'd) F. R. Henn, 'Guidelines for Peacekeeping—Another View', *British Army Review* no. 67 (April 1981), pp. 35–36; *Toronto Star*, 30 July 1974,

indicates that the first reinforcements for the Canadian contingent did not leave Canada until two weeks after the start of the crisis. Lively, detailed accounts of the airborne regiment's experience in Cyprus may be found in: Canadian Airborne Regiment, *Airborne Regiment Tenth Anniversary Journal 1968–1978* (Canadian Forces Base Petawawa, 1978), pp. 16–17, 26, 42, 62, and *Fragments of 1 Airborne Battery* (CFB Petawawa, 1978), pp. 53–54, 62–65.

45. Lieutenant Colonels R. McLean and A. Desroches, 'The Canadian Forces in Internal Security Operations', in *The Management of the Police Response to Crisis Situations: the Proceedings of the Tactical Unit Workshop* (Ottawa: Canadian Police College, 1982), pp. 61, 63; John Gellner, *Bayonets in the Streets: Urban Guerrilla at Home and Abroad* (Toronto: Collier MacMillan, 1974), p. 131. The most complete account on the use of Canadian troops in aid of the civil power is Jean Pariseau, *Forces Armées et Maintien de l'ordre au Canada, 1867–1967: un Siècle d'Aide au Pouvoir Civil* (unpublished doctoral thesis, Université Paul Valery, France, 1981), 5 volumes.
46. See Dan G. Loomis, *Not Much Glory: Quelling the F.L.Q.* (Toronto: Deneau, 1984), pp. 14, 46–47, 51, 70–71, 73, 76, 112, 114–23; see also David A. Charters, 'The October Crisis: Implications for Canada's Internal Security,' in Brian MacDonald, ed., *Terror. CISS Proceedings Spring 1986* (Toronto: Canadian Institute of Strategic Studies, 1986), pp. 56–57.
47. This is the central thesis of Loomis's book *Not Much Glory*.
48. Denis Smith, *Bleeding Hearts . . . Bleeding Country: Canada and the Quebec Crisis* (Edmonton: Hurtig, 1971), pp. 12–14, 20–21, 34–37.
49. *Montreal Star,* 13 October 1970: John Saywell, *Quebec 70: A Documentary Narrative* (Toronto: University of Toronto Press, 1971), pp. 78, 81. See also David A. Charters, 'The October Crisis: Implications for Canada's Internal Security', in Brian MacDonald, ed., *Terror. CISS Proceedings, Spring 1986* (Toronto: Canadian Institute of Strategic Studies, 1986), pp. 63–67, which suggests that an 'intelligence failure' contributed to the strain on the police.
50. Major Guy Morchain, 'Peacekeeping at Home', *Canadian Forces Sentinel* (February-March 1971), p. 2.
51. *ibid.*, pp. 3–4.
52. *ibid.*, p. 3; Saywell, *op. cit.* p. 81; powers under the War Measures Act cited in Ron Haggart and Aubrey Golden, *Rumours of War* (Toronto: New Press, 1971), Appendix C, pp. 283–86.
53. Morchain, *op. cit.* pp. 4–6, 9. One soldier was killed when his own rifle discharged accidentally.
54. Captain Bill Aikman, 'The Beginnings', *Canadian Forces Sentinel Olympic Triple Issue* vol. 13, no. 1 (January, 1977), p. 5.
55. *ibid.*; Lieutenant Colonel Pierre Senecal, 'La Securité aux jeux Olympiques 76', *Canadian Defence Quarterly* vol. 5, no. 2 (Autumn 1976), p. 26.
56. Arthur B. Fulton, *Countermeasures to Combat Terrorism at Major Events: A Case Study for Senior Seminar on Foreign Policy* (Washington, D.C.: Department of State, 1976), p. 41.
57. *ibid.*, p. 40; *Toronto Star,* 19 July 1975.
58. Aikman, *op. cit.* p. 6; Senecal, *op. cit.* p. 27; Canada Department of National Defence, *Defence 1976* (Ottawa: Department of Supply and Services, 1977), p. 64 (annual report).
59. See Task Force and other accounts in *Sentinel Olympic Issue,* pp. 13–44 *passim*, 48–50; Fulton, *op. cit.* pp. 42, 46–47. A brief, but colourful account may be found in: Lieutenant Andy Pittendrigh, 'Portrait of the Life of a Paratrooper in Montreal', *Junior Officer's Journal* vol. 1, no. 1 (January 1977), pp. 14–15.
60. Fulton, *op. cit.* pp. 44–45; *Montreal Star,* 8 June 1976.

61. See *Sentinel Olympic Issue*, pp. 66–73.
62. Canada, Department of the Solicitor-General, *Annual Report 1975–1976* (Ottawa: Supply and Services, 1976), p. 8; see also Senecal, *op. cit.* p. 28; Fulton, *op. cit.* pp. 45–46; and Aikman, *op. cit.* p. 9.
63. Senecal, *op. cit.* p. 28; Aikman, *op. cit.* p. 8; *Toronto Star,* 19 July 1975.
64. J. D. Murray, 'Military Aspects of Peace-keeping: Problems and Recommendations', in Henry Wiseman, *Peacekeeping: Appraisals and Proposals* (New York: Pergamon Press, 1983), pp. 180–81.
65. *ibid.*, pp. 184–85; R. B. Byers and Michael Slack, eds., *Canada and Peacekeeping: Prospects for the Future* (Downsview, Ontario: Research Programme in Strategic Studies, York University, 1984), pp. 29–30.
66. Wiseman, *op. cit.* 'Has New Life . . . U.N. Peacekeeping?', p. 24.
67. *ibid.*, pp. 24–25; Murray, *op. cit.* pp. 187–89; Lieutenant Colonel James H. Allan, 'The Future of Peacekeeping for Canada', *Canadian Defence Quarterly* vol. 8, no. 1 (Summer 1978), p. 32.
68. McLin, *op. cit.* p. 208; Canada, *White Paper on Defence* (1964), p. 16; Lecture by the Right Honourable Lester B. Pearson, Carleton University Ottawa, 7 May 1964, in Stewart, *Canadian Defence Policy,* pp. 156–57; Larry L. Fabian, *Soldiers Without Enemies: Preparing the United Nations for Peacekeeping* (Washington, D.C.: Brookings, 1971), pp. 134–35.
69. Brigadier General Clayton E. Beattie, 'Preparations for Peace-keeping at the National and International Level', *Canadian Defence Quarterly* vol. 8, no. 2 (Autumn 1978), pp. 28–29.
70. SCEAND, no. 31 (21 May 1970), 'Eighth Report to the House—Subcommittee on United Nations and Peacekeeping', pp. 75–77.
71. Beattie, *op. cit.*, p. 29.
72. SCEAND, no. 31 (1970), 'Eighth Report', pp. 73–74.
73. *ibid.*, p. 75.
74. See 'Exercise New Crusader', *The Canadian Guardsman* (1966), pp. 59–60; and 'Exercise Park Bandit', *The Canadian Guardsman* (1967), pp. 86, 88–89.
75. John Walker, 'What was the Exercise About?', *Montreal Gazette,* August 1969; see also Loomis, 'Not Much Glory', *op. cit.* pp. 114–15.
76. Cuthbertson, *op. cit.*, p. 251.
77. *ibid.*, pp. 250–51.
78. Loomis, *Not Much Glory, op. cit.* pp. 144–45.
79. SCEAND, no. 31 (1970) 'Eighth Report', pp. 72–73; Major S. R. Elliott, *Scarlet to Green: a History of Intelligence in the Canadian Army, 1903–1963* (Toronto: Canadian Intelligence and Security Association, 1981), pp. 518–57.
80. Canada, Commission of Inquiry Concerning Certain Activities of the Royal Canadian Mounted Police, *Third Report: Certain RCMP Activities and the Question of Governmental Knowledge* (Ottawa: Supply and Services, 1981), pp. 201–206.
81. Allan, *op. cit.* p. 31; Rod B. Byers, 'Peacekeeping and Canadian Defence Policy: Ambivalence and Uncertainty', in Wiseman, ed., p. 131.
82. See news reports in *Globe and Mail,* 22, 24, 26 July, 5 August 1974; *Toronto Star,* 23, 29 July 1974.
83. David A. Charters, 'Canadian Security Intelligence Problems in Historical Perspective', Paper presented at Conference on Intelligence and Policy, Defense Intelligence College/American Political Science Association, August 1986, Appendix 2, pp. 6–8; *Ottawa Citizen,* 13 March 1985.
84. 'Taking on Terrorists', *Macleans,* 24 March 1986.
85. David Charters, 'Organization, Selection and Training of National Response Teams—a Canadian Perspective', *Conflict Quarterly* vol. 1, no. 3 (Winter 1981),

pp. 26–30, and *Armed Forces and Political Purpose: Airborne Forces and the Canadian Army in the 1980s* (Fredericton, N.B.: Centre for Conflict Studies, University of New Brunswick, 1984), pp. 98–101; Lt. Col. G. Davidson-Smith (Ret'd), 'A Positive Approach to Terrorism: the Case for an Elite Counter-Force in Canada', *RUSI Journal* vol. 129, no. 3 (September 1984), pp. 17–22.

86. Solicitor General Canada, 'Notes for a Speech by the Honourable Perrin Beatty, Solicitor General of Canada, to the Law Faculty of the University of Toronto', 10 March 1986; Garry Saunders, 'The RCMP Special Emergency Response Team', *RCMP Gazette* vol. 49, no. 3 (1987), pp. 1–6; 'A Team Against Terror', *Macleans*, 26 May 1986; *Ottawa Citizen,* 13 May 1986; *Globe and Mail*, 17 May 1986.

6

From Palestine to Northern Ireland: British Adaptation to Low-Intensity Operations

DAVID A. CHARTERS

> To make war upon rebellion is messy
> and slow, like eating soup with a knife.
> T. E. Lawrence*

'Britain world leader in anti-guerrilla methods'.[1] Written in the wake of the successful hostage rescue operation at the Iranian embassy in London, that headline expressed a view that most observers probably took for granted. The article that accompanied it, however, said almost nothing about how Britain had come to acquire or to deserve such a reputation. This chapter will attempt to shed some light on this matter, by analysing the way in which the British Army has learned to adapt to counter-insurgency and anti-terrorist operations in the period since 1945.

The study will consist of three sections. The first will examine the British Army as an institution in this period—its development as an organisation and a professional force, and its approach to conducting its military tasks. The insights thus gained should give an indication of the Army's ability to cope with changing operational requirements. The second section will explain the adaptation process: what the Army learned, and how it learned—the means by which the Army was able to incorporate both experience and innovation. The focus here will be on basic principles, training methods, development of tactical skills and other capabilities. The final section will attempt

NORTHERN IRELAND

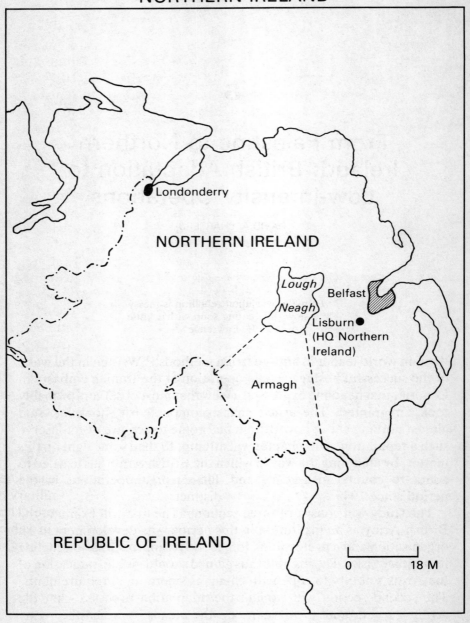

- Londonderry

NORTHERN IRELAND

Lough

Neagh

Belfast

Lisburn●
(HQ Northern
Ireland)

Armagh

REPUBLIC OF IRELAND

0   18 M

to draw conclusions about the British Army's ability to adapt to low-intensity operations and about the consequences of successful adaptation for the Army's ability to fight in conventional war.

Considerable emphasis will be placed on the army's efforts to adapt to the conflicts in Palestine and Malaya—for two reasons. First, together they comprised a watershed of experience in the approach to low-intensity operations after 1945; and also primary and secondary source material is more readily available for the study of these campaigns than for others. Nevertheless, there are enough data to discuss the latter in detail sufficient to make comparative observations. Before turning to discussion of the Army itself, something should be said about the nature of these campaigns, by way of describing the operational environment of low-intensity operations.

Britain has been officially at peace for the last 40 years. Paradoxically, the British Army probably has never been busier; up to the end of 1982 it had carried out 94 operational commitments worldwide. Of these, only three—Korea, Suez, and the Falklands—involved combat in conventional, if undeclared, wars. All but 14 of the remainder consisted of low-intensity operations: internal security duties, peace-keeping or peace-restoring operations, or counter-insurgency campaigns.[2] These operations spanned a considerable period of time, a diverse collection of countries, cultures, terrains and climates, and a wide variety of political circumstances and operational environments. Nevertheless, the nine principal conflicts[3] shared a number of common features which distinguished them significantly from conventional wars.

First, the political dimension dominated all military considerations and activities down to the lowest level.[4] In conventional war the soldiers at the sharp end—the sections, platoons, companies or battalions in direct contact with the enemy—needed to concern themselves only with the military task at hand: defeating the enemy troops immediately in front of them and seizing the unit's objectives by military means alone. The politics of the war was left to the politicians and the 'brass'—the military high command. By contrast, the frequently complex political circumstances of low-intensity conflicts meant that even relatively minor military actions, such as an ambush, could have a significant political impact, even if only at the local level. This meant that the individual soldier had to be made aware of the political nature of his actions and the consequences of ill-advised or excessive application of force. At least in theory this applied to both sides in such conflicts, even if in practice the principle was respected more in the breach than in the observance, particularly by those whom the British were fighting. For the British Army it translated into strict political control of operations, necessitating a close if not always comfortable working relationship with the civil power, and political limits on the use of violence—the weapons that could be used and the circumstances in which their use would be considered appropriate.[5]

In fact, operations took on a policing character, wherein the capture or arrest of individuals—the collection of evidence and bringing suspects to trial—was more important than killing them; indeed, killing them was often politically unacceptable. Troops might have to adapt from acting as soldiers in a traditional ambush, able to 'shoot to kill' under certain circumstances, to acting as 'peace officers' enforcing the law in others—and both in the same campaign. Political and legal constraints often left the initiative in the hands of the opposition, who could strike at will, while the Army had to wait until the 'crime' had been committed before being permitted to act. This, and the fact that the final outcome of any conflict is determined largely by political and other intangible factors and not by military action, understandably produced frustration for the soldiers and a certain degree of civil-military friction.

The second distinctive characteristic of this spectrum of warfare is implicit in the concept itself—low-intensity. A number of points illustrate this aspect. First, the number of troops engaged in combat at any one time was usually measured in dozens or less, and only rarely in scores or hundreds. Pitched battles involving battalion-size or larger forces occurred infrequently. These conflicts have been described aptly as 'platoon commanders' wars'.[6] Second, as noted earlier, political constraints frequently set limits on the levels of violence, especially as used by the British Army. In Malaya, on the other hand, it was the terrain—the jungle—more than anything else that dictated which weapons could be used. Air power was used sparingly in Malaya and elsewhere. Consequently, Army (and usually insurgent) casualties in such campaigns were light when compared with those suffered in conventional operations. For example, three years of predominantly conventional combat in Korea resulted in 7,268 British Army casualties, including more than 1,200 dead. The 12-year Malayan Emergency, on the other hand, cost less than half that number of British Army casualties, with only 509 killed.[7]

Paradoxically, although the major low-intensity conflicts usually involved combat between units of section or platoon size, the campaigns as a whole consumed large numbers of troops: two-and-a-half divisions in Palestine for nearly three years; 45,000 Commonwealth troops (25,000 from Britain alone) in Malaya at the peak in 1954; 21,000 at the time of Operation MOTORMAN in Northern Ireland (1972).[8] These represented significant commitments of forces in peacetime, even if they pale by comparison with the size of forces fielded in recent Middle East wars. But these examples serve effectively to illustrate Frank Kitson's rule of thumb that 'the number of troops required to control a given situation goes up as the amount of force which it is politically acceptable for them to use goes down'.[9] The nature of the fighting and the manpower requirements that flowed therefrom dictated that these were primarily infantry operations, with a relatively small input from the other two principal combat arms.[10] In some instances, notably in Northern Ireland, the demand for troops and a shortage of infantry resulted in some armoured, artillery and other units being used in the infantry role. Auxiliary and 'proxy' forces featured in some campaigns.

The third feature which sets these conflicts apart from conventional war is the largely clandestine nature of the enemy. In rural areas guerrillas were indistinguishable from the peasantry and based themselves in less accessible areas, avoiding contact with the security forces except under circumstances where they could bring superior force to bear. In urban centres insurgents organised themselves into small, carefully selected, highly secure and anonymous 'cells'. Security was ensured by the ruthless liquidation of traitors and informers. Military and political hierarchies seldom overlapped except at the level of the high command or central committee.[11] The task of defeating the enemy then, as Kitson has observed, consisted mainly of finding him.[12] This, in turn, put a premium on intelligence operations and close co-operation between the police and the Army—something which did not always develop in practice. Without accurate and timely intelligence, security force operations against insurgent forces and their political infrastructures were futile. When such information was available on a consistent basis, it probably meant the difference between victory and defeat.[13] In this regard, Palestine and Malaya stand out as examples of worst and best case scenarios respectively.

The fourth distinctive characteristic of these conflicts is the importance of the psychological dimension. Although psychological warfare can and does play an occasionally significant role in conventional wars—particularly in the field of deception—it consistently plays a leading, even dominant, role in low-intensity conflict. Characteristically, revolutionary or nationalist insurgents are militarily and often politically weak, especially at the outset of their campaigns. It is essential, therefore, for them to develop, to portray and to reinforce an image of strength beyond their numbers, omnipotence, cleverness, magnanimity towards the common man, and manifest destiny.[14] Propaganda played a significant part in virtually all of the major post-war low-intensity conflicts and this forced the British Army, and the various governments it served, to get into the psychological warfare struggle themselves. This was not always undertaken either with great skill or with great enthusiasm; the insurgents frequently proved more adept at using or manipulating the news media and the images their coverage provided. The Army, for its part, was not accustomed to having its operations examined under the media microscope. Learning to cope with this, and with the challenge of psychological warfare generally, was for the British Army one of the unique features of low-intensity warfare after 1945.

The fifth and final feature of low-intensity warfare in this period concerns the nature of the fighting. The enemy employed irregular or unconventional methods of warfare: guerrilla ambushes or hit-and-run raids; terrorist assassinations, bombings or kidnappings. Riots, hijacking and hostage-taking were also part of this spectrum of conflict.[15] Furthermore, regardless of ideological or nationalist motivation, the guerrilla, terrorist or insurgent was usually deeply committed to his cause. The close-knit nature of the clandestine life, the shared experience of hardship, and constant indoctrination by morale-building propaganda gave the enemy considerable staying power. These factors had two implications for the British Army; first, in such operations it must change its conventional approach to warfare not only to include the policing dimension noted earlier, but also to adopt some unconventional methods itself, in order to meet the enemy on equal terms on his own ground. Moreover, as these operations were undertaken largely in the outer reaches of the empire, where the climate and the terrain favoured the enemy, the Army had to develop innovative ways of conducting operations in otherwise inaccessible areas. Second, defeating the enemy would require more persuasion than mere superiority of arms. This gave these wars, campaigns and operations a protracted, open-ended character with the outcome never clearly in sight. Unlike conventional wars, these campaigns rarely experienced a single battle which could be identified at the time—or in retrospect—as the turning point at which victory or defeat became inevitable. The Malayan Emergency was terminated after 12 years of fighting during which there was no single significant engagement. Patience, therefore, was another method the Army had to learn.

To close this section, it may be useful to summarise the distinctive characteristics of low-intensity operations, with a view to highlighting their implications for the way the British Army would conduct its operations.

1. *Characteristic* – the political nature of the conflicts and operations.
   Implications – political control of operations and limits on the use of force, which turned military operations into policing tasks and ensured that the final outcome would be determined by political, not military, considerations.
2. *Characteristic* – the 'low-intensity' level of combat.
   Implications – small-unit operations with relatively low casualties which required large numbers of infantry to keep the violence from escalating beyond politically acceptable limits.
3. *Characteristic* – clandestine nature of the enemy.
   Implications – considerable emphasis on intelligence collection.
4. *Characteristic* – important role of psychological warfare.
   Implications – scrutiny of the Army's methods by domestic and foreign critics, and Army involvement in psychological warfare.
5. *Characteristic* – unconventional methods of warfare.
   Implications – the need for the Army to acquire the patience demanded by protracted operations, and to develop unconventional, innovative methods for bringing the enemy to battle on equal terms in extremes of terrain and climate.

These characteristics show clearly how much low-intensity operations differ from those of conventional war, and place in perspective the nature of the challenge facing the British Army after 1945. It should be borne in mind, however, that these patterns have been identified in retrospect; they were not necessarily apparent in 1945.

There was no reason for the Army to assume that the campaign in Palestine was anything but the exception to the rule.

The British Army Since 1945

For the British Army the period since 1945 has been one of constant change and adjustment in the face of evolving defence commitments, financial and manpower constraints, technological advances and organisational and professional development. By 1984 it had been an all-volunteer force for more than 20 years, thoroughly professional in its organisation, training, combat and technical skills. Advances in weapons development have made it a more technically-oriented army, demanding more, intellectually, of its officers and men. It is better educated, paid, clothed, housed and fed than its World War II counterpart. It may even be more democratic. Man for man, it is certainly more expensive. And yet, as Henry Stanhope observed in 1979, 'The most remarkable thing about the Army is not perhaps that it has changed so much, but that it has changed so little'.[16] The veteran of World War I would still recognise the basic features of the Army that fought in the Falklands. This part of the study will attempt to identify those features or characteristics, to discuss their interplay with major trends for change after 1945 and thereby explain the Army's development as an institution and profession capable of adapting to the requirements of low-intensity warfare.

Operational History and Institutional Character

The British Army, Dominick Graham argues, has always been a professional force. It 'has never regarded itself as a cadre for a national army that will fight a major war'.[17] Moreover, it has been, historically, an imperial army, whose principal role since the 18th century has been to defend the outposts of the Empire.[18] Although it played a lengthy part in support of the civil power until civilian police forces emerged in the 19th century, the Army was not really needed for defence of the homeland; that was the job of the Royal Navy. Instead, it served overseas, fighting an endless series of minor battles and major campaigns in out-of-the-way places against usually primitive opponents. Continental conventional wars, including the two world wars of this century, were aberrations—the exception, rather than the rule. From the end of the Napoleonic period, low-intensity warfare was the predominant experience of the British Army.[19] Nor, as noted earlier, did this pattern change significantly after 1945.

This historical experience has had a significant impact on the British Army as an institution. Largely forgotten by its countrymen in Britain, it evolved in a way that was insulated from them. It never became a citizen army. Anthony Verrier, a critic of the Army in the 1960s, wrote then that from the imperial experience the Army had acquired 'habits and practices which not only distinguish it sharply from most other armies . . . but from many of the attributes which we now associate with British life'.[20] These are probably most singularly manifest in the regimental system. Regimental organisation preceded by a wide historical margin the peak period of the British Empire, but imperial requirements in the latter half of the 19th century shaped regimental organisation and the character of the British Army thereafter. The residual effects may still be seen today, even in the much-diluted modern British regiments. The Cardwell system, introduced in 1873, reorganised the infantry into paired battalions so as to provide permanent forces for overseas duty, plus a home-based rotational reserve garrisoned and recruited on a territorial basis.[21] The system survived largely intact until its virtual collapse during World War II, owing to the demand for a vastly expanded army.

It was hoped that localised basing, recruiting, and links to the militia would go some way to bridge the gulf between the nation and its overseas Army. To a certain extent it did so. Yet, a considerable social gulf remained and does so to this day, although to a much reduced extent; the Army still filled its ranks from the lower orders of society, while the officers continued to be drawn from an upper class that failed to reflect the considerable changes taking place in British society. What bound these two groups together into a closed family, especially overseas, was the regiment. The pervasive impact of this institution cannot be overstated. More than one observer has described the British Army as 'not so much an army as a collection of regiments'.[22] Regimental loyalties, however diluted by several decades of amalgamations, have remained strong. They have fostered, even encouraged, the individualism that runs through the regiments, and through their officers in particular, and have precluded the development of a national 'officer corps'.[23]

This approach has some obvious limitations. To this day the Army is a conservative institution, resistant to change, neither deeply intellectual nor self-critical. Until comparatively recently, it was not good at retaining and learning from historical experience.[24] The regimental system, designed for small imperial wars, has not worked well in preparing the Army for large conventional wars. It has probably hindered the kind of thinking that would see the Army as a functional whole, greater than the sum of its component parts. Where individualism prevails, combined arms thinking falls short. Traditionally shy of 'doctrine' in its approach to the study and practice of war, the British Army remains today 'an unprofessional coalition of arms and services'.[25]

On the other hand, the imperial/regimental experience has given it some advantages, especially where low-intensity warfare is concerned. Overseas commanders traditionally were allowed a fair degree of latitude in the formulation of strategy, execution of policy and devising of tactics for local situations. A certain independent habit of mind was both required and permitted. This lent itself neatly to the individualistic nature of overseas regimental life, but also meshed with operational necessity; the army was frequently 'outnumbered by its enemies and . . . more impoverished than its friends'.[26] The need to concentrate on the immediate requirements of practical, down-to-earth soldiering in such circumstances made it a master of improvisation, flexibility, on-the-job learning and training—making do with what was available. This is reflected in the rather untidy nature of the modern British Army. For emotional as well as for practical operational reasons it has resisted the kind of managerial revolution which would do away with something as 'inefficient' as the regiment, preferring the cohesion and flexibility that a regimental-based army offers.[27]

There is no question that it required such attributes in the post-war period, when it was subject to constant changes and reductions while being required to carry out a variety of commitments. These developments did not occur in an orderly fashion; rather, they were the product of a degree of deliberate planning, some decisions of expediency, and numerous unforeseen contingencies. Each had its impact on the Army's ability to adapt to and fulfil its commitments. Before looking at these in depth, it may be instructive to examine how the Army prepared itself professionally to cope with warfare in this period.

Having just described the British Army as 'unprofessional' in its approach to the study and practice of war, it may seem contradictory now to call it a professional force. Yet, since 1962, when the last national servicemen were released, the British Army has been a professional force in every technical sense. It has been all-volunteer, with high standards of recruitment, training and discipline. The Army includes the requisite combat arms and services, command and staff organisations, training establishments and courses. Moreover, its officers conform to those basic characteristics which are deemed to constitute 'professionalism': expertise, responsibility and corporateness.[28]

The means by which to instil and enhance professionalism improved considerably after World War II. The two officer schools, Woolwich and Sandhurst, were merged into a single academy at Sandhurst, and education there was provided solely at government expense. With the end of the distinction between those whose families paid and those paid for by the public purse, the candidate selection base broadened substantially. In the first decade after the war, two-thirds of the cadets were public school boys; one in eight had been educated at Wellington or Eton. By the late 1970s the public school component had dropped to 40 percent. However, after the end of conscription the Army had difficulty in attracting the required number of suitable candidates for Sandhurst. Business and the public service appeared to offer more promising careers to those who, in other times, might have gone into the Army as officers. Nor is it clear that the broader social base changed the Army's social or professional outlook. Sandhurst—only a one-year course for a regular commission—is merely the first step in an educational, training and socialisation process which consumes most of an officer's career. Correlli Barnett remarked in 1970 that 10 years' service was enough to make an officer of grammar school origin indistinguishable from a son of the rural gentry.[29]

The Staff College at Camberley grew in stature after the war. Along with the arms schools (infantry, armour, artillery) it now constitutes one of the repositories of knowledge and experience that provides the Army with a 'historical memory'. Anthony Verrier noted that while at one time to enter staff college was a sign of considerable ambition, now, not to do so is seen as a sign of idleness. The competition for admission is intense. All young officers, at the rank of captain, attend the Junior Command and Staff Course, introduced in 1969, which provides a general introduction to organisation, staff duties, logistics and combined arms training. Only about a third of all officers are selected to attend the full Command and Staff Course at Camberley. Without it, the chances of promotion beyond the rank of major are diminished considerably. Selection is determined by performance on the captain-to-major promotion exams, which a Staff Candidate may sit twice. If the officer does not make it to Staff College he may still become 'staff qualified' by virtue of good performance in a series of staff appointments, but he is unlikely to be given a battalion command or higher. The selected candidate spends 3–15 months at the Royal Military College of Science at Shrivenham, and a year at Camberley. The course is very demanding, intellectually, and in terms of sheer work. In five terms it covers all aspects of conventional warfare; one term is devoted to out-of-area operations, desert, jungle and arctic combat, and low-intensity operations.[30]

Beyond Staff College, the officer's career consists of alternating command, staff and regimental appointments. Promotion above the rank of major is determined by a combination of reports and promotion boards. His career may also include further specialised courses relating to his branch, and he may attend one or both of the joint service colleges. The first of these is the Joint Services Defence College (JSDC). It was founded in 1948 (as the Joint Services Staff College) with the aim of improving joint staff training and promoting mutual understanding and common 'doctrine' between the three services. Army officers usually attend at the rank of lieutenant colonel. Only one in 17 is selected to attend. In 1978 the course was shortened from 10 to 6 months. The following year the college incorporated the Joint Services Warfare School, which runs a series of short courses on amphibious and other combined operations distinct from the JSDC course itself. The truly promising officer, perhaps one in 50, may be selected to attend the Royal College of Defence Studies (RCDS) (formerly the Imperial Defence College). It is not a teaching or training course *per se*. It is assumed that the officers who attend, usually at the rank of brigadier in the case of the Army, already know their jobs; the RCDS attempts to prepare them for high command by broadening their outlook. The approach is relaxed and quasi-academic—lectures, seminars, debates, and thesis writing—and includes a considerable amount of travel. Almost half the students are foreigners.[31]

For the other ranks, there is a less demanding but complicated career structure, involving as many as 180 different patterns, depending largely upon the branch. Basic and special-to-arms training is followed by alternating unit postings, trades and specialised courses, and promotion through the ranks. Some may be commissioned; since 1967, nearly a third of all officers have come up through the ranks.[32]

There are other organisations, both internal and adjunctive to the armed forces, that play a role in shaping the Army's professional outlook. Bidwell and Graham noted with satisfaction that the Army followed Liddell Hart's suggestion that a branch of the Staff be established solely for the purpose of studying the lessons of past wars and the potential significance of advancing technology on future conflicts. An army 'think tank' was established after the war, and in 1971 was expanded into the Defence Operational Analysis Establishment. It carries out wide-ranging analysis on aspects of broad strategy, tactics and equipment, defence management, research and development. The Army now has directors for each of the combat arms, tactical employment wings at the arms schools, the Royal Armaments Research and Development Establishment, a directorate of combat development, and the Training directorate. In 1971, a tactical doctrine retrieval office was established at the Staff College, to provide a central repository of papers and studies useful for professional development. Even so, the historical dimension, say Bidwell and Graham, does not get sufficient attention.[33]

This imbalance is at least partly redressed by the professional journals and independent research institutes. Officers intent on broadening their professional knowledge in the fields of military history and strategic studies face no shortage of reading material or outlets for professional writing and debate; indeed there is probably a surfeit from British sources alone.[34] Officers based in London have access to the Royal United Services Institute for Defence Studies (RUSI), the International Institute for Strategic Studies (IISS), and the Royal Institute of International Affairs (RIIA), to name only three. The RUSI frequently serves as a forum for enunciation of policy. A small number of officers are sent annually on Defence Fellowships to one of the several civilian universities that offer graduate degree programmes in military, strategic or defence studies.

Taken together, these opportunities for professional development offer considerable scope for officers to become steeped in the lore of their chosen calling. Yet the Army is not known for turning out rigorous intellectuals: General Sir Frank Kitson and Field Marshal Lord Carver are two who do come to mind, and they are exceptions to the rule. The physical demands that the job makes on an officer, the closed nature of the regimental system, and the need to concentrate on 'practical' soldiering leave little time for deep reflection until retirement. These factors have made the officers of the British Army less inquisitive about the theoretical or philosophical aspects of the profession of arms. The system produces, by and large, a 'regimental' officer, whose concerns will be those of his unit and his immediate superiors, wherever and whatever the circumstances might be. The tactical or organisational problem he confronts in an overseas conflict will probably be handled locally with the resources—material, human and intellectual—he has at hand. Historical experience has probably conditioned him not to expect a flood of assistance from Britain—there was usually little to be spared—nor to look to some sacrosanct body of 'doctrine' for advice: there was none. Instead, he must make do, improvise if necessary, use his imagination and initiative, relying on the skills he and the officers and men of his unit have acquired in years of training. In short, he must adapt.

The British Army's ability to adapt was probably never more thoroughly tested than during the period since 1945. The conditions under which Britain carried out its operational commitments demanded ingenuity and initiative at every level. Considerable responsibility for conducting operations devolved upon relatively junior commanders. This situation can be attributed to several policy, financial and organisational factors which combined to limit the resources available for operations.

Defence Policies, Budgets and Manpower

The shape and size of the Army and the commitments it undertook after 1945 were determined by an uneven interplay of colonial, foreign and defence policy objectives and decisions. These, in turn, were decided largely, but not exclusively, by financial considerations. This is not to suggest that decisions were taken in a strategic vacuum. Policy or strategy notwithstanding, however, economic constraints underlay the fundamental aspects of defence decision-making in the post-war period.[35] To a greater or lesser extent, they defined the tasks which could be undertaken, for how long, how many men could be made available, and how they would be equipped and supported. This is true, of course, for most countries, but particularly so for Britain which, bankrupted by the war, did not have the economic base after 1945 to support its global military commitments. Cost-driven policies had a significant impact on the British Army as an organisation and a profession. Three periods of strategic readjustment stand out.

In the first five years after the war, demobilisation reduced the Army from a strength of more than two million in 1945 to just 354,000 in 1950.[36] This rundown coincided with the termination of significant imperial responsibilities. In 1947 Britain granted independence to the Indian sub-continent. India had been the cornerstone in the concept of imperial defence and, although British leaders were slow to recognise the fact, without India the rationale for British Middle and Far East strategies simply evaporated. But it freed 55,000 British troops to return home. Shortly thereafter, the British government announced its intention to withdraw from Palestine, which at that time was garrisoned by some 100,000 British troops.[37] These decisions allowed demobilisation to continue at a rapid pace, and in October 1947 every regiment of the line—except for the Guards and the Parachute Regiment—was reduced (temporarily, as it turned out) to a single battalion. Similar reductions affected the other arms and services.[38]

Yet, it had already become clear that the rundown could not continue indefinitely without seriously undermining British interests worldwide. The dilemma facing Britain was that it could afford neither to abandon its overseas commitments with undue haste, nor to maintain a purely voluntary army of a size sufficient to discharge all of Britain's military tasks. The only viable alternative was to continue conscription, and to this end the National Service Act was proclaimed in July 1947, with effect from the beginning of 1949. The objective was to make available to the Army about 100,000 recruits per year for a tour of duty that eventually was extended to two years on active service. Neither the British public, the conscripts, nor the Army's professional soldiers viewed conscription with much enthusiasm. One senior officer was said to have remarked that it 'nearly killed the British Army'.[39] In fact, it probably saved the Army. Without conscription it could not have fulfilled the heavy commitments imposed upon it in the early 1950s—in Korea, Malaya, and for NATO. National Service allowed the Army in this period to expand to a peak strength of 446,000. National Servicemen provided a larger proportion of junior officers and NCOs than the regulars. Moreover, the conscripts propped up the regimental system which, strained beyond the breaking point by wartime expansion, had been almost discarded after the war.[40]

The second period of adjustment followed from the 1957 Defence White Paper. Impelled by a desire to bring defence spending into line with the nation's economic capabilities, the government proposed to reduce the armed forces as a whole by one third. That Britain felt it could justify such a massive reduction on military grounds rested at least in part on the assumption—however specious—that nuclear weapons had revolutionised defence; that they could keep the peace and, if necessary, fight a war more economically than conventional forces. Furthermore, the Suez fiasco was taken to mean that Britain could no longer mount large-scale independent conventional military operations overseas. Instead, such future operations would be undertaken only in conjunction with allies (principally the United States), while residual British overseas interests could be protected by a small, home-based, air-transportable, strategic reserve. National Service, therefore, could and would be abolished.[41]

The decision to opt for an all-volunteer Army meant, of course, a leaner organisation because such a force is more expensive: it must be better paid, equipped, fed and housed. Not surprisingly, Army strength was reduced by about 50 percent, from about 400,000 in 1956 to just over 200,000 by 1961. Simultaneously, the regimental system went through another painful period of disbandments and amalgamations required to accommodate a smaller Army.[42] Colonel J. C. M. Baynes has suggested that the years which followed, from 1962–66, 'may well be regarded by future military historians as some of the best in the history of the British Army'.[43] The period marked the return of the small professional army whose high standards were highlighted by the 'Confrontation' with Indonesia, arguably the best-conducted campaign of the post-war era.[44] Yet it was also a period of considerable strain on the limited resources of the Army. Recruiting fell short of filling the ranks depleted by departing National Servicemen. By 1964, when the Army was heavily committed in Borneo, Cyprus and South Arabia, it was still five percent below its intended establishment. The Strategic Reserve was fully deployed and Rhine Army, already under strength, was threatened with further reductions to meet overseas contingencies. Of the Army's 60 battalions, more than 24 were committed to overseas operations, and 20 to Rhine Army. The remainder had to provide for home defence, training, rotational forces, and replenishment of the Strategic Reserve. The battalions themselves were seriously under strength. This was plainly visible at the 'sharp end' in the Far East: a Guards battalion was deployed to the region in the early 1960s with one company found from another regiment, and with volunteers from a battalion just returned from Kenya. One line battalion in Borneo was reinforced by Gunners, REME troops, and young soldiers on 'adventure training'.[45]

The constraints were also clearly highlighted by the Army's

frustrating experience in attempting to create a strategic reserve during this period. In spite of initial talk of a force of more than two divisions, by 1957 only a single brigade had been designated for the role. In March 1959 the 3rd Division was earmarked and its training programme amended to meet the requirements of limited war overseas. However, reports from the early 1960s suggest that the formal composition of the division was of limited significance, and that the Strategic Reserve never constituted more than a loose organisation of the three brigade groups. Between 1963 and 1966 it fell below brigade strength.[46]

The fundamental problem with the attempt to form a home-based strategic reserve was that it was not suited to Britain's military requirements; 'as soon as a start was made assembling troops for the strategic reserve, the units involved would be posted overseas to meet the demands of operational commitments'.[47] Furthermore, it was not until the mid-1960s that the Royal Air Force (RAF) had appropriate aircraft in sufficient numbers to support a Strategic Reserve. By that time political sensitivities in the Third World had raised barriers to rapid deployment by air. Together, these factors served to disperse the Strategic Reserve and its air-lift resources to bases in East Africa, the Middle East and Southeast Asia. Frustrating as this must have been to military planners in Whitehall, it is possible to argue that thus dispersed, the Strategic Reserve was more useful, because its component parts were deployed closer to where they might be required.[48]

The Labour government of Harold Wilson (1964–70) initiated the third phase of adjustment. Guided by ideological precepts as much as by a perceived need to maintain a ceiling on defence spending, the government reviewed defence policy in 1966. The review coincided with the end of the Confrontation in Indonesia, which released from operations some 17,000 troops. This was followed shortly by the decision to withdraw from South Arabia, where two brigades and a large regional command headquarters were tied down. Then, in January 1968, the government announced that all British forces would be withdrawn from the Far East and the Gulf by the end of 1971, and that Britain would retain no capability to intervene in those areas. Army strength declined from 182,900 in 1964 to 168,600 in 1970, accompanied by yet another wave of regimental reorganisation. Although a strategic reserve remained in place, designated Army Strategic Command in 1968, the decision to terminate 'East of Suez' commitments undercut its role from the outset. It was then offered to NATO as a reserve force for the flanks, although it is not clear that as composed (the 3rd Division and the Parachute Brigade) the force actually fulfilled NATO's requirements.[49]

That was not the end of the cuts. After a brief interlude of stability under the government of Edward Heath, the Army experienced further reductions during the subsequent Labour administrations. But these appear to have been founded almost solely on ideological grounds; the government could offer no strategic justification for them, and the economic case was not as compelling as its earlier counterparts. A combination of planned reductions and increased resignations owing to low morale (induced by poor pay and benefits) reduced the Army's strength by 15,000 to 150,400 by 1979. Only the scale of the commitment to Northern Ireland spared the Army deeper cuts than those prescribed in 1975. The Army's force structure was reorganised—the brigade being replaced temporarily by the 'field force'—and oriented solely towards NATO requirements. The Army's strategic 'reach' was severely curtailed; the Joint Airborne Task Force (a two-battalion parachute brigade with integral air support) was replaced by a field force of three airportable battalions, but only one parachute battalion. The RAF's strategic 'heavy lift' capacity was cut in half. At the end of the 1970s the Army had more but slimmer infantry battalions and a smaller amount of artillery. The Conservative government of Margaret Thatcher restored virtually all the manpower the Army had lost since 1975. At the time of the Falklands War, Army strength stood at 164,000.[50]

One final constraint is worth mentioning: the British Army of the Rhine (BAOR). From its inception in the early 1950s, it represented something entirely new in British military history—a 'continental' army permanently organised and deployed in peace-time. Moreover, although it did not constitute the majority of the Army, it was—and is—the largest single commitment. It was subject to frequent organisational changes in order to cope with declining manpower, constrained budgets and the need for new strategic and tactical thinking to adapt to NATO requirements for combat in a nuclear environment. These organisational changes were also imposed on the rest of the Army. Anthony Verrier suggests that this caused a degree of resentment, because the reasons for being in Germany were, in historical terms, new and because 'the answers to them imply change in British military organisation and *métier*'[51]—anathema to so conservative an institution as the British Army.

Certainly, there is no question that initially BAOR divided the Army, organisationally if not intellectually, for it required most of the armoured regiments and artillery, while the 'imperial' army consisted predominantly of infantry. There was a distinct difference in outlook between those forces normally committed to BAOR and those whose role was principally in overseas emergencies of the Malaya type. The latter was the preferred role because, in the 1950s and 1960s, it represented not only the opportunity for genuine combat, but also because it traditionally had been the Army's *raison d'être*. BAOR, on the other hand, was more like garrison life in Britain and was administratively top-heavy with successive levels of headquarters reporting to NATO and to the Ministry of Defence.[52]

It may be suggested that by the end of the period under study the distinctions between Rhine Army and the rest were probably less striking for two reasons. First, the overseas role had been all but terminated, the Army had been 'brought home' and committed almost entirely to NATO. Second, the prolonged campaign in Northern Ireland consumed units from all parts of the Army, thereby providing a cross-regimental body of common experience. In short, the entire British Army returned ultimately to its traditional role, but at home instead of abroad.

The significant characteristics of the British Army in this period can therefore be summarised as follows. First, it was an Army with a long history of involvement in low-intensity operations in the Third World, but in the post-war period it had to be organised and trained for conventional, continental war in addition to its traditional role. This limited the manpower available for low-intensity operations overseas, and placed the burden largely upon the infantry. Strategic reserves and mobility were limited. Second, although a mixed force of conscripts and volunteers for the first decade and a half after the war, it developed and maintained professional standards of training, discipline, unit cohesion and morale, much of which can be attributed to the regimental system. Third, the regimental system, combined with the experience of imperial defence and the constraints on its size after 1945, produced an army whose units and officers were forced to rely on individual initiative and practical, flexible solutions to military problems at the local level. Relatively junior commanders were encouraged, or forced by circumstances, to improvise tactics or organisations to meet operational requirements. Yet, the Army as a whole, because of its internal 'regimental' make-up, remained a conservative institution, not always willing or able to absorb new ideas or to learn from experience.

The foregoing suggests that in many aspects the British Army was well suited to adapt to the characteristics of low-intensity warfare as described in the introduction to this chapter. The next section of this study will examine the adaptation process through several major campaigns. It will attempt to show what was learned, and how it was learned.

Adaptation to Low-Intensity Operations

Understanding Insurgency

> The first, the supreme, the most far-reaching act of judgement that the statesman and commander have to make is to establish . . . the kind of war on which they are embarking; neither mistaking it for, nor trying to turn it into, something that is alien to its nature. This is the first of all strategic questions and the most comprehensive.
>
> (Clausewitz, *On War*)[53]

Writing in 1965 Lieutenant General Sir Kenneth Darling said: 'We do not want to allow ourselves to be persuaded by upstarts such as Mao Tse-tung that he has produced some original thought in this field. In fact, we British in some degree or another have been promoting insurgency all around the world for centuries'.[54] His sentiments were echoed the following year by Richard Clutterbuck who, in the introduction to his study of the Malayan Emergency, drew a comparative analogy between comments about the Emergency and the American Revolution in order to show that 'the British have been learning the same lessons about counter-insurgency for nearly 200 years'.[55]

Both men are correct—up to a point. For example, the British government, by means of the enigmatic Colonel T. E. Lawrence, stimulated the Arab rebellion during World War I. And, as noted earlier, the Army's traditional role through the 19th century and into the 20th was the suppression of colonial rebellion. Yet the record suggests that the British Army had some difficulty in comprehending the nature of the conflicts in which it became involved after 1945. J. Bowyer Bell suggests that the British were almost always taken by surprise, even outraged, by the outbreak of colonial insurrections, and that they were quick to blame the trouble on a small group, dismissing out of hand the possibility that the rebellion might have deep and widespread political support.[56] There were several reasons for this. First, it was neither apparent nor widely perceived that

World War II had transformed the imperial relationship, that the rising tide of nationalism would make the British unwelcome foreign occupiers amongst hostile populations. It was the rare officer indeed who could comprehend this change and suggest that the British could learn some useful lessons about combating resistance from the wartime occupiers of Europe.[57]

Second, although the Army had long been involved in providing aid to the civil power in Britain and in suppressing colonial insurrection, there was little in this body of experience to give it guidance in combating an enemy whose organisation was clandestine and whose tactics were political in intent and criminal (rather than military) in method. The Irish rebellion of 1919–21 was a case in point. In its rural aspects the campaign bore some slight resemblance to earlier colonial insurrections such as the Boer War,[58] but urban terrorism and propaganda added an entirely new dimension to this form of warfare. There was much to be learned from the Irish experience, but there was no reason for the British to suppose that the campaign was anything but an aberration. Moreover, the atmosphere prevailing in the inter-war Army militated against thoughtful inquiry into the crucial political-military-psychological dimensions of insurgency and counter-insurgency. Thus Army literature from the period exhibited only a modicum of comprehension of the nature of the problem. The tendency—quite understandable—was to look for answers in familiar methods; theory and practice coalesced along purely military lines.[59]

In 1937 H. J. Simson, a retired officer, published the first considered analysis of modern insurgency and counter-insurgency. Drawing on the Irish experience, Simson observed that the insurgents used terrorism and propaganda to achieve two objects: first, to support a carefully orchestrated political-psychological war against the government; and second, to isolate the police from the population, thereby ensuring a secure subversive organisation, and to disperse the security forces on defensive duties, thus denying them the initiative. Simson recognised that existing army tactics had not been framed to deal with this type of war. To remedy this he favoured the application of martial law, but if that was not possible he recommended the appointment of a single director of operations, assisted by a joint civil, police and military staff to direct both the emergency and the normal administration. Most important, he felt the security forces had to destroy the clandestine subversive organisation and they needed, therefore, improved intelligence services.[60] Simson did not have all the answers. He gave little consideration to the negative aspects of martial law, despite the limitations obvious from the Irish case. He said nothing about how to respond to propaganda. Nonetheless, the study was remarkable for its sophistication; it clearly defined insurgency as a form of political warfare, requiring both a political and a military response, and offered solutions to some of the problems posed by this form of conflict.

Yet, officers assigned to internal security duties in Palestine in 1945 were urged to read, not Simson, but Sir Charles Gwynn's *Imperial Policing*,[61] published at about the same time. While Gwynn recognised the importance of intelligence to both sides and the need for close co-operation between all elements of the security forces, his study revealed no understanding of the political nature of insurgency. For reasons he never makes clear, he deliberately avoided drawing upon the Irish experience; instead, the case studies focused on either rural insurrection or riot control operations in urban areas. Gwynn's approach, with its emphasis on firepower and mobility, was little different from Callwell's 30 years earlier.[62]

The British Army in India continued to echo this theme after World War II. This was apparent in the series of field trials designed to test the viability of tried and true imperial policing methods enhanced by modern technology. The guerrilla opponent was described in purely military terms, to be defeated by military means in the shortest possible time. In the absence of a political context, maximum force was emphasised. Moreover, successful military operations were considered to be the Army's best propaganda weapon.[63] This is not to suggest that methods such as mobile columns, employing armoured vehicles, heavy weapons and tactical air support, were necessarily inappropriate in all circumstances; for example, they proved to be both effective and appropriate in the Radfan campaign in 1964.[64] However, campaigns in such isolated locations, where the guerrilla enemy could be clearly identified and unrestricted use of force was permitted, were probably the exception after 1945. More usually, the opponent was indistinguishable from the population as a whole, operated in a clandestine fashion in small numbers, and the political context and media access made the unrestrained use of force unacceptable and inappropriate.

Yet, it was the 'imperial policing' school of thought that informed preparations for Palestine. There the Jewish underground was expected to launch the kind of insurrection that could be suppressed by traditional methods.[65] In March 1945 the War Office issued to Middle East Forces a study on guerrilla warfare prepared in December 1944 for the forthcoming allied occupation of Germany. The paper discussed the strengths, weaknesses and tactics of guerrilla forces, and advised that offensive action by security forces—drives against centres of resistance, pursuit of sabotage bands, and searches—was the most effective weapon against guerrillas. Counter-guerrilla operations were seen as purely military.[66] GHQ Middle East Forces published *Middle East Training Pamphlet no. 9*, Part 13, 'Notes for Officers on Internal Security Duties' to provide the Army in Palestine with a body of tactical methods.[67] What is significant about the pamphlet is that it said nothing about the political context of the Palestine problem, which was considered to be beyond the Army's purview. More important, it made no attempt to define or explain 'the threat'. The three underground groups—the *Haganah*, the *Irgun* and the *Lechi*—had carefully crafted military strategies designed to fulfil the political objective of independence by undermining simultaneously the British right, will and ability to govern Palestine.[68] There is nothing in the written record to suggest that the Army—not to mention their political masters—even grasped the nature of the war being waged by the Jewish underground. Indeed, a fundamental misunderstanding of the conflict lay at the heart of a long-running dispute between the High Commissioner, who was cognizant of the political context, and the CIGS, Field Marshal Montgomery, who saw the problem only in traditional military-imperial policing terms. Based on his experience in Ireland and Palestine (during the Arab revolt, 1938–39), he favoured the application of more ruthless military measures, and his view ultimately prevailed with the British Cabinet. Although in the short term these measures produced some satisfactory results, they were unable to reverse the gradual deterioration of the British position, applied as they were in a political vacuum.[69]

It is not clear to what extent the lessons of the Palestine experience permeated the Army as a whole. In 1947, the first full post-war Staff College course devoted seven days to the study of internal security operations; the programme included a lecture on Palestine by General Barker, formerly GOC Palestine.[70] No official history of the campaign was undertaken, but in 1949 Major R. D. Wilson, who had served in a staff position in Palestine, published a history of the 6th Airborne Division's role in the campaign. In its opening chapter it described in general terms the political setting, the underground groups, and the political constraints on Army operations.[71] The remainder of the book discussed in considerable detail the counter-insurgency campaign itself, but did not attempt to extract tactical lessons or general principles that might be applied elsewhere. One article from the period that did, confined itself to military aspects.[72]

Nonetheless, even if the Palestine experience was lost to the Army's 'historical memory', there was growing awareness of the nature of revolutionary guerrilla strategy in general terms. As early as 1940 the *Army Quarterly* had published an article on Mao Tse-tung's strategy,[73] but the impetus for considering the problem seriously clearly came from the outbreak of the communist insurrection in Malaya in June 1948. Consequently, the 1949 internal security manual described in some detail the Maoist 'model' of revolutionary war. The manual identified the potential sources of unrest—political, economic, racial, or religious—but instigation and exploitation by propaganda means were laid at the door of 'outside influences'. The objectives to be attained by terrorism were described accurately, although terrorism itself was not defined or described. Resistance organisations were said to consist of 'a hard core surrounded by a much larger number of hangers-on'.[74]

This was scarcely appropriate. While conceding that insurgents operated amongst the civil population, the manual stopped short of recognising that a solid base of popular support was essential to the survival and success of the insurgents. A year after the outbreak of the Malayan Emergency, observers were only just beginning to grasp that fundamental point.[75] Once recognised, however, it became virtually an article of faith within the body of knowledge which passes for British doctrine of insurgency and counter-insurgency. In Malaya, it pointed British thinking and intelligence collection in the appropriate direction. By 1952 the Combined Intelligence Staff were building up—although not without considerable difficulty—a detailed and accurate picture of the insurgent organisation.[76] This information was conveyed to the Army not only in the form of routine operational intelligence but also in consolidated form in the Army's manual, first issued that year. *The Conduct of Anti-Terrorist Operations in Malaya* (the ATOM pamphlet) provided officers down to platoon commander level with a comprehensive handbook which covered in considerable detail the topographic, demographic and political background of Malaya and, more important, the origins, organisation, policies, strategy and tactics, strengths and weaknesses of the insurgents.[77]

Some observers since have criticised the Army for failing to develop a strategic doctrine for counter-insurgency.[78] Their criticism seems misdirected in two respects. First, it fails to take account of the non-doctrinaire nature of the Army itself. Second, closer examination suggests that, in fact, the Malayan experience came very close to providing a doctrine of insurgency and counter-insurgency—undoubtedly because of the Army's successful campaign.[79] Its influence can be seen in the way insurgent threats were defined subsequently. This is not to suggest that the Army saw the insurgencies in Kenya, Cyprus or Northern Ireland as communist-inspired; most who considered the subject recognised the diverse sources and inspirations of rebellion.[80] But the Army did seize upon the communist revolutionary *technique*—exemplified mainly by Malaya, but latterly by Vietnam—almost exclusively as the 'model' for the organisational, politico-military and tactical aspects of the insurgent.[81] This was not necessarily inappropriate; after all, insurgents learned from the experience of other conflicts, and for some time the Maoist model was favoured, even though it was never applied successfully outside China. So, although the Provisional Irish Republican Army (PIRA) borrowed more from the tradition of the original IRA, as well as the Irgun and the Greek Cypriot guerrilla movement, EOKA, in terms of organisation and tactics,[82] the British Army had by the 1970s a very clear understanding of the kind of threat the PIRA posed: a terrorist campaign based on a clandestine politico-military organisation, closely co-ordinated with political action and propaganda.[83]

This is not to suggest that mistakes were not made; old ways of thinking and acting die hard. Richard Clutterbuck reports that even in the late 1950s new brigade commanders would arrive in Malaya 'nostalgic for World War II, or fresh from manoeuvres in Germany', and conclude that the guerrilla unit in their area could be eliminated by a simple four-battalion sweep.[84] Misjudgements in Northern Ireland could be attributed to a number of factors: first, the fact that the Army's initial role in the province was of a peace-keeping nature, and was welcomed by the Catholic population; terrorism was not the problem at that time, and was not anticipated. It emerged as a threat in a desultory, haphazard way, forcing the Army to adjust its thinking and its mission in mid-stride.[85] In these circumstances, errors are inevitable. Second, when the terrorist threat arose, the Army found that police intelligence on the IRA was wholly inadequate.[86] Without adequate intelligence the Army could not selectively and effectively contain the terrorist threat. The consequent escalation of violence brought political pressure to undertake meaures—such as intern-

ment—which played straight into the hands of PIRA propagandists.[87] The Ulster experience confirms the point that a theoretical
understanding of the nature of a particular conflict is insufficient by
itself; 'models' do not fit perfectly because the circumstances of each
conflict are different. There is no substitute, then, for timely and
accurate intelligence on the actual threat confronting the Army, and
more will be said later of the importance of adapting quickly and
effectively to the intelligence task. In a broader sense, the experience
from Palestine onwards pointed to the need for the Army to develop
a body of operational principles and tactical skills appropriate for the
particular political circumstances of one conflict, but readily transferable and adaptable to another.

Basic Operational Principles

In Palestine, the basic operational principles were the familiar axioms
of aid to the civil power: the use of minimum force and the need for
close co-operation between the Army and the civil authorities,
specifically the police. The legal powers of the troops under the
Emergency Regulations were explained in detail, and the supremacy
of the civil power affirmed.[88] These were fine, so far as they went, but
they did not really get to grips with either the political dimension of
the problem or the tactical aspect of cracking the insurgent organisation. The High Commissioner's mandate was 'to keep the peace in
Palestine',[89] and that clearly defined and constrained the Army's
role; it was not a directive to defeat the insurgents. Thus it was from
Malaya, where the nature of the conflict was clearly grasped, rather
than from Palestine, that a set of operational principles evolved.

First among these was the requirement for a clear statement by the
civil authority, in Britain or in the territory, defining the political aim
of the campaign. This political directive, in turn, was supposed to
define the purpose and scope of the military contribution to the long-
term political effort.[90] Desirable as that might be, it was not always
forthcoming. When the political aim was clear, as it was in the
Malayan Emergency, and in the Confrontation with Indonesia,[91]
effective military campaigns could be conducted, even if they had to
be improvised at the outset. Where the political aim was less certain,
non-existent, or completely at odds with local aspirations, the Army
was left holding the ring, and the military dimension was affected
accordingly. This was the case in Palestine; the directive to 'keep the
peace' was enunciated and pursued in a policy vacuum, and in the

face of violent opposition from the Jewish community. The political response to the Mau Mau uprising in Kenya was hesitant and poorly co-ordinated, and more than a year passed before the military commander was in a position to draft a clear campaign plan.[92] In Cyprus, the British government was forced to reverse its policy, first ruling out the possibility of Cypriot independence, and later being persuaded to grant it.[93]

In Northern Ireland, the political problem has proved so intractable that it has not been possible to define a clear political aim. Moreover, the nature of the conflict changed over time from communal violence to terrorist insurgency. In theory, the Army's role there has been to buy time and a degree of stability in order to allow the political process to go forward; in reality, no viable political progress is anticipated. So the Army has had to function in a situation of close political direction and high visibility but lacking long-term political objectives.[94] It has had to adjust its operational style to cope with that uncertainty, while at the same time conducting a full-scale counter-insurgency campaign.

A clear political directive, then, has been the exception rather than the rule since 1945. The challenge facing the British Army, therefore, has been to learn to adapt military measures designed for dovetailing with political strategy to campaigns where such a strategy was clearly lacking.

The remaining principles will be discussed with respect to their application in greater detail in subsequent sections of the study; here they will be merely identified. Second only in importance to the need for a clear political aim was the requirement for complete co-operation between the civil authorities, the police and the armed forces.[95] The third principle was to retain or regain the confidence and support of the population. This requirement was defined succinctly in Field Marshal Templer's now famous phrase: 'The answer lies not in pouring more troops into the jungle, but rests in the hearts and minds of the Malayan people.'[96] The concept of winning hearts and minds underlay virtually all subsequent thinking about the importance of the psychological warfare dimension of counter-insurgency.[97] The Army's Malayan pamphlets stressed that 'the importance of intelligence in the campaign . . . cannot be overemphasised'.[98] Historians and other analysts since have concurred in this assessment, believing that the key to disrupting the insurgent organisation and destroying its military components lay primarily in identifying and locating them; that done, appropriate military measures could be applied in a selective and effective manner against the insurgent enemy. Hence the requirement for a single, integrated intelligence effort.[99]

Richard Clutterbuck and others emphasised the need for specialised training in counter-insurgency, to attune soldiers' minds to the problem as well as providing them with the basic skills and techniques of conducting operations and directing a campaign. This, too, was reflected in army manuals.[100] Finally, at the tactical level, where the army would engage in combat insurgent units or attempts to capture individual members, the manuals stressed the application of the basic principles of war: surprise, security, concentration, economy of force, selection and maintenance of the aim, flexibility, and morale.[101]

Guided by these principles, operations were supposed to achieve two objectives: first, protection of the population and, second, isolation of the insurgent. The former would facilitate restoration and continuity of government, administration and rule of law, and the latter, effective offensive action against the insurgents.[102] No two campaigns were exactly alike, however, and the circumstances peculiar to each locale and conflict dictated necessarily uneven applications of these principles. Nor was it in the nature of the British Army to adhere rigidly to a prescribed doctrine. Together these factors enhanced the importance of the principle of flexibility. The Army's attitude was perhaps best summarised in General Erskine's Foreword to the operations manual for the Kenyan Emergency: 'This is much more a book of ideas than a book of rules.'[103]

Command by Committee

One factor sets the British experience apart from that of the Americans or the Israelis: Britain was the governing colonial (or, in the case of Northern Ireland, constitutional) power in virtually all the countries or territories where it became involved in counter-insurgency. In some cases, Malaya, for example, British rule had been a long-standing institution with roots implanted deep in the fabric of the country. This was not the case in Palestine, which Britain administered on a League of Nations Mandate. Britain's position conferred upon it several distinct advantages with respect to the management of conflict in those areas. First, it gave the British government—either directly from London or through its local representatives (the governor or high commissioner)—a relatively free hand in running the colony or territory. Second, and perhaps more important for this study, colonial rule gave the British control of an existing government and administrative structure: executive and/ or legislative councils; civil services; regional or municipal administrations; police forces; social services; transportation and communication networks. All the means to direct an emergency were in British hands; it was merely a case of adapting these structures to meet emergency requirements. H. J. Simson seems to have been the first to suggest that this could best be achieved by means of a joint civil-police-military committee system, with one person designated to direct emergency measures.[104]

In Palestine, the Central Security Committee, and its counterpart at District level, were intended to enhance co-operation between the civil government and the security forces. Both committees met weekly. The Central Security Committee, frequently chaired by the High Commissioner, consisted of the Chief Secretary (the senior executive officer of the administration), the Inspector-General (Chief) of Police, the senior officer of GSI (military intelligence), and the Defence Security Officer. The GOC British Troops Palestine, who exercised operational control of the Army and the police, was not a member but attended as required, which was often. His formal exclusion seems curious and has never been adequately explained. There is no evidence to suggest, however, that his views were not heard nor that his formal inclusion at the 'top table' would have made a significant difference in the way the campaign was conducted. That the British ultimately did not prevail in Palestine could hardly be blamed on the committee system which, on the whole, functioned rather well.[105]

A survey of both the official and unofficial literature suggests that the Malayan model of Emergency command and control had a significant impact on Army thinking. This is all the more surprising once it is recognised that in its most important manifestation—the appointment of Field Marshal Templer as 'Supremo', combining civil and military authority—the command arrangement was in every sense unique. It lasted only two years, 1952–54. Yet, perhaps because the period was seen in retrospect as central to the eventual victory, and because it bore the unmistakable stamp of Templer's per-sonality,[106] it impressed upon the Army, as no previous experience had, the importance of civil-military-police co-operation. This is particularly noticeable in the emphasis placed on the need for a single director of operations, operations staffs, war councils and joint

committees.[107] Certainly, Anthony Short's official history of the
Malayan Emergency gives no indication that the Army resisted or
encountered significant difficulties adapting to a committee form of
command and control. This is not to suggest that the British got it
right from the start or that it worked perfectly; it was reorganised
several times during the Emergency to make it less cumbersome and
more effective. Moreover, troop deployments did not always
facilitate Army co-location with the police and this hampered
co-operation.

However, the military and the civil authority were agreed on the
need for a single Director of Operations.[108] The hardest part for the
Army, probably, was to adjust its way of thinking about the conduct
of operations. Simon Hutchinson has observed that the soldier sees
the guerrillas as a military force which must be defeated; his police
counterpart sees them as highly organised, dangerous criminals, who
can only be eliminated by the lengthy, methodical, investigative
process that will produce results in court, even if it infuriates his
Army colleagues in the meantime.[109] It is not surprising, then, that
one officer who served in Malaya made the following comment:

> Warfare by committee is positive anathema to the soldier, who has been trained all
> his life to make up his own mind on the conduct of operations and to carry them out
> . . . [in Malaya] the soldier, like everyone else, had to submit his plans to the
> committee and try and persuade them of the soundness of his ideas. No doubt it
> was very good for him, though at times he could be forgiven for thinking that the
> frustrations he encountered helped only to hasten his journey to an early grave.[110]

This system of command and control was applied with varying
degrees of success in most other emergencies. In Kenya, the Mau
Mau uprising had been active for six months before the existing
committee system was restructured in February 1953 to provide a
'triumvirate' (civil, police, military) down to district level, and a
Military Adviser (later Director of Operations) was appointed. But
at the higher levels the committee system proved cumbersome, and
Major General Hinde (D/Ops), who was operating through police
headquarters, could not exert effective operational control of the
forces in the field. In short, the system was, in one critic's words,
'complicated and indecisive'. It was overhauled in June 1953, when
General Sir George Erskine was appointed C-in-C East Africa
Command and Director of Operations with Army, police, colonial
and auxiliary security forces under his command. Hinde became
Deputy D/Ops for the anti-Mau Mau campaign. He moved from
Police to Army Headquarters, whence he co-ordinated security force

activities with the civil government and represented Erskine on all committees. A streamlined War Cabinet and Emergency joint staff were created to facilitate quick and effective decision-making.[111]

Again, the system was not flawless, even at the 'sharp end'. General Erskine noted that because Army deployments changed frequently, there was a lack of continuity in Army representation at the Provincial and District levels.[112] Sometimes the system just broke down under the strain of day-to-day operations. Frank Kitson recalled Christmas Day 1953, in Thika District: the District Commissioner was away on a visit, and the military commander had been shot dead in an ambush the previous afternoon. The Division Chief of Police had arrived only a few weeks earlier. The Commandant and Assistant Commandant of his Police Reserve had been wounded in the same skirmish which killed the Army company commander. In the interval between the incident and the arrival from Nairobi of the new company commander, the woman manning the radio in the joint operations room 'had exercised the supreme command with great skill, but by midnight affairs were a bit beyond her control'.[113] At that point, a police officer took command of the situation.

When Field Marshal Sir John Harding took up the post of Governor of Cyprus in October 1955, he also assumed the role of Director of Operations. His position was thus similar to that of Templer in Malaya, but without the same degree of political responsibility. Harding delegated actual operational control of the security forces to his Chief of Staff, and appointed a civilian Under-Secretary for Internal Security to facilitate liaison between the military, the police and the civil administration. The Chief of Staff, who became D/Ops in 1957, was assisted by a Joint Staff and triumvirate District Security Committees. Information from secondary sources suggests that the British successfully applied their operative campaign theme: 'Cooperation is not enough; there must be integration.'[114]

This axiom was not so easily applied in the Aden campaign, owing to divisions of civil government responsibility between London, the High Commissioner, the Aden State government and that of the South Arabian Federation, of which Aden was a member while still remaining a British colony. To complicate matters further, the military command in Aden was initially divided between four components, only one of which was directly responsible for internal security in Aden State. The emergency had been under way for a year and a half before the GOC Middle East Land Forces (whose HQ was in Aden) was appointed security commander for the colony in June

1965. A system of six committees put in place to manage the campaign worked effectively in the initial stages but, according to Julian Paget, it became more cumbersome as terrorism increased. Finally, in February 1967, the Security Commander assumed complete and sole responsibility for internal security. The committees were abolished, replaced by the normal military chain of command.[115] But the decision to abandon Aden had already been taken a year earlier, and all British forces were withdrawn by the end of 1967.

Until the imposition of direct rule from Westminster in March 1972 the command and control situation in Northern Ireland was almost as complex as that of Aden. In August 1969 the GOC Northern Ireland was given responsibility for maintaining law and order in the province; to accomplish this he was given operational control of the police for security operations, in addition to the Army. But simplicity ended there. Because of divided constitutional and administrative responsibility for Ulster, the GOC was serving at least two masters: the Northern Ireland government at Stormont, which made the laws under which the security forces functioned, and the United Kingdom government, which provided the military forces required to enforce the laws from August 1969. The GOC was directly responsible to the Ministry of Defence in London, but had to work in close co-operation with the Stormont government. It was a highly unsatisfactory arrangement, because the two governments disagreed on many aspects of policy. Richard Clutterbuck suggests that it was the issue of divided control and responsibility for security that finally forced the UK government to impose direct rule. From then on it provided unified direction of political and security policy through the Secretary of State for Northern Ireland and the Northern Ireland Office.[116]

A triumvirate committee system had been established at the outset, and became institutionalised as time passed. Brigade and unit areas were established to correspond to police regional and divisional areas. Joint Army-police committees met constantly to co-ordinate operations. This did not wholly eliminate co-operation problems, however. Chairmanship of the Operational Policy Committee alternated between the police and the Army, resulting in concern about balance of military and police viewpoints in the direction of policy. After the Mountbatten and Warrenpoint incidents in 1979, the security forces were offered a 'Supremo' to be responsible for the whole political and security operation. They rejected this in favour of a civilian co-ordinator. In October 1979 Sir Maurice Oldfield, former head of MI6, was appointed to this task. Although his role was not clearly defined and he lacked executive powers, he made the committee more effective by allowing the Army and the police to make their cases to an independent chairman. This was a catalyst to improve co-operation between the Army and the police.[117]

Below the senior committee level there were other problems. By October 1970, for example, the Army had recognised that in Belfast a closer link was needed between the police and the Army on the one hand, and the civil administration—at the level of police division—on the other. Such a link would enhance co-ordination of security operations and civil affairs. Headquarters Northern Ireland, however, declined to act on the request for civil service advisers at that time, and individual commanders and staff officers were left to deal on a case-by-case basis with the various civil service departments, each with its own field of responsibility. It was not until September 1971, after the internment operation had caused such a violent response from the Catholic community, that a single civil affairs representative was appointed, initially only for Belfast. The scale of the task quickly became apparent, however, and by autumn 1972, each police division had its own civil representative. Yet, even after direct rule, problems continued. Robin Evelegh attributes this to the continued physical separation of Army, police, and civil administration headquarters which, he says, 'sometimes led to three different campaigns being waged'.[118]

Northern Ireland, perhaps more than any previous campaign, illustrates the significant differences in Army command 'styles' between conventional and low-intensity conflict. As Lieutenant Colonel Michael Dewar points out, in Northern Ireland the senior officer is more of a manager and co-ordinator than a commander. Real operational 'command', in the sense of 'leading troops', has devolved downward, through the battalion and company commanders to the junior NCOs.[119] More often than not, it is these men who are confronted with the most difficult operational decisions. The consensus is that they have adjusted to this responsibility very well.

Training Methods

Major General Anthony Deane-Drummond wrote in 1975:

> the change in role from conventional military operations to internal security and para-military duties is neither rapid nor easy. Intense—and time-consuming—periods of training are required to prepare troops tactically and psychologically for

a role which although less lethal in terms of overall casualties than conventional war is equally demanding and stressful.[120]

As noted earlier, the British Army that was committed to internal security (IS) duties in Palestine in 1945 had been immersed in conventional war for the previous six years. So, although the IS mission represented in historical terms a return to the Army's traditional role, for most officers and other ranks it constituted a significant break with recent experience in terms of outlook, training and operational methods. Consequently, the Army in Palestine in 1945 had to embark on an extensive training programme. Initial training was conducted in two phases. First, training teams from GHQ Middle East Forces taught street and house clearing and command and control of a company-sized mobile column. Then, formations and headquarters carried out signals exercises and tactical exercises without troops, covering cordon and search operations and suppression of large-scale insurrection. Two brigades, however, had not yet had the time to organise exercises before the first incidents at the end of October.[121]

The Army tried to compensate for such gaps as existed in procedures or training by a continuous process of revising techniques on the basis of operational experience. Formations constantly refined roadblock techniques, as this was felt to be the best weapon against the highly mobile insurgents. The new methods included pre-designated road-block locations which would be occupied rapidly following an incident, and mobile road-blocks which could be mounted briefly at random locations on principal roads.[122] Headquarters Palestine constantly stressed the need for close co-operation between the Army and the police, for two reasons: first, because the police were under strength and needed the Army's manpower to help them to carry out their tasks; and secondly, because the co-operation demanded by internal security theory did not always materialise in practice. Apart from providing additional manpower, efforts to improve collaboration included the designation of specific Army units to advise and assist in the physical security of individual police stations and to monitor constantly police radio frequencies in order to provide immediate assistance in the event of attack. While in Egypt the 2nd Infantry Brigade held a two-day study period on tactical problems and procedures for internal security.[123]

The series of search operations conducted in June 1946 proved valuable in exposing inadequacies in search procedures. Reports by the 1st Guards Brigade indicated requirements for unarmed troops to deal with passive resistance; for special equipment and expert searchers to locate hidden arms; for improved techniques and Hebrew interpreters to expedite identification and interrogation; for reserve troops to relieve weary search teams; and above all, for secrecy and surprise in executing operations.[124] Several factors conspired to interfere with re-training and thus with tactical adaptation and innovation. The most important of these were time and turbulence. Constant operational commitments reduced to a minimum the amount of time available to analyse operational lessons and to incorporate these into re-training programmes. The demobilisation process, then well underway, brought constant changes in the leadership and manpower of units, and the unit composition of formations. Experience gained was not retained, and such training as could be arranged within the time constraints necessarily had to be confined to basics.[125] As noted earlier, even these were imperfectly understood and applied.

Malaya presented a different tactical problem. Whereas the predominant threat in Palestine had been terrorism in densely packed urban areas, in Malaya the Army confronted guerrillas operating in or near the jungle. British strategy under the 'Briggs Plan' was to sever the guerrillas' tenuous links to the population as a whole, first by resettling the Chinese squatters—the guerrillas' principal source of supply—in protected villages away from the jungle fringe, and second, by interposing the security forces between the insurgents and the population, thereby forcing the guerrillas to operate in the security forces' domain when they tried to re-establish their presence amongst the population. The system did not work perfectly; it was conceived and carried out in haste and without sufficient security force resources to seal off the barrier between the guerrillas and the population. Nonetheless, it allowed the security forces gradually to identify and arrest the insurgents' supporters in the resettled areas, and freed the Army and police to operate against the terrorists themselves outside the protected areas and in the jungle.[126]

The nature of the enemy and the terrain dictated that the Army concentrate on small-unit actions. It was quickly recognised that a degree of specialised training was required to make soldiers effective in this role. The majority of those troops arriving in Malaya knew little of small-group tactics. Some, having had a little experience, became convinced that they already knew everything there was to know about jungle warfare. In fact, they demonstrated poor planning ability, inappropriate section movement organisation, and a reluctance to consider night operations. Moreover, heavy operational commitments precluded proper training courses at battalion level.[127] To remedy these shortcomings, the Far East Land Forces (FARELF) Training Centre at Kota Tingii near Johore Bahru established in September 1948 a Basic Jungle Warfare course. Staffed by Australians, Gurkha officers and others with war-time fighting experience in Malaya or Burma, the course programme covered all aspects of relevance to the soldier: it started with lectures on the history of the Emergency, on insurgent organisation and methods, on the organisation and roles of the security forces, on living in the jungle, jungle navigation and silent movement, tactics and many other subjects. There were also classroom and outdoor demonstrations of patrolling techniques, immediate-action drills and ambush methods. Considerable emphasis was placed on shooting quickly and accurately. Course members were later tested in these skills on exercises against jungle-wise Gurkhas attached to the school. Battalions deploying to Malaya would send advance parties of officers and NCOs to take the course; these, in turn, would provide a cadre of instructors who would train battalions on their arrival in Malaya, with assistance from the staff of the school. Battalion training took four weeks.[128]

That was not, however, the end of the training. The National Service system meant there was a need for constant training of new arrivals. Battalions were advised to continue training while on operational duties. They were advised to build ranges and training areas in their base camps where shooting and other jungle warfare skills could be rehearsed. Retraining immediately upon return from patrols or actions was undertaken right down to platoon level in some units. Battalions also regrouped for thorough retraining after long periods of operational duty. The FARELF Training Centre also offered courses for Junior Leaders, upon whom so much of the operational responsibilities devolved. Refresher courses were also offered to keep forces current on conventional 'all-arms' techniques. Nor was tactical thinking 'frozen in stone'. The FARELF Training Centre instructors emphasised that they could teach only the basics, and that the soldiers would have to learn for themselves what worked and what did not. Operational experience was incorporated into their training procedures, and tactical development continued at unit and sub-unit level.[129]

The Army went to considerable lengths to institutionalise the training methods and content of the Malayan campaign and subsequent emergencies. Units were encouraged to submit to the Army Training Directorate reports on their operations and training so as to extend valuable lessons to the Army as a whole. *Notes and Information on Training Matters* (NITM), the Army's training circular, drew on the Malaya and Kenya campaigns to stress the importance of marksmanship, fieldcraft, night movement, patrolling and ambushes. It also emphasised the point that successful anti-terrorist operations depended upon individual skills, the efficiency of platoons and sections, and the initiative and self-reliance of Junior Leaders.[130]

Officers were encouraged to write about their operational experience with a view to extracting useful lessons. The *British Army Journal* (later the *British Army Review*), published by the Training Directorate, provided one such forum; regimental journals or histories and personal accounts yet another.[132] In 1960, the *Army Quarterly*, a privately-published journal, chose for its annual prize essay competition the subject of the requirement for special training in 'unconventional operations' to meet the Army's Malaya-type emergencies. The winner that year was Lieutenant Colonel Richard Clutterbuck,[133] who went on to become one of the foremost thinkers, writers and teachers in the field.

The effect of this can be seen in subsequent campaigns. In terms of tactical training emphasis, the Kenya Emergency manual was a carbon copy of the Malayan publication. Moreover, East Africa Command followed the Malayan example and established a Battle School to teach the required skills to incoming units. Officers and advance parties attended the course, subsequently spending four weeks training their units.[134] By the end of the Confrontation campaign in Borneo, the British Army had raised jungle warfare techniques to the status of an art form.[135] But not all campaigns were fought in the jungle. In Cyprus, Aden and Northern Ireland, as in Palestine, the Army operated largely or frequently in urban areas where it might confront rioters one day and search a town or a city block the next. In Northern Ireland troops had to be able to change from riot control procedures and formations to street fighting tactics at a moment's notice, sometimes in the middle of an operation. There is some evidence to suggest that the Army welcomed the appearance of the PIRA gunman because dealing with snipers was a military task for which the Army was properly trained. Nevertheless, rapid changes in tactics required a high degree of flexibility, and it is noteworthy that, even with the experience of Palestine, Cyprus and Aden before them, some soldiers in Northern Ireland felt that the existing IS pamphlets were inadequate for operations in a modern city.[136] As the conflict consumed more and more British Army units, including many non-infantry arms and services, it became clear that a new training programme was needed.

Initially, preparation for Northern Ireland involved the distribution of briefing packages which contained lists of suggested reading and reports of study periods. This was to be supplemented by the dispatch of reconnaissance parties to Northern Ireland and the showing of a film on Ulster. It was recommended that units establish a briefing-room with appropriate materials to familiarise their troops with the situation. Tactical training emphasised the entire spectrum of IS operations from community relations and riot control to patrolling, cordon and search operations, and street fighting, both day and night. Eventually, the Ministry of Defence established two training teams, staffed by officers and NCOs experienced in Northern Ireland, to assist units in preparation and training for Northern Ireland. Positions on infantry IS training courses were also set aside for non-infantry officers.[137] This last point is very important. Traditionally, the infantry was the repository of IS experience; as noted earlier, infantry units had provided the largest proportion of troops for post-war emergencies. Because Northern Ireland drew in so many non-infantry units just to maintain sufficient manpower, by 1973 every arms group was affiliated for training to an infantry battalion. By this means and those mentioned above, the other combat arms and services were able to absorb knowledge and skills that were second-nature to experienced infantrymen.[138]

The most important training innovation was the creation of urban training areas—'tin cities'—designed to look and feel like the cities and towns of Northern Ireland. These allowed troops to develop tactical skills in an appropriate setting, complete with drunks, rowdies, rioters, slogans and songs, and all the hazards and unexpected situations the soldier was likely to encounter. The Close Quarter Battle Range gave units a chance to test their troops under simulated sniper fire in an urban setting as they attempted to carry out their patrols, searches and other duties. This training could then be followed up by Command Post Exercises and other drills to bring the requisite skills up to scratch before departure for Northern Ireland.[139] Although most preparatory training was confined to about nine months prior to deployment, the entire process of readying a unit for service in Ulster could consume as much as two years.

Training and learning also continued at higher levels at, for example, the Staff College. There the Counter Revolutionary Warfare section covered basic principles such as the development of a revolutionary situation and the government response; intelligence and handling of information; the use of force and the soldier's powers under the law; information services; offensive and defensive tactics; and training. However, the time devoted to the subject represented only a small proportion of the entire course, most of which covered conventional operations.[140]

The need for specialised skills was recognised at all levels, in the attention given to intelligence and information services in the Staff College course, and in the provision of special courses for members of all ranks going to Northern Ireland: for example, radar; driving and maintenance of the Humber 'Pig' armoured truck; intelligence courses; sharp-shooters; search teams; and television training.[141] Yet, long before Northern Ireland—indeed, shortly after the war—the case was made forcefully and successfully that some specialised skills and techniques should be concentrated within a single unit.

Special Forces and Special Operations

The British Army has a long history of special forces and operations. During the Seven Years' War and the American War of Independence, the British raised 'ranger' units from among the local population, often led or advised by a few regular officers and men. These units carried out long-range reconnaissance and raiding operations behind enemy lines, using unconventional tactics learned from the North American Indians. Not all these actions were successful, nor were they always viewed favourably by the military establishment of the day. However, they appear to have exerted some influence on the late 18th century British Army, notably in the creation of regular light infantry units whose equipment and tactics were specifically adapted to skirmishing and forest warfare.[142]

In World War I Colonel T. E. Lawrence was instrumental in raising an irregular Arab force which helped the British liberate the Middle

East from Ottoman rule—a large return for a small investment in manpower, munitions and money.[143] But Lawrence did not find favour with the traditionally-minded inter-war army, which did not keep useful files on some of Lawrence's innovative operations. As noted earlier, Ireland was overlooked. Consequently, planners had to start from scratch when forming special forces during World War II.[144] The British established a large number of special forces during the war; not all of them in or from the Army. The principal special forces were the Commandos and the Special Air Service (SAS). The former operated as raiding forces; the latter, behind the lines and in conjunction with resistance units. These, like the other special forces, had a mixed record of success and were the subject of considerable controversy and criticism relating to their operational effectiveness, command and control, and their relationship to traditional Army structures. A subcommittee of the War Office Directorate of Tactical Investigation was critical of the tendency of special forces to 'drift away' from the normal channels of command, to become private armies and a law unto themselves. As a result, the British Army disbanded virtually all its special forces at the end of the war.[145]

The Army did recognise that it was useful to have some capacity for special operations, so in 1947 a Territorial Army SAS unit was created. It struggled to keep alive the skills of its wartime parent. Indeed, its role was conceived to be solely within the framework of conventional war.[146] Therefore, it was not involved in the initial attempts to develop special operations capabilities for low-intensity operations.

The Army's capability might be said to have evolved along concurrent informal and formal lines. With regard to the former, there are two examples which bear discussion. The first of these took place in Palestine in 1947. There, at the instigation of Bernard Fergusson, a Black Watch and former Chindit officer on secondment to the Palestine Police, a special unit of undercover counter-terrorist operatives, consisting largely of former SAS and Commando troops, was formed by the police. This example is instructive because it undoubtedly confirmed all the grave reservations that conventionally-minded soldiers held about special forces. After some initial success against the Jewish underground, the operation went off the rails. It was 'blown' and accused of carrying out an alleged atrocity. Roy Farran, one of the leaders and a highly decorated SAS veteran, was tried and acquitted on a murder charge, much to the embarrassment of the British government. Even if the circumstances surrounding the case are never fully explained, one aspect is clear; the special squads operated in a 'grey' legal, moral and political environment, without clear guide-lines as to their mission, powers and constraints.[147]

The second example was more positive. Frank Kitson, then a young Rifle Brigade officer serving in Kenya as an intelligence officer, developed a technique for penetrating the Mau Mau forest gangs. In 1955, using loyal Kikuyu tribesmen, surrendered Mau Mau, and British troops in disguise, he created 'counter-gangs' to collect intelligence and to capture insurgents. They had some considerable success, and earned General Erskine's wholehearted support. They were not uncontroversial, however, and eventually were placed under centralised operational control, despite Kitson's protests. A similar unit in Malaya—the Special Operations Volunteer Force— composed of several hundred surrendered guerrillas, was commanded by police officers, but included soldiers as well.[148]

These informal or independent initiatives raised the issue of control, unwittingly reinforcing wartime criticisms. This may have contributed, at least in part, to the decision to concentrate special operations capabilities within a formally-constituted regular regiment of the Army. Yet, even the permanent establishment of the regular SAS was not a foregone conclusion when the embryo unit was formed in 1950.

The impetus came from Lieutenant Colonel Michael Calvert, a former Chindit commander, in discussions with General Sir John Harding, then C-in-C FARELF, early in 1950. Harding commissioned Calvert to study the Malayan situation and to produce a report offering solutions to the problem. Calvert produced his report in April 1950; among the recommendations was a proposal to create a special force for deep jungle operations beyond the normal reach of Army and police units. Although officially conceived for reconnaissance purposes, the force Calvert had in mind would have the broader mission of denying the bandits rest or sanctuary in the jungle; in short, an offensive, harassment role.[149] In the event, Calvert was vindicated, and his perception ultimately shaped the role of the SAS in Malaya.

Both Harding and General Briggs endorsed the proposal for a special force. Simultaneously, support for the idea of such a force came unexpectedly from the Australian Prime Minister, Robert Menzies. The Army high command agreed, with the usual provisos that the force be kept small, that it should not milk other units of their best men and that, above all, it should not become a 'private army'. It initially authorised an establishment of a regimental headquarters and one company, totalling 16 officers and 126 other ranks. Calvert was appointed commander of the new unit, which was designated the Malayan Scouts (SAS). It began forming on 1 August 1950. A two-month training programme was initiated, and Calvert began an extensive recruiting drive. He got volunteers from other units in the theatre, including veterans of wartime special forces. A squadron was provided by the Territorial regiment, and another was recruited in Rhodesia. By the end of 1951, the unit consisted of a regimental headquarters, a headquarters squadron, and four operational squadrons totalling 906 officers and other ranks.[150]

Initially the regiment deployed squadrons and troops into the jungle on long patrols (one of them lasted 103 days) tracking the insurgents, laying ambushes and adapting to long-term jungle operations. The aim was to find and destroy small bands of insurgents, and to prevent the return of insurgents to cleared areas. In 1952–53, the regiment's role was modified to include food denial (raiding and destroying insurgent cultivation), and winning the hearts and minds of the jungle tribes by protecting them from the guerrillas and providing assistance, such as medical aid, to the tribes. But the deep jungle tracking and ambush mission remained the principal focus throughout the campaign. During this time the SAS introduced several innovations in addition to deep jungle patrolling: river patrols in inflatable boats; use of helicopters for resupply (later thought to be too noisy for maintaining operational security and replaced by parachute); booby-trapping of insurgent weapons supplies, food caches, and jungle 'letter boxes'; and parachuting into the jungle. This last technique was abandoned at the end of the campaign because of the casualties incurred.[151]

There is no question that the regiment ultimately became very effective in long-range offensive operations against the insurgents in the deep jungle. This was not achieved without problems over the unit's proper function and its standards of training and discipline. For instance, from March to June 1951, the unit did not have the resources to train two new squadrons to the same high level as the first. This led to the SAS being concentrated in Johore, where the insurgents operated close to civilised areas, and being used like infantry. The unit's role was reviewed in September, and from October 1951 to April 1952 the tactics were changed again; the SAS was used in conjunction with police and Royal Marine Commandos to saturate selected targets. This, too, proved less effective than the deployment of small patrols.[152] The SAS found its proper niche only when the unit returned to deep jungle operations.

The training and discipline problems were interwoven. The SAS Malayan Scouts was an *ad hoc* organisation, hastily recruited and trained. It was weak in regimental administration. The unit contained many thoroughly professional soldiers, but it was in its nature that it also included some who were completely unsuitable for special forces. Regular soldiers posted to the unit were appalled at lapses of discipline. Over several years a series of strong-willed commanding officers weeded out the misfits and imposed professional standards of conduct on the rest. Simultaneously, efforts were made to place the regiment on a more permanent footing. The name Malayan Scouts was dropped and the unit became 22 Special Air Service Regiment. The tour of service was extended to two years for regulars (one for National Servicemen). Volunteers were put through a special selection course to eliminate unsuitable candidates, and trained thoroughly in the special skills required for SAS operations—jungle navigation, aerial resupply, jungle parachuting and small boat-handling. The Rhodesian squadron returned home, replaced by one from New Zealand and a fifth squadron from the Parachute Regiment. But the regiment was not yet part of the permanent establishment of the Army; that only came about as a result of lobbying and good fortune. A committee on the role of special forces concluded that there was an appropriate role for the SAS in conventional war—long-term, deep penetration, an extension of its Malayan role. Thus the SAS survived the regimental reductions that followed the 1957 Defence White Paper and joined the permanent establishment of the British Army.[153]

Tony Geraghty has suggested that implicit in the decision to retain the regiment was the assumption that it would not be constantly engaged in operations in the Third World. This view is disputed by others who argue that it was just that sort of operation—the first Oman campaign is specially mentioned—that saved the regiment from eventual extinction.[154] The fact is that the regiment, like other units of the British Army, was drawn into further campaigns in the Third World. These, in turn, provided it with experience and skills which would prove valuable for the tasks to be undertaken in the 1970s. Late in 1958 the SAS, now comprising only two squadrons, deployed from Malaya to Oman where, in January 1959, they defeated a guerrilla force many times larger by a daring and risky night-time climb and assault on the rebels' mountain redoubt, previously thought to be invulnerable.[155] The operation was carried out in secret, and was not announced to the British public until some months later. This operation, perhaps more than any other, may have instilled in the regiment the reputation as a 'silent service', a reliable covert military arm of British diplomacy.

The regiment returned to Oman in 1970 to combat yet another rebellion. In the meantime, it served with considerable effect in the Confrontation campaign in Borneo, and in Aden and the Radfan. The SAS role in the Confrontation was a variant of its Malayan counter-part: long-range reconnaissance, tracking, guiding raiding parties, and ambushing enemy patrols. The difference between these opera-tions and those in Malaya was that in this case, first, the enemy consisted of tough Indonesian regular forces, themselves experienced jungle fighters, and second, offensive operations against them involved covert raids across the border into Indonesian territory though not officially acknowledged. Much more important, however, was the creation by the SAS of a frontier intelligence network amongst the border tribesmen. This allowed the British to concentrate their relatively slim resources where and when required to meet Indonesian incursions across the 1,000-mile jungle-clad frontier.[156]

In South Arabia, the SAS was involved in two campaigns. The suppression of a tribal rebellion in the rural Radfan mountain area bore some similarity to the earlier Oman campaign. In addition to reconnaissance patrolling, the SAS was used to provide target identi-fication parties operating covertly behind rebel lines and calling down artillery fire on their positions. In Aden, the regiment had its first experience of urban counter-terrorist warfare. According to Tony Geraghty, the SAS carried out a number of plain-clothes undercover operations aimed at a team of insurgent assassins, but with only limited success. Unlike Kenya, there were no rebels to be 'turned' and used for 'counter-gangs'. Instead, the SAS was operating in a manner similar to Roy Farran's squads in Palestine. Geraghty con-cludes that the SAS felt that 'little of tangible value came out of the experiment except the acquisition of new experience and knowledge'.[157]

When the SAS returned to Oman in 1970, it was in a largely advisory role, to assist the Omani government in suppressing a tribal rebellion in Dhofar province that was supported by the neighbouring Marxist regime in South Yemen. Operating under the thin official cover of British Army Training Teams, elements of several SAS squadrons were instrumental in raising, training and leading the

Firquats, Dhofari irregular forces composed of loyal tribesmen and surrendered guerrillas who had been 'turned' to fight for the new Sultan. By the end of the campaign they numbered some 3,000, of whom about one third were surrendered guerrillas. The *Firquats* provided the counter-revolutionary infrastructure—intelligence and distribution of civil aid, in addition to their defensive policing-type role—that bought enough time for the regular forces to defeat the insurgents. As in the Confrontation campaign, the SAS role was *very* low-profile; their participation in the battle of Mirbat in July 1972, a turning point in the campaign and an occasion on which the SAS suffered fatalities, was not acknowledged publicly until later.[158]

By the time the SAS was deployed to Oman it had proven its value in low-intensity operations to the Ministry of Defence. The 1969 manual of counter-revolutionary operations formally acknowledged the special capabilities of the SAS in such campaigns: 'SAS squadrons are particularly suited, trained and equipped for counter-revolutionary operations.'[159] The manual went on to institutionalise the following tasks as those for which the SAS was particularly capable:

a. The collection of information on the location and movement of insurgent forces;
b. The ambush and harassment of insurgents;
c. Infiltration of sabotage, assassination and demolition parties into insurgent-held areas;
d. Border surveillance;
e. Limited community relations;
f. Liaison with, and organisation, training and control of, friendly guerrilla forces operating against the common enemy.[160]

On the face of it, these were just the sort of capabilities that Britain would need in the then-developing conflict in Northern Ireland. Not surprisingly, the PIRA and other critics of the British role in Ulster were quick to blame the SAS for a variety of atrocities early in the conflict.[161] However, Tony Geraghty suggests that, in fact, the Dhofar commitment and the reluctance of the British government to exacerbate an already delicate politico-military conflict precluded deployment of the SAS as a unit in the early stages, with the exception of a limited patrolling operation lasting several weeks in 1969 and aimed at suspected Protestant extremist gun-running. Instead, Geraghty says, undercover work during the first several years was undertaken by Army intelligence. SAS officers and NCOs were posted as individuals to intelligence positions from

1972 to stiffen Army capabilities for intelligence collection. The first full squadron deployment took place in 1974. It was a covert operation intended to enhance the Army's plain-clothes operations. It was not until January 1976 that the British government was prepared to announce publicly the deployment of an SAS squadron to Ulster.[162]

At that time the SAS was deployed into South Armagh, a border county with a high proportion of PIRA sympathisers and a high level of PIRA activity and sectarian murders. There the SAS established covert observation posts and ambushes which eliminated some of the key terrorists in the area and forced others to flee to the Irish Republic. They also made a significant number of arrests and captured a substantial number of weapons. The problem of adaptation confronting the SAS—and other undercover operations—in this conflict was not so much one of learning new tactics as adjusting those tactics to the peculiarities of the situation. For the first time the SAS had to operate in a campaign covered extensively by the news media. So, when mistakes were made, they tended to gain a significance out of all proportion to the circumstances of the incident itself. This gave the SAS much unwanted publicity which did not always do the regiment credit. The other dimension was the legal one; in common with the rest of the Army, the SAS had to be accountable in the courts for its use of lethal force. This, too, was difficult for a force accustomed to treating the opposition—whether in Malaya, Oman, Aden or Borneo—as military co-belligerents subject to normal wartime rules of engagement rather than to the legal niceties of civilian police-type arrest.[163]

Simultaneously with the Dhofar and Northern Ireland campaigns, the British government had to cope with terrorism in Britain itself. Some of this was a spill-over from Northern Ireland, the rest largely associated with the violent politics of the Middle East. The 1972 Munich Olympics massacre convinced many Western governments, Britain amongst them, of the need for special forces to deal with the modern manifestations of terrorism: airliner hijackings and hostage-taking sieges at embassies and other locations. The SAS was assigned to this role almost by accident. In the interval between the end of the Confrontation and the beginning of the Dhofar campaign they had been training bodyguards of foreign heads of state. This training was part of the range of skills required for anti-terrorist operations, and the fact that the regiment made an effort to keep these skills alive after 1970 meant that the British government had a ready-made force when the Munich incident convinced it of the need for such a capability. The SAS were given the resources needed to prepare fully for the role. The embryonic counter-revolutionary warfare (CRW) wing was expanded and put on a permanent footing. New weapons were designed or tested and purchased on the recommendation of a regimental operational research team. Squadrons were assigned to the CRW role on rotation, and put through a rigorous training programme with monthly siege-breaking exercises. In London at the Balcombe Street siege (1975) and at Mogadishu (1977) the SAS gained operational experience in the role. Clearly, duty in Northern Ireland had provided some beneficial lessons as well. Consequently, the regiment probably could not have been better prepared when the Iranian embassy siege occurred in London in 1980. The exemplary performance of the SAS in that siege-breaking and hostage rescue operation is a matter of record.[164]

Intelligence

In his excellent historical survey of British counter-insurgency intelligence, Keith Jeffery pointed to conflicting intelligence methods and requirements as a source of strain in army-police relations, and to the need for 'careful management and close co-ordination' to deal with the problem.[165] The historical record amply bears out Jeffery's thesis; indeed, with few exceptions, the intelligence co-ordination 'problem' was a recurring theme. In Palestine, intelligence was deemed to be largely a police responsibility. The subject was not covered in *Notes for Officers on Internal Security Duties*, and official army thinking discouraged soldiers from undertaking 'duties of a detective or secret service nature'.[166] This attitude is not surprising given that historically the Army had never been entirely comfortable with the intelligence task. After the war there was substantial opposition to the creation of even a small permanent army intelligence corps.[167] The Palestine Police, however, were overworked, undermanned, isolated from the Jewish community, and penetrated, compromised and intimidated by the insurgents.[168] Consequently, the Army was drawn into the intelligence task.

All formations, from battalion to division level, had their own intelligence staffs, as did Army headquarters in Jerusalem. The head of Army intelligence (GSI), Lieutenant Colonel The Hon. Martin Charteris, felt that one of his main tasks, given the Army's non-political nature, was 'to make sense for the soldiers out of the tangle of the Palestine problem, so that they may see things in their true perspective'.[169] This was necessary, he felt, because the soldiers, who were in Palestine temporarily and who regarded IS duties there as an interference with proper soldiering, did not have the time or incentive to get to grips with the problem. But devoting attention to this task may have diverted GSI from a more important mission— directing the flow of operational intelligence to units and formations. One thing is clear; it had a rather mixed record of accuracy in its intelligence assessment. By contrast, the Defence Security Office, staffed by officers with lengthy service in Palestine and represented in all the main cities, frequently provided more accurate reports.[170]

As a result, *ad hoc* arrangements were made. Some senior commanders developed personal contacts with highly-placed and influential members of the Jewish community. Field Security Sections, which normally provided physical security for Army formations and installations, were often called upon for operational or special intelligence work. And the Special Investigation Branch of the Military Police conducted some intelligence work related to internal security in the context of investigation of criminal offences within units and installations, such as thefts of arms.[171]

This is not to suggest that there was no Army-police co-operation in intelligence matters. As noted earlier, Army, police and Defence Security intelligence officers sat on the Security Committees. Combined Army-police intelligence courses were conducted to share knowledge and experience. The Army, police and Security Intelligence Middle East collaborated in the use of the Army's Detailed Interrogation Centre for in-depth interrogation of captured terrorists.[172] But in spite of the fact that the Army GOC exercised operational control of the police, there was no single body to collect or integrate intelligence from police, Army or other sources. Furthermore, the Army was wary of lax police security and frequently resorted to deceiving the police in order to ensure the security of planned joint operations.[173] This, of course, was a highly unsatisfactory state of affairs. It allowed the insurgents considerable freedom of action to plan and carry out their operations in secrecy, thereby retaining the tactical and the strategic initiative. It meant further that security force operations were often launched with insufficient information and thus only rarely produced significant results in terms of arrests, prosecutions or a reduction in the level of insurgent activity. In short, the security forces lost the intelligence battle, in Menachem

Begin's view, 'the decisive battle in the struggle for liberation'.[174]

The Army did learn from this experience. The 1949 IS manual placed considerable emphasis on the need for accurate, up-to-date intelligence; all possible sources were to be consulted. The commander was urged to consider the scrutiny of his intelligence system as his first duty upon taking up a posting. Likely deficiencies in the allotment of intelligence staffs were noted, and this was taken to mean that the Army should not try to do the job of the police Special Branch, which should be the principal source of information for operational planning; rather it placed more weight on the need for close co-operation and mutual confidence. This was to be achieved by regular—even daily—intelligence conferences.[175] Although such thinking still saw the Army and police intelligence tasks as distinct and separate, it went some way towards preparing the ground intellectually for the more integrated approach that eventually characterised the Malayan and subsequent campaigns.

After being almost completely surprised by the outbreak of the communist insurrection, owing largely to the intelligence priorities of the Malayan Security Service (MSS), the Malayan government reacted with astonishing speed to correct the intelligence situation. At the urging of the Commissioner-General Malcolm Macdonald, a Combined Intelligence Staff was created in July 1948. This brought MSS, police and armed forces intelligence together at the highest level, reporting at that time to the Local Defence Committee. At the state level, joint intelligence centres were set up, attached to police chiefs' headquarters. Army and police were directed to pass their information to the nearest police headquarters.[176]

Even so, it took some time for the intelligence picture to improve, principally because of weakness in the police force. Nor, as noted earlier, was it always possible for the Army and police to be co-located. It was not until the initiation of the Briggs Plan that the Federal War Council had a joint intelligence advisory committee to assist it, and a Director of Intelligence was appointed only towards the end of 1950. He lasted less than a year, retiring in the autumn of 1951. Field Marshal Templer, who took over as High Commissioner in 1952, was himself a former Director of Intelligence at the War Office, and placed considerable emphasis on the intelligence task. He appointed the regional MI5 representative, John Morton, as Director of Intelligence with his own intelligence staff and responsibility for co-ordinating the existing services. He sat as a full member of the Director of Operations Committee, and chaired the Federal Intelligence Committee, the co-ordinating body. Although he exercised no executive authority over the Services themselves, he served as Templer's principal intelligence adviser and thus wielded considerable influence, which was immediate, positive, and lasting.

By this time the flow and quality of intelligence had improved cumulatively, and the Combined Intelligence Staff (CIS) was doing a better job of collating it. The CIS at this time consisted of four representatives from the Civil Service, police, Army and RAF, working directly under the new Director of Intelligence. Their job was to co-ordinate intelligence products and make recommendations to the D/OPs committee. The Army's contribution to the effort at this level included the secondment of military intelligence officers to work inside the police Special Branch on tactical intelligence, insurgent order of battle and to provide a channel for passing operational intelligence to the Army. This freed the Special Branch officers to concentrate on clandestine investigations. At brigade and battalion level, the Army intelligence staffs were integrated with the police in joint operations rooms. Special Branch remained the principal intelligence-producing body.[177]

At the operational level the most valuable intelligence source was the surrendered guerrilla. Considerable efforts were made to 'turn' these persons to work for the security forces; in fact, most took very little persuading to lead the Army or police to the guerrilla units or camps from which they had just defected. The local Army unit had to be prepared to mount patrols, ambushes or other operations at short notice if Special Branch decided that the surrendered guerrilla could best be exploited for immediate operational intelligence.[178] It was, after all, the effective exploitation of intelligence—regardless of source—that was the key to successful anti-guerrilla operations at the patrol, platoon and company level. In retrospect, Richard Clutterbuck observed that

> Our best commanders in Malaya were the ones who set themselves the task of managing the war in such a way that their small patrols came face to face with the guerrillas on favourable terms; in other words, with good intelligence. This meant long hours of tactful discussions with police officers, administrators, rubber planters, tin miners, and local community leaders, getting them to co-operate with the soldiers, and to promote the flow of information to them.[179]

From Malaya onwards, the importance of intelligence as the key to success in counter-insurgency, the need for a single integrated intelligence organisation based on the police Special Branch, the need for a single director of intelligence and the integration of military intelligence liaison officers into Special Branch, became articles of faith in Army counter-insurgency doctrine.[180] Inevitably, the application of these principles in subsequent campaigns varied considerably.

Prior to the Harding reorganisation of the Cyprus command structure in 1955, there had been little co-ordination of police and military intelligence staffs; existing intelligence was not being properly collated or distributed. Upon reorganisation Harding appointed a Director of Intelligence responsible for co-ordination of all intelligence services. The intelligence picture improved considerably thereafter,[181] although never to the point where EOKA could be completely eliminated. A similar situation prevailed in Aden. There, the intelligence organisation was initially almost as complex as the politico-military structure. The High Commissioner, the Army and the police each had separate intelligence services—in fact, there were more than 10 in all in South Arabia—and there was no single director. The principal source was Special Branch, which operated under the commissioner of police but its effectiveness decreased as the Arab officers were intimidated or eliminated. In 1964 an army brigadier was appointed director of intelligence and an intelligence centre established to collate information from all sources. Military Intelligence liaison officers were assigned to each brigade headquarters to maintain close contact with Special Branch. Army units gave intelligence collection a high priority and patrolling, searches and other operations did increase the flow of information somewhat. However, as in Cyprus, even the improved intelligence organisation could not compensate for the lack of co-operation from the local population. Consequently, the supply of intelligence was never sufficient.[182] In both campaigns the Army tried to overcome this problem by resorting to coercive interrogation methods, which will be discussed briefly later.

In the Confrontation campaign the Director of Operations, General Walker, recognised the importance of intelligence from the outset, and gave priority to the expansion of Special Branch. The SAS was used to provide an early-warning intelligence system along the frontier. Small detachments were air-lifted into the jungle near the border where they would remain for several weeks, not attacking the enemy but watching him, sending back information by radio. The SAS also helped to raise and train the Border Scouts, who were supposed to be a civilian, indigenous tribal irregular force, tasked to live amongst their people and bring back information to the security forces. Initially, however, they were organised as a uniformed, armed militia—and not a very good one at that—so a considerable effort was made by Major John Cross to convert them back to the originally intended role. Eventually, some remained in uniform, guarding tribal longhouses and guiding Army patrols, but an increasing number acted in the appropriate surveillance role, in plainclothes—or in no clothes at all.[183]

Finally, in Northern Ireland the Army had to run the intelligence system virtually unaided from the start because the police, the Royal Ulster Constabulary (RUC), were politically discredited, unable to function in the Catholic areas, under strength and demoralised.[184] The task confronting the Army was daunting, for the police intelligence organisation had long been neglected. The RUC's files were out of date, and their intelligence network in the Catholic areas almost non-existent. One officer observed:

> Financial constraints and lack of foresight led, in Ulster, to insufficient attention being paid to the activities of the Special Branch and other intelligence-gathering agencies. These agencies were insufficient in size to cope with the situation once the conflict started and it is an unfortunate fact that any terrorist organisation can expand at a faster rate than the agencies responsible for providing information on them.[185]

Because the campaign is still continuing there is much that is not known about the intelligence dimension of the Northern Ireland campaign; reliable source material is hard to come by. Much of what follows should be considered educated guesswork.

The British hastily assembled an intelligence organisation based on the Army, with input from RUC Special Branch and the Security Service. Army Intelligence Corps officers were seconded to Special Branch. A diplomat was apparently appointed to co-ordinate intelligence. Even so, there was apparently some confusion over who had supreme authority in intelligence, and inter-agency rivalry continued, even after direct rule was imposed and a new intelligence 'supremo' appointed.[186] At unit level, the priority given to intelligence-collection meant that much operational activity was oriented towards gathering information. The Army mounted constant foot and mobile patrols, snap searches and vehicle check-points to familiarise troops with their areas of responsibility and to pick up background information. This allowed the intelligence staffs to carry out a kind of local census, building up a street-by-street population register, and a card index of known or suspected terrorists, their families, friends and habits. This index was cross-referenced to reports and intelligence summaries so that a complete dossier could be put together for any suspect. The Army and the RUC maintained joint operations centres and conducted joint patrols. A combined Army-RUC murder investigation squad was formed to deal with sectarian killings.[187]

Political considerations, however, dictated changes in these methods in early 1972. Following the imposition of direct rule, the Army was ordered to adopt a 'low-profile' in the Catholic areas of Belfast and Londonderry. Street patrols were reduced; some areas were patrolled only at night, and later not at all. The Army stopped 'hot pursuit' of known terrorists and restricted arrests and searches. At the same time, the government began to phase out internment. Together, these decisions (temporarily) reduced the pressure on the PIRA, and jeopardised both the intelligence networks and the intelligence 'picture' that the Army had constructed painstakingly for nearly three years. Overt intelligence did not begin to flow again until after Operation MOTORMAN in August 1972 permitted the security forces to re-establish a presence in the Catholic ghettos. From 1972–76 the security forces searched nearly 250,000 houses, recovering substantial quantities of arms and ammunition. But as Jeffery points out, there was an immeasurable political cost to these operations, and in recent years house searches have been far more selective, yet proportionately more productive.[188]

The 'low-profile' phase placed a greater premium on the Army's covert operations. One of the best known of these was the Military Reconnaissance Force (MRF). Several sources suggest that the SAS had a hand in setting up and running the MRF, although Geraghty denies this, citing the political considerations noted earlier. What is known is that the MRF units consisted of small detachments of plain-clothes British soldiers who carried out covert surveillance, guided to likely targets by captured PIRA members who had been 'turned' to work for the British. It was highly dangerous work; the former terrorists faced torture or death if recaptured by their erstwhile PIRA comrades, and MRF patrols shot at each other on several occasions. Innocent bystanders were also occasionally caught in the cross-fire. Then, in the deteriorating intelligence environment of 1972, the MRF's most profitable intelligence channel—'the Four Square Laundry'—was blown by a defector from the MRF. The PIRA ambushed the van and killed the soldiers operating it.[189]

That was not the end of covert actions; indeed, they were stepped up in scope and intensity by the end of the 1970s. In addition to the introduction of the SAS in squadron strength in 1976, SAS officers were drafted to control agents in the field. Soldiers from line regiments were trained for undercover operations, but there is some question of whether they were properly trained and a few came to grief, the best known case being that of Captain Robert Nairac, who was abducted and killed.[190]

More controversial by far has been the use of interrogation techniques to extract intelligence from captured or arrested terrorists or suspects. The use of in-depth interrogation in British low-intensity operations goes back at least as far as the Palestine campaign. Experience since World War II had cast some doubt on the value of centralised interrogation by professional specialists, suggesting instead that more informal, relaxed questioning by personnel closely familiar with the prisoner's milieu was more likely to produce results.[191] Yet, in Cyprus and Aden the Army was accused of employing more brutal methods of extracting information. Jeffery suggests that 'the likelihood of ill-treatment increases in a poor intelligence environment', where priority is given to acquiring operational intelligence, and when the 'interrogation becomes excessively specialised within the security effort'.[192] This state of affairs prevailed in both colonies. An investigation of the situation in Aden led the government to decide that Army personnel should not carry out interrogation of prisoners in these campaigns. In Ulster, the RUC was responsible for in-depth interrogation, but the Army provided the training. It was thus indirectly involved in the charges of 'torture' laid against the security forces in that province.[193] How the Army came to be involved can be traced to several sources: first, the Army's own requirement for extracting information quickly from captured enemy in any form of warfare; the unimaginative, impatient intelligence officer or NCO might revert to brutality as a short-cut, simply because it produces quick results. Second, during the Korean War, captured allied soldiers were subjected to sophisticated 'group dynamics' techniques, stress manipulation and other pressures, the aim of which was to produce not just confessions but conversions. The British Army trained its soldiers to resist this kind of interrogation, but in turn used it against insurgent suspects in several conflicts.[194]

It has been argued that these methods produced windfalls of intelligence that might not have been acquired by any other means. Moreover, PIRA propaganda about torture so frightened their own members that many suspects readily 'spilled all' upon capture.[195] Robin Evelegh challenges the notion of the importance of windfall benefits by asserting that the real purpose of interrogation should be to 'turn' captured insurgents into informers or 'moles', who will keep the security forces informed of insurgent plans and activities in advance, from within the ranks of the organisation. The development of 'supergrass' informers inside the PIRA in the 1980s, albeit with mixed results, indicates that Evelegh's arguments were not lost on the authorities.[196] In any case, it is clear that whatever benefits were gained by 'in-depth' interrogation, they were achieved at a price in the propaganda war. This dimension of low-intensity operations will be discussed next.

Information Services

Although propaganda had played a major role in World War II on the home front and against the enemy, and an even more significant part in post-war conflicts, the British Army has dealt with psychological operations only sporadically and tangentially. The reason is simple: 'Political Warfare', as it was called in World War II, was a civilian task, and remained so after the war; the Army played a relatively small role in most psychological campaigns. In Northern Ireland the Army demonstrated greater interest in the subject, but with only a small apparatus for information services—as opposed to public relations—and in the absence of a doctrine and a body of relevant experience, this interest did not translate into a sustained or effective strategy.

In Palestine, the Army dealt with insurgent propaganda by first attempting to protect its own integrity. The main objective was to deny the insurgents material with which to make propaganda. First, formation commanders explained to their troops the aims and effects of propaganda, and impressed upon them the need to avoid taking unnecessarily provocative actions. Above all, they were not to lose their 'sense of proportion'.[197] Second, the Army encouraged good relations with the press. The security forces gave all possible assistance to the accredited correspondents consistent with safety and operational security. Public relations officers were appointed to sector, brigade and divisional headquarters to assist the press. Correspondents were permitted to move freely through curfew and restricted areas and to accompany the troops on operations. They were allowed on several occasions to visit internment camps. However, until 1947 officers were forbidden to give interviews to the press. It was then decided that the senior military commander on the scene of an operation could give an interview to, or answer questions from, the press. Officers concerned were encouraged to give the fullest possible account of the operations but were to confine their remarks to statements of fact that the correspondents could check; they were not to comment on policy or express opinions.[198]

Third, the Army gave some thought to 'managing' news coverage of incidents. Instructions emphasised the speed and accuracy needed to 'beat Reuters' in order to prevent or correct inaccurate news reports. One staff officer suggested that the Army should try to influence press reporting by providing them with information before the insurgents did, thereby ensuring that the press would give 'the right angle to the story'. It was not until August 1947, however, that the Central Security Committee decided that the Palestine Public Information Office should colour its reporting by emphasising successful security force operations.[199]

The Army, however, was not accustomed to conducting operations under the glare of publicity and its inexperience caused some difficulties. Despite the best of intentions and the co-operative arrangements, the Army's press relations were less than satisfactory. British correspondents complained of being 'held up, searched and refused admittance to places where, with their passes, they have every right to go.'[200] It is not surprising, then, that the security forces had few defenders in the news media. The problem was probably self-sustaining, since hostile reporting generated a hostile attitude towards the press on the part of the Army.

In Malaya the British mounted an intensive psychological warfare campaign as part of the 'Briggs Plan'. The Psychological Warfare Section had a civilian head and a largely civilian staff, on which one member each of the Army and RAF were represented. This apart, the Army's role was limited to the distribution of leaflets designed to undermine insurgent morale and to encourage surrenders. At the outset of the campaign Army thinking on this subject tended to discourage press interviews with junior officers and soldiers, routing the flow of information solely through the most senior commander or his public relations officer. By the mid-1950s this view had changed slightly in recognition of the fact that a complete ban on access to junior leaders might be counter-productive. It was left to the public relations officer to arrange such interviews, given the approval of the high command.[201]

In the decade between the end of the Malayan campaign and the start of the Northern Ireland operation, the Army paid desultory attention to psychological warfare. While its importance was recognised, it was not seen as a major Army task, and rightly so. The Army did offer short courses, and the manuals indicate that a limited Army role was anticipated; but overall direction was to remain in civilian hands. By 1970, the Army's resources consisted of information staff officers at three overseas headquarters and one at the Ministry of Defence, two officers running courses at the Joint Warfare Establishment, a 12-man team in Hong Kong, and an embryonic reserve team being formed as part of one infantry battalion. The Army units were designed to conduct loudspeaker and leaflet distribution operations.[202]

This low-key approach changed radically during the Northern Ireland campaign. Prior to direct rule, the Home Office was the ministry responsible for Northern Ireland affairs. Unlike the Foreign and Commonwealth Office (FCO), which had worked closely with the Army in many overseas campaigns, providing the necessary expertise and resources, the Home Office had virtually no experience in such matters. It consented to the posting to Ulster of one FCO official but resisted advice favouring a much more aggressive information effort. This left the propaganda initiative in the hands of the PIRA. From the outset every action of the security forces was scrutinised by the news media, and mistakes, errors of judgement, unsuccessful operations or disproportionate use of force provided the PIRA with useful propaganda, quite apart from material the PIRA conjured up on its own. Maurice Tugwell suggests that for some time the Army maintained a detached disdain for responding to PIRA propaganda, and that it was pressure from officers and soldiers, who felt that their every act had been misrepresented, that persuaded the Army to get into the psychological battle in a significant way.[203] However, the Army initiated some *ad hoc* efforts as early as 1969. A 'Hearts and Minds' offensive was launched in November of that year, wherein the Army initiated community projects, bi-sectarian youth clubs, dances, sporting events, and even a meals-on-wheels service for the elderly in Londonderry. From October 1970, the Army and its civil representatives appointed to police divisions co-ordinated their efforts to win over the population. The civil representatives acted as 'trouble-shooters' and sat with representatives from the Army, the police and local councils on committees to hear complaints and to deal with local problems. The Army also appointed press relations officers at headquarters and units to handle the greatly increased news media coverage.[204] This *ad hoc* approach changed with the rapid deterioration of the political and security situation following the introduction of internment in August 1971.

First, the Ministry of Defence added a new Chapter, on 'Public Relations', to the Army's manual *Land Operations 3/1*. This Chapter identified three requirements: to provide information that would convince national and international opinion that the Army's cause was good; to foster good relations with the local community; and to preserve and improve the Army's image. It pointed out that the media would attempt to get the news whether or not the Army helped them; since fair, accurate reporting would always be in the Army's interest, the media should be given full access to the scene of any incident and to the information they require, subject to security considerations. However, the Chapter warned those officers and soldiers permitted to speak to the media to 'confine their answers to matters of fact and . . . avoid comment on political or controversial issues'.[205]

Second, in line with this thinking, the Army relaxed restrictions on soldiers speaking to the media, recognising that on television the private soldier might be more likeable and hence more credible than the GOC.[206] To enhance this capability, the Army and the Ministry of Defence increased the media and information services training programme. By the end of 1971 more than 200 officers had been put through courses on how to be interviewed on television. The media was introduced as a subject into the Sandhurst curriculum in 1972. It was also studied at the higher defence colleges. From 1977 officers designated for assignment as unit press officers attended special courses; by 1982, nearly 400 a year were receiving this training. From 1973–76, 212 Army officers attended the information services course at the Joint Warfare Establishment.[207]

Third, in September 1971, the Army established an Information Policy office at headquarters in Lisburn. The role of this PR 'think tank' was to analyse trends in PIRA propaganda and in media coverage of the conflict in order to allow the Army to keep abreast of developments in the 'propaganda war'. Richard Clutterbuck suggests that the office had a more activist role as well: 'to take a positive initiative in presenting the news to the best advantage of the security forces'.[208] This included private, 'off-the-record' or 'deep background', unattributable briefings to journalists by senior officers. The Information Policy unit also apparently became involved in some propaganda operations of doubtful effectiveness. This ended in 1975 with a reorganisation of Army and police information services in the province.[209]

The results of these Army efforts cannot yet be fully analysed. Although the Army modified its tactics to accommodate intensive media scrutiny—for example, by making 'retrospective arrests' after an incident rather than during it[210]—it was rarely able to 'beat Reuters' or the PIRA propagandists. Complete freedom of the press meant that the first, and usually the most sensational, story of any incident was the one most likely to be believed, even if it was subsequently shown to be inaccurate or misleading. The authorities always felt that 'the truth will out' in the end, to the satisfaction of all concerned, but this was not always so. Thorough investigation of incidents takes time and, by the time a report appeared, the damage already done by PIRA propagandists might be irreparable. Internment, interrogation and 'Bloody Sunday' are classic examples of issues which were exploited effectively by the PIRA before the government could respond in detail. In 1977 the Army had to modify its information policy yet again to emphasise Army successes and to report incidents only when specifically requested to provide details.[211] In so far as, at the time of writing, the British Army remains in Ulster, enjoying broad support from its domestic public, including that considerable section of the public that would be delighted to see the Army out of Ulster, its PR campaign can be termed a success, at least to the extent that it has protected the integrity of the Army as an institution. But this does not mean the Army has worked miracles. Even an elaborate and sophisticated public relations programme designed primarily for the domestic UK audience failed to make any inroads among the Northern Ireland Catholic minority—the water in which the PIRA fish swim. As one officer remarked early in the campaign, 'it would take an advertising campaign of genius to sell the British Army in the Catholic ghettos. . . .'[212] If Ulster had been an overseas colony, far from Westminster and under FCO control, no doubt an experienced team of 'Psy-Warriors' might have found ways of persuading the minority population to withdraw support from the insurgents. But this was the United Kingdom: the FCO had no mandate and the Army even less in terms of psychological manipulation. To be sure, the surrender rate among PIRA members in recent years, and the willingness of some to give evidence against erstwhile comrades, suggests some successful psychological action against 'the enemy'. But a wider campaign addressed to Catholics would be an essentially political act, and in the absence of a sustainable political policy for the Province, this key target audience remains neglected.

Technological Adaptation

Low-intensity operations are not 'technology intensive', not at least to the same extent as with conventional war. So, adaptation to new technology did not figure too significantly in these campaigns. There are two exceptions to this proposition. The first is in the field of riot control. After the Amritsar incident of 1919, the Army standardised its regulations and drills for providing military aid to the civil power in riot situations. These procedures were adopted for use in Britain and were gradually extended for use throughout the Empire. They were predicated upon the use of minimum, but lethal, force, the soldiers being armed only with rifles.[213] Over the years tactics were not altered significantly but by the mid-1950s the Army recognised that it might have to replace the police in certain riot situations and required a graduated response of its own where lethal force might not be appropriate. Thus tear gas, batons and shields made their appearance in Cyprus, though not without arousing criticism. Vehicles were modified to function in such situations while still providing protection to their occupants.[214] The outbreak of communal rioting in Northern Ireland drew the Army directly into riot control because the police were unable to do the job, and this presented the Army with a dilemma. In a situation where the rioters were British, and were perceived to be a victimised minority, and where the British and international news media provided immediate coverage and commentary for the domestic audience, 'the traditional box formation and its associated "one round at the man in the red hat" was something of a non-starter'.[215] The Army modified its tactics as much as it could, but also came to rely more heavily upon 'technological' means to control riots: CS gas, water cannon and rubber bullets. The first and the last of these had operational limitations and characteristics which made them controversial, particularly when their use produced casualties—circumstances which could lend themselves to exploitation by PIRA propagandists. However, by the time that these methods were becoming controversial, the nature of the conflict had changed, and riot control operations declined in frequency.[216]

The second area in which the Army adapted successfully to technological innovation was in air-mobility, particularly at the tactical level. Helicopters were first used in 1950 in the casualty evacuation role in Malaya; in 1952–53, the Army began to use them for operations. The helicopters themselves were operated by the RAF or the Royal Navy, and were severely limited in numbers and serviceability. These factors undoubtedly ensured that the Army never became too dependent on air-mobility, always bearing in mind that it was 'not a substitute for feet on the ground'.[217] Insertion of troops by air posed problems in any case; helicopters were noisy and required cleared landing zones, and parachuting into jungle from aircraft was dangerous. Aerial resupply of deep jungle patrols, on the other hand, proved very effective. Still, the helicopter provided an element of tactical flexibility and speed the Army might not otherwise have had and most officers were prepared to exploit it when the resources could be made available.[218] Nor was adaptation confined to helicopters; early in the Brunei revolt, British troops hastily organised and mounted successfully two air-landing operations from fixed-wing aircraft.[219] The importance of integral tactical air-mobility was formally recognised with the re-creation of the Army Air Corps in 1957 (although the Army remained largely dependent on RAF and Navy resources until the 1970s), and the increasing prominence given to transport air support in the Army manuals thereafter.[220] Again, it is significant that the innovations in this regard originated largely with the forces in operational theatres, thereby demonstrating the Army's ability to improvise and adapt without the benefit of a 'pre-cooked' doctrine.

Conclusions

In general, the British Army adapted effectively, if not always easily, to the conditions and requirements of low-intensity operations. That said, it also had a mixed record of success in its post-war campaigns. In short, effective adaptation and victory were not necessarily one and the same. The distinction is at least partly semantic. Dennis Duncanson has observed that 'the test of validity of experience in armed conflict ought to be victory or defeat. However, victory or defeat are not always easy to measure under conditions of decolonisation, the end result of which was, by definition, surrender of the colonials' power's mandate sooner or later'.[221] In these circumstances—applicable in the cases of Palestine, Malaya, Kenya, Cyprus and Aden—the outcome of the campaigns was determined by political considerations, at home and in the colony, of which the military-

security campaign was merely one of many. The relative significance
of the military-security dimension varied from one campaign to the
other; it was very important in Malaya, rather less so in Palestine.
However, the extent to which the Army adapted effectively to the
requirements of the situation could determine to a considerable
extent the character of the British surrender of authority: either an
orderly transfer of power, as in Malaya, or chaos—as in Palestine and
Aden.

In this context, J. Bowyer Bell's view that 'military tactics in the
field . . . could be learned, could be applied, could in the long run be
largely effective; but only if used in a cunningly prescribed political
formula'[222] is simplistic at best. The British Government rarely, if
ever, was guided by such a political formula (the Malayan case was
exceptional in this regard) and the Army proved able to adapt
effectively to operational conditions regardless of the political
circumstances. In any case, some different criteria are surely required
to assess the Army's performance where clear political direction was
absent—as in Northern Ireland—or was in the hands of an
independent government, such as Malaysia during the Confrontation, and Oman. Only in the latter case was there a 'formula' which
involved something more than merely resisting the insurgents. A
more sophisticated political approach was not really necessary in the
Confrontation and was simply not possible in Northern Ireland. So, if
there is a key to understanding the Army's ability to adapt to low-
intensity operations, it lies largely outside the political dimension.
The answer, surely, is to be found in the nature of the British Army
itself.

Because of the large number of commitments and the relatively
small size of the Army, it could not afford to confine counter-
insurgency expertise to a single specialised unit or even to a relatively
small number of units. These skills were required throughout the
infantry, and had to be transferable to the artillery and the armoured
corps as well as the other supporting arms. This forced the Army to
develop, to write down, and periodically to revise a body of collective
wisdom based on experience, to provide all arms and services with
standardised tactical procedures. This is as close as the Army came to
developing a counter-insurgency doctrine, and it is wholly in keeping
with its traditions that the first and probably most significant effort in
this regard, the ATOM pamphlet, originated in a theatre of operations, not in a Ministry of Defence 'doctrine' committee. Concur-
rently, the Army developed training courses 'in theatre', based on

accumulated experience and oriented towards the local situation. These courses taught the required classics—the standard drills and survival skills; after that, it was up to the individual soldier and unit to learn and to adapt on-the-job. Whether the soldiers and the unit became highly proficient in the task or merely adequate depended upon unit leadership, particularly the junior officers and NCOs. None of this would have been possible, however, had not the Army already instilled high standards of professional conduct, leadership qualities, and basic skills at arms training at the outset of the soldier's service.

The regimental system accorded several advantages. First, it enhanced unit cohesion in stressful operational conditions; this was particularly important during the National Service period, when the small number of regular officers and soldiers had to struggle to maintain a sense of continuity for successive drafts of conscripts. Second, it turned out officers and NCOs who, by tradition and experience, were at their best in small unit and sub-unit operations, battalion and below. This is extremely important because these campaigns were most effectively conducted at that level. Moreover, the relative paucity of resources and manpower forced commanders to 'think small', to conceive methods and operations that would allow relatively small numbers of men to become effective out of all proportion to their numbers. This, in turn, forced the Army to recognise the importance of accurate intelligence, and to adapt their organisation, personnel and operations to enhance the process of collecting, developing and exploiting intelligence.

In this context, the colonial and Commonwealth dimension gave the British a further advantage—additional manpower in the form of auxiliaries and allies. In virtually every territory, the British were able to draw upon or, if necessary, create local auxiliary, irregular, or paramilitary forces of varying degrees of competence.[223] As village and settlement guards (in Malaya and Kenya) they freed British troops to concentrate on offensive operations; as frontier scouts and guides, in the Confrontation, they enhanced the Army's intelligence-gathering capabilities and thus contributed directly to successful operations. Regular colonial or Commonwealth regiments from East Africa, Rhodesia, Australia, New Zealand and Fiji provided extra battalions where the British could not.

The resurrection of the SAS was a significant innovation, which allowed the Army to concentrate and refine specialised capabilities that were particularly appropriate for low-intensity operations. Yet, establishing the SAS did not diminish the requirement for, nor the Army's ability to adapt, line battalions to undertake basic counter-insurgency tasks. Many such units proved very adept at this. Moreover, the recent years of the Northern Ireland campaign have demonstrated that troops from line battalions can be properly trained for more sophisticated, covert operations. In this context, the SAS has proved its value as a repository of expertise and a training formation upon which the rest of the Army can draw to hone its specialised skills.[224] However, the end of the imperial commitment and the focus on NATO meant that the much smaller Army could not afford to maintain a special forces unit solely for imperial policing; the SAS had to justify its retention on the order of battle by finding a role appropriate for conventional operations. It did so, and sub-sequently found an additional role—countering terrorism—that was a logical extension of its imperial role in the post-imperial era. Far from being too narrowly focused or too specialised, the SAS has proved to be one of the most flexible, adaptable elements of the British Army.

Where the Army proved least adaptable or comfortable was in the psychological warfare dimension. This is hardly surprising, since it was traditionally the domain of civilians and was seen as highly political—with all the pitfalls that entailed. For a very long time, the Army eschewed deep involvement in it. It was drawn into the task in Northern Ireland in a significant way relatively late in the struggle, only after the campaign had changed from peace-keeping to counter-insurgency. Once it became clear that the Army had become the target of bullets, bombs, abuse and propaganda, and that the civilian infrastructure to counter these attacks did not exist, the Army moved to fill the vacuum. It can scarcely be criticised for making this effort when no one else would do it for them, but in the absence of political guidance from Westminster it is not surprising that the Army's efforts proved controversial and had only limited success. Given the exigencies of the situation, however, the Army adapted quickly, if imperfectly, to the task.

Finally, how did prolonged involvement in low-intensity opera-tions affect the Army's ability to perform its conventional role? Unfortunately for the historian, the occasions which would provide the evidence to answer this question have been few, and the open source evidence itself is scant. Suez is the first case. It is widely acknowledged that the operation was planned and mounted slowly and inefficiently; that much is beyond question.[225] Whether this can be attributed to a decade of involvement in low-intensity operations is less than clear. The ponderous planning phase probably had more to do with the need to co-ordinate operations with the French and the Israelis and with the normal administrative sluggishness of peacetime military planning at the Ministry level. The British Government itself was hesitant. James Wyllie does suggest that the orientation of British defence policy—towards nuclear forces on the one hand and low-intensity imperial policing on the other—adversely affected Britain's intervention capabilities.[226] On the other hand, the units then engaged in counter-insurgency operations in Cyprus, which were deployed subsequently at Suez, the paratroops and the Royal Marine Commandos, adapted quickly and performed creditably. Neither of the last-mentioned units had conducted routine training in its conventional role for a year. The paratroops were withdrawn from anti-terrorist operations, flown back to the UK for refresher airborne training, whence they returned to Cyprus and to their counter-insurgency task virtually up to the eve of the invasion. Low-intensity operations continued even while the commander of 3rd Parachute battalion and his staff planned for the conventional operation. The battalion ceased its Cyprus operation only a few days before the airborne assault. The Commandos also withdrew from operations in Cyprus in August and trained for the invasion in Malta, whence they departed for Egypt. If the larger Suez operation itself was characterised by inefficiency and ponderous preparation and execution, at least those charges could not be laid against the paratroops and Commandos, who made an effective transition from low- to high-intensity operations. Their performance is even more impressive since few of the paratroops had any experience of combat airdrops, much of their equipment was obsolete, and the aircraft from which they jumped were unsuitable for airborne operations. The troops of 45 Commando, too, had to adapt to something they had never tried— a helicopter-borne combat assault into hostile territory, in helicopters which were too few and not designed for the task.[227] That the two forces performed as well as they did is testimony to their ability to adapt under highly adverse conditions.

The same could be said, in general terms, about the performance of British Army units in the Falklands War. When the war broke out, 2 Para had just returned from several weeks training in Kenya, and was due to depart for Belize. Prior to Kenya, it had completed a two-year tour of duty in Northern Ireland.[228] The Royal Marine Commandos were dispersed on training or leave, and only one squadron of the

SAS could be made available immediately[229] (elements of another squadron were deployed in Northern Ireland, and yet another was committed to the anti-terrorist role). The Commandos, like 2 and 3 Para, had seen repeated intermittent duty in Northern Ireland since 1969. None of the units had been involved in conventional war for more than 25 years. All turned in highly professional performances on operations in the Falklands. In short, they adapted to high-intensity operations very well, although the same could not be said for all Army units in the task force.

The length of time the task force took to deploy south to the Falklands gave the units time to prepare for the battle ahead. Units were able to polish their skills at arms, and communications, and improve their physical fitness aboard ship, and adapted to new equipment and increased scales of issue. During the stopover at Ascension Island, amphibious drills were conducted, and battalions fired their personal and crew-served weapons.[230] Even so, a number of problems emerged in the course of the war: first, the *ad hoc* organisation of 5 Brigade proved unsatisfactory; such practices might have been acceptable for low-intensity operations, but they did not work as well for conventional war. Nor were some of its assigned units trained for the rigours of winter war. Second, while the Northern Ireland commitment provided invaluable training and leadership experience for junior officers and NCOs, it left a legacy of 'minimum force' thinking and behaviour—a tendency to react like policemen when what was required was genuine aggressiveness. Third, the infantry had not received sufficient training in co-operation with artillery.[231] On the other hand, the Army was more experienced in developing relations with the news media on the scene than was the Navy or the Ministry of Defence.[232] In terms of media awareness, Northern Ireland was a watershed in British Army experience: it is doubtful if there has ever been an armed force so well informed about the news media, its methods and its power.

This awareness has operated at two levels. For senior commanders, it has introduced a 'public opinion factor' into military planning for low-intensity operations; for the junior leaders, rank-and-file, it has created a sensitivity over what their actions are likely to look like on the television news that evening, and a willing, even eager, preparedness to justify and explain these actions before cameras and microphones. Such attitudes clearly paid considerable dividends for the Army in terms of the media coverage it received during and after the Falklands campaign. This, and the limitations noted above, could be attributed directly to its experience in low-intensity operations. That these problems could be overcome to produce a victory most experts attribute to the quality of leadership, training, and unit cohesion—the product of the regimental system—and the capacity to improvise,[233] of the British Army.

Notes

* T. E. Lawrence, 'The Evolution of Revolt', *Army Quarterly* vol. 1, no. 2 (October 1920), reprinted in Michael Elliott-Bateman *et al.*, eds., *The Fourth Dimension of Warfare, Volume 2: Revolt to Revolution* (Manchester: Manchester University Press, 1974), p. 150.

1. Nick Davies, 'Britain world leader in anti-guerrilla methods', *Manchester Guardian Weekly*, 17 May 1981.

2. Henry Stanhope, *The Soldiers: An Anatomy of the British Army* (London: Hamish Hamilton, 1979), Appendix 6, pp. 343–47, lists 92, to which should be added the London Embassy Siege (1980) and the Falklands War (1982). The 14 exceptions consisted of rescue and relief work which required the use of military manpower and resources, but did not involve armed conflict, and hence are not discussed further in this study.

3. Palestine, Malaya, Kenya, Cyprus, Borneo, South Arabia/Aden, Northern Ireland, Oman (twice).

4. David Charters, Dominick Graham and Maurice Tugwell, *Trends in Low-Intensity Conflict*, ORAE Extra-Mural Paper no. 16 (Ottawa: Department of National Defence, August 1981), p. 28.

5. Frank Kitson, *Low Intensity Operations: Subversion, Insurgency, Peacekeeping* (London: Faber, 1971), pp. 51–52, 89–90.

6. For the importance of operations at platoon level see Julian Paget, *Counter-Insurgency Campaigning* (London: Faber, 1967), p. 166.

7. Stanhope, *op. cit.* Appendix 6, p. 343.

8. David Anderson Charters, *Insurgency and Counter-Insurgency in Palestine, 1945–1947* (unpublished Ph.D. dissertation, University of London, 1980), Appendix 4; Michael Carver, *War Since 1945* (London: Weidenfeld and Nicolson, 1980), p. 24; Institute for the Study of Conflict (ISC), *Northern Ireland: Problems and Perspectives,* Conflict Studies no. 135 (London: ISC, 1982), p. 21.

9. Kitson, *op. cit.* p. 90.

10. Lieutenant Colonel J. C. M. Baynes, *The Soldier in Modern Society* (London: Eyre Methuen, 1972), p. 91 notes that between 1950 and 1967, infantry provided 70 percent of the manpower for 'Emergency' operations, while the artillery and the armoured corps contributed 18 percent and 12 percent respectively.

11. Bard E. O'Neill, 'Insurgency: A Framework for Analysis', in O'Neill *et al.*, eds., *Insurgency in the Modern World* (Boulder, Colo.: Westview Press, 1980), pp. 11–13; see also Paul Wilkinson, *Terrorism and the Liberal State* (London: Macmillan, 1977), pp. 133–34.

12. Kitson, *op. cit.* p. 95.

13. Sir Robert Thompson, *Defeating Communist Insurgency* (London: Chatto and Windus, 1966), pp. 84–89.

14. The themes of revolutionary insurgent propaganda from several recent campaigns, including Palestine, Northern Ireland and Oman, are analysed in detail in Maurice A. J. Tugwell, *Revolutionary Propaganda and Possible*

Counter-measures (unpublished Ph.D. dissertation, University of London, 1979).

15. O'Neill, *op. cit.* pp. 4–5.
16. Stanhope, *op. cit.* pp. 3–4, 30–40, 45–46, 67, 78–79, 321.
17. Dominick Graham, 'England', in Richard A. Gabriel, ed., *Fighting Armies: NATO and the Warsaw Pact—A Combat Assessment* (Westport, Conn.: Greenwood Press, 1983), pp. 64, 76.
18. Baynes, *op. cit.* pp. 10–13 emphasises the latter part of the imperial era, but the proposition stands for the period before 1891 as well.
19. It is not possible to list here the great number of low-intensity campaigns in which the British Army was involved before 1945. Descriptions of the more significant of these may be found in Colonel Charles E. Callwell, *Small Wars: Their Principles and Practice* (London: His Majesty's Stationery Office, 1909), and Sir Charles Gwynn, *Imperial Policing* (London: Macmillan, 1939).
20. Anthony Verrier, *An Army for the Sixties: A Study in National Policy, Contract and Obligation* (London: Secker and Warburg, 1966), p. 27.
21. Correlli Barnett, *Britain and Her Army: 1509–1970: A Military, Political and Social Survey* (New York: William Morrow, 1970), pp. 306–7.
22. *ibid.*, pp. 278, 306, 313–14; Stanhope, *op. cit.* p. 28.
23. Dennis Barker, *Soldiering On: An Unofficial Portrait of the British Army* (London: Sphere Books, 1981), pp. 119–31 provides an insightful look at the intricacies and peculiarities of the regimental system in the modern British Army.
24. Stanhope, *op. cit.* p. 321; Verrier, *op. cit.* pp. 43, 47, 83, 157, 165; also comments by the late Colonel Jonathan Alford, then Deputy Director, International Institute for Strategic Studies, London, interview with author, 28 June 1984.
25. Shelford Bidwell and Dominick Graham, *Firepower: British Army Weapons and Theories of War, 1904–1945* (London: George Allen and Unwin, 1982), pp. 2–3, 295. An effective critique of the current approach to war studies in British Army education may be found in Hew Strachan, 'The British Army and the Study of War—A Personal View', *Army Quarterly and Defence Journal* vol. 111 (1981), pp. 134–48.
26. Graham, 'England', in Gabriel, *op. cit.* p. 76; Verrier, *op. cit.* pp. 46–47.
27. Stanhope, *op. cit.* pp. 321–22.
28. Samuel P. Huntington, *The Soldier and the State: The Theory and Politics of Civil-Military Relations* (New York: Vintage, 1957), pp. 7–18; see also Graham, 'England', in Gabriel, *op. cit.* p. 74; Stanhope, *op. cit.* pp. 56, 66.
29. Peter J. Dietz and J. F. Stone, 'The British All-Volunteer Army', *Armed Forces and Society* vol. 1, no. 2 (February 1975), pp. 175–81; Barnett, *op. cit.* p. 488; Graham, 'England', in Gabriel, *op. cit.* p. 74; Stanhope, *op. cit.* pp. 56, 66.
30. Colonel J. N. Somerville, 'The Junior Command and Staff Course', *British Army Review* no. 37 (April 1971), pp. 22–24; see also Alford, *op. cit.* interview; Barker, *op. cit.* p. 200; Baynes, *op. cit.* pp. 130–31; Stanhope, *op. cit.* pp. 70–71; and Verrier, *op. cit.* pp. 43, 56.
31. Franklyn A. Johnson, *Defence by Ministry: The British Ministry of Defence, 1944–1974* (New York: Holmes and Meier, 1980), p. 24; Stanhope, *op. cit.* pp. 74–76; Verrier, *op. cit.* p. 165.
32. Baynes, *op. cit.* pp. 148–52; Stanhope, *op. cit.* pp. 76–78.
33. Bidwell and Graham, *op. cit.* p. 293; Johnson, *op. cit.* pp. 155, 160–61.
34. In addition to regimental magazines and journals, the list includes: *Journal for Defence Studies (RUSI)*; *Army Quarterly and Defence Journal*; *British Army Review* (produced by the Training Directorate); *Survival* and the *Adelphi Papers* (both published by the IISS); and *Janes Defence Weekly*. The *RUSI Journal* tends to cover broad issues, including higher defence policy, military history and

strategic analysis. The *Army Quarterly* will usually carry accounts of operations and discussions of tactics and equipment.

35. William P. Snyder, *The Politics of British Defence Policy, 1945–1962* (Columbus, Ohio: Ohio State University Press, 1964), pp. 9, 33. This theme is developed further and in detail in Michael Chichester and John Wilkinson, *The Uncertain Ally: British Defence Policy, 1960–1990* (Aldershot: Gower, 1982), pp. 3–73 *passim*.

36. Baynes, *op. cit.* p. 27; R. N. Rosecrance, *Defense of the Realm: British Strategy in the Nuclear Epoch* (New York: Columbia University Press, 1968), p. 298.

37. Philip Darby, *British Defence Policy East of Suez, 1947–1968* (London: Oxford University Press, 1973), pp. 1, 11; and C. J. Bartlett, *The Long Retreat: A Short History of British Defence Policy, 1945–70* (London: Macmillan, 1972), p. 23.

38. Gregory Blaxland, *The Regiments Depart: A History of the British Army, 1945–1970* (London: William Kimber, 1971), pp. 8–9.

39. Remarks attributed by Baynes, *op. cit.* p. 75 to General Sir Richard Hull, Chief of the Imperial General Staff (CIGS) in 1957, citing Anthony Sampson's *The Anatomy of Britain Today*, p. 349. For other sources on National Service, see: Trevor Royle, *The Best Years of Their Lives: the National Service Experience 1945–63* (London: Michael Joseph, 1985); Barnett, p. 487; Bartlett, pp. 26–27; Graham, 'England', in Gabriel, p. 64; Snyder, p. 36; and Stanhope, pp. 26–27.

40. Blaxland, *op. cit.* pp. 6–10, 330–40; Stanhope, *op. cit.* pp. 12–14, 18–19; Verrier, *op. cit.* p. 55. Baynes, *op. cit.* pp. 28–29 shows the peak figure being reached in 1952 and 1954. Snyder, *op. cit.* p. 37, and Rosecrance, *op. cit.* p. 298 show different peak strengths, reflecting different ways of calculating strengths from official sources.

41. James. H. Wyllie, *The Influence of British Arms: An Analysis of British Military Intervention Since 1956* (London: George Allen and Unwin, 1984), pp. 50–51; Great Britain, House of Commons, Command Paper Number 124, 'Defence: Outline of Future Policy', *British Parliamentary Papers*, Session 1957; see also Rosecrance, *op. cit.* pp. 219–26, 238; and Snyder, p. 21.

42. Again, the figures do not quite agree. For 1956, Baynes, *op. cit.* p. 29 says 426,800, while Rosecrance, *op. cit.* p. 298 gives the figure 393,000. For 1961, Baynes, p. 31 gives the Army's strength as 211,100; Rosecrance, 217,400. The difference in detail does not detract from the general thrust of the argument. On regimental reorganisation, see Blaxland, *op. cit.* pp. 330–40.

43. Baynes, *op. cit.* p. 32.

44. Denis Healey, Labour Minister of Defence, stressed this point himself: Blaxland, *op. cit.* pp. 409–10.

45. Bartlett, *op. cit.* p. 172; Blaxland, *op. cit.* pp. 331, 842; Baynes, *op. cit.* (for recruiting figures) pp. 183–84. 1964 saw 18 battalions in Borneo, 6 in Cyprus, and elements of several more in South Arabia and scattered throughout East Africa. See also Verrier, *op. cit.* p. 33.

46. Neville Brown, *Strategic Mobility* (London: Chatto and Windus, 1963), pp. 54–55; see also Bartlett, *op. cit.* pp. 120, 138, 161, 186; Darby, *op. cit.* pp. 77–78; and Snyder, *op. cit.* p. 11.

47. Darby, *op. cit.* p. 78.

48. Brown, *op. cit.* pp. 156–57, 161–62; Wyllie, *op. cit.* pp. 54–55; Snyder, *op. cit.* pp. 12–15; Darby, *op. cit.* pp. 78–82, 97, 109–10, 180–89, 258–61.

49. Chichester and Wilkinson, *op. cit.* pp. 9–10, 14–15, 18–24, 70; Darby, pp. 305, 314–15, 323–26; see also, Peter Nailor, 'Denis Healey and Rational Decision-Making in Defence', in Ian Beckett and John Gooch, eds., *Politicians and Defence: Studies in the Formulation of British Defence Policy, 1845–1970* (Manchester: Manchester University Press, 1981), pp. 158, 161, 165–66. For

troop strength figures from the Confrontation, see, Harold James and Denis Sheil-Small, *The Undeclared War: The Story of the Indonesian Confrontation, 1962–1966* (London: Leo Cooper, 1971), pp. 191–92.

50. Bartlett, *op. cit.* pp. 221, 235; Baynes, *op. cit.* p. 92; Chichester and Wilkinson, *op. cit.* pp. 43–48, 50–53, 59–61, 70, 153–56; Stanhope *op. cit.* pp. 22–24. The relevant Command Papers are 4891 (1972), 5231 (1973), 5976 (1975), 6432 (1976), 6735 (1977), 8212 (1981).

51. Verrier, *op. cit.* p. 20; see Bidwell and Graham, *op. cit.* p. 294 on the significance of the organisational changes.

52. Alford, *op. cit.* interview; Barker, *op. cit.* p. 102; Baynes, *op. cit.* p. 91; Blaxland, *op. cit.* p. 71; Stanhope, *op. cit.* p. 120.

53. Carl Von Clausewitz, *On War*, trans. and ed. by Michael Howard and Peter Paret (Princeton: Princeton University Press, 1976), pp. 88–89.

54. Lieutenant General Sir Kenneth Darling, 'British Counterinsurgency Experience', *Military Review* vol. 45, no. 1 (January 1965), p. 9.

55. Richard Clutterbuck, *The Long Long War: The Emergency in Malaya 1948–1960* (London: Cassell, 1966), p. 3.

56. J. Bowyer Bell, 'Revolts Against the Crown: The British Response to Imperial Insurgency', *Parameters* vol. 4, no. 1 (1974), pp. 31–46.

57. Major P. N. M. Moore, 'The Other Side of the Kampong', *Army Quarterly* vol. 52 (July 1946), pp. 248–52.

58. Charles Townshend, *The British Campaign in Ireland, 1919–1921: The Development of Political and Military Policies* (London: Oxford University Press, 1975), pp. 85, 151–53.

59. The problem then, and even now, resides in part in the anomalous legal-constitutional status of insurgency, which is not recognised in British law. See Charles Townshend, *Britain's Civil Wars: Counterinsurgency in the Twentieth Century* (London: Faber and Faber, 1986), pp. 13–23; On the anti-intellectual character of the inter-war Army, see Brian Bond, *British Military Policy Between the Two World Wars* (Oxford: Clarendon Press, 1980), pp. 36–37, 44, 52–53, 56–57, 67–71. One article from the period which clearly perceived the nature of the Irish conflict was Major B. C. Dening, 'Modern Problems of Guerrilla Warfare', *Army Quarterly* vol. 13 (October–January 1926–27), pp. 347–54. More typical in the sense that it concentrated solely on tactical matters was Brevet Major T. A. Lowe, 'Some Reflections of a Junior Commander Upon the Campaign in Ireland 1920 and 1921', *Army Quarterly* vol. 5 (October-January 1922–23), pp. 50–58.

60. H. J. Simson, *British Rule, and Rebellion* (London: William Blackwood, 1937), pp. 16, 33–36, 40–49, 54–55, 66–77, 81–98, 105–6, 121–26.

61. GHQ Middle East Forces, G (Training) Branch, *Middle East Training Pamphlet no. 9*, Part 13, 'Notes for Officers on Internal Security Duties', 1945, War Diary GHQ MEF, WO 169/19521, Public Record Office, UK (PRO).

62. Gwynn, *op. cit.* pp. 20, 24, 28–32.

63. Brigadier T. L. T. Miller, 'Report—Experimental Frontier Brigade—Mountain Warfare Against Guerrilla Enemy', April 1947, WO 231/34.

64. See Julian Paget, *Last Post: Aden, 1964–1967* (London: Faber, 1969), pp. 51–110 *passim* for an account of the campaign and an assessment of its military lessons.

65. Joint Intelligence Committee, GHQ Middle East Forces, 'Probable Jewish Reactions and the Potential Threat of Jewish Forces in Palestine in Certain Eventualities', 11 January 1945, CAB 119/147. See also Bruce Hoffman, *The Failure of British Military Strategy Within Palestine 1939–47* (Tel Aviv: Bar-Ilan University Press, 1983), pp. 18–19.

66. War Office, 'Guerrilla Warfare', December 1944, issued to Middle East Forces, 14 March 1945, WO 169/19521.

67. *ibid.*

68. The strategies of the three groups differed considerably, but the unity of political objectives and military means, and the ultimate objective of independence, were common to them all. See David Anderson Charters, *The British Army and the Jewish Insurgency in Palestine 1945–57* (London: Macmillan, 1988), Chapter 3.

69. *ibid.*, Chapters 4–5, based principally on minutes of the Chiefs of Staff Committee, and the Cabinet Defence Committee, and on correspondence in CO 537/1731 (PRO), and in the diaries for 1947 of Major General H. E. Pyman, Liddell Hart Centre for Military Archives, King's College, London. On Ireland and Palestine, see Nigel Hamilton, *Monty: The Making of a General* (London: Hamilton, 1981), pp. 157–60, 292–94, 296–97.

70. K. M. White. Librarian, Staff College, letter to author, 8 February 1979.

71. Wilson, *op. cit.* pp. 8–18.

72. Brigadier Richard N. Anderson, 'Search Operations in Palestine: The Problem of the Soldier', *Army Quarterly* vol. 55 (October-January 1947–48), pp. 203–208.

73. Lieutenant Jack W. Rudolph, 'Partisan Warfare', *Army Quarterly* vol. 40 (April–July, 1940), pp. 255–67, was in fact a reprint from the US Army's *Infantry Journal*.

74. War Office, Army Council, *Imperial Policing and Duties in Aid of the Civil Power 1949* (London: War Office, 13 June 1949), pp. 6–9.

75. See for example, L. B. Oatts, 'Guerrilla Warfare', *RUSI Journal* (May 1949), p. 192.

76. Anthony Short, *The Communist Insurrection in Malaya, 1948–1960* (London: Frederick Muller, 1975; repr. 1977), pp. 360–65.

77. *ibid.*, p. 369; HQ Malaya Command, *The Conduct of Anti-Terrorist Operations in Malaya* (hereafter ATOM), 2nd ed. (Kuala Lumpur, 1954), Chapters 1 and 2. The manual was largely the brainchild of Field Marshal Sir Gerald Templer—the 'Supremo' of Malaya—who believed it was essential to pool the wealth of jungle fighting knowledge and to make it available to those who needed it most. He was convinced that the manual was a major factor in the defeat of the insurgents. See John Cloake, *Templer: Tiger of Malaya* (London: Harrap, 1985), p. 242.

78. Verrier's criticism, p. 158, is cited and amplified in Darby, *op. cit.* pp. 49–51.

79. This is reflected both in the official literature: see for example, War Office, Directorate of Military Training, *Notes and Information on Training Matters (NITM)* no. 11 (1955), p. 5; no. 13 (1956), p. 5; no. 24 (1962), p. 5; and Ministry of Defence, Defence Council, *Land Operations Volume III—Counter-Revolutionary Operations* (London: MOD, 29 August 1969), Part I 'Principles and General Aspects', pp. 1, 5, 22–40; and in the voluminous secondary literature. No other similar British campaign has been so widely studied for its lessons. Apart from Anthony Short's excellent history cited above, other significant campaign studies include: Richard Clutterbuck, *The Long Long War: The Emergency in Malaya 1948–1960* (London: Cassell, 1966); Sir Robert Thompson, *Defeating Communist Insurgency: Experiences from Malaya and Vietnam* (London: Chatto and Windus, 1966); and Julian Paget, *Counter-Insurgency Campaigning* (London: Faber, 1967).

80. Captain T. Leaske, 'The Problems of Cold War Operations', *Army Quarterly* vol. 74 (1957), p. 162 claimed to see communist inspiration in every case, but this was not the official Army view. See War Office, Army Council, *Keeping the Peace (Duties in Aid of the Civil Power) 1957* (London: War Office, 10 April

1957), p. 30. Nor was it accepted by serious analysts of the subject. See, for example, Paget, *Counter-Insurgency Campaigning*, pp. 15–16.

81. MOD, *Land Operations Volume III*, Part I, *op. cit.*

82. Martha Crenshaw, 'The Persistence of IRA Terrorism', in Yonah Alexander and Alan O'Day, eds., *Terrorism in Ireland* (New York: St. Martin's Press, 1984), pp. 249–51, 254–56.

83. MOD, *Land Operations Volume III*, Part I, pp. 4, 19–21, 31–32, 34; see also Frank Kitson, *Low Intensity Operations: Subversion, Insurgency, Peacekeeping* (London: Faber, 1971; repr. 1972), pp. 29–43, 127–28.

84. Clutterbuck, *op. cit.* p. 51.

85. Major Michael Banks, 'The Army in Northern Ireland', *Brassey's Annual* (1972), pp. 148–50; for a detailed scholarly analysis of the implications of the army's changing role see, Randall W. Heather, *The British Army in Northern Ireland, 1969–72* (unpublished MA thesis, University of New Brunswick, 1986).

86. David A. Charters, 'Intelligence and Psychological Warfare Operations in Northern Ireland', *RUSI Journal* vol. 122, no. 3 (September 1977), p. 23.

87. *ibid.*, pp. 24–25.

88. 'Notes for Officers on Internal Security Duties', WO 169/19521; G Branch, HQ Palestine, 'Operational Instruction (hereafter OI) no. 21', 27 October 1945, WO 169/19745.

89. 'Extract from Note on Points Raised with the Secretary of State by the High Commissioner', 14 November 1945, Papers of the British Colonial Office (CO) 733/461, PRO.

90. Thompson, *op. cit.* pp. 50–51; Paget, *Counter-Insurgency Campaigning, op. cit.* p. 156; Darling, *op. cit.* p. 5.

91. Short, *op. cit.* pp. 327, 333–34; Michael Carver, *War Since 1945* (London: Weidenfeld and Nicolson, 1980), pp. 83, 89–92, 94; Wyllie, *op. cit.* pp. 68–69.

92. Charters, *The British Army and the Jewish Insurgency*, Chapter 2; Carver, *op. cit.* pp. 32–36.

93. Charles Foley and W. I. Scobie, *The Struggle for Cyprus* (Stanford: Hoover Institution Press, 1975), pp. 23, 50–51, 126, 128–29, 132, 140, 155–56.

94. Institute for the Study of Conflict, *Conflict Studies Number 135 Northern Ireland: Problems and Perspectives* (London: ISC, 1982), pp. 3, 14–16, 29, 36, 37–44.

95. HQ Malaya Command, *ATOM*, 3rd ed. (1958), Chapter 3, p. 1; War Office, *Keeping the Peace Part 1—Doctrine* (1963), p. 3; Paget, *op. cit.* pp. 157–59; Thompson, *op. cit.* p. 55.

96. Paget, *op. cit.* p. 65, citing C. Northcote Parkinson, *Templer in Malaya* (Singapore, 1954), p. 23. Clutterbuck, *op. cit.* p. 3 gives 1952 as the date of the quote itself.

97. W.O., *Keeping the Peace 1* (1963), pp. 2, 64–66; MOD, *Land Operations 3/1* (1969), pp. 41, 43, 97, 103–5, 107–8; General the Lord Bourne, 'The Direction of Anti-Guerrilla Operations', *Brassey's Annual* (1964), pp. 210–11, 213; Paget, pp. 64–67, 76–77, 176–79.

98. HQ Malaya Command, *ATOM*, 2nd ed. (1954), Chapter 14, p. 1.

99. Keith Jeffery, 'Intelligence and Counter-Insurgency Operations: Some Reflections on the British Experience', *Intelligence and National Security, op. cit.* vol. 2, no. 1 (January 1987), pp. 118–49; see also Short, *op. cit.* p. 502; Clutterbuck, *op. cit.* pp. 4–5, 52, 86–111 *passim*; Kitson, *op. cit.* p. 95; Thompson, *op. cit.* pp. 84, 89; Paget, *op. cit.* pp. 162–64; Bourne, *op. cit.* p. 213; WO, *Keeping the Peace 1* (1963), p. 3; MOD, *Land Operations 3/1* (1969), pp. 69–70.

100. Lieutenant Colonel Richard L. Clutterbuck. 'Bertrand Stewart Prize Essay

1960', *Army Quarterly and Defence Journal* vol. 81 (October 1960), pp. 161, 169–70, 173, 177–79; see also Paget, *Counter-Insurgency Campaigning*, pp. 165–67; Kitson, *op. cit.* pp. 165–67; WO, *Keeping the Peace 2* (1963), pp. 91–93; and MOD, *Land Operations 3/1* (1969), p. 88.

101. WO, *Keeping the Peace 1* (1963), pp. 3–4.

102. Thompson, *op. cit.* pp. 51–53, 56–57, 112–13, 141–49.

103. GHQ East Africa Command, *A Handbook on Anti-Mau Mau Operations*, 2nd ed. (Nairobi, [1954?]).

104. Simson, *op. cit.* pp. 122–23.

105. The District committees included the District Commissioner, the District Superintendent of Police, the Area Security Officer, and a military intelligence officer. Sources: HQ Palestine, 'OI 21', WO 169/19745; HQ 21 Area, 'OI 21', 21 November 1945, WO 169/19821; GSI, HQ Palestine, *Short Handbook of Palestine* (Jerusalem, 1944), p. 7, in Private Papers, Mr. John Briance, London; Minutes of the Conferences of the Central Security Committee for 1946–47 may be found in the Papers of General Sir Alan Cunningham, St. Anthony's College, Oxford. The author also conducted interviews with Mr. John Briance and Sir Richard Catling (ex-Palestine Police), 3 March 1977, 28 May 1976 respectively, and Mr. R. W. D. Pawle, formerly personal secretary to the High Commissioner (Cunningham), 18 May 1978.

106. Townshend, *Britain's Civil Wars*, pp. 27, 58–60; on the significance of Templer's appointment and actions in the Emergency see, Cloake, *op. cit.* pp. 205–8, 212, 216–25, 227–79, 300–307, 310–15, 326–27.

107. WO, *Keeping the Peace* (1957), pp. 30–32; WO, *Keeping the Peace 1* (1963), pp. 24–26; MOD, *Land Operations 3/1* (1969), pp. 45–49; see also David Galula, *Counter-insurgency Warfare: Theory and Practice* (London: Pall Mall, 1964), pp. 87–91; Bourne, *op. cit.* p. 213; Darling, *op. cit.* pp. 5–6; Kitson, *op. cit.* pp. 54, 57; Paget, *Counter-Insurgency Campaigning, op. cit.* pp. 158–62; Thompson, *op. cit.* pp. 81–83; and Bell, *op. cit.* pp. 41–42.

108. Short, *op. cit.* pp. 117–24, 234–40, 248–51, 322–26, 329, 334–38, 352–53.

109. Simon Hutchinson, 'The Police Role in Counter-Insurgency Operations', *RUSI Journal* vol. 114, no. 4 (December 1969), pp. 57–58.

110. Richard Miers, *Shoot to Kill* (London: Faber, 1959), p. 39.

111. Blaxland, *op. cit.* pp. 269, 271–72, 277; Paget, *Counter-Insurgency Campaigning, op. cit.* pp. 93–94; General Sir Cameron Nicholson, CINCMELF, to Lieutenant General H. Redman, VCIGS, 18 May 1953, WO 216/852; General Sir George Erskine, CINC East Africa Command, to General Sir John Harding, CIGS, 14 June 1953, WO 216/853; Erskine, 'Report by General Erskine—Kenya—Operations Against Mau Mau', [1956?], Papers of General Sir George Erskine, WO 236/16; GHQ, E. A. Command, *Handbook on Anti-Mau Mau Operations*, pp. 6–7.

112. Erskine, *op. cit.* 'Report—Operations Against Mau Mau'.

113. Frank Kitson, 'The Turning Tide', in Maurice Tugwell, ed., *The Unquiet Peace: Stories from the Post War Army* (London: Allan Wingate, 1957), pp. 125–28.

114. Blaxland, *op. cit.* p. 298; Paget, *op. cit. Counter-Insurgency Campaigning*, pp. 122–23, 150–51, 184; Major E. A. Cooper-Key, 'Some Reflections on Cyprus', *British Army Review* no. 5 (September 1957), pp. 42–43. Townshend, *Britain's Civil Wars, op. cit.* p. 27.

115. Paget, *Last Post: Aden, op. cit.* pp. 121–32.

116. Robin Evelegh, *Peace-Keeping in a Democratic Society: The Lessons of Northern Ireland* (Montreal: McGill-Queens University Press, 1978), pp. 16, 110; Richard Clutterbuck, *Protest and the Urban Guerrilla* (London: Cassell,

1973), pp. 76, 124–25; Institute for the Study of Conflict, *Conflict Studies no. 36 Ulster: Politics and Terrorism* (London: ISC, 1973), p. 6.

117. David Charters, 'The Changing Forms of Conflict in Northern Ireland', *Conflict Quarterly* vol. 1, no. 2 (Fall 1980), p. 35. This article drew in part upon information provided in briefings to the author by HQ Northern Ireland during a visit to the province in August 1980.

118. Evelegh, *op. cit.* pp. 57, 110; Kitson, *Low Intensity Operations, op. cit.* p. 93; Banks, *op. cit.* pp. 153–54; Lieutenant Colonel P. W. Graham, 'Low Level Civil/Military Coordination, Belfast, 1970–73', *RUSI Journal* vol. 119, no. 3 (September 1974), pp. 80–82.

119. Lieutenant Colonel Michael Dewar, *The British Army in Northern Ireland* (London: Arms and Armour Press, 1985), pp. 177–78.

120. Anthony Deane-Drummond, *Riot Control* (London: RUSI, 1975), p. 64 .

121. 12 GHQ Training Team, War Diary, 1945, WO 169/19621; see also formation war diaries in WO 169/19656, 19697, 19699, 19701, 19703, 19743.

122. HQ Palestine, 'Directive—Searches and Road Checks', January 1946, WO 169/23–21; HQ 3 Inf. Div., 'Directive no. 1—Information from IS Ops', 23 Jan. 1946, 'Directive no. 3—Further Lessons of Recent Ops', 6 Feb. 1946, 'Directive no. 5—Further Lessons: Roadblocks', 19 Feb. 1946, WO 169/22967; HQ 3 Inf. Bde., 'Roadblocks', 5 April 1946, WO 169/22995.

123. HQ Palestine, 'OI no. 67—Military Cum Police Operations', 17 June 1946, WO 169/23022; HQ Palestine, *Combined Military and Police Action* (June 1947), pp. 8–9, in Private Papers of Mr. John Briance, London; HQ 3 Inf. Div., 'Directive no. 1' and 'Directive no. 7—Wireless Communications—Coordination with Palestine Police Network', 25 Feb. 1946, WO 169/22967; HQ 9 Inf. Bde., 'Internal Security Instruction no. 5', 2 March 1946, WO 169/23003; HQ 2 Inf. Bde., 'Brigade I.S. Study Period—General Summary and Notes', 6 March 1946, WO 169/22993.

124. Brigadier E. H. Goulburn to HQ 1 Inf. Div./North Palestine District, 21 June 1946, and 1 Guards Bde., 'Report on Op AGATHA 29 June–1 July 1946', WO 169/22989.

125. Charters, *The British Army and the Jewish Insurgency, op. cit.* Chapter 5.

126. Resettlement actually had begun some time before Briggs arrived, but he gave the programme a strategic purpose and focus. See Short, *op. cit.* pp. 173–202 *passim*, 235–38, 246, 391–94.

127. Lieutenant Colonel W. C. Walker, Commandant, FARELF Training Centre, 'Interim Training Report—FTC—Sept. 48–Jan. 49', in FARELF Training Centre, *Quarterly Historical Report*, Quarter Ending March 1949, pp. 1–4, WO 268/116.

128. FARELF Training Centre, QHR, Quarter Ending March 1949, p. 1. WO 268/116; see also Miers, *op. cit.* pp. 30–35; Oliver Crawford, *The Door Marked Malaya* (London: Rupert Hart-Davis, 1958), pp. 57–61.

129. HQ Malaya, *ATOM*, 2d ed. (1954), Chapter 15, pp. 2–9; see also Crawford, *op. cit.* pp. 58, 74, 186–90; Major J. B. Oldfield, *The Green Howards in Malaya (1949–1952): The Story of a Post-War Tour of Duty by a Battalion of the Line* (Aldershot: Gale and Polden, 1953), pp. 4, 32, 36, 43–44, 46, 68–69, 78, 107, 113–14, 127; Frank Kitson, *Bunch of Five* (London: Faber, 1977), pp. 85–87, 150–51.

130. W.O., no. 13 (October 1956), pp. 5–6. No. 17, pp. 15–17, contained a section on 'Lessons From Operations', which discussed the laying of an ambush, based on experience in Cyprus.

131. See, for example, Major P. E. Crook, 'A Subaltern's War in Malaya', *British Army Journal* no. 9 (January 1953), pp. 21–24.

132. Oldfield's, *The Green Howards in Malaya, op. cit.* is the regimental history most frequently cited. Tugwell's, *The Unquiet Peace*, consisted of a collection of personal accounts of operations or actions from several postwar campaigns. F. Spencer-Chapman's, *The Jungle is Neutral* (London: Chatto and Windus, 1949; repr. 1957–73) was regarded as a classic account of jungle warfare in Southeast Asia, based on the author's experience in World War II.

133. Clutterbuck, 'Bertrand Stewart Prize Essay 1960' (full citation in note 48). Leaske's 'Problems of Cold War Operations', *Army Quarterly* (1957), won the Clowes Memorial Prize Essay competition for his suggestions on organisation, equipment and methods for combating guerrillas and terrorists.

134. GHQ East Africa Command, *Handbook on Anti-Mau Mau Operations*, Foreword, and pp. 15–24, 34–65 *passim*, 73–77, 85–90.

135. James and Sheil-Small, *op. cit.* pp. 30–35.

136. Lieutenant Colonel M. B. Farndale, 'To Belfast as Infantry', *Journal of the Royal Artillery* (September 1970), p. 126; Brigadier G. L. C. Cooper, 'Some Aspects of Conflict in Ulster', *British Army Review* no. 43 (April 1973), pp. 73–74; see also Banks, pp. 149–50. The limitations of the existing pamphlets with respect to Northern Ireland were acknowledged in MOD, *NITM* 42 (March 1971), p. 13.

137. MOD, *NITM* 42 (March 1971), pp. 13–15; *NITM* 43 (September 1971), pp. 17–18; *NITM* 45 (September 1972), pp. 5–6.

138. Lieutenant Colonel Jonathan R. Alford, 'Holdfast Foxhounds I', *Royal Engineers Journal* vol. 88 (June 1974), p. 92.

139. *ibid.*, pp. 95–100.

140. Alford, interview with author. The author also consulted the Army Staff College course Precis(s) on Counter Revolutionary Warfare.

141. MOD, *NITM* 45 (1972), p. 5.

142. Both the primary and secondary literature on these forces and actions is extensive. For concise accounts and a useful guide to the source material, see the entries for John and Walter Butler, Robert Rogers, and Thomas Gage, in *Dictionary of Canadian Biography Volume 4 1771–1800* (Toronto: University of Toronto Press, 1979).

143. Lawrence's two main works, *Revolt in the Desert* (London: Jonathan Cape, 1927) and *The Seven Pillars of Wisdom* (London: Jonathan Cape, 1935) remain classic accounts of the Arab revolt, even if Lawrence's achievements have come to be regarded more critically in recent years. See also Michael Elliott-Bateman, 'The Age of the Guerrilla', in Elliott-Bateman *et al.*, eds., *The Fourth Dimension of Warfare, Volume 2: Revolt to Revolution—Studies in the 19th and 20th Century European Experience* (Manchester: Manchester University Press, 1974), pp. 9, 20.

144. M. R. D. Foot, 'Special Operations, 2', in Michael Elliott-Bateman, ed., *The Fourth Dimension of Warfare, Volume 1: Intelligence, Subversion, Resistance* (Manchester: Manchester University Press, 1970), p. 37. Charles Townshend's very thorough history of the campaign indicates clearly that extensive records were retained. What is less clear is whether the Army ever organised or consulted them with a view to extracting 'lessons'. The official *Record of the Rebellion in Ireland* (4 vols.) remains classified.

145. A detailed account of SAS operations in World War II may be found in the 'authorised' regimental history: John Strawson, *A History of the S.A.S. Regiment* (London: Secker and Warburg, 1984), Chapters 1–12. See also Foot, 'Special Operations, 2', pp. 42–45; Eliot A. Cohen. *Commandos and Politicians: Elite Military Units in Modern Democracies* (Cambridge, Mass.: Harvard Center for International Affairs, 1978), pp. 22–23, 37–40, 58–62, 71, 83–85;

Tony Geraghty, *Who Dares Wins: The Story of Special Air Service 1950–1980* (London: Arms and Armour Press, 1980), pp. 10–15; Michael Calvert, *Prisoners of Hope* (London: Jonathan Cape, 1952; repr. 1971), p. 259; War Office, Directorate of Tactical Investigation, 'Report of a Working Party on Control of Special Units and Organisations', September 1946, WO 232/10B.

146. B. A. Young, *The Artists and the SAS* (London: 21 Special Air Service Regiment, 1960), pp. 53–55; Lieutenant Colonel L. E. O. T. Hart, 'The Special Air Service' [c. 1957?], p. 2, and 21 SAS Regiment (Artists) TA, 'Annual Report', 31 October 1948, in the Papers of General Sir Roderick McLeod, Liddell Hart Centre for Military Archives, King's College, University of London.

147. A detailed account of the case may be found in David Charters, 'Special Operations in Counter-Insurgency: The Farran Case, Palestine 1947', *RUSI Journal* vol. 124, no. 2 (June 1979), pp. 56–61.

148. Frank Kitson, *Gangs and Counter Gangs* (London: Barrie and Rockliff, 1960), pp. 2–6, 19, 74–76, 94, 170–88, 209; Short, *op. cit.* p. 364; Edgar O'Ballance, *Malaya: The Communist Insurgent War* (London: Faber, 1966), p. 130.

149. Geraghty, *op. cit.* pp. 23, 25; Captain J. M. Woodhouse, 'Some Personal Reflections on the Employment of Special Forces in Malaya', *Army Quarterly* vol. 66 (April–July 1953), p. 69; FARELF to War Office, 17 May 1950, Chiefs of Staff Committee Papers, DEFE 11/36, PRO. Strawson, *op. cit.* p. 158 puts more emphasis on the 'hearts and minds' role envisaged for the regiment.

150. Geraghty, *op. cit.* pp. 25–26; Woodhouse, *op. cit.* p. 69; FARELF to War Office, 17 May 1950, War Office File 098/4586 'Special Force Malaya', 18–19 May 1950, and Prime Minister (Australia) to Prime Minister (United Kingdom), telegram, 26 May 1950, DEFE 11/36; William Elliot to Secretary of State for War, 'Use of Special Operations Techniques in Malaya', 13 June 1950, DEFE 11/37; CINC FARELF to Under Secretary of State, War Office, 'Malayan Scouts—Special Air Service Regiment', 22 December 1951, WO 216/494.

151. Geraghty, *op. cit.* pp. 26–27, 29–34, 30–38; Woodhouse, *op. cit.* pp. 68–72; Short, *op. cit.* pp. 366–67, 449–50, 455; Clutterbuck, *op. cit. Long Long War*, pp. 150–55.

152. Woodhouse, *op. cit.* pp. 72–73; Strawson, *op. cit.* pp. 161–64.

153. Major C. L. D. Newell, 'The Special Air Service', *British Army Review* no. 1 (September 1955), pp. 41–42; Geraghty, *op. cit.* pp. 27–29, 31, 34–35, 39–41; 'Malayan Scouts—Special Air Service Regiment' (1951), WO 216/494. On the role envisaged for the SAS in a European War see Hart, 'The Special Air Service', pp. 3–5, and 'Notes on the Organisation, History and Employment of Special Air Service Troops' (undated), both in McLeod papers, Liddell Hart Centre.

154. Geraghty, *op. cit.* pp. 41, 43; Wyllie, *op. cit.* p. 60; and Peter Dickens, *SAS— The Jungle Frontier: 22 Special Air Service Regiment in the Borneo Campaign, 1963–1966* (London: Arms and Armour Press, 1983), p. 37.

155. Lieutenant Colonel A. J. Deane-Drummond, 'Operations in the Oman', *British Army Review* no. 9 (September 1959), pp. 7–14; Geraghty, *op. cit.* pp. 106–10.

156. See Geraghty, *op. cit.* pp. 42–43, 47–59, for a general survey of the SAS role in the Confrontation; a more detailed account is provided by Dickens, *SAS—The Jungle Frontier, passim;* see also James and Sheil-Small, *op. cit.* pp. 66–70.

157. Paget, *Last Post: Aden, op. cit.* pp. 62–67, 79; Geraghty, *op. cit.* pp. 79–83.

158. Colonel Tony Jeapes, *SAS: Operation Oman* (London: William Kimber, 1980), pp. 36–38 and *passim*, 143–57; Geraghty, pp. 131–32; Penelope

Tremayne, 'End of a Ten Years' War', *RUSI Journal* vol. 122, no. 1 (March 1977), p. 45.
159. MOD, *Land Operations 3/1*, p. 60.
160. *ibid.*
161. See, for example, Roger Faligot, *Britain's Military Strategy in Ireland: The Kitson Experiment* (London: Zed Press, 1983), pp. 28–30, 37–38, 41–43; Kennedy Lindsay, *The British Intelligence Services in Action* (Dundalk: Dunrod Press, 1980), pp. 17–83, *passim.*
162. Geraghty, *op. cit.* pp. 139, 141, 143–47, 149, 151.
163. *ibid.*, pp. 150–61.
164. *ibid.*, pp. 164–81, 214.
165. Jeffery, *op. cit.* p. 119.
166. WO, 'Guerrilla Warfare', WO 169/19521.
167. Jock Haswell, *British Military Intelligence* (London: Weidenfeld and Nicolson, 1973), pp. 12, 192–94. See also F. H. Hinsley *et al.*, *British Intelligence in the Second World War: Its Influence on Strategy and Operations*, vol. 1 (London: HMSO, 1979), pp. 6–11, 13; and Thomas G. Fergusson, *British Military Intelligence 1870–1914: The Development of a Modern Intelligence Organisation* (Frederick, Maryland: University Publications of America, 1984).
168. Charters, 'Insurgency and Counter-Insurgency in Palestine', *op. cit.* pp. 42–44, 46–47, 49, 51–56.
169. The Hon. M. M. C. Charteris, 'A Year as an Intelligence Officer in Palestine', *Middle East Society Journal* vol. 1 (1946), pp. 17, 18, 20.
170. To cite just one example: the Defence Security Office, 'Monthly Summary no. 8', May 1946, WO 169/23031, accurately predicted a revival of terrorism on a major scale in June 1946, while Army Headquarters 'Fortnightly Intelligence Newsletter no. 16', 10 June 1946, WO 169/23022, discounted the possibility on the very eve of the insurgent offensive. Details of the organisation of the Defence Security Office may be found in Defence Security Officer Palestine, war diary 1945–46, WO 169/19758.
171. General Sir Richard Gale, *Call to Arms* (London: Hutchinson, 1968), pp. 163, 166–69; see also Haswell, *op. cit.* pp. 167–68; GHQ Middle East Forces, 'Directive no. 245—Internal Security', 23 June 1945, WO 169/19510; 3 Field Security Section, War Diary 1945, WO 169/21414; A. V. Lovell-Knight, *The Story of the Royal Military Police* (London: Leo Cooper, 1977), pp. 275–89.
172. 1 Infantry Division, 'Intelligence Course Programme', 17–30 January 1946, WO 169/22956; 'Establishment of Interrogation Centre for Examination of Terrorists', CO 537/1838; GSI; GHQ Middle East Forces, War Diary, February, May 1946, WO 169/22882; interview with Sir Richard Catling, 14 February 1979.
173. 3 Infantry Division, 'Directive no. 2 Combined Ops Police and Mil', 23 January 1946, WO 169/22967; HQ Palestine, 'OI no. 67', 17 June 1946, WO 169/23022; Goulburn to HQ 1 Infantry Division/North Palestine District, 21 June 1946, WO 169/22989; 1 Infantry Division/North Palestine District, 'OI no. 7', 28 June 1946, WO 169/22957; interviews: Brigadier Maurice Tugwell, 3 November 1976; Lieutenant General Sir Napier Crookenden, 9 June 1976; Major General H. E. N. Bredin, 28 June 1976.
174. Menachem Begin, *The Revolt: Story of the Irgun* (London: W. H. Allen, 1951), p. 100.
175. WO, *Imperial Policing and Duties in Aid of the Civil Power* (1949), pp. 6, 9–11, 14.
176. Short, *op. cit.* pp. 77–90, 139–40.
177. *ibid.*, pp. 240, 248, 275–76, 343, 360, 363; HQ Malaya, *ATOM*, 2d ed. (1954),

Chapter 14, pp. 1–3; Jeffery, *op. cit.* pp. 123–25; Cloake, *op. cit.* pp. 228–30.

178. Short, p. 364; HQ Malaya, *ATOM*, 2d ed. (1954), Chapter 14, pp. 3–4; Richard Clutterbuck, *Long Long War, op. cit.* pp. 101–111, 122–31, and 'The SEP— Guerrilla Intelligence Source', *Military Review* vol. 42, no. 10 (October 1962), pp. 13–21; Oldfield, *op. cit.* pp. 120–22; Crook, *op. cit.* pp. 21–24; F.J.C.P., 'All in a Week's Work', *British Army Review* no. 2 (March 1956), pp. 16–19.

179. Clutterbuck, *Long Long War, op. cit.* p. 52.

180. WO, *Keeping the Peace* (1957), pp. 44–46; *Keeping the Peace Part 1* (1963), pp. 59, 62; MOD, *Land Operations 3/1* (1969), pp. 69–72, 74–76; Paget, pp. 163– 64; Kitson, *Low Intensity Operations, op. cit.* pp. 71, 73–74, 95, 99–100.

181. Paget, *Counter-Insurgency Campaigning*, pp. 124, 184; Jeffery, *op. cit.* p. 125 asserts that the intelligence effort was crippled from the outset by a 'pitifully weak' Special Branch and an almost uniformly hostile Greek population.

182. Paget, *Last Post: Aden, op cit.* pp. 128–29, 149–50.

183. James and Sheil-Small, *op. cit.* pp. 66–70, 193; Dickens, *op. cit.* pp. 55, 57–58, 60–118 *passim*.

184. Charters, 'Intelligence and Psychological Warfare Operations in Northern Ireland', *op. cit.* p. 23.

185. Cooper, 'Some Aspects of Conflict in Ulster', *op. cit.* p. 72; see also David Barzilay, *The British Army in Ulster, Volume 2* (Belfast: Century Services Limited, 1975), p. 89; and Faligot, *op. cit.* p. 97.

186. Jonathan Bloch and Patrick Fitzgerald, *British Intelligence and Covert Action* (London: Junction Books, 1983), p. 212; Geraghty, *op. cit.* pp. 145–47; Jeffery, *op. cit.* pp. 126–27 states that the Army so distrusted the RUC Special Branch that it withheld information from it, and that a wholly co-operative atmosphere was not achieved until 1980.

187. Charters, 'Intelligence and Psychological Warfare Operations in Northern Ireland', *op. cit.* p. 23; on patrol tasks and importance, see Dewar, *op. cit.* pp. 180–83.

188. Charters, 'Intelligence and Psychological Warfare Operations in Northern Ireland', *op. cit.* p. 23.

189. Geraghty, *op. cit.* pp. 141, 143, 147; see also Bloch and Fitzgerald, *op. cit.* pp. 216–17; and Faligot, *op. cit.* pp. 29–31.

190. Geraghty, *op. cit.* pp. 147, 149; Faligot, *op. cit.* pp. 45–48; ISC, *Northern Ireland: Problems and Perspectives, op. cit.* p. 35.

191. Evelegh, *op. cit.* pp. 133–35; Cyril Cunningham, 'International Interrogation Techniques', *RUSI Journal* vol. 117 (September 1972), pp. 32–33.

192. Jeffery, *op. cit.* p. 134.

193. Charters, 'Intelligence and Psychological Warfare Operations in Northern Ireland', *op. cit.* p. 24; Charles Foley, *Island Revolt* (London: Longmans, 1962), pp. 76, 130–32; Paget, *Last Post: Aden, op. cit.* pp. 129, 168–69.

194. Cunningham, *op. cit.* pp. 32–33; Banks, *op. cit.* pp. 151–52; Evelegh, *op. cit.* pp. 134, 137–38.

195. Clutterbuck, *Protest and the Urban Guerrilla, op. cit.* p. 101; Thompson, 'Northern Ireland to 1973', *op. cit.* p. 77.

196. Evelegh, *op. cit.* p. 138; The Supergrass system was not, strictly speaking, an Army operation, being in the purview of the RUC. Its importance, however, warrants mention here. For a thorough and critical analysis, see Steven C. Greer, 'The Supergrass System in Northern Ireland', paper presented to the Academic Conference on Research on Terrorism, University of Aberdeen, April 1986.

197. 1 Inf. Div., 'Divisional Commander's Directive no. 1', Nov. 1945, WO 169/ 19656; 3 Para. Bde., 'Training Instruction no. 1', (undated), 'Notes on Cordon

Check Searches', 16 Oct. 1945, 'ISUM no. 2, 3', 21, 28 Nov. 1945, WO 169/ 19705; 6 Airlanding Bde., 'Notes on Confirmation of Brigade Commander's Conference', 11 Oct. 1945, WO 169/19706; 2 Inf. Bde., 'IS Appreciation', 24 Oct. 1945, WO 169/19699; HQ Palestine, 'OI no. 67', 17 June 1946, WO 169/ 23–22; Wilson, *Cordon and Search, op. cit.* pp. 19–20.
198. HQ Palestine, 'OI no. 56—Press', 31 Dec. 1945, WO 169/19745; 1 Inf. Div., 'Report on Operation ELEPHANT', pp. 102–5; 1 Armoured Division, 'IS Instruction no. 4', 6 June 1947, WO 261/178; 1 Inf. Div., 'Report on Operation TIGER', WO 261/181; Farrar-Hockley, interview, 13 Sept. 1976; HQ Palestine, 'OI no. 56—Press', WO 169/19745; 3 Para. Bde., 'OI no. 38— Appendix: Relations with Press', 30 April 1947, WO 261/219.
199. 6 AB Div., 'OI no. 4—Passing of Information', 17 Oct. 1945, WO 169/19685; HQ Palestine, 'Lessons From Ops 25/26 Nov. 1945', 7 Dec. 1945, WO 169/ 19745; 1 Infantry Division, 'Publicity', 8 May 1946, WO 169/22957; Minutes of Security Conference, 22 August 1947, Cunningham Papers.
200. 'Bad Tempered Censorship', *Evening Standard*, 25 November 1946.
201. Short, *op. cit.* pp. 416–24; HQ Malaya, *ATOM* 2d ed. (1954), Chapter 3, pp. 15–17; 3d ed. (1958), Chapter 3, pp. 16–18; WO, *Imperial Policing and Duties in Aid of the Civil Power* (1949), p. 16; WO, *Keeping the Peace* (1957), pp. 52–53.
202. WO, *NITM*, no. 28 (1964), p. 6; no. 29 (1964), p. 6; WO, *Keeping the Peace— Part 1* (1963), pp. 64–68; MOD, *Land Operations 3/1* (1969), pp. 107–12; Kitson, *Low Intensity Operations, op. cit.* p. 188.
203. Tugwell, *Revolutionary Propaganda . . ., op. cit.* pp. 215, 225, 229–31, and comments by Tugwell (December 1984).
204. Charters, 'Intelligence and Psychological Warfare Operations in Northern Ireland', *op. cit.* p. 25, and note 16, p. 27; see also Liz Curtis, *Ireland: The Propaganda War. The British Media and the Battle for Hearts and Minds* (London: Pluto Press, 1984), p. 231.
205. MOD, *Land Operations 3/1* (1969), Amendment no. 1 (Nov. 1971), pp. 118C–E.
206. Richard Clutterbuck, *The Media and Political Violence* (London: Macmillan, 1981), p. 98; Charters, 'Intelligence and Psychological Warfare Operations in Northern Ireland', *op. cit.* p. 25.
207. Curtis, p. 233; Bloch and Fitzgerald, p. 29, citing House of Commons, *Hansard* (4 November 1976); and Alan Hooper, *The Military and the Media* (Aldershot: Gower, 1982), pp. 186–89, 193, 200–201.
208. Banks, *op. cit.* p. 154; Clutterbuck, *Media and Political Violence, op. cit.* p. 96.
209. Curtis, *op. cit.* pp. 232–33, 235–42; Bloch and Fitzgerald, *op. cit.* pp. 214–15.
210. Colonel Robin Evelegh, interview with Max Hastings, cited in Curtis, *op. cit.* p. 234; see also Evelegh, *op. cit.* p. 38.
211. Tugwell, *Revolutionary Propaganda . . ., op. cit.* pp. 249–50, 254–62; Chris Ryder, 'Army Plans to Stress Successes', *Sunday Times*, 27 February 1977; Charters, 'Intelligence and Psychological Warfare Operations in Northern Ireland', *op. cit.* p. 25. Tugwell was in charge of Information Policy in Northern Ireland, 1971–73.
212. Banks, *op. cit.* pp. 152–54.
213. Deane-Drummond, *Riot Control, op. cit.* pp. 13–15; Keith Jeffery, 'The British Army and Internal Security, 1919–1939', *Historical Journal* vol. 24, no. 2 (1981), p. 388; for a description of Operation BELLICOSE, a typical riot control operation of this type in Palestine, see 3 Parachute Brigade, 'Intelligence Summary no. 3', 28 November 1945, WO 169/19705, and Wilson, *Cordon and Search, op. cit.* pp. 27–29.

214. WO, *Keeping the Peace* (1957), pp. 15–16, 72–75; Verrier, *op. cit.* p. 130; MOD, *Land Operations 3/2* (1969), pp. 15–19, 27–39, and Annexes E, G–N.
215. Millman, *op. cit.* p. 20.
216. *ibid.*, pp. 20–21, 24; Clutterbuck, *Protest and the Urban Guerrilla, op. cit.* pp. 39–40; *Sunday Times*, 'Ulster', p. 204; Deane-Drummond, *Riot Control, op. cit.* pp. 115, 117, 126; Barzilay, *British Army in Ulster, op. cit.* vol. 1 (1973), pp. 69–75, vol. 2 (1975), pp. 65–68, 75, 77.
217. Lieutenant Colonel Napier Crookenden, GSO1 (Plans), 'Planning Section Paper no. 5—Notes on HQ Malaya Paper on Helicopters', Kuala Lumpur, 29 April 1952, and covering note 'Helicopters in Malaya', WO 216/542; Short, pp. 369–70, 372; Thompson, *Defeating Communist Insurgency, op. cit.* p. 107.
218. Anthony Crockett, *Green Beret, Red Star* (London: Eyre and Spottiswoode, 1954), pp. 66–68; Crawford, *op. cit.* p. 170; Miers, *op. cit.* pp. 147–49; 'Use of Helicopters in Cyprus', *NITM*, no. 18 (1959), pp. 5–6.
219. James and Sheil-Small, *op. cit.* pp. 17–19; see pp. 86–91 on the importance of helicopters to the campaign.
220. Blaxland, *op. cit.* p. 342; WO, *Keeping the Peace* (1957), pp. 34–36; WO, *Keeping the Peace Part 1* (1963), pp. 46–49. Note: the Army Air Corps helicopter fleet now exceeds that of the Navy and the RAF, although not all of the army's helicopters can be used for troop lift.
221. Dennis Duncanson, 'Lessons of Modern History: The British Experience', in Sam C. Sarkesian and William L. Scully, eds., *U.S. Policy and Low-Intensity Conflict: Potentials for Military Struggles in the 1980s* (New Brunswick: Transaction Books, 1981), p. 100.
222. Bell, 'Revolts Against the Crown', *op. cit.* p. 40.
223. See James Lunt, *Imperial Sunset: Frontier Soldiering in the 20th Century* (London: Macdonald, 1981) for an account of 18 prominent colonial units which served with British forces in Africa, Asia and the Middle East.
224. It is instructive to note that the recent successful ambushes sprung on Irish terrorists have been conducted by members of 'close observation platoons' of line battalions, trained by but not part of the SAS.
225. Wyllie, *op. cit.* pp. 33–35; Blaxland, *op. cit.* pp. 236–42; Brown, *op. cit.* pp. 60, 66.
226. Wyllie, *op. cit.* p. 34; Major George Fielding Eliot, 'Lessons From Suez', *British Army Review* (March 1958), (repr. from March–April issue of *Ordnance*, a US publication), pp. 79, 81; Kenneth Love, *Suez: The Twice Fought War* (New York: McGraw-Hill, 1969), pp. 370, 382, 392–94, 397–98, 424, 457–60; Robert Jackson, *Suez 1956: Operation Musketeer* (London: Ian Allan, 1980), pp. 20–22; Roy Fullick and Geoffrey Powell, *Suez: The Double War* (London: Hamish Hamilton, 1979), pp. 20–23, 26–29, 30–32, 38–41.
227. See 'Cyprus' and 'Suez', drafts for recordings in the Airborne Forces Museum, in the Papers of Major-General C. W. Dunbar, Liddell Hart Centre, Kings College, London; see also, Jackson, *op. cit.* pp. 15, 20–23, 55–56, 66–67; Lieutenant Colonel P. E. Crook, 'Operation Musketeer: Capture of Gamil Airfield by 3 Para Bn Gp', *British Army Review* no. 4 (March 1957), pp. 10–11; '33rd Parachute Field Regiment—Cyprus and Suez 1956', *Journal of the Royal Artillery* vol. 84, no. 4 (1957), pp. 285–89, 291; Fullick and Powell, *op. cit.* pp. 48, 124–25, 144–49. Valuable insights on the problems surrounding the mounting of these operations may be found in two personal accounts: Sandy Cavenagh, *Airborne to Suez* (London: William Kimber, 1965), and D. M. J. Clark, *Suez Touchdown: A Soldier's Tale* (London: Peter Davies, 1964).
228. Major General John Frost, *2 Para Falklands: The Battalion at War* (London: Buchan and Enright, 1983), p. 13.

229. Max Hastings and Simon Jenkins, *The Battle for the Falklands* (London: Michael Joseph, 1983), pp. 68, 85.

230. Frost, *op. cit.* pp. 17–22; Hastings and Jenkins, *op. cit.* pp. 91–92, 180–82, 235.

231. Secretary of State for Defence, *The Falklands Campaign: the Lessons*, Cmd 8758 (London: HMSO, 1982), pp. 16–18; see also David Charters, 'Lessons to be Learned From the Falklands War', in Brian Macdonald, ed., *War in the Eighties: Men Against High Tech—CISS Proceedings Fall 1982* (Toronto: Canadian Institute of Strategic Studies, 1983), pp. 26–28, 30–31; Hastings and Jenkins, *op. cit.* pp. 267–69; Colonel R. F. Vincent, 'Meeting Our Internal Security Commitments in Northern Ireland, and Maintaining Acceptable Gunnery Standards', *Journal of the Royal Artillery* (March 1974), pp. 5–6.

232. Hooper, *op. cit.* pp. 157–64, 197; Hastings and Jenkins, *op. cit.* pp. 331–34.

233. See, for example, Jeffrey Record, 'The Falklands War', *Washington Quarterly* vol. 5, no. 4 (Autumn 1982), pp. 46–47; Lawrence Freedman, 'The War of the Falkland Islands 1982', *Foreign Affairs* vol. 61, no. 1 (Fall 1982), p. 207; Wyllie, *op. cit.* p. 100.

Conclusions

'Low-intensity conflict' is a valuable term, but one that embraces a host of quite different conflict forms. The five case studies in this book illustrate many of the challenges which Western armies have had to meet since World War II. They vary from the major operations mounted by the French and later the Americans in Indochina, the prolonged withdrawal-from-empire campaigns of Britain and France, short and sharp cross-border raids and anti-terrorist operations conducted by Israel, operations in Northern Ireland, and the ubiquitous peace-keeping operations performed by Canada's Armed Forces. All five armies are today expected to perform at all levels of intensity, from—at the highest—full-scale war between the major powers to—at the lowest— providing 'aid to the civil power' or breaking a terrorist siege.

Within their own territories, each army's responsibilities at the lower end of the scale differ according to national law, tradition and organisation. In France there are several levels of force available to the government before the use of the military need be contemplated. In the USA the jurisdictional confusion is awesome, and state governors are required to employ their National Guard before appealing for federal military assistance. But in Britain, where there are strict controls on the issue of arms to the police, and where the Territorial Army may not, by law, be used for internal security operations, any serious escalation of violence is likely to result in the regular army being ordered into action. Consequently, exposure to domestic conflict is uneven. Overseas, all five armies have to be prepared to deal at every level. But even there, the existence of an agency such as the CIA's Clandestine Action Service separates the

US Army from certain roles which might otherwise fall to it.

Although, for obvious reasons, armies are forced to concentrate the bulk of their training, equipment and attention on the major threat of an all-out attack by a well-equipped enemy (for Israel, the combined Arab armies; for the NATO countries, the Warsaw Pact armies), it is mistaken and potentially dangerous to assume that lower levels of threat and conflict pose only minor challenges. Limited war which is skilfully orchestrated for unlimited strategic aims could conceivably undermine the West's ability to resist the major conventional threat. Even while this book has been in preparation, France, Belgium and West Germany had begun to experience a terrorist campaign explicitly aimed at weakening NATO. It begins to be possible to see a seamless web across the spectrum of East–West conflict, just as this continuum in Arab hostility has for long been obvious to Israel. Adaptability in the face of a wide range of military and politico-military threats is therefore just as important for all five now, as it was for France and Britain in the colonial era.

In both the French and the Israeli case studies we have seen how good adaptation against relatively low threats resulted in those threats escalating. Low-intensity conflicts left unchecked may prove extremely damaging; confronted and controlled, they may become higher-intensity threats. As early as the 1940s, Britain discovered that the inventiveness of the *Irgun* in mandated Palestine posed severe technological challenges. Today, when great power provision of the most sophisticated weapons and techniques to terrorists is a matter of record, the small size of a hostile group is no guarantee of its insignificant performance. In the types of minor war that France has fought in Africa in recent years, the introduction of shoulder-launched ground-to-air missiles and anti-armour guided missiles could possibly raise the costs to unacceptable levels. The IRA's probable acquisition of SAMS, for example, could seriously erode the security forces' advantage in Northern Ireland.

The evidence presented in the preceding Chapters suggests that the British, French and Israeli armies have adapted effectively to the conditions of low-intensity conflict. They have done so by modifying conventional small-unit tactics and techniques to suit the political and military conditions of the operational environment. Several points stand out in this regard. First, the ability of these armies, and particularly their commanders, to learn from experience and to adapt accordingly, which is attributable largely to the latitude given to theatre, local and even relatively junior commanders to develop doctrines and tactics appropriate to the situation. Second, each of these armies placed considerable emphasis upon small-unit leadership, intelligence, surprise, and mobility—in other words, upon those very assets normally associated only with their insurgent opponents. In short, they attempted to beat their opponents at their own game. Third, each concentrated certain roles and skills within specialised units, which then served as repositories of expertise that could be shared with the rest of the army. This was important because, with the exception of a few clearly delineated missions, all or most army units, particularly the infantry, had to be able to operate effectively in the low-intensity role. Finally, each of the armies was aware, to a greater or lesser degree, of the political context in which its military operations were being conducted, and tailored its actions accordingly. This is not to suggest that these three armies have solved the problems of adapting. The challenges which continue to face them will require a constant response.

The US Army adapted for Vietnam with the energy and enthusiasm characteristic of the nation. In technological terms, adaptation was remarkable. At certain stages of the war, particularly when it more closely resembled a conventional conflict in the mountainous border regions, doctrinal innovation which exploited the mobility of the helicopter was effective and impressive. But in the populated regions, where the conflict was essentially political, the Americans seemed least successful in their efforts to adapt. Neither the American political nor military leaderships ever seemed to understand the political context of revolutionary and counter-revolutionary war. The Army devoted its attention almost solely to the military aspects of unconventional warfare. Moreover, wedded to an operational concept of attrition by fire-power, it was unable to shed the perception that unconventional warfare was merely an adjunct of conventional operations performed by smaller units. Such politico-military expertise as was developed was almost totally confined to the Special Forces, and never really permeated the US Army as a whole.

On the face of it, the Canadian Army appears to have adapted effectively to its low-intensity roles. Its methods of adaptation are similar to those of the British, and to a lesser extent to those of the French and Israelis. The Canadian Army demonstrated the ability to modify its conventional tactics and standard procedures to suit the peace-keeping and internal security operational requirements. However, it must be said that its operational experience in these roles has not tested the army in prolonged combat. So the significance of the Canadian experience is at least an open question.

The five case studies do, however, suggest some general criteria for effective adaptation. The first of these is flexibility. An army which is open to change or accustomed to making *ad hoc* adjustments to its tactics and methods will be more likely to adapt effectively than one which is doctrinaire or inclined to operate only according to standard operating procedures. The army must be able to learn from on-the-job experience. Political sensitivity is the second criterion. It is a characteristic that can be instilled by proper training but, as a rule, requires a degree of guidance and direction from the relevant political authorities. It follows, as well, that political sensitivity requires high standards of discipline, both in terms of behaviour and with respect to the use of force. This points to two more important criteria: good junior leadership, at the officer and NCO levels; and high standards of training in basic military skills. Together these can instil adequate—and on occasion, excellent—standards of performance even from a conscript army. They are also essential for unit cohesion, an important factor in the prolonged, stressful and debilitating operational conditions that characterise low-intensity conflicts. The regimental system, whether of the French or the British pattern, appears to offer genuine, if intangible, benefits in this regard. Next, the army requires an effective intelligence capability. It should be flexible enough to operate either in conjunction with police and other intelligence agencies, or on its own in a hostile environment. The intelligence personnel, moreover, must have a clear understanding of the nature of threat, and must be able to communicate relevant information to the commanders who need it most. Only in this way will the army—and the rest of the security forces—be able to locate, anticipate and pre-empt the enemy by exploiting the principle of surprise to his disadvantage. Finally, the army requires mobility; again, flexibility is the operative consideration. The army must be capable of deploying in force or by stealth, over short distances and long, by a variety of means. That said, mobility must not be over-emphasised; helicopters and armoured vehicles are no substitute for feet on the ground and, where appropriate, a semi-permanent presence.

The consequences of adaptation are less easily identified. In the case of both the British and the French, that portion of each army committed to low-intensity operations overseas evolved into an institution that was somewhat distinct from the remainder of the army which was committed to conventional war. This produced genuine, but not necessarily insurmountable, organisational and doctrinal divisions within the armies concerned. These were most pronounced in the French Army, less so in the British, and the divisions have been largely overcome since the 'end of empire'. In the United States, the concentration of low-intensity roles, skills and experience in the Army's Special Forces tend to isolate those units from the mainstream Army. Such divisions were not characteristic of either the Canadian or Israeli armies, owing to different operational circumstances and the requirement for all elements of those armies to be multi-capable. The British and Israeli experiences, moreover, suggested that prolonged commitment to low-intensity operations would not necessarily adversely affect the army's ability to conduct conventional operations; rather the reverse.

The most severe potential consequence of low-intensity conflict is the risk of politicisation of the army concerned. This was demonstrated in a most pronounced fashion by the French Army in Algeria. There it was the product of the historic tradition of the French Army which combined military and administrative powers in its imperial duties, concurrent with a doctrinal commitment to conducting counter-revolutionary war by revolutionary means. In a vacuum created by weak government at home, the Army moved into the realm of political and psychological action in a manner that superseded the authority of the civil power and placed the Army in opposition to it. The British experience, by contrast, has traditionally separated the civil and the military power, even in the colonies. Consequently, the British Army was never politicised to the same extent; on the other hand, neither did it become truly effective in the psychological warfare dimension, leaving it vulnerable to that form of attack. Inevitably, however, it is in the nature of such conflicts that, if prolonged, they become politically volatile for the nation which has committed its army to fight in them. The army may or may not adapt effectively, but that in itself can only partly determine the outcome. For democratic countries, the political will and wisdom of the government, and the cohesion of the 'home front' are likely to be more significant factors. Where these are lacking, even the most effective army cannot guarantee success.

Three lessons stand out from these studies: the importance of allotting the right amount of emphasis on low-intensity conflict in the doctrine and training of an army as a whole; the need to retain small specialist cadres for the most challenging roles; and the danger of imagining that either can act as a substitute for the other. The experience of the US Marines in the Lebanon, where, apparently, a commitment to a peace-keeping role blinded the leadership to other threats, illustrated in the grimmest manner the need for every soldier to be alert and at least basically trained to handle such dangers. In Europe today, NATO troops must be ready for both the Soviet Army and a terrorist attack. Israel's performance against a sustained guerrilla-terrorist threat has emphasised the need for the expert counter-terrorist. He is kept at a state of readiness which the line battalion could not possibly match: he undertakes the impossible. But he does not relieve the line units of their responsibility to perform excellently at the same level of conflict, though in a more straight-forward way.

Index

Aden   see *Warfare, Low-Intensity:*
Campaigns, Incidents, and
Operations: *Middle East*
Aeroplane/aircraft   see *Warfare,
Conduct of:* airmobility; Weapons:
airpower
Africa   79–81, 84, 89, 93–95, 99, 100,
102–10, 114–17, 119, 124, 126–28,
132 n.43, 135 n.70, 185, 231, 237
n.45, 248 n.223, 252; see also
Warfare, Low-Intensity:
Campaigns, Incidents, and
Operations: *Africa*
Africa, East   185, 231, 237 n.45; see
also *Warfare, Low-Intensity:*
Campaigns, Incidents, and
Operations: Africa, Kenya
Africa, North   79, 80, 82, 93, 94, 96,
102, 104; see also *Warfare, Low-
Intensity:* Campaigns, Incidents,
and Operations: Africa, Algerian
Campaign; Morocco; Western
Sahara
Africa, West   91, 94, 109; see also
Warfare, Low-Intensity:
Campaigns, Incidents, and
Operations: *Africa*, Cameroon;
Chad; Dahomey; Gabon; Senegal;
Togo
Aid to the Civil Power   see *Warfare,
Low-Intensity:* Aspects and
Concepts: Internal Security
Operations

Algeria (Algerians)   12, 14, 51, 62,
71, 79–81, 83, 88–97, 99, 102, 115,
129 n.5, n.6; see also *Armies,
National:* French Army; *Warfare,
Low-Intensity:* Campaigns,
Incidents, and Operations: Africa,
Algerian Campaign
Algiers   77, 82, 86, 95
Allon, Yigal   53
America (Americans)   see *Armies,
National:* United States Army;
United States
Amman (Jordan)   66
Angola   102
Anti-terrorist operations   see *Warfare,
Low-Intensity:* Aspects and
Concepts: Counter-terrorist
operations
Arabs   11, 13, 52, 53, 56, 57, 61–63,
66, 69, 88, 93, 95, 126, 129 n.6,
n.8, 188, 207, 219; see also
Middle East; *Warfare, Low-
Intensity:* Aspects and Concepts:
terrorism, Campaigns, Incidents,
and Operations: Middle East
Arab states   54–56, 61–62, 252; see
also Egypt; Iraq; Jordan;
Lebanon; Saudi Arabia; Syria;
Warfare, Low-Intensity:
Campaigns, Incidents, and
Operations: Middle East
Armagh (Northern Ireland)   170
(map); see also *Warfare, Low-*

257

Armagh (*cont.*)
  Intensity: Campaigns, Incidents,
  and Operations: Europe,
  Northern Ireland
Armies, organisation of   4, 5, 19, 21,
  22, 28, 29, 35, 37, 42, 44–46, 49,
  51, 54–55, 59, 110–13, 139, 141–
  47, 150–51, 156–57, 163 n.3, 169,
  172–73, 176–87, 207–15, 225–27,
  229, 231, 233–34, 238 n.51, 243
  n.133, 251, 254–55; see also
  Armies, National
force types airborne forces: 31, 35,
  51, 55–60, 64, 74 n.28, 108, 111–
  15, 135 n.66, 141, 144–45, 162,
  166 n.44, 183, 186, 190, 208–15,
  219, 221–22, 231–34, 244 n.153,
  n.156, 248 n.224; airmobile
  forces: 112–13, 135 n.66, 141,
  144, 146, 161, 184–86, 209–15,
  229, 231–33; amphibious forces:
  51, 67–69, 79, 84, 86, 101, 111–12,
  144, 180, 208, 210–11, 233–34;
  armoured forces: 34, 51, 69, 86,
  101, 107, 111–13, 135 n.66, 142,
  146, 148–49, 173, 179, 187, 190,
  230, 235 n.10; artillery units: 1–3,
  57, 69, 81, 83, 94, 111–13, 142,
  173, 179, 184, 186, 187, 212, 230,
  234, 235 n.10; cavalry: 2–4, 82–83,
  93; commando forces: 34, 37, 42,
  51, 67–68, 208, 210, 233–34;
  communications (signals) units:
  112, 148, 154–55; elite units: 30,
  32, 43, 53–54, 57, 60, 64, 71, 207–
  15, see also commando forces,
  special forces; engineer units:
  111–13, 157, 184; infantry: 1–2,
  33, 35, 51, 55, 58, 60, 93, 100,
  101, 111–13, 135 n.66, 142, 145–
  46, 148–49, 153–54, 157, 160, 171–
  73, 175, 177, 179, 183–87, 193,
  202–4, 206–7, 218, 225, 230–32,
  234, 235 n.10, 253; light infantry:
  71, 82, 100, 207, see also airborne
  forces; medical units: 148, 210;
  military police: 148, 216; special
  forces: 9, 19, 29–40, 42–45, 48
  n.58, 49, 51, 56–57, 67–68, 70, 71,
  81, 91, 93, 110–13, 207–15, 219,
  221–22, 230–34, 253, 255–56; see
  also *Armies, National,* formations
  and units

formations: battalions: 5, 58, 85,
  149, 171–72, 177, 180, 183–84,
  186, 193, 201, 204, 206, 215, 218,
  225, 231–34, 237 n.45, 248 n.224,
  256; brigades: 51, 58, 60, 64, 111–
  13, 141–42, 144–46, 149, 185–86,
  200, 202, 218; companies: 5, 171,
  184, 199, 201, 202, 218; divisions:
  5, 27, 29, 59, 64, 101, 147, 185–
  86, 190, 215; platoons: 5, 58, 85,
  171–73, 192, 204–5, 218, 248
  n.224; regiments/regimental
  system: 5, 93, 112–13, 145, 177–
  78, 180–87, 205, 211, 222, 230–31,
  235, 236 n.23, 254; sections: 171,
  173, 204–205; squadrons: 210–15,
  233
manpower: 28, 42, 49, 51–55, 71,
  79, 85–86, 91–95, 115, 120–23,
  141–45, 147, 155, 161–63, 163 n.4,
  172–73, 175, 176, 179, 182–87,
  202–3, 208–11, 230–32, 235 n.10;
  non-commissioned officers
  (NCOs): 64, 96, 160, 183, 201,
  204–6, 213, 222, 231, 234, 254;
  officers/officer corps: 8, 31–32,
  34–36, 43, 54–55, 57, 64–65, 81,
  91, 96–99, 115, 119, 155, 160–61,
  171–72, 176, 177–83, 187, 192–93,
  197–202, 204–6, 208–11, 215–26,
  231, 234, 253–54; rank structures:
  4, 96, 179–80; mobilisation and
  recruitment: 3, 6, 44, 91–99, 120,
  132 n.41, 141, 146, 176–79, 183–
  87, 209–11, 231; conscription
  (national service): 6, 54–56, 58–
  59, 64, 92, 94–95, 122–23, 138
  n.108, 178–79, 183–84, 187, 204,
  211, 231, 237 n.39, 254; levée en
  masse: 5, 12, 81; volunteer
  service: 91, 94, 122–13, 137 n.106,
  141, 176, 179, 183–84, 187, 209–
  11; career patterns: 32, 36, 46, 48
  n.58, 97–99, 115, 133 n.51, 177–
  84, 187, 211, 226, 231: see also
  Armies, National
Educational and Training:
  professional education: 5–6, 32,
  37, 38, 40–41, 55, 114–15, 146,
  160, 177–81, 201–7, 223–26, 230
  232, 236 n.25; conservatism: 32,
  43, 177–82, 187, 189, 208; service
  colleges and schools: 31, 96–98,

105, 115, 132 n.44, 146, 160, 179–81, 191, 207, 225–26, 243 n.140; training: 5, 22, 28, 33, 38–40, 42, 45, 53, 58–59, 73 n.13, 74 n.28, 96, 105, 113–14, 143, 145–46, 151, 156–63, 169, 176, 178–82, 184–85, 187, 191, 196, 201–7, 210–11, 213–16, 219, 222, 225–26, 228, 230–35, 248 n.224, 252, 254–56; doctrine: 1–3, 5–6, 19, 21, 22, 27–29, 32–33, 37–40, 42, 44–46, 49, 51–55, 58–59, 74 n.28, 80–128, 143, 145, 155–60, 163, 178, 180–82, 188–98, 202–7, 213, 215–19, 223, 226, 230–31, 253–55; doctrine, experience as source of: 169, 171, 177–79, 181–82, 187–94, 196, 202–5, 215–17, 223, 229–31, 235, 252–54; drills: 5, 204, 228, 231, 234; exercises: 114, 146, 155, 158–60, 202, 204, 206; manuals: 37, 160, 190–92, 195–96, 205–6, 213, 215, 217, 225–26, 229, 230, 239 n.77, 243 n.136; standardisation: 157, 203–6, 228, 230, 254; training teams: 202, 204–6

Adaptation: x, 1–14, 27–40, 42, 45–46, 51, 56–58, 62, 64, 70–72, 82–83, 114–16, 119, 121, 128, 139, 141, 155–63, 171, 176, 178, 182, 188–235, 251–56; innovative adaptation: 1–4, 34–35, 39, 64, 70, 82, 83, 156, 169, 174–75, 178, 182, 187, 189–90, 197, 203–4, 206, 208–10, 214–15, 221–22, 226, 229, 231–33; reactive adaptation: 1–3, 5, 7, 27–28, 32–33, 37–39, 45–46, 51, 56–58, 82, 178, 182, 193–94, 201–206, 217–18, 220–21, 223–27; technological adaptation: 1–3, 5–7, 26–29, 51, 59, 68, 77, 84, 96, 101, 116, 119, 121, 128, 176, 190, 228–29, 252–54

Combat Effectiveness: 1–7, 10, 28–29, 33, 36, 51, 53, 55–58, 60, 61, 64–65, 69, 70, 71, 79, 95–96, 101, 111, 114–16, 127, 138 n.119, 145, 156–63, 169, 173–75, 178, 182–88, 193, 198, 201–16, 218–22, 228–35, 252–56; cohesion: 4–5, 57, 64, 96, 178, 187, 231, 235, 254; discipline: 4, 28, 54, 57, 68, 83–84, 114–15, 155, 158, 179, 187, 204, 210–11,

223, 254; morale and motivation: 3, 5, 8–11, 55–56, 58–59, 65, 70, 72, 74 n.28, 83, 115, 138 n.119, 174, 186–87, 198, 224–25; professionalism: 71, 88, 91, 97–99, 122, 151, 163, 169, 176, 178–82, 184, 187, 211, 218, 231, 234–35

Armies, National: British Army: 14, 54–55, 58, 149, 156, 169–249, 251–55; *Organization,* formations and units: British Army of the Rhine (BAOR): 184, 186–87; Middle East (Land) Forces: 190–91, 199, 202: Strategic Reserve/Army Strategic Command: 184–87; 3rd Division: 185–86; 6th Airborne Division: 190; 1st Guards Brigade: 203; 2nd Infantry Brigade: 202; 5th Brigade: 234; Chindits: 208–9; Joint Airborne Task Force: 186; Parachute Brigade: 186; Army Air Corps: 229, 248 n.220; Black Watch: 208; Guards Regiments: 183–84, 203; Gurkhas: 204; Parachute Regiment: 183, 186, 211, 233–34; Royal Electrical and Mechanical Engineers (REME): 184; Rifle Brigade: 209; Royal Military Police: 216; Special Air Service Regiment (SAS): 208–15, 219, 221–22, 231–34, 244 n.153, n.156, 248 n.224; Territorial Army: 208, 210, 251; auxiliary forces: 173, 209, 213, 218, 221, 231; *Education and Training*: Army Staff College (Camberley): 179–81, 191, 207, 243 n.140; Royal Military Academy (Sandhurst): 179, 226; Training Directorate: 205; Close Quarter Battle Range: 206; Far East Land Forces (FARELF) Training Centre (Johore Bahru, Malaya): 204; jungle warfare training: 203–4, 210–11; doctrine (counter-insurgency): 188–98, 202–7, 213, 215–19, 223, 226, 230–31; manuals: (1) *The Conduct of Anti-Terrorist Operations in Malaya* (ATOM): 192, 195, 230, 239 n.77; *Land Operations, Volume 3: Counter-Revolutionary Operations*: 213, 226; *Middle East*

Armies, National (*cont.*)
  Training Pamphlet no. 9, 'Notes for Officers on Internal Security Duties': 191, 215; *Operational Commitments:* 171, 173, 176, 178, 182–87, 193, 202–6, 210–15, 219–22, 229–30, 232–35.
  Canadian Army: 14, 139–68, 251, 253–55; *Organisation:* 141–47, 150–51, 163 n.3; integration/unification: 139, 142–43, 145–47, 150–51; Total Force/Corps Concept: 146; formations and units, Active Force: 141; brigades (brigade groups): 141–42, 144–46, 149; combat groups: 144–46, 151, 153–54; Mobile Command: 143–45, 147, 151, 153–54; Mobile Striking Force: 141; armoured units: 142, 146, 148–49; communications (signals) units: 148, 154–55; infantry: 142, 145–46, 148–49, 153–54, 157, 160; 2nd Combat Group: 145, 151, 154; 5th Combat Group: 151, 153; Special Service Force: 145; Canadian Airborne Regiment: 144–46, 149, 151–54, 162, 166 n.44; Canadian Guards: 159; 1st Battalion, Royal Canadian Regiment (1 RCR): 160; 1st Canadian Signals Regiment: 155; Queen's Own Rifles: 148; Intelligence Corps: 160; NATO forces: 142–47; reserve forces (militia): 141, 146–47; *Training:* 156–60; doctrine (peace-keeping, internal security): 143, 155–60, 163; *Operational Commitments:* 141–42, 144, 146–55; roles and missions: 139, 141–47, 161–62
  French Army: 77–138, 251–55; *Organisation:* leadership (officers): 81, 91 96–99, 115; general chief of staff: 101, 137 n.106; formations and units, airborne forces: 57, 108, 111–15, 135 n.66; armoured forces: 86, 101, 107, 111–13, 135 n.66; artillery: 94, 111–13; cavalry: 82–83, 93; command elements: 112–13; engineers: 111–13; infantry: 93–94, 108, 111–13, 135 n.66;

Marine units: 94, 108, 111–13, 122, 135 n.66; special forces: 81, 91, 93, 110–13; First Army (Corps): 112–13; Rapid Assistance Forces (FAR): 107–8, 113, 122, 128, 135 n.66, 136 n.79; 4th Aeromobile Division: 113, 135 n.66; 10th Airborne Division: 111; 11th Airborne Division: 111–13, 122; 25th Airborne Division: 111; 27th Alpine Division: 113; 11th Infantry Division: 111; 6th Light Armoured Division: 113; Light Division of Intervention: 111; 9th Marine Infantry Division: 111–13, 122, 135 n.66; Foreign Legion: 93, 112, 114, 117, 132 n.35; 2nd Foreign Paratroop Regiment: 114; 31st (Demi-)Brigade: 112–13; commandos de chasse: 86, 101; groupes mobiles: 84; Special/Urban Administrative Sections: 90; native troops: 84, 89, 91–96, 131 n.32, n.43, 133 n.50; Armée d'Afrique: 93–94; Armée Coloniale: 94; *Education and Training:* Saint-Cyr (military academy): 97–98, 115, 132 n.44; doctrine: (1) 'Guerres Africaines': 99–128, (2) 'Guerre Algérienne': 80–101; *Operational Commitments:* 77, 79, 81, 83–91, 94, 99–102, 105–6, 109–10, 113–14, 116–18, 121, 123–28
  Israeli Army: 14, 49–76, 251–53, 255–56; *Organisation:* leadership, officers: 54–57, 64–65, 68; general staff: 55, 60, 62; chief of staff: 54, 56–57, 65, 68; chief of infantry and paratroops: 59; manpower, conscripts: 54–56, 58–59, 64, 71; formations and units: airborne forces: 51, 55–60, 64–70, 74 n.28; armoured forces: 51, 59–61, 67–70; artillery: 60–61, 65, 69; infantry: 51, 55, 58–59, 61, 64–65; intelligence: 51, 56, 63; logistics troops: 51, 70; reconnaissance units: 64; reserve forces: 51, 55, 59, 64, 70; special forces: 51, 64–65, 67–70; 890th Parachute Battalion: 57; Golani Brigade: 59, 64, 70; No'ar Halutzi Lohemet

(NAHAL): 55, 58; Sayaret: 51, 64, 65, 68, 70; Unit 101: 56–57, 71; Unit 202: 57–58; *Doctrine:* 51–55, 58–59; *Operational Commitments:* 51, 56–70, 72

United States Army: 19–48, 251–53, 255; *Organisation:* leadership, officers: 31–32, 34–36, 43; formations and units: 8240th Army Unit: 33, First Special Service Force: 36; Office of the Chief of Psychological Warfare: 34; Psychological Warfare Center (Fort Bragg): 35; Rangers: 21, 30–35, 37, 42, 44; Special Forces: 22, 29–40, 42–43, 45, 253, 255; 1st Special Forces Group: 36; 10th Special Forces Group: 35–36; 77th Special Forces Group: 36: First Special Operations Command: 42; Strategic Services Unit: 30; Wolfpack 33; *Doctrine:* 27–29, 32–34, 38–40, 42, 44–45; *Operational Commitments:* 26, 28, 33–40, 42

Other Armies: Egyptian: 58, 61, 67; Indonesian: 212; Jordanian: 61, 65–66; Libyan: 100, 115, 126, 138 n.112, n.119; Syrian: 60, 70; Turkish: 149, 161; Vietnamese Communist (Viet Cong/Viet Minh): 24, 37, 40

Army Quarterly (and Defence Journal) 192, 205, 236–37 n.34

Ascension Island 234

Asia 2, 23, 24, 26, 93, 248 n.223

Asia, Southeast 23–25, 37–40, 81, 94, 100, 183–85, 243 n.132; see also *Warfare, Low-Intensity:* Campaigns, Incidents, and Operations

Assassination see *Warfare, Low-Intensity:* Aspects and Concepts, Terrorism

'A Team' see *Armies, National: United States Army*

Atlantic Ocean 80, 103

d'Aumale, Duc 88

Australia (Australians) 25, 204, 209, 231

Baratier, General 87

Barker, General Sir Evelyn 191

Bar-Lev, General Chaim 65

Barnett, Correlli 179

Barre, Raymond 128

Baynes, Colonel J. C. M. 184

Beattie, Brigadier-General Clayton 157

Begin, Menachem 216

Beirut 68, 70, 118, 121, 137 n.95; see also *Warfare, Low-Intensity:* Campaigns, Incidents, and Operations: Middle East, Lebanon

Belfast 170 (map), 201, 221; see also *Warfare, Low-Intensity:* Campaigns, Incidents, and Operations: Europe, Northern Ireland

Belgium 92, 118, 127, 252

Bell, J. Bowyer 188, 230

Ben-Gurion, David 54, 57

Bidwell, Brigadier R. G. S. 181

Bokassa, Emperor Jean, B. 106

Bolshevism see Communism; see also Marxism-Leninism

Bonaparte, Napoleon (Napoleonic Wars) 1, 3, 5, 6, 13, 79, 81–82, 91–92

Borneo see *Warfare, Low-Intensity:* Campaigns, Incidents, and Operations: Southeast Asia, Confrontation campaign

Bourget, General Pierre 5

Briggs, Lieutenant-General Sir Harold 209, 242 n.126; see also *Warfare, Low-Intensity:* Campaigns, Incidents, and Operations: Southeast Asia, Malayan Emergency

Britain (British) see Great Britain

British Army Journal/Review 205, 236 n.34

Bromont (Quebec, Canada) 140 (map), 153

Bugeaud, Marshal Thomas R. 81–86, 88, 90–91, 97–98, 129 n.8

Bujumbura (Franco-African summit) 124–25, 128

Burns, Major-General E. L. M. 148

Cadieux, Leo 159; see also Canada; Minister of Defence

Cairo 26

Callwell, C. E.   190
Calvert, Lieutenant-Colonel
   Michael   209–10
Cameroon   79, 90, 105, 125
Canada   14, 139–68, 251; defence
   policies, commitments, and
   budgets; 141–47, 157, 161–63;
   Department of National Defence
   (DND): 143, 145–46, 152–53,
   157–58, 161–62; Minister of
   National Defence: 142, 143, 147,
   159; National Defence
   Headquarters: 152, 158; Combat
   Development Committee: 146;
   Director-General Military Plans
   and Operations: 157; Mobilisation
   Planning Task Force: 146; Task
   Force on the Unification of the
   Canadian Forces: 145; Canadian
   Armed Forces: 14, 139–68; Air
   Force (Royal Canadian Air Force/
   Air Command): 144, 148, 153,
   157; Communications Command:
   154; Navy (Maritime Command):
   144, 153, 154; Senate Sub-
   committee on National Defence:
   145; Solicitor-General of Canada:
   152, 155; War Measures Act: 150–
   51, 166 n.52; see also *Armies,
   National:* Canadian Army
Cannon   see *Weapons and Equipment*:
   artillery
Carver, Field Marshal Lord
   (Michael)   181
Castro, Fidel   24
Catroux, General Georges   85
CCRAK   see United States, armed
   forces
Central African Republic   77, 106,
   109–10, 125, 133 n.52, 135 n.65
Central America   24, 42
Central Intelligence Agency
   (CIA)   see *Warfare, Low-
   Intensity:* Aspects and Concepts:
   Intelligence
Central Treaty Organisation
   (CENTO)   24
Challe, General Maurice   86, 101
Charteris, Lieutenant-Colonel The
   Hon. (Lord Martin)   215
Cheysson, Claude   124
China   2, 4, 12, 23–25, 27–28, 37–38,
   43, 79–80, 84, 193

Clausewitz, Carl von   42, 82, 116, 188
Cline, Ray   23, 30
Clutterbuck, Lieutenant-Colonel
   Richard   188, 193, 196, 200, 205,
   218, 226, 243 n.133
Collins, General J. Lawton   35
Communism   23–26, 37, 62, 91, 193,
   239 n.80; see also Bolshevism;
   Marxism-Leninism
Confédération Economique des Etats
   d'Afrique Occidental
   (CEDEAO)   127
Congo-Brazzaville   79
Conventional war see *Warfare,* types
   (other than low-intensity)
Coups d'état   11, 23, 106
Cross, James   150
Cross, Major John   220
Cuba   24, 115–17
Cuthbertson, Brian   160

Dacko, David   106
Dakar (Senegal)   100, 109, 127
Daly, Most Reverend Dr.   14
Darlac (Vietnam)   39
Darling, Lieutenant-General Sir
   Kenneth   188
Dayan, Moshe   53, 56–58, 62, 65
Dead Sea   64, 66
Deane-Drummond, Major-General
   Anthony   201
Decker, General George H.   49
Delbruck, Hans   87
Dewar, Lieutenant-Colonel
   Michael   201
Diego-Suarez (Madagascar)   109
Diplomacy   4, 56, 89, 105, 117, 124–
   28, 156, 212
Djibouti   100, 105, 109–10, 133 n.52,
   135 n.65
Dodds, General Alfred   84
Dominican Republic   159
Donovan, William J.   30
Druze   56, 67
Duchemin, General   84, 89
Duncanson, Dennis   229

Edmonton (Alberta, Canada)   145,
   151
Egypt   25, 56, 58–61, 67, 79, 92, 148,
   156, 202, 233

Eitan, Colonel Rafael 68
El Fatah 60, 63, 65
Ellul, Jacques 11, 14
EOKA 193, 219
Erskine, General George 196, 198–99, 209
d'Estaing, Valery Giscard 108, 117
Europe, Eastern 8, 22–24, 26, 34, 36, 38, 115
Europe, Western 22–24, 26–27, 34, 41, 43, 77, 79, 101, 104, 141–42, 144–46, 252, 256
Evelegh, Robin 201, 222–23

Faidherbe, Governor 83, 93, 101
Far East see Asia, Southeast; see also *Warfare, Low-Intensity:* Campaigns, Incidents, and Operations, Southeast Asia
Farran, Roy 208, 212
Fedayeen 58–59, 61–63, 65–66, 68–69
Fergusson, Bernard 208
Fiji 231
Flexible Response see United States, national security policy
Fort Bragg (North Carolina, USA) 34–36
FOSH see Plugoth Sadeh
France (French) 3, 5–6, 11, 13–14, 24–26, 37, 51, 57, 59, 71, 77–138, 233, 251, 252; government of: 25, 117, 118, 134 n.57; Minister of Defence: 110; Minister of Foreign Affairs: 124; Départements et Territoires d'Outre-mer: 103; defence policy and budget: 111–13, 119–23, 137 n.103; security policy and Africa: 102–7, 109–10, 114, 116–19, 125–28, 133–34 n.57; Air Force: 111, 114, 120–21, 124–26; Navy: 111. see also *Armies, National:* French Army.
Front de Libération du Québec (FLQ) 150, 160

Gabon 79, 100, 105–6, 109–10, 125; see also *Warfare, Low-Intensity:* Campaigns, Incidents, and Operations, Africa
Gal, Reuven 71
Galilee 64

Gallieni, General Joseph 84, 86–87, 89–90, 131 n.28
de Gaulle (Gaullist) 103–4, 107–8, 110
Geraghty, Tony 211–13, 221
Germany (Germans) 6, 12, 22, 36, 92, 96, 102, 147, 186, 191, 193, 252
Giap, Vo Nguyen 38
Giraud, General Henri 85
Gneisenau, General N. von 6
Graham, Dominick 176, 181
Gray, Colin 144
Great Britain (British) 1, 3, 6–7, 11, 25, 51–53, 59, 87, 92, 95–96, 105, 116, 169–249, 251–52; government of: 25, 182, 185–86, 188, 191, 195–96, 199–200, 208, 212–14, 225, 227, 232; Foreign and Commonwealth Office (FCO): 225, 227; Home Office: 225; Ministry of Defence: 187, 200, 206, 213, 225–26, 230, 233–34; War Office: 190, 208, 217; defence policy and budget: 176, 181–86, 208, 211–12, 230, 232–33, 236 n.34; Defence White Paper (1957): 183, 211; Defence Operational Analysis Establishment: 181; armed forces, Royal Air Force (RAF): 185–86, 218, 224, 229, 233, 248 n.220; Royal Marine Commandos: 208, 210, 233–34; Royal Navy: 176, 229, 234, 248 n.220; service schools: Joint Service Warfare School (Joint Warfare Establishment) 180, 225–26; National Defence College 180; Royal College of Defence Studies 180; Royal Military College of Science 180; see also *Armies, National:* British Army
Green Berets, see *Armies, National:* United States Army, Special Forces
Guerre Algérienne, Guerres Africaines see *Armies, National:* French Army, *Education and Training:* doctrine
Guevara, Ernesto 'Che' 38
Guiana 103
Guillaume, General 101

GUNT (Government of National Unity) 124–25, 138 n.112, 119; see also *Warfare, Low-Intensity:* Campaigns, Incidents, and Operations, Africa: Chad
Gwynn, Sir Charles 190

Habré, Hissène 100, 124–25, 134 n.57
Haganah (Defence) 52–53, 191
Haifa 53
Harding, Field Marshal Sir John 199, 209, 219
Heath, Edward 186
Hebron 61
Hellyer, Paul 142, 144
High commissioner (British colonial official) 191, 194, 196–97, 199, 219
Hinde, Major-General W. R. N. 198
Hong Kong 225
Hull (Quebec, Canada) 140 (map), 160
Hungary 23, 36
Huré, General 85
Hussein, King (of Jordan) 66
Hutchinson, Simon 198

Ideology 3, 10–13, 22, 52, 55, 59, 87, 89, 91, 127, 131 n.30, 185–86
Imperialism 10–11, 13
India 79, 148, 183, 190
Indian Ocean 80, 99, 103, 109–10
Indochina (Indochinese) 12–13, 24, 26, 37–38, 51, 71, 79, 80–81, 84–86, 89–91, 93–95, 99, 102; see also *Warfare, Low-Intensity:* Campaigns, Incidents, and Operations, Southeast Asia
Indonesia 184–85, 194, 212; see also, *Warfare, Low-Intensity:* Campaigns, Incidents, and Operations, Southeast Asia: Confrontation campaign
International Institute for Strategic Studies 181
Iran 3, 11, 23–25
Iraq 11, 24, 53
Irgun Zevai Leumi 52, 54, 191, 193, 252
Islam 11–13, 83, 129 n.6

Israel 14, 25, 49–76, 196, 233, 251–52, 255–56; government: 25; Minister of Defence: 54, 62, 65, see also Dayan, Moshe; defence policy: 52, 54–56, 58–61, 65–70; Defence Service Law: 54–55; armed forces, air force: 51, 54, 59, 61, 65, 69; navy: 51, 54, 67; naval commandos: 51, 67–68; see also *Armies, National: Israeli Army*
Ivory Coast 105, 109–10, 124

Jeffrey, Keith 215, 221–22
Jewish insurgent groups 52–54, 190–91, 239 n.68; see also Haganah; Irgun Zevai Leumi; Lechi; Palmach
Joint Advisory Commission Korea (JACK) see United States, Central Intelligence Agency
Joint Chiefs of Staff (JCS) see United States, armed forces
Jordan 62–64, 66

Kader, Emir Abd el 82, 88, 93, 95
Katanga (Zaire/Congo) 113–14, 119
Kelly, Colonel Francis J. 32
Kennedy, United States President John F. 29, 37–38, 41
Khartoum conference 116
Kibbutzim 53–54
Kingston (Ontario, Canada) 140 (map), 153–54
Kitson, General Sir Frank 173, 181, 199, 209
Kleber, General 92
Krepinevich, Andrew 38
Krim, Abd el 85
Kyrenia (Cyprus) 149

Lansdale, Major-General Edward G. 39, 48 n.52
Laporte, Pierre 150
Lawrence, Colonel T. E. 169, 188, 207–8, 243 n.143
Lechi 191
Lenin (Vladimir Ilich Ulyanov) 12; see also Bolshevism; Communism; Marxism-Leninism

Leopoldville (Congo) 148
Libreville (Gabon) 100, 109
Libya 100, 102, 116–17, 123–27, 134 n.57, 136 n.88, 138 n.113, see also *Warfare, Low-Intensity:* Campaigns, Incidents, and Operations, Africa: Chad
Liddell Hart, B. H. 181
Lisburn (Northern Ireland) 170 (map), 226
Lomé conference 125, 128
Londonderry (Northern Ireland) 170 (map), 221, 225
Loomis, Major-General D. G. 146, 150–51
Lyautey, Marshal Louis 81, 84–85, 87, 90, 97, 101

Macdonald, Malcolm 217
Makarios, Archbishop 149
Makleff, General Mordechai 56–57
Malagasy 80, 84, 86, 89, 93, 95, 100, 109
Malaysia 230
Malta 233
Mangin, General Charles 84, 131 n.32
Mao Tse Tung 24, 37–38, 188, 192–93
Marxism-Leninism 12–14, 22, 49, 104
M'Ba, Leon 106
McArthur, General Douglas 9
McClure, General Robert 35
McLin, Jon 142
McNeill, William H. 2–4
Media, news 139, 174, 190, 207, 214, 223–28, 234
Menzies, Robert 209
Messmer, Pierre 110, 138 n.110
Mexico 79–80
Middle East 3, 24–25, 49–76, 79, 84, 94–95, 100, 148, 173, 183, 185, 190–91, 197, 199, 202, 205–8, 211–16, 219, 229, 233, 248 n.223; see also *Warfare, Low-Intensity:* Campaigns, Incidents, and Operations, Middle East
Minh, Ho Chi 24, 37
Mitterrand, François 103–4, 106, 117, 123–25, 134 n.57
Moltke, General Helmut von 6
Montgomery, Field Marshal Lord (Bernard Law) 191

Montreal (Quebec, Canada) 140 (map), 150–54
Moslems 4–5, 11, 13; see also Islam

Nairac, Captain Robert 222
Napoleon see Bonaparte, Napoleon
Nasser, Egyptian President Gamal Abd el 25, 58, 61
Nationalism 10, 12–14, 89, 91–92, 129 n.6, 174, 189, 192
National Liberation Front (FLN, Algeria) 86, 89
National Security Council (NSC) see United States
NATO see North Atlantic Treaty Organisation
Netherlands 87
New Brunswick (province of Canada) 154
New Zealand 25, 231
Nicosia (Cyprus) 149
Niger 106, 124, 138 n.113
Nigeria 116
Nile River 67
North Atlantic Treaty Organisation (NATO) 23, 25, 29, 34, 104–5, 112–13, 117, 141–47, 156, 158, 183, 185–87, 232, 252, 256; Allied Command Europe Mobile Force 146
North Korea 28, 32–33
North Vietman 40
Norway 25

Oldfield, Sir Maurice 200
Ontario (province of Canada) 140 (map), 145, 151, 153–54
Organisation of African Unity (OAU) 125, 127
Osgood, Robert 26
OSS (Office of Strategic Services) see *Warfare, Low-Intensity:* Aspects and Concepts: Intelligence Ottawa (Canada) 140 (map), 150–51, 154, 160 162 Oueddei, Goukouni 124–25

Pacific Ocean 80, 103
Paget, Lieutenant-Colonel Sir Julian 200

Pakistan 24–25, 148
Palestine Liberation Organisation (PLO) 60, 62–63, 65–70, 75 n.66; see also El Fatah; Fedayeen; Popular Front for the Liberation of Palestine
Palmach 53–54, 57, 65, 73 n.12
Persia see Iran
Petawawa (Ontario, Canada) 140 (map), 145, 151
Plugoth Sadeh 52
Polanyi, Karl 79
Police forces and duties 8, 52, 56, 63, 67, 69, 150–54, 161–62, 173, 176, 189, 193–95, 197–203, 208–9, 215–21, 225, 227–28, 251, 254; Canada: Montreal Urban Community Police 153; Ontario Provincial Police 153; Quebec (Provincial) Police 151, 153; Royal Canadian Mounted Police (RCMP) 151, 153–54, 162; Israel: 56, 63, 67, 69; Palestine: Jewish Settlement Police 52; Palestine Police Force 197, 202, 208, 215–16; Northern Ireland: Royal Ulster Constabulary (RUC) 200–201, 220–22, 246 n.186; police tactical units; 161–62
Polisario 100, 111
Politics 4, 7–8, 13, 24, 32, 38–46, 71, 87–88, 91, 96, 106, 115–16, 119, 121, 127, 152–53, 171–75, 182–86, 188–95, 200, 213, 221, 223–24, 226–30, 232, 252–55
Polynesia 103
Popular Front for the Liberation of Palestine (PFLP) 66, 68, 70
Preston, Richard 8
Protestant extremist groups (Northern Ireland) 213
Provisional Irish Republican Army (PIRA) 193, 206, 213–14, 221–23, 225–28, 248 n.224, 252

Qaddafi, Colonel Muhammar 123–24, 126
Quebec (province of Canada) 140 (map), 147, 150–54, 160
Quebec City 140 (map), 152

Radios see Weapons and Equipment

Rangers see Armies, National: United States Army
Reid, Major-General Roland 153
Religion 11, 14; see also Islam; Moslems
Réunion (Indian Ocean) 109
Revolution 11–14, 21–24, 36–40, 44–46, 49; see also Warfare, Low-Intensity: Aspects and concepts, revolutionary warfare
Rhodesia 210–11, 231
Richardson, James 143
Ridgway, General Matthew B. 27–28
Rikhye, Major-General Indar 165 n.33
Royal Institute of International Affairs 181
Royal United Services Institute for Defence Studies (RUSI) 181; RUSI Journal 236 n.34
Russia see Soviet Union

Sadeh, Yitzhak 52–53, 73 n.13
Saudi Arabia 56
Scharnhorst, General Gerhard von 6
Senegal (Senegalese) 79, 83–84, 89–91, 93–95, 105, 110, 135 n.65; see also Warfare, Low-Intensity: Campaigns, Incidents, and Operations, Africa
Shaba see Warfare, Low-Intensity: Campaigns, Incidents, and Operations, Africa: Zaire
Sharon, General Ariel 56–57
Shia see Moslems
Short, Anthony 198
Simson, H. J. 189–90, 197
Sinai Desert 59, 61
Soult, Marshal 88
Southeast Asia Treaty Organisation 25
South Yemen 212
Soviet Union 7–8, 13, 22–28, 34, 36, 43, 59, 87, 102, 104, 115, 117, 137 n.98; armed forces 26, 34, 121, 141, 256
Spanier, John 22
Special Air Service Regiment (SAS) see Armies, National: British Army
Special branch see police; see also Warfare, Low-Intensity: Aspects and Concepts, intelligence

Special forces see *Armies*
Special Night Squads 53; see also
  Haganah; Palmach
Special operations see *Warfare, Low-
  Intensity:* Aspects and Concepts
Stanhope, Henry 176
Straits of Tiran 59, 61
Strategy see *Warfare*
Suez Canal 61, 67, 99
Syria 53, 58, 60–61, 63, 66

Tactics see *Warfare*
Tanks see *Weapons and Equipment*
Taylor, General Maxwell D. 48 n.52
Templer, Field Marshal Sir
  Gerald 195, 197, 199, 217, 239
  n.77, 241 n.106
Thatcher, British Prime Minister
  Margaret 186
Third World 26, 37–38, 42, 45–46,
  103, 185, 211
Treaty of Tripoli 123–25, 136 n.88
Tugwell, Brigadier Dr. Maurice 225,
  247 n.211
Tunisia (Tunisians) 93, 95, 99

Ulster see *Warfare, Low-Intensity:*
  Campaigns, Incidents, and
  Operations, Northern Ireland
United Nations 22, 142, 144, 148–49,
  155–61, 165 n.33; see also
  Warfare, Low-Intensity: Aspects
  and Concepts, peace-keeping;
  Campaigns, Incidents, and
  Operations, Europe: Cyprus;
  Middle East: United Nations
  Emergency Forces (UNEF)
United Nations Partisan Infantry
  Korea (UNPIK) 33
United States 7, 13, 14, 19–48, 51,
  59, 62, 65, 70–71, 79, 92, 116–18,
  121, 141, 154, 159, 196, 251, 253,
  255; Department of Defense 30–
  31; Assistant Secretary of Defense
  for Special Operations and Low-
  Intensity Conflict 42;
  Department of State 30;
  National Security Council
  (NSC) 30–31; national security
  policy (foreign and defence
  policies) 22–27, 29–30, 41–46;

armed forces: 19, 21, 22, 26–29,
  38, 41–42, 44–45, 77, 251–56;
  Joint Chiefs of Staff 31, 48 n.52;
  Air Force 29, 117, 121, 123;
  CCRAK (Covert, Clandestine and
  Related Activities in Korea) 33;
  Delta Force 21; Marine
  Corps 27, 256; National
  Guard 251; Navy 27, 29;
  Unified Special Operations
  Command 42; see also *Armies,
  National: United States Army*
USA see United States
USSR see Soviet Union

Vallières, Pierre 150–51
Verrier, Anthony 177, 179, 186

Walker, General Sir Walter 219
Warfare, Concepts and Principles:
  firepower 2, 3, 6, 28, 49, 53, 65,
  86, 101, 112–13, 121, 190, 253;
  flexibility 114–15, 142, 178, 187,
  196, 206, 229, 232, 254;
  initiative 86, 115, 156, 172, 182,
  187, 189, 205, 216, 225;
  leadership 3, 32, 35, 53–55, 83,
  115, 155–56, 160–61, 163, 172,
  177–83, 187, 197–201, 203–6, 211–
  12, 218, 231, 234–35, 253–54;
  mobility 1–3, 6–7, 28–29, 60, 64,
  70, 81–84, 86, 111–13, 144, 187,
  190, 253–54; operational
  security 196, 203, 216; speed 1,
  83–84, 86, 111, 229; surprise (and
  shock effect) 1, 53, 57, 60, 84,
  86, 96, 111, 196, 203, 253–54
Conduct of: administration 156–
  58, 179–80, 182, 187, 211, 255;
  command, control and
  communications 3–7, 22, 33–34,
  49, 59, 83, 86, 89, 96, 112, 114,
  151–56, 158, 164 n.10, 171, 173,
  178–80, 187, 189, 191, 194–202,
  208, 211, 215–16, 218–19, 224,
  231, 233–35; command – general
  staff system 6, 55, 179–81, 198–
  200, comand – joint civil-
  military 151–55, 158, 171–72,
  175, 189–91, 194–202, 215–22,
  225, 227; communications 3–4,

Warfare, (*cont.*)

6–7, 83–84, 96, 148–49, 154–55, 157, 159, 197, 199, 202, 219, 224, 234; logistics 3–4, 6, 9, 49, 82–84, 107–11, 126, 148, 156–57, 159, 179, 210–11; logistics – deployment and basing 3, 77, 79, 105, 109–10, 115, 121, 144, 149–50, 152–53, 157, 184–87, 198, 254; logistics – pre-positioning 110, 146; logistics – strategic mobility 3, 110–11, 121–23, 144, 146–47, 156–58, 161, 184–87; operations 2–9, 21, 28–29, 32–33, 37–40, 42, 56–58, 60–61, 64–70, 79, 82–86, 100, 111–17, 121, 143, 146–63, 169, 171–75, 180, 184–85, 187, 190–91, 194–206, 208–16, 218, 220–24, 228–29, 231–35, 235 n.10, 237 n.34, 248 n.227, 253; operations – types: *airborne* 67, 79, 100, 106, 114, 141, 210–11, 229, 233; *airlanding* 229; *airmobile* (*airmobility, airlift*) 3, 64, 66, 68, 86, 101, 110–14, 121–23, 144, 146–47, 151–53, 157–58, 161, 164 n.18, 184–86, 210–11, 219, 228–29, 233, 248 n.220, 253–54; *ambush* 53, 64, 171–72, 174, 204–5, 210, 212–14, 218, 221, 242 n.130, 248 n.224; *amphibious* 67–69, 79, 84, 86, 101, 144, 180, 210–11, 233–34; *armoured* 27, 59–61, 66, 69, 86; *artillery* 60–61, 65, 68–70, 81, 212, 234; *assault* 65, 84–86, 154–55; *close air support (air strikes)* 60–61, 65, 68–70, 79, 100, 111, 124–26, 190; *commando* 31–33, 35, 44, 65, 67; *engineering* 157, 159; *invasion* 149, 161, 233; *jungle warfare* 172, 195, 203–5, 209–12, 219–20, 229; *mining* 60–61, 63–64; *mountain warfare* 83, 85; *night* 53, 57–58, 204–6, 221; *pre-emptive strikes* 65, 68–69, 119; *raids* 33, 38, 44, 53, 56–57, 67–68, 82–83, 112, 152, 174, 207, 212, 251; *sealift* 144, 146, 158, 161; *street-fighting* 202, 205–6; operations – casualties 35, 56–58, 60–61, 65–66, 68–70, 82, 118, 152, 166 n.53, 172, 175, 202, 210, 213–14, 221–22, 228–29; planning 6, 22, 26, 28–29, 31, 35–38, 40, 45, 60, 83, 84, 86, 142, 145–46, 152–53, 155–58, 172, 178, 180, 182–207, 216–20, 223–24, 226, 233–34; strategy 6, 22–27, 29, 42–45, 82–83, 85–87, 102–7, 109–10, 114, 116–19, 125–28, 178, 180–201, 203, 223–26, 232–33, 239 n.68; tactics 5, 8, 28–29, 33, 37, 41, 53, 57–58, 62, 64–65, 71, 81–84, 86, 157–59, 169, 172, 174, 178, 181–82, 186–87, 189–94, 196, 202–7, 210, 212, 214, 216, 218, 220, 227–28, 230, 234, 237 n.34, 252–54

Types other than Low-Intensity: conventional (high-intensity) 8–9, 21, 26–29, 32–34, 36, 40–43, 49, 51, 58–62, 64, 68–69, 71, 112–13, 128, 145–46, 161, 163, 171–72, 174–76, 178, 180, 184, 187, 201–2, 206–7, 211, 228, 232–35, 251–53, 255; limited 8–10, 14, 21, 40–42, 157, 185, 252; nuclear (and nuclear deterrence) v, 21, 29, 43, 99, 120, 128

Low-Intensity (low-intensity conflict): v, 8–9, 19, 21–22, 32, 36–40, 42–46, 49, 51, 53, 58, 60, 62, 64, 67–68, 70–72, 77, 79–80, 82, 87, 99–102, 113, 123, 126, 127–28, 139, 146–52, 162–63, 169, 171–77, 180, 187–96, 202–35, 235 n.10, 236 n.19, 251–56. Aspects and Concepts: civil-military relations 4, 41, 44, 46, 54–55, 59, 70–72, 91, 116–17, 151–55, 157–58, 171–72, 177, 183, 189, 191, 194–203, 206, 210, 213, 215–28, 232; Civil-Military Relations – public opinion and criticism 40, 57, 67, 69–72, 116–18, 138 n.108, 139, 175, 214, 222–28, 232, 234; civil war 8, 66, 125; Counter-Insurgency v, 37–38, 42–43, 49, 62, 69–70, 81–99, 159, 169, 171, 188–207, 210, 212–27, 230, 232–33, 243 n.133, see also Counter-Revolutionary Warfare, Counter-Terrorism; counter-insurgency measures: *arrest/capture* (of insurgents) 172, 196, 203, 214, 216, 221–23; *civic action* 88–90, 210, 213; *'counter-gangs'* 209, 212; *deportation* 63, 91; *food denial* 210; *information services* 174–75, 207, 210, 223–28, 247 n.211, see also separate entry for Psychological Warfare; *intelligence* see separate entry; *internment* (detention without trial) 151, 193–94, 201, 221, 223, 227; *joint command and planning* (civil-military committees) 151–55, 171–72, 189–91, 194–202, 215–22, 225, 227; *pacification* 40, 66, 85, 94, 97, 101, 129 n.10, 131 n.28; *patrolling* (patrols) 21, 33, 44, 59–60, 63–64, 67, 70, 148–49, 155, 159–60, 204–6, 210, 212–13, 218–21, 229; *resettlement* 203, 242 n.126; *searches* 23, 67, 151–52, 159–60, 191, 202–3, 205–7, 219–21; Counter-Revolutionary Warfare 21–22, 36, 38–40, 42, 44–46, 72, 80–99, 171–75, 188–96, 203, 207, 210, 212–15, 217–28, 230, 232, 243 n.140, 253, 255; Counter-Terrorism v, 21, 42, 51, 60–70, 75 n.62, 159, 161–62, 169, 205, 208–9, 212, 214–15, 232–34, 251, 256, see also Covert Action, Special Operations; counter-terrorism – hostage-rescue/siege-breaking v, 21, 42, 69–70, 79, 100, 106, 114, 155, 162, 169, 215, 235 n.2, 251; Covert Action 30, 32, 67, 73 n.12, 208–14, 218–23, 232; Guerrilla forces 32–33, 37, 60, 65–66, 69, 71, 173–74, 190–93, 198, 202–4, 207, 209–11, 213, 218, 256, see also separate entries for specific groups; Guerrilla Warfare 29, 32–36, 38–39, 44–45, 49, 51–52, 61–62, 70, 256; Insurgency (insurgents) 23, 37, 39–40, 44–45, 62–63, 173–74, 188–96, 202–4, 209–19, 224, 230, 235 n.14, 238 n.59; Insurrection 11, 150, 188–90, 192, 202; Intelligence 6–7, 22, 30–32, 34–35, 38, 60, 63, 70, 75 n.67, 84, 86–88, 111, 154–55, 160, 166 n.49, 173, 175, 189–90, 192–97, 206–7,

209–10, 212–23, 231, 245 n.170, 246 n.181, 253–54; intelligence activities: *close observation platoons* 248 n.224; *informers* 173, 218, 221, 223, 227, 246 n.196; *interrogation* 203, 216, 219, 222–23, 227; *observation posts* 64, 155, 160, 214; *reconnaissance* 31, 84, 111, 152, 206–7, 209–10, 212–13, 219–21 *target identification* 212; *torture* 91, 222; intelligence services: *Canada* RCMP Security Service 154; *France* Bureaux Arabes 88–89; *Great Britain* Army intelligence: GSI (General Staff, Intelligence) 197, 213, 215–16, 218–22, 241 n.105; Field Security Sections 216; Intelligence Corps 215; 220; military intelligence liaison officers 218–19; Military Reconnaissance Force (MRF) 221; Border Scouts 219–20; Combined Intelligence Staff (CIS) (Malaya) 192, 217–18; Combined Services Detailed Interrogation Centre 216; Defence Security Office/Officer 197, 216, 241 n.105, 245 n.170; Director of Intelligence 217–20; Joint intelligence centres 154, 217–21; Malayan Security Service 217; MI5 217; MI6 200; Security Intelligence Middle East 216; Special Branch (police) 217–20, 246 n.181, 186; *Israel* 51, 63, 68; General Security Service 63; Mossad 68, 75 n.67; *United States* Central Intelligence Agency (CIA) 27, 30–31, 33, 39, 68, 251; Joint Advisory Commission Korea (CIA) 33; Office of Strategic Services (OSS) 29–33, 35–36, 44; Internal Security Operations v, 7–8, 14, 139, 147, 150–55, 159–62, 171, 176, 189–91, 193–94, 200–203, 205–6, 216, 220–21, 228, 253; *'Aid to the Civil Power'* 151, 160, 166 n.45, 172, 176, 189, 194, 228, 251; border security 153–54; convoy escort/

Warfare (*cont.*)
protection 149, 154;
curfews 223; 'minimum force
principle' 155, 158, 172–73, 194,
228, 234; roadblocks (vehicle
check points) 202, 220; riot
control 159–61, 190, 205–6, 228,
247 n.213; route security and
surveillance 154; VIP
protection 151, 153–54, 159–60;
vital points protection 151–54,
159–61; '*Imperial Policing*' 172,
176, 188–91, 202, 212, 231,233;
emergency regulations 194;
martial law 189–90; military
control 159; mobile
columns 81–85, 101, 190, 202;
reprisals 56–58, 60–61, 63, 65,
68, 69; *Police-style
operations* 72, 94, 100–01, 106,
172–76, 189, 194, 196, 200–02,
205–6, 213, 215–21, 228, 234;
Intervention 41, 59, 79, 100,
105–11, 113–20, 122–23, 126–28,
133 n.52, 137 n.103, 138 n.109,
149, 159; Legal aspects 172,
189–90, 194, 196–98, 200–01, 207–
9, 214, 216, 221–22, 227–28, 238
n.59, 251; Military Assistance 21,
42, 105, 113, 127; Peace-
Keeping v, 59, 116, 127, 139,
141–42, 146–50, 155–62, 171, 193,
232, 251, 253, 256;
Propaganda 13, 38, 45, 68, 87,
89, 174, 189, 190, 192–94, 222–23,
225–28, 232, 235 n.14;
Psychological Warfare 30–31,
34–35, 38, 42, 45, 81, 87–91, 173–
75, 189, 195, 207, 210, 223–28,
232, 244 n.149, 255; see also
Counter-Insurgency, *Information
services*; Propaganda;
Revolutionary Warfare 5, 8, 10–
11, 14, 22, 32, 42, 49, 61, 87, 91,
174, 188–89, 192–93, 207, 223,
253; Rioting 174, 205, 228;
Sabotage 53, 56, 60, 62, 191,
213; Special Operations v, 19,
21, 29, 31, 33–36, 38, 40, 44–45,
51, 67–71, 162, 207–15, 219–22,
231–32; Terrorism 11, 38, 42,
45, 49, 51–53, 58, 60–63, 66–69,
91, 118, 147, 150, 152, 154–55,

161–62, 173–74, 189, 192–93, 195,
200, 212, 214–15, 221–22, 245
n.170, 248 n.224, 252, 256;
international terrorism 66, 68–69,
162, 214–15; *terrorism methods*
assassination 56–57, 173–74,
212–14, 221–22; hijacking 174,
214; hostage-taking/
kidnapping 11, 69, 150–51, 155,
162, 174, 214, 222;
Unconventional Warfare v, 29–
40, 42–43, 80, 174–75, 207, 253
Campaigns, Incidents, and
Operations: *Africa* Algeria 12,
14, 51 62, 71, 79, 86, 89–90, 99,
101, 115, 129 n.5, 130 n.16, 255;
Battle of Algiers 86; French 'oil
patch' strategy in 85;
quadrillage 94; see also *Armies,
National: French Army*, doctrine,
Guerre Algérienne; Kabylie
campaign (Algeria) 83, 85–86,
129 n.10; Operations (Jumelles,
Trident) 86; Cameroon 79, 90,
133 n.52; Chad 77–78 (map), 84,
100–02, 112, 115–18, 121–28, 133
n.52, 134 n.57, 135 n.65, 136
n.88, 137 n.103, 138 n.109, n.112;
Aouzou Strip (Chad) 78 (map),
125; N'djamena (capital of
Chad) 77–78 (map), 109, 122,
125; Opération *Epervier* 125–28;
Opération *Manta* 100–01, 112,
118, 121, 124–25, 138 n.119;
Ouadi Doum (Chad) 78 (map),
125–26; 'Red Line' (16th Parallel,
Chad), 78 (map), 125–26, 137
n.94; Tibesti mountains (Chad) 78
(map), 125; Ziguey (Chad) 78
(map), 124, 126; (Belgian) Congo
(civil war/peacekeeping
operations) 148–49, 157, 159,
162; Gabon 79, 100, 106, 133
n.52; Horn of Africa 77, 109;
Kenya (Mau Mau campaign/
Emergency) 184, 193, 195–96,
198–99, 205, 209, 212, 229, 231,
235 n.3; 'counter-gang' operations
in 209, 212; Mauritania 79, 83,
133 n.52; Mogadishu (hostage-
rescue operation at) 215;
Morocco 79–80, 84–85, 93–95,
97, 100–01; Riff War in 84–85,

101; see also Western Sahara; Senegal 79, 83, 89–91, 93, 114; Shaba see Zaire; Entebbe (Uganda) 70; Western Sahara 77, 100, 111; Zaire 77, 79, 100, 113–14, 116–17, 119, 133 n.52; Kolwezi (Shaba, Zaire) 106, 113–14, 117–18, 121

Canada October Crisis (Quebec, Canada 1970) 150–52, 160–61; Operations ESSAY, GINGER 151–52; see also Front de Libération du Québec; Olympic security (Operation GAMESCAN) 152–55, 160–61

Europe anti-NATO terrorism 252, 256; Cyprus 142, 144, 146, 148–50, 156–57, 159–62, 165 n.33, 184, 193, 195, 199, 205–6, 219, 222, 228–29, 233, 235 n.3, 237 n.45, 242 n.130; Nicosia airport (Cyprus) fighting at (1974) 149–50; Great Britain: Balcombe Street siege (London 1975) 215; Iranian embassy rescue operation (London 1980) 169, 215, 235 n.2; Northern Ireland 14, 51, 152, 169, 170 (map), 173, 186–87, 193–96, 200–01, 205–7, 213–15, 220–23, 225–28, 230, 232–34, 235 n.3, 243 n.136, 247 n.211, 251–52; HQ Northern Ireland 201, 226, 242 n.117; Information Policy office 226, 247 n.211 Northern Ireland Office 200; Secretary of State for Northern Ireland 200; atrocities, accusations of 213, 227; 'Bloody Sunday' 227; Catholic population 193, 201, 220–21, 227; 'Four Square Laundry' (covert intelligence operation) 221; internment 193–94, 201, 221, 226–27; Mountbatten, Lord Louis (assassination of) 200; Operation MOTORMAN 173, 221; 'supergrass' informers 223, 246 n.196; Warrenpoint (Northern Ireland) bombing 200; see also Provisional Irish Republican Army; Irish Republic, rebellion (1919–21) 189–91, 193, 208, 238 n.59; West Germany Munich

Olympics terrorist incident (1972) 152, 214–15

Middle East Aden (South Arabia, 1964–67) 184–85, 199–200, 205–6, 212, 214, 219, 222, 229–30, 235 n.3, 237 n.45; Arab Rebellion (World War I) 188, 207–8, 243 n.143; Egypt (Israeli raids on: Green Island, Ras Garib) 67; Gaza Strip 51, 58, 61–62, 66–67, 69, 72; Golan Heights 58, 60–61; Israel (attacks on: Beit Shean, Kiryat Shemona, Maalot) 64, 69; Jordan 56, 58–63, 65–66; Israeli attacks on, (Karameh, salt) 65–66; Lebanon 11, 51–52, 60, 63, 66–72, 75 n.66, 77, 99, 102, 115, 117–18, 121, 137 n.103, 156–57, 256; Beirut, Israeli raids on (1968, 1973) 68; Sidon, Tripoli (Lebanon) 68, 70; Oman (1958–59 campaign) 211–12, 214, 235 n.3; (Dhofar campaign 1970–76) 212–14, 230, 235 n.3; British Army Training Teams in 212; *Firquats* (Dhofari irregulars) 213; Mirbat (Dhofar, Oman), battle of (1972) 213; Palestine 52–54, 169, 171, 173, 176, 183, 190–92, 194, 196–97, 202–3, 205–6, 208, 212, 215–17, 222–24, 229–30, 235 n.3, 247 n.213, 252; Arab revolt in (1936–39) 52, 191; 'Farran case' (1947) 208, 212; General Officer Commanding (British Troops Palestine) 191, 197, 216; Public Information Office 224; security committees 197, 216, 224, 241 n.105; special anti-terrorist operations in 208–9; Radfan (South Arabia, 1964) 184, 190, 212; United Nations Emergency Forces (1 and 2) in Sinai 59, 61, 142, 148, 156–57; West Bank 51, 58, 60–67, 72; Israeli military government of 62–63, 69; Jerusalem 61, 69; Kibya 57; Nablus 63; Samua 61; Operation Ring 63; see also El Fatah; Fedayeen; Palestine Liberation Organisation

Southeast Asia Amritsar massacre

Warfare (*cont.*)
(India 1919)   228; Brunei revolt (1962)   229; Confrontation campaign (Borneo 1962–66) 184–85, 194, 205, 212–14, 219–20, 230–31, 235 n.3, 237 n.45, 238 n.49, 244 n.156; Malayan Emergency (1948–60)   171–73, 175, 183, 187–88, 192–99, 203–5, 209–12, 214, 217–18, 224, 229–31, 235 n.3, 239 n.77; 'Briggs Plan' 203, 217, 224; committee/council system   197–98, 217–18; intelligence in 217–18; operations and training   203–5, 209–11; psychological warfare operations in 224; Special Operations Volunteer Force   209; Philippines   25, 29, 39–40; Vietnam wars   9, 12–14, 19, 24, 26, 28–29, 37–42, 51, 62, 71, 79, 81, 84–86, 90, 91, 94–95, 99, 101, 119, 146, 193, 251, 253; Dien Bien Phu   24, 126; U.S operations   28, 39–40; Civilian Irregular Defense Groups (CIDG)   39–40

Wars   (other than low-intensity) American Revolutionary war 188, 207; Crimean War 80; Falkland Islands War (1982)   21, 171, 176, 186, 233–35; Franco–Prussian War   80, 93, 96; Israeli War of Independence (1948–49)   54; Korean War   9, 21, 23–26, 28–29, 31–36, 43, 141–42, 148, 160, 171–72, 183, 222; October War (1973)   69; Peninsular campaign   82; Seven Years' War 207; Sinai campaign (1956) (Operation KADESH; see Suez Crisis/War; Six Day War (1967)   51, 61; Suez Crisis/ War   24–25, 58–59, 148, 171, 184, 232–33; War of Attrition (1967–70)   70; World War I   1, 6, 9, 44, 52, 80, 84–85, 95–96, 99, 139, 176, 188, 207; World War II   v, 6, 9, 12, 19, 24, 27–31, 33, 43–44, 54, 73 n.12, 77, 86, 90, 104, 139–40, 176–77, 179, 189–90, 193, 202, 208, 222–23, 243 n.132, n.145, 251

Weapons and Equipment   2–7, 9, 26, 28–30, 35, 37, 41, 55–57, 59, 62, 67, 69, 77, 85, 96, 101–02, 105, 111–13, 127, 135 n.65, 142–43, 145–47, 155, 157, 161, 163, 172, 176, 179, 181, 186, 190, 203, 207, 210, 213, 215, 228–29, 233–34, 237 n.34, 243 n.133, 251–54; air defence   67, 141, 252; airpower (aircraft)   3, 6, 27–29, 51, 61, 65, 69, 84, 85, 100, 101, 111, 117, 121–22, 144, 152, 154, 172, 184–86, 190, 210, 228–29, 233; armoured vehicles (all types)   2, 3, 6–7, 27, 59–61, 66, 69, 86, 101, 112–13, 144, 146, 161, 164 n.18, 190, 207, 154; artillery   1–3, 57, 69, 81, 83, 164 n.18, 212; batons 228; blockhouses   83, 86; electronic detection devices   64, 112; gases (riot control) 228; helicopters   64, 86, 101, 112–13, 151, 154, 210, 229, 233, 248 n.220, 253, see also *Warfare, Conduct of: operations, airmobile*; machine guns   1, 96, 112; mines   60–61, 63–64; missiles, precision-guided   101, 112–13, 252; multiple rocket launchers 70; nuclear weapons/forces   8–9, 24–28, 30, 77, 103, 107–9, 113, 128, 135 n.66, 184, 186, 233; radar   67; rifle   84; rubber bullets   228; water cannon   228
Weizman, General Ezer   60–61
Wellington, Arthur Wellesley, Duke of   8, 14
Weyand, General Fred C.   41
Wilson, British Prime Minister Harold   185
Wilson, Major R. D.   191
Wingate, Major Orde Charles   53
Wise, Sydney   8
Wyllie, James   233

Zaire   77, 79, 100, 105–6, 113–14, 116–17, 119, 127; see also *Warfare, Low-Intensity: Campaigns, Incidents, and Operations, Africa*
Zionism   12, 52, 54–55, 59